It's been a year since I moved into my current apartment and I just recently realized something... I can see Mt. Fuji from my porch. It took me this long to notice!

—*Masashi Kishimoto, 2004*

岸本斉史

Author/artist Masashi Kishimoto was born in 1974 in rural Okayama Prefecture, Japan. After spending time in art college, he won the Hop Step Award for new manga artists with his manga **Karakuri** (Mechanism). Kishimoto decided to base his next story on traditional Japanese culture. His first version of **Naruto**, drawn in 1997, was a one-shot story about fox spirits; his final version, which debuted in **Weekly Shonen Jump** in 1999, quickly became the most popular ninja manga in Japan.

NARUTO VOL. 23
The SHONEN JUMP Manga Edition

STORY AND ART BY MASASHI KISHIMOTO

Translation/Kyoko Shapiro, HC Language Solutions, Inc.
English Adaptation/Ian Reid, HC Language Solutions, Inc.
Touch-up Art & Lettering/Gia Cam Luc
Design/Yvonne Cai
Editor/Joel Enos

Editor in Chief, Books/Alvin Lu
Editor in Chief, Magazines/Marc Weidenbaum
VP of Publishing Licensing/Rika Inouye
VP of Sales/Gonzalo Ferreyra
Sr. VP of Marketing/Liza Coppola
Publisher/Hyoe Narita

Printed in the U.S.A.

Published by VIZ Media, LLC
P.O. Box 77010
San Francisco, CA 94107

SHONEN JUMP Manga Edition
10 9 8 7 6 5 4 3 2
First printing, November 2007
Second printing, November 2007

www.viz.com

THE WORLD'S
MOST POPULAR MANGA

www.shonenjump.com

SHONEN JUMP MANGA EDITION

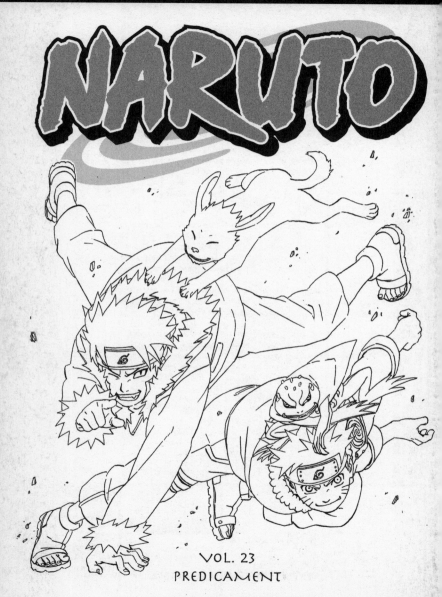

VOL. 23
PREDICAMENT

STORY AND ART BY
MASASHI KISHIMOTO

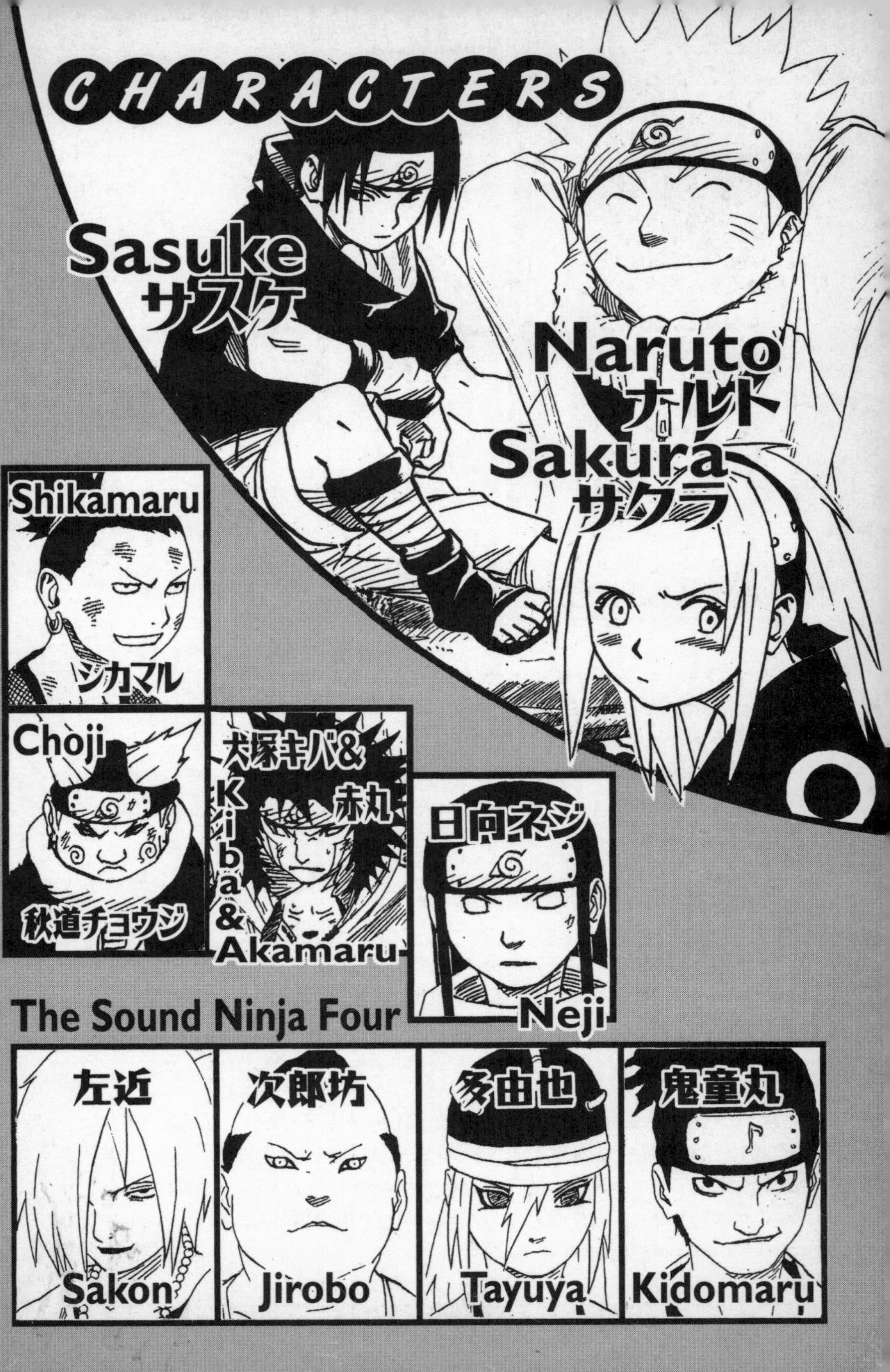
CHARACTERS
Naruto ナルト
Sasuke サスケ
Sakura サクラ
Shikamaru シカマル
日向ネジ Neji
犬塚キバ&赤丸 Kiba & Akamaru
Choji 秋道チョウジ
The Sound Ninja Four
鬼童丸 Kidomaru
多由也 Tayuya
次郎坊 Jirobo
左近 Sakon

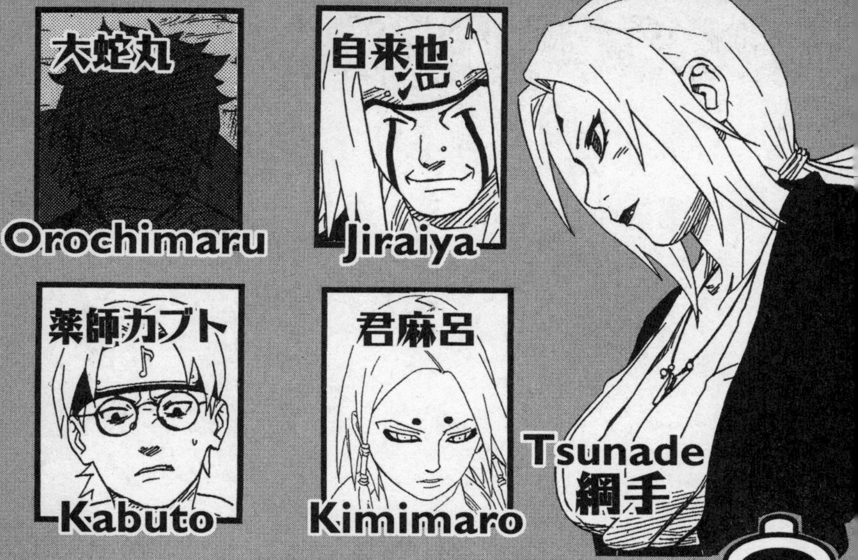
大蛇丸
Orochimaru
自来也
Jiraiya
薬師カブト
Kabuto
君麻呂
Kimimaro
Tsunade
綱手

The Story So Far...

Twelve years ago a destructive nine-tailed fox spirit attacked the ninja village of Konohagakure. The *Hokage*, or village champion, defeated the fox by sealing its soul into the body of a baby boy. Now that boy, Uzumaki Naruto, has grown up to be a ninja-in-training, learning the art of ninjutsu with his cellmates Sakura and Sasuke.

Naruto and company take on the Chûnin Selection Exams but suffer a sudden attack from Orochimaru in the Forest of Death. Orochimaru leaves a curse mark on Sasuke's body and vanishes, only to return during the final round to launch *Operation Destroy Konoha!* While Naruto battles Gaara, the Third Hokage falls to Orochimaru.

After the funeral, the mysterious Tsunade becomes Fifth Hokage. Sasuke flees Konohagakure with the Sound Ninja Four. Shikamaru and a cell hurry to pursue Sasuke, but Choji and then Neji are struck down by the Sound Ninja. Can Sasuke be saved from himself?!

NARUTO

VOL. 23
PREDICAMENT

CONTENTS

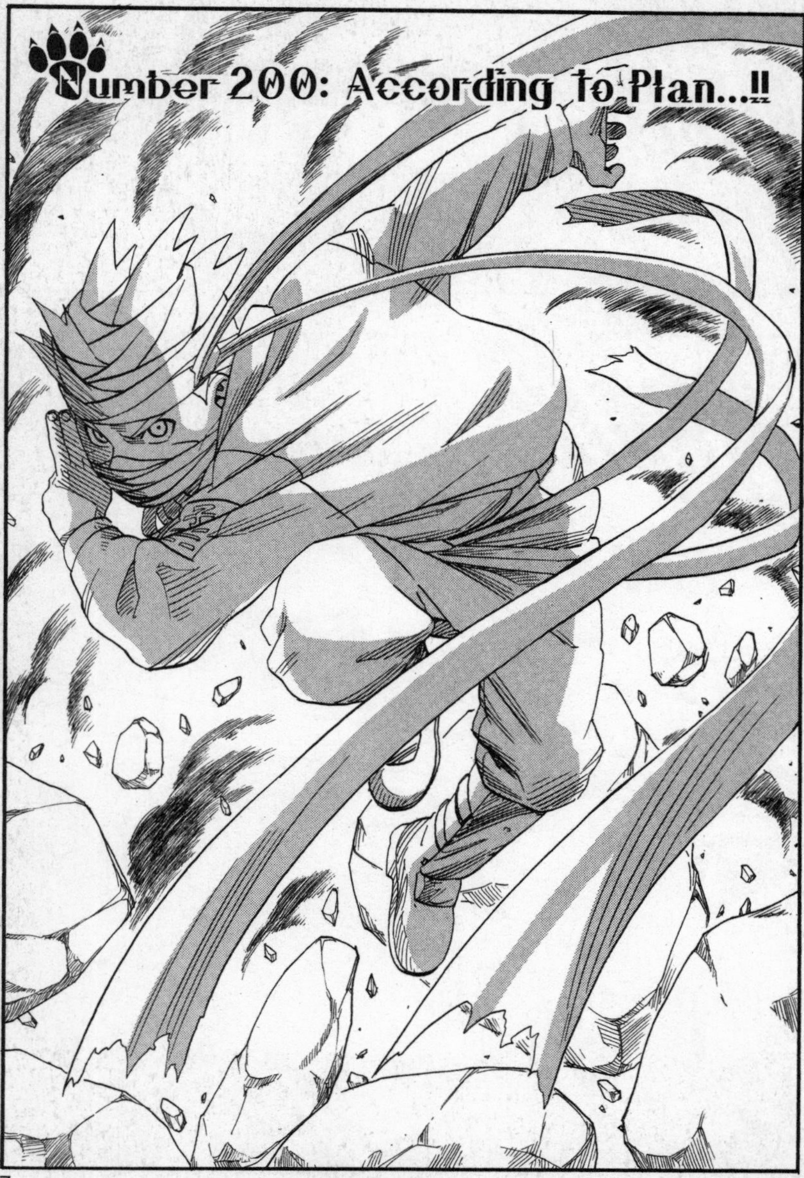
Number 200: According to Plan...!!

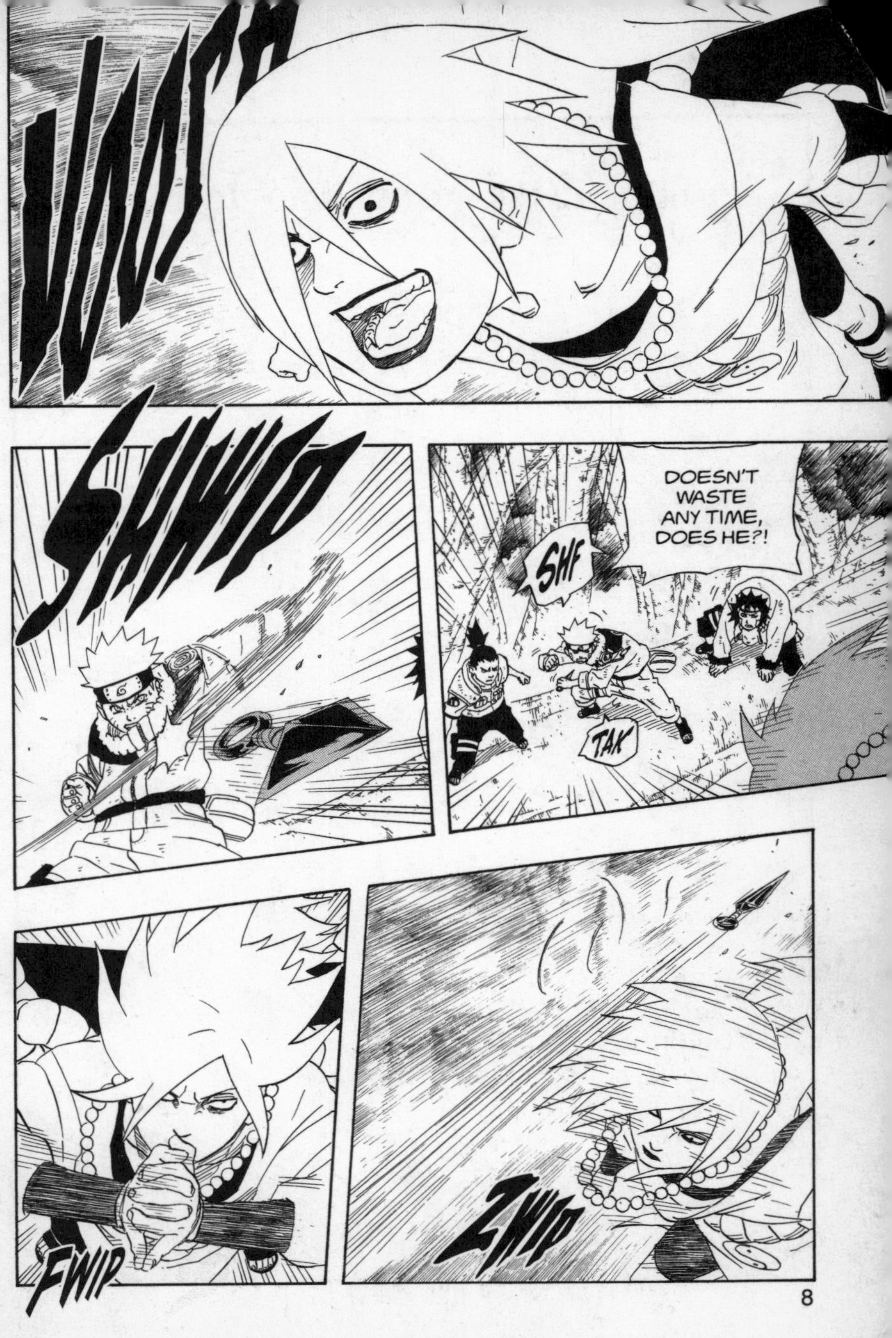
SHF
DOESN'T WASTE ANY TIME, DOES HE?!
TAK
SHWIP
ZWIP
FWIP

READ THIS WAY

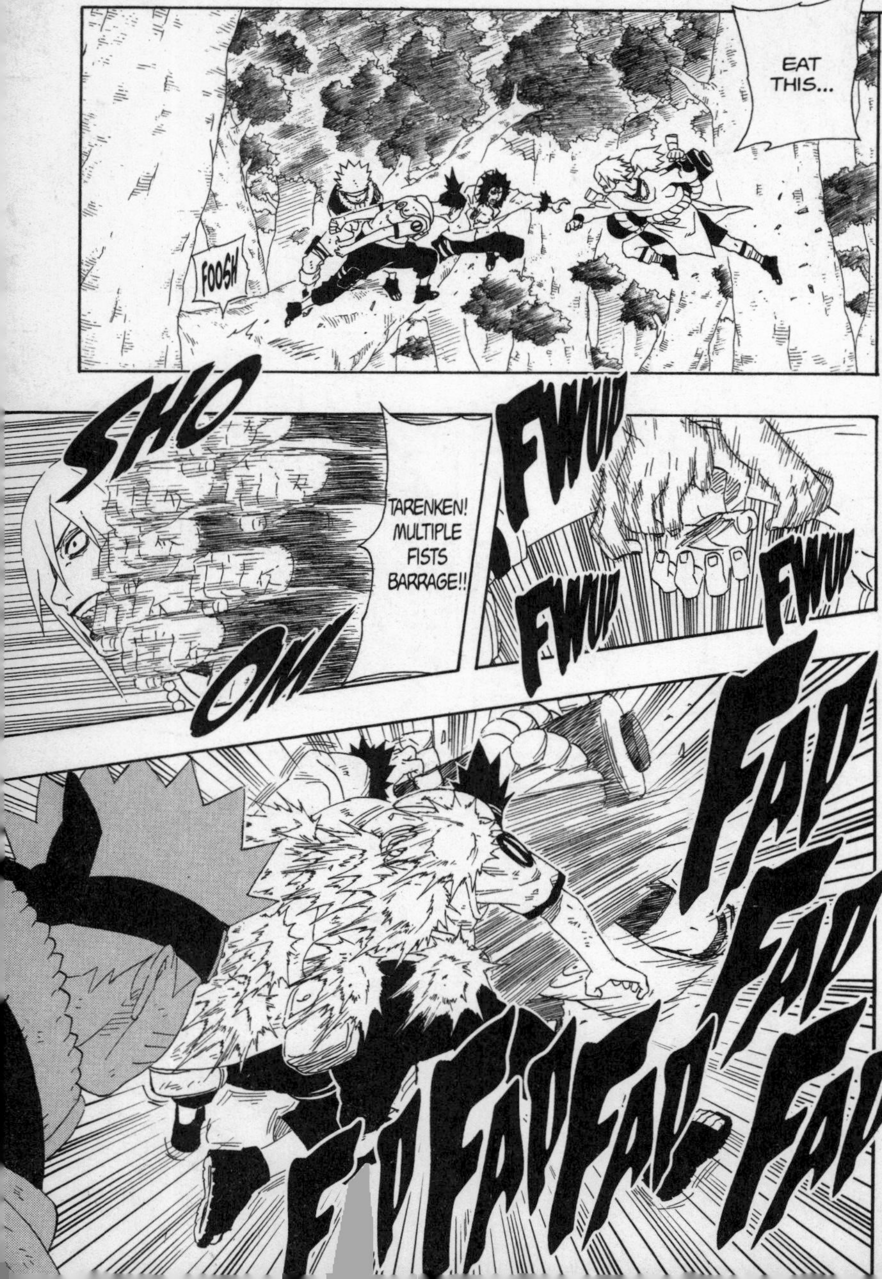
EAT THIS...
FOOSH
FWUP
FWUP
FWUP
TARENKEN! MULTIPLE FISTS BARRAGE!!
SHOOM
FAP
FAP
FAP FAP FAP-FAP

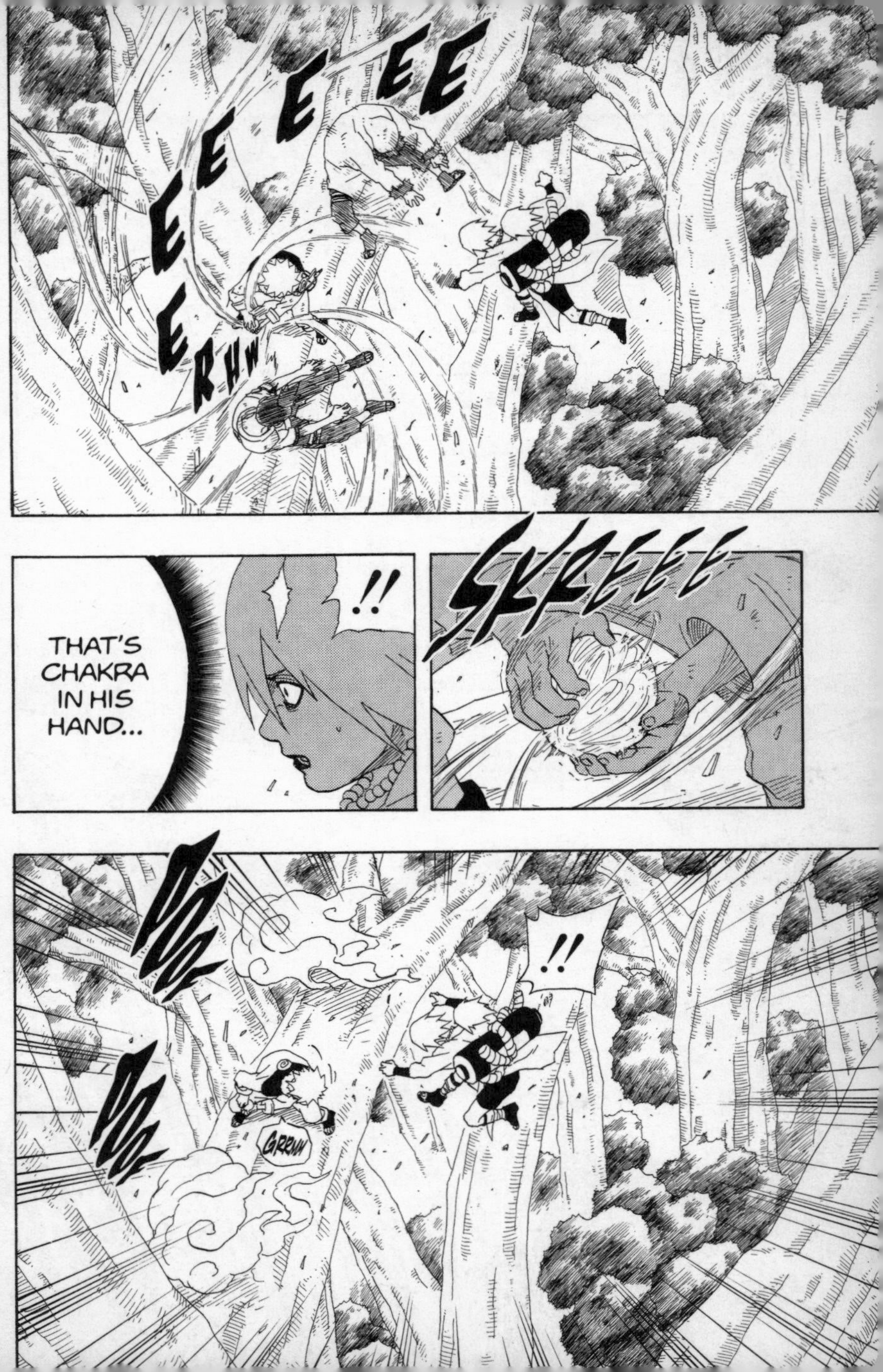
WHREEEEEEEE
SKREEEE
!!
THAT'S CHAKRA IN HIS HAND...
!!
GRRNN

READ THIS WAY

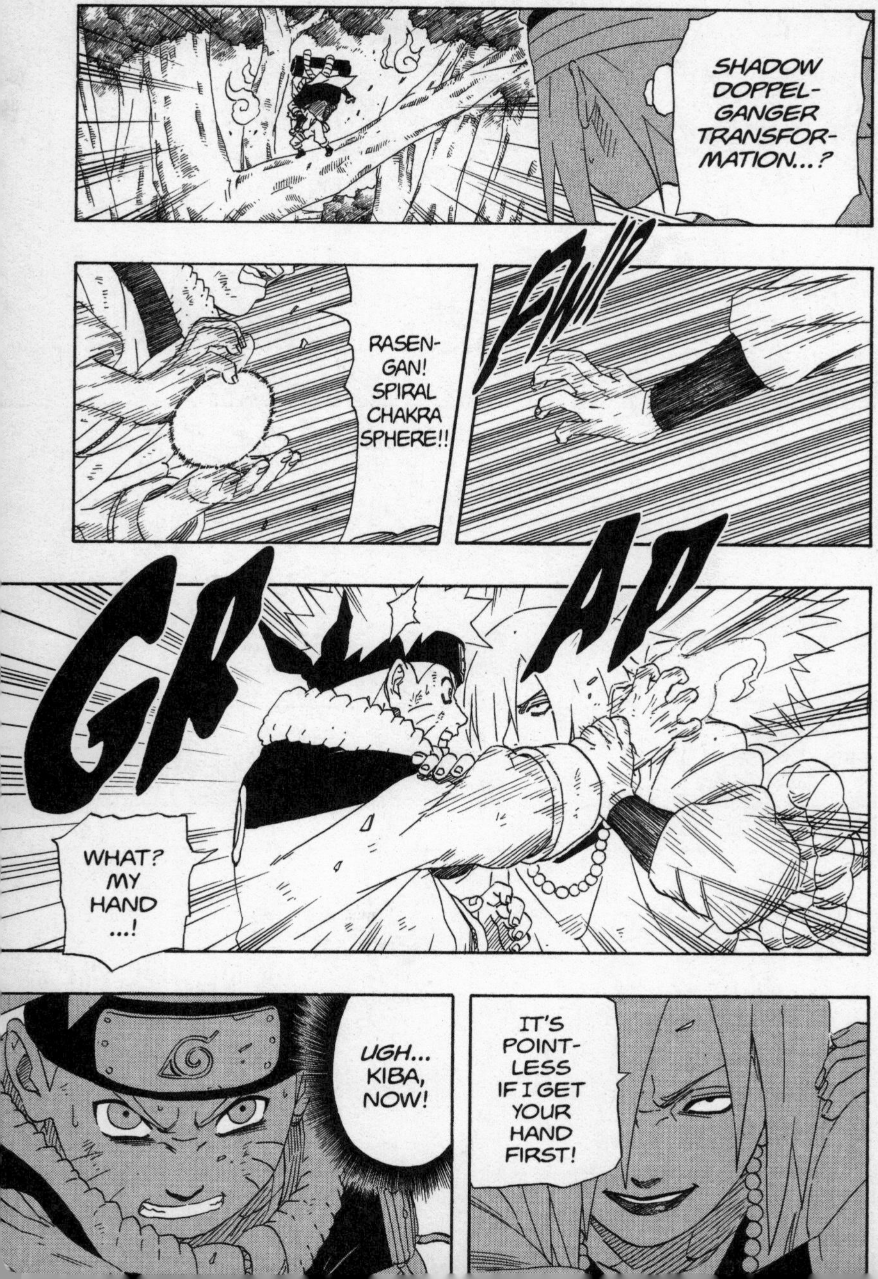
SHADOW DOPPEL-GANGER TRANSFOR-MATION...?
FWIP
RASEN-GAN! SPIRAL CHAKRA SPHERE!!
GRAB
WHAT? MY HAND ...!
IT'S POINT-LESS IF I GET YOUR HAND FIRST!
UGH... KIBA, NOW!

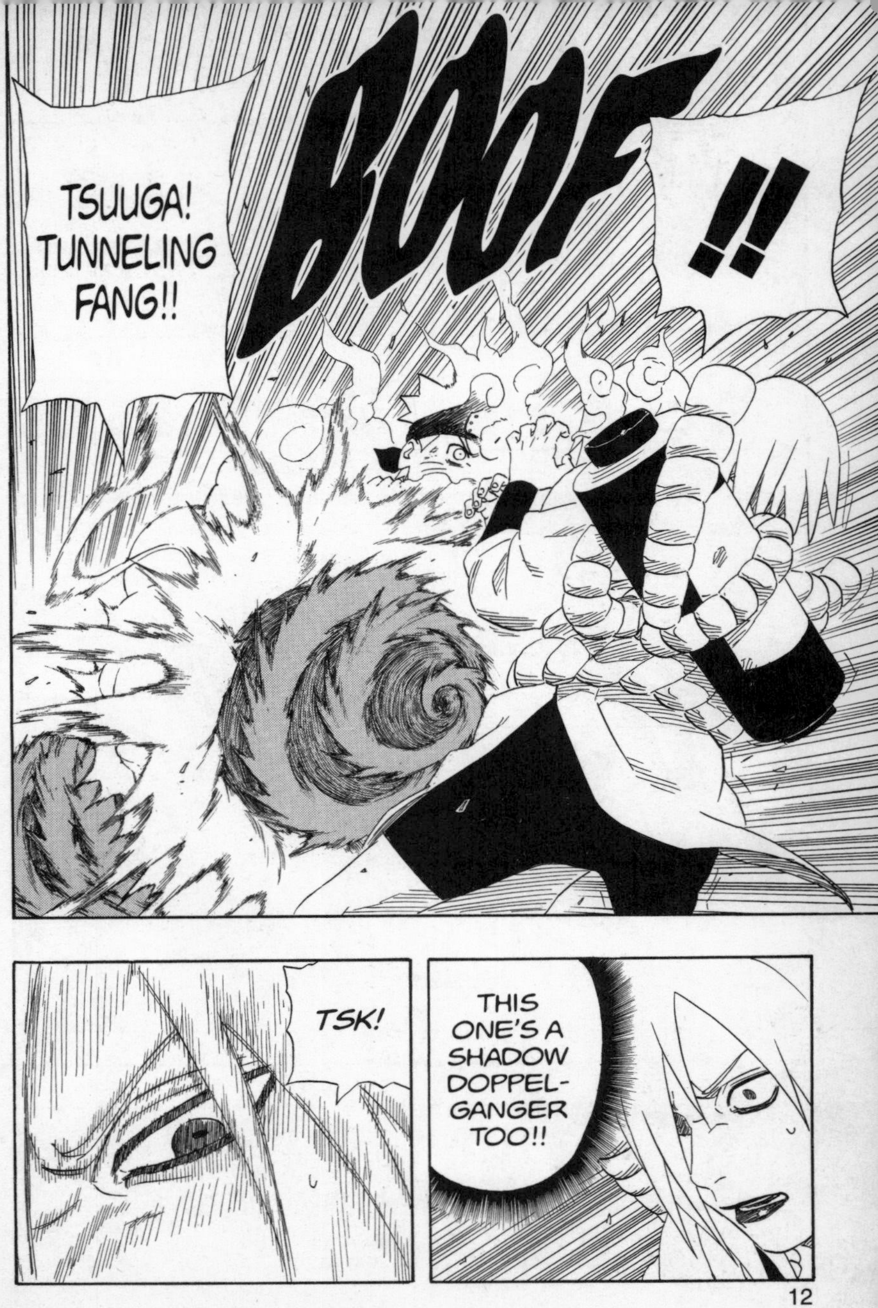
BOOF!!
TSUUGA! TUNNELING FANG!!
THIS ONE'S A SHADOW DOPPEL-GANGER TOO!!
TSK!

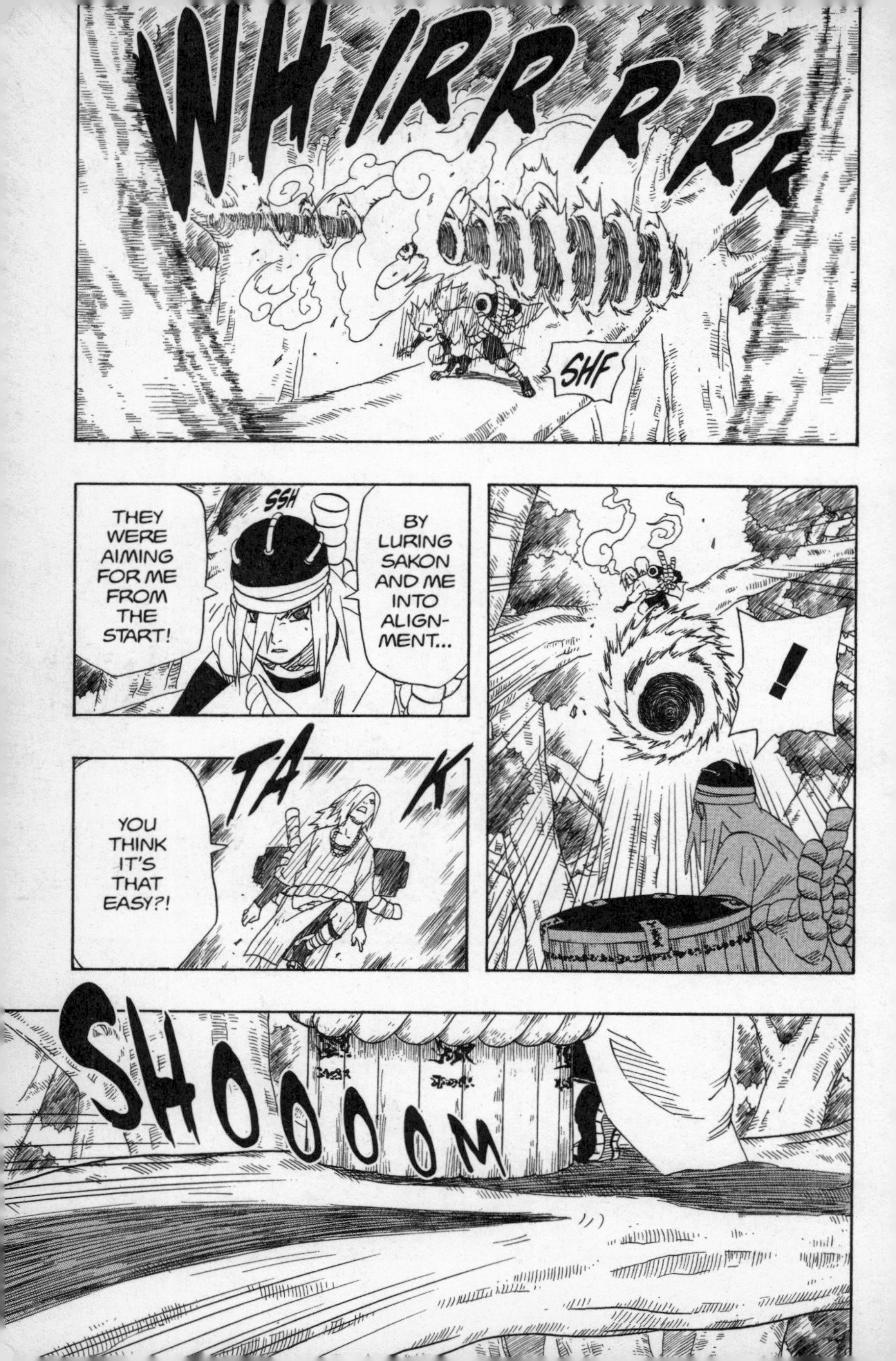
WHIRRRRRK
SHF
!
SSH
BY LURING SAKON AND ME INTO ALIGNMENT...
THEY WERE AIMING FOR ME FROM THE START!
TAK
YOU THINK IT'S THAT EASY?!
SHOOOOM

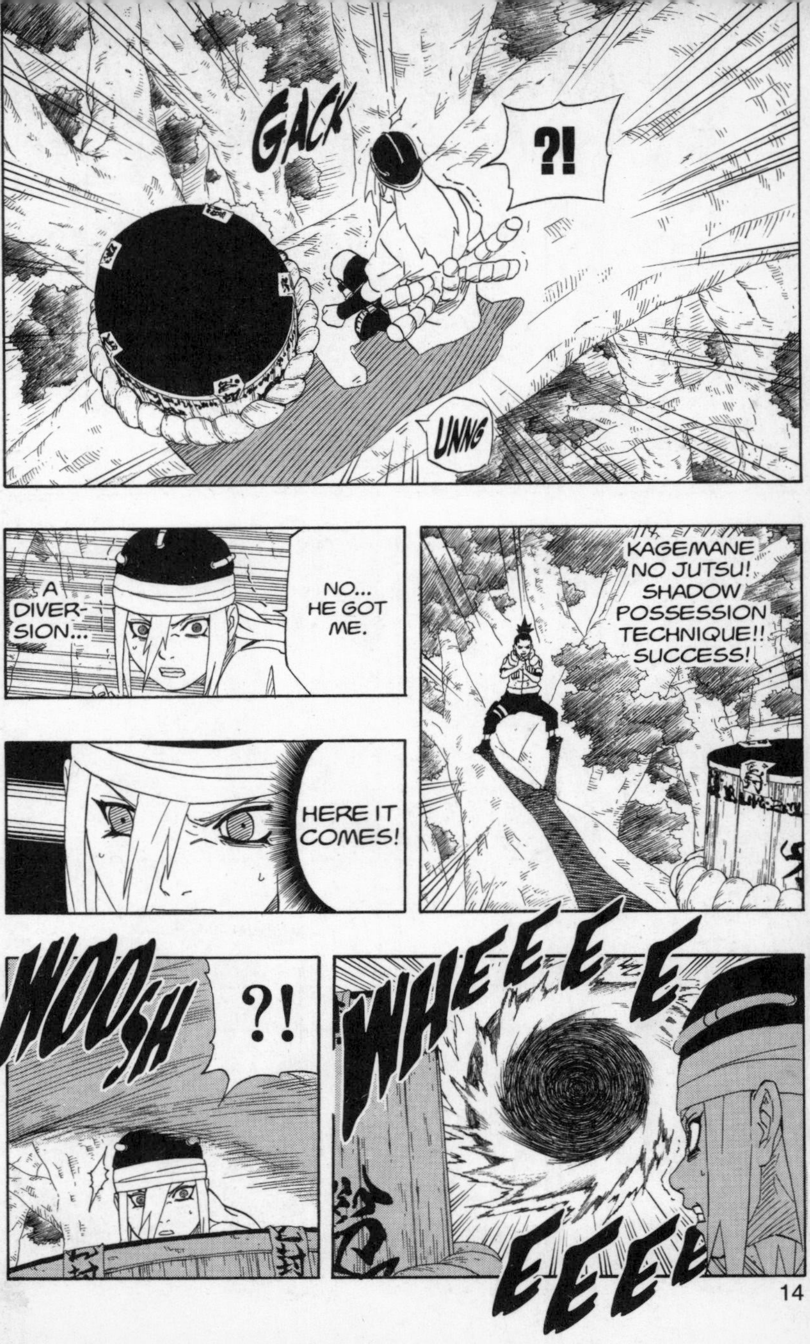
?!
GACK
UNNG
KAGEMANE NO JUTSU! SHADOW POSSESSION TECHNIQUE!! SUCCESS!
NO... HE GOT ME.
A DIVER-SION...
HERE IT COMES!
WHEEEEE
EEEE
?!
WHOOSH

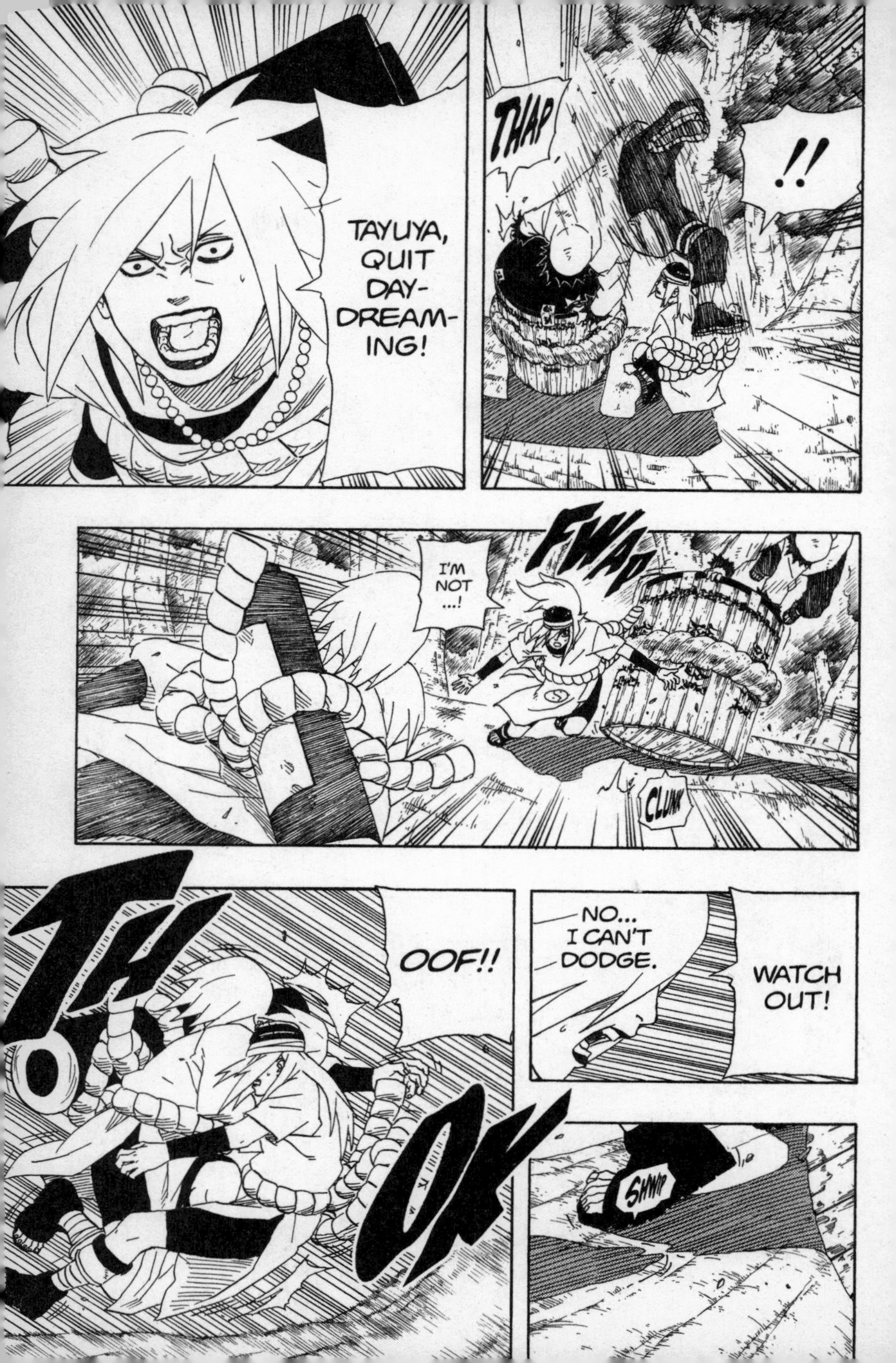
THAP
!!
TAYUYA, QUIT DAY-DREAMING!
FWAP
I'M NOT ...!
CLUNK
WATCH OUT!
NO... I CAN'T DODGE.
SHWIP
OOF!!

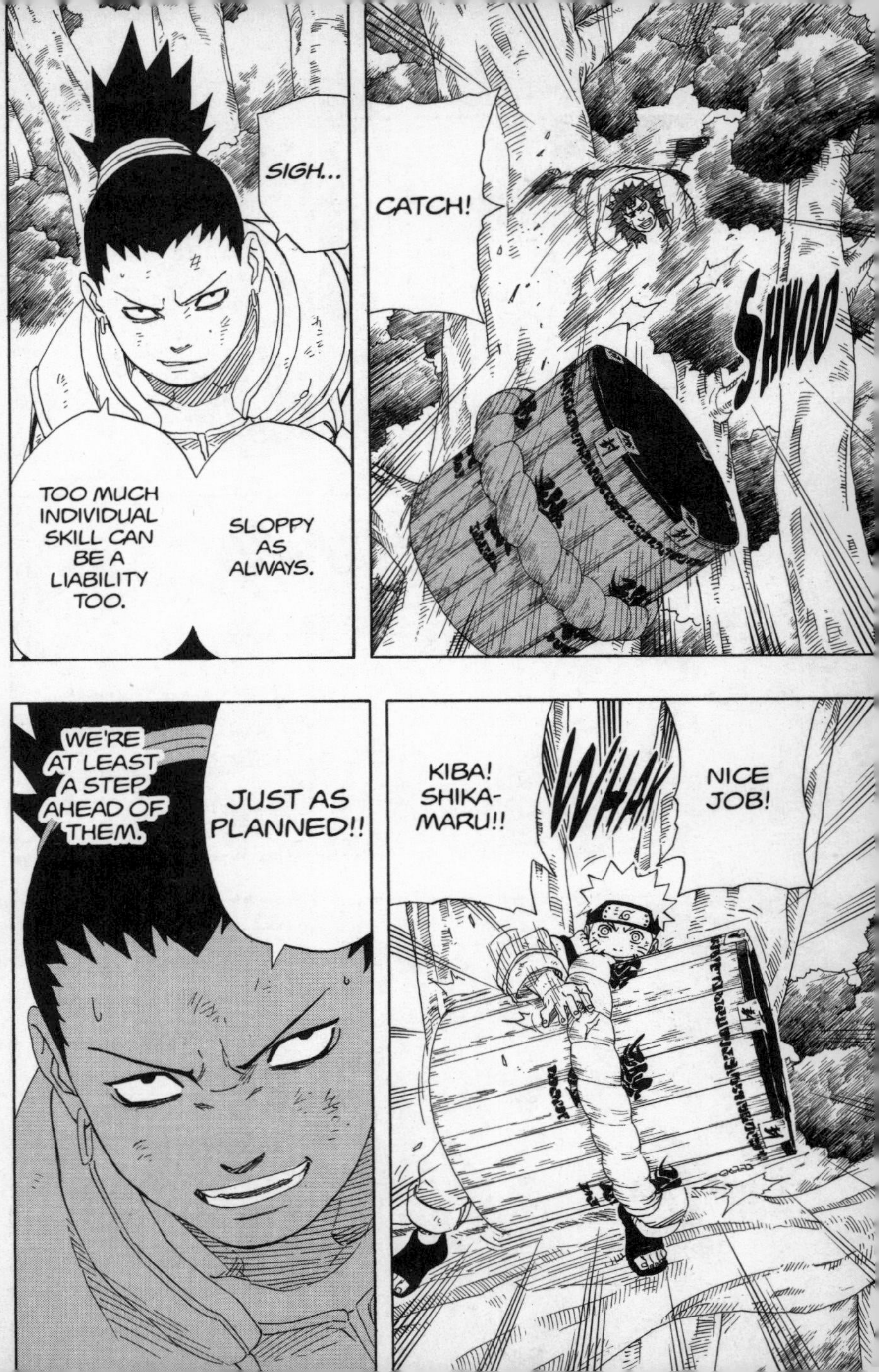
CATCH!
SHWOO
SIGH...
SLOPPY AS ALWAYS.
TOO MUCH INDIVIDUAL SKILL CAN BE A LIABILITY TOO.
NICE JOB!
WHAK
KIBA! SHIKA-MARU!!
JUST AS PLANNED!!
WE'RE AT LEAST A STEP AHEAD OF THEM.

READ THIS WAY

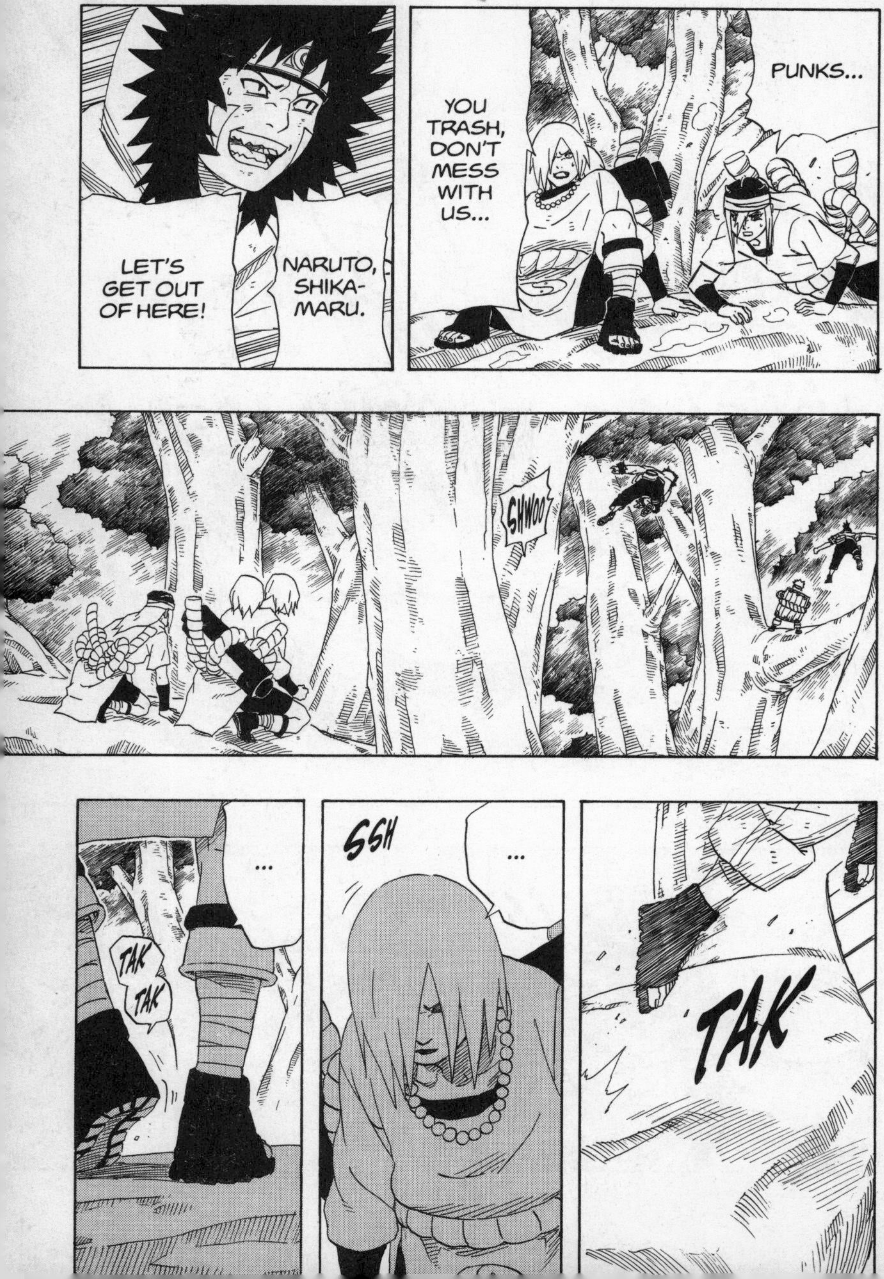
PUNKS...
YOU TRASH, DON'T MESS WITH US...
NARUTO, SHIKA-MARU.
LET'S GET OUT OF HERE!
SHWOO
TAK
SSH
...
...
TAK TAK

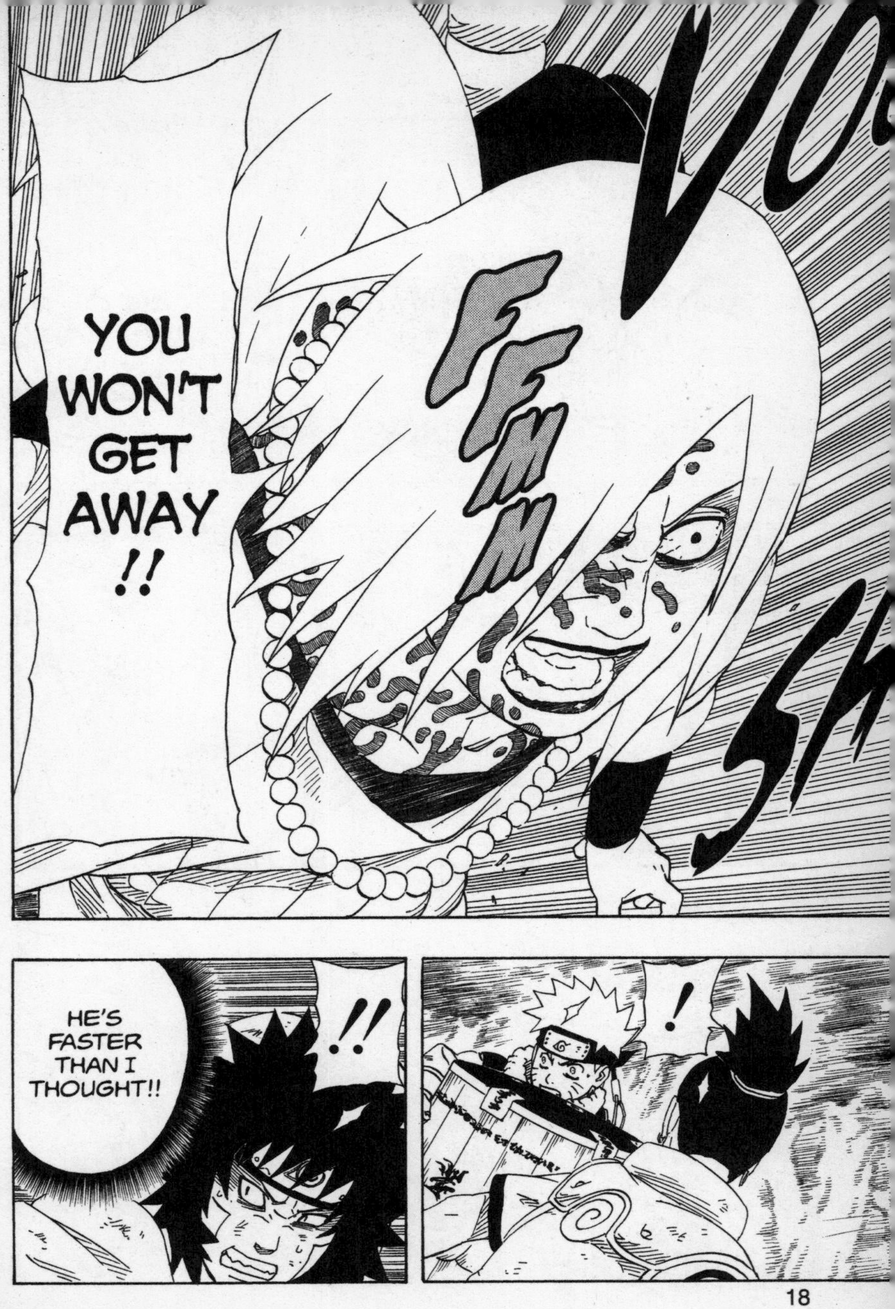
FFMM
YOU WON'T GET AWAY!!
!
!!
HE'S FASTER THAN I THOUGHT!!

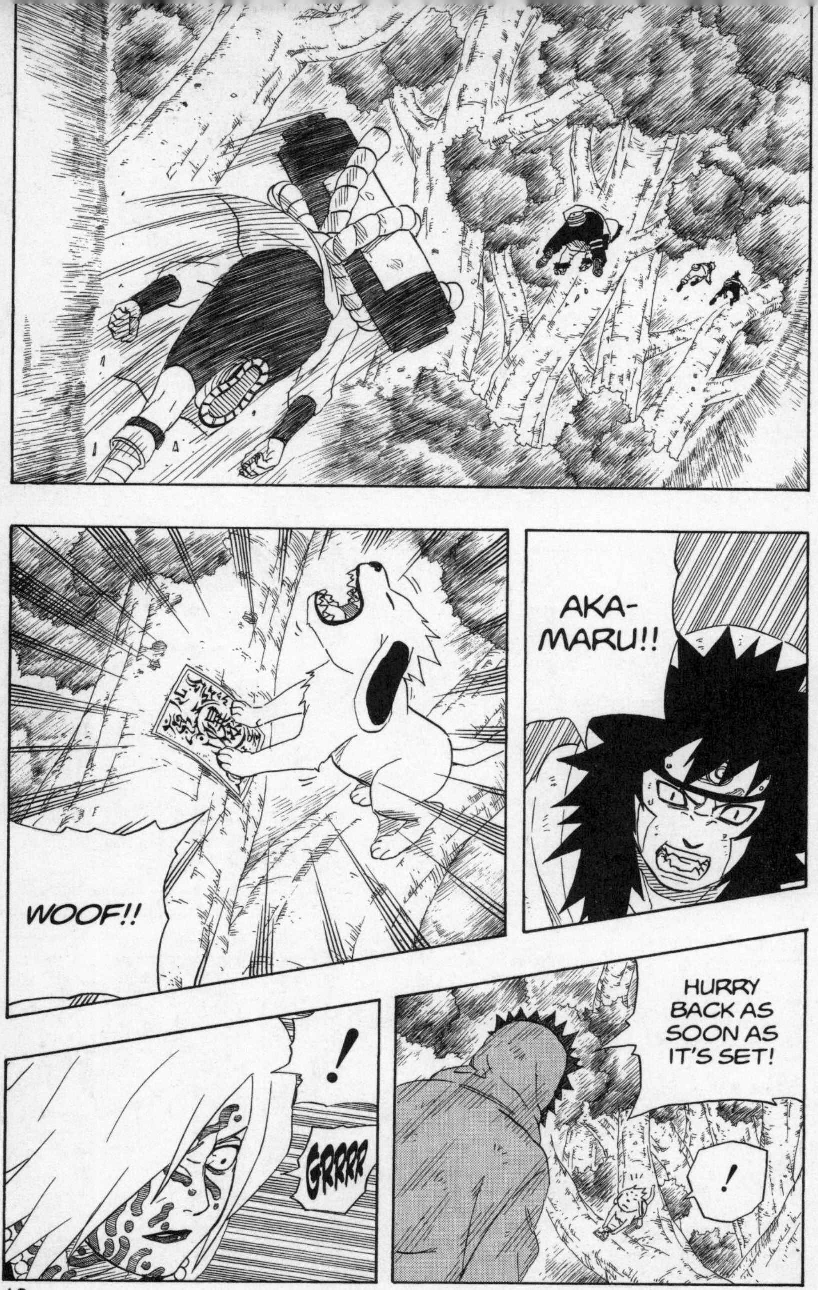
AKA-
MARU!!
WOOF!!
HURRY BACK AS SOON AS IT'S SET!
!
!
GRRRR

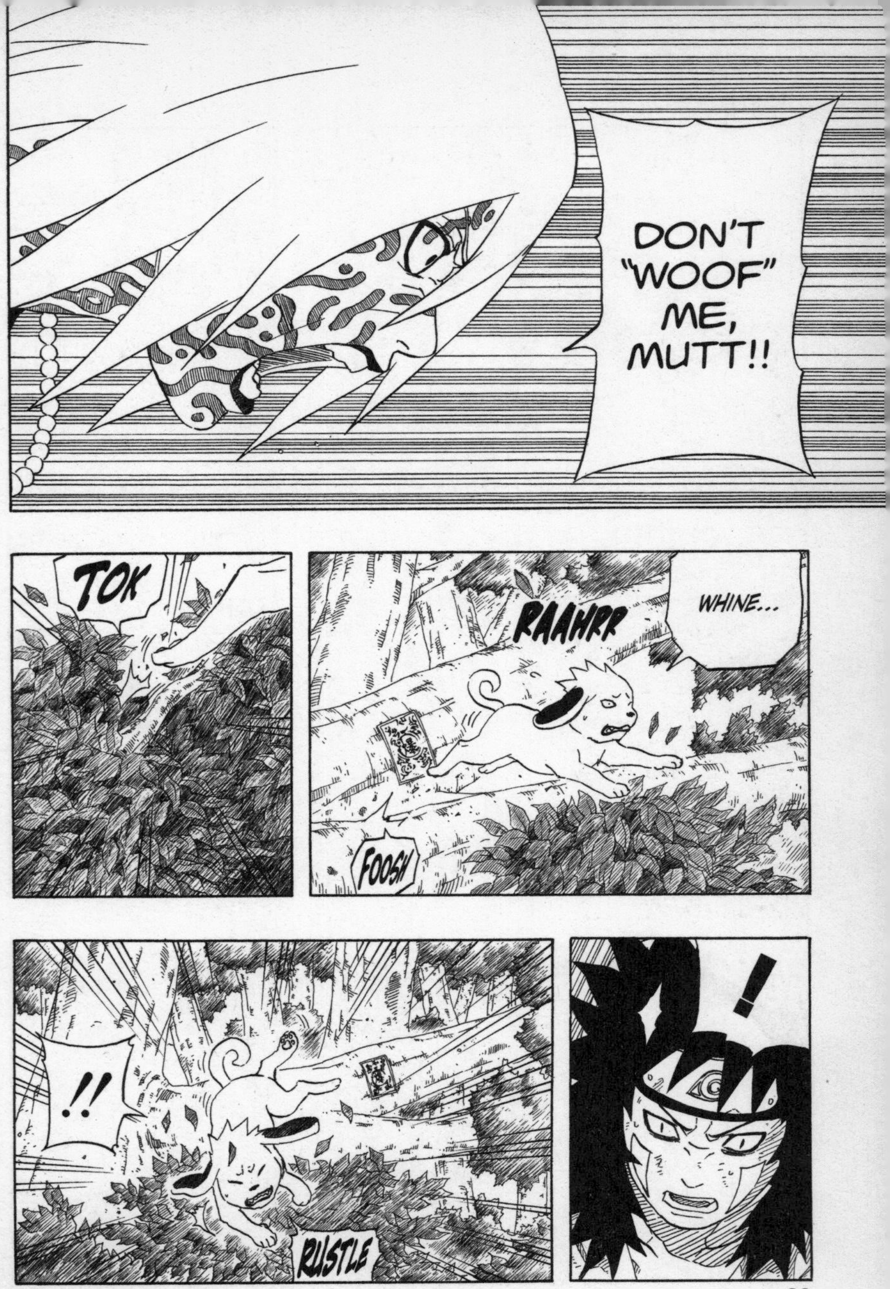

DON'T "WOOF" ME, MUTT!!
WHINE...
RAAHRR
FOOSH
TOK
!
!!
RUSTLE

READ THIS WAY

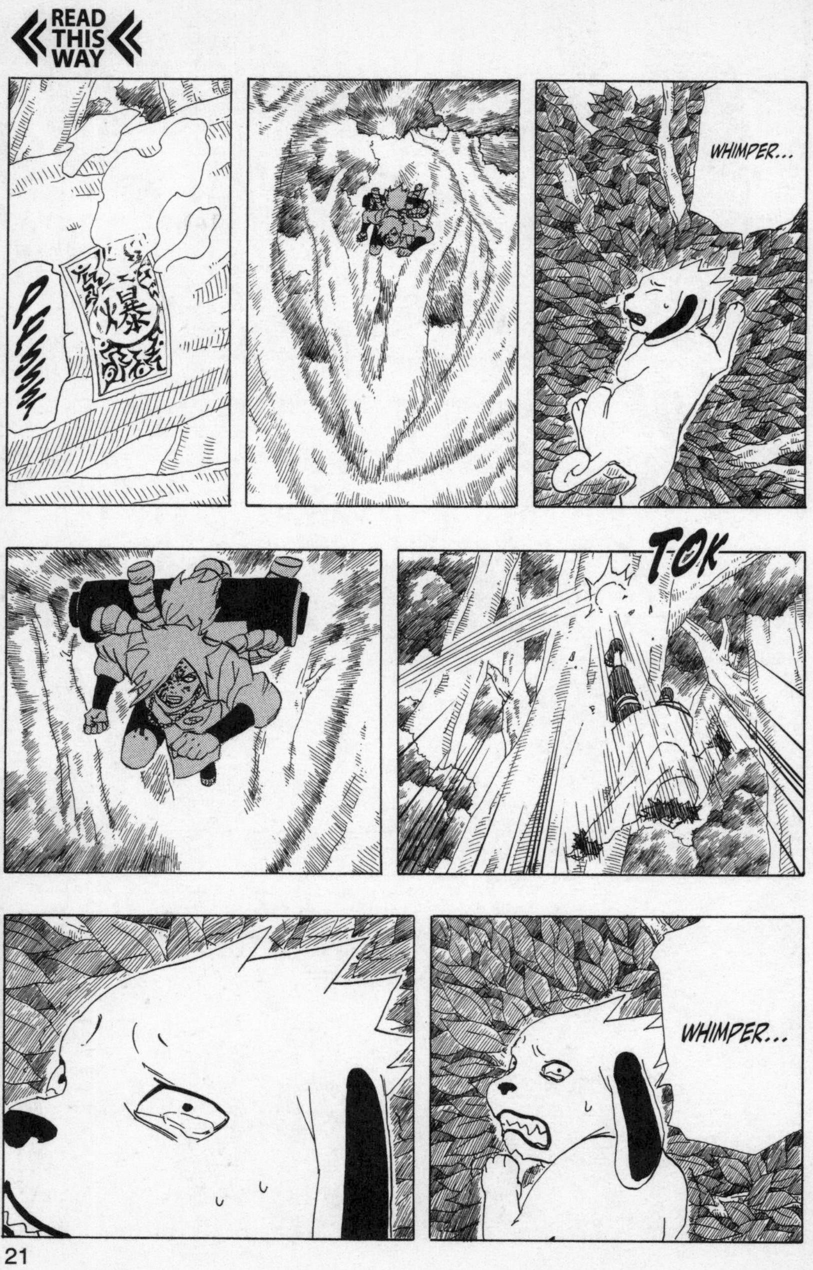
WHIMPER...
TOK
WHIMPER...

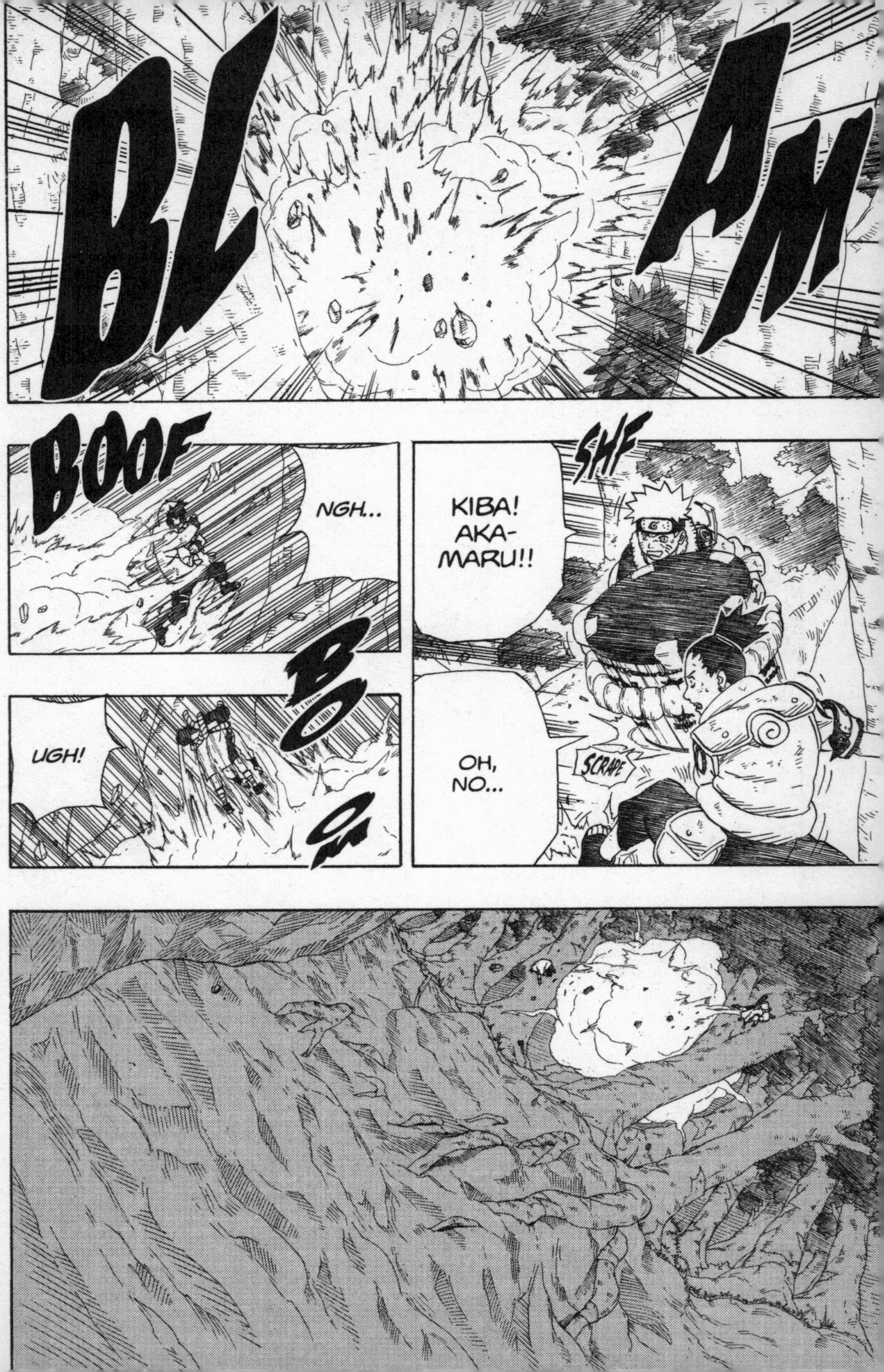
BLAM
SHF
KIBA! AKA-MARU!!
SCRAPE
OH, NO...
BOOF
NGH...
BOOM
UGH!

READ THIS WAY

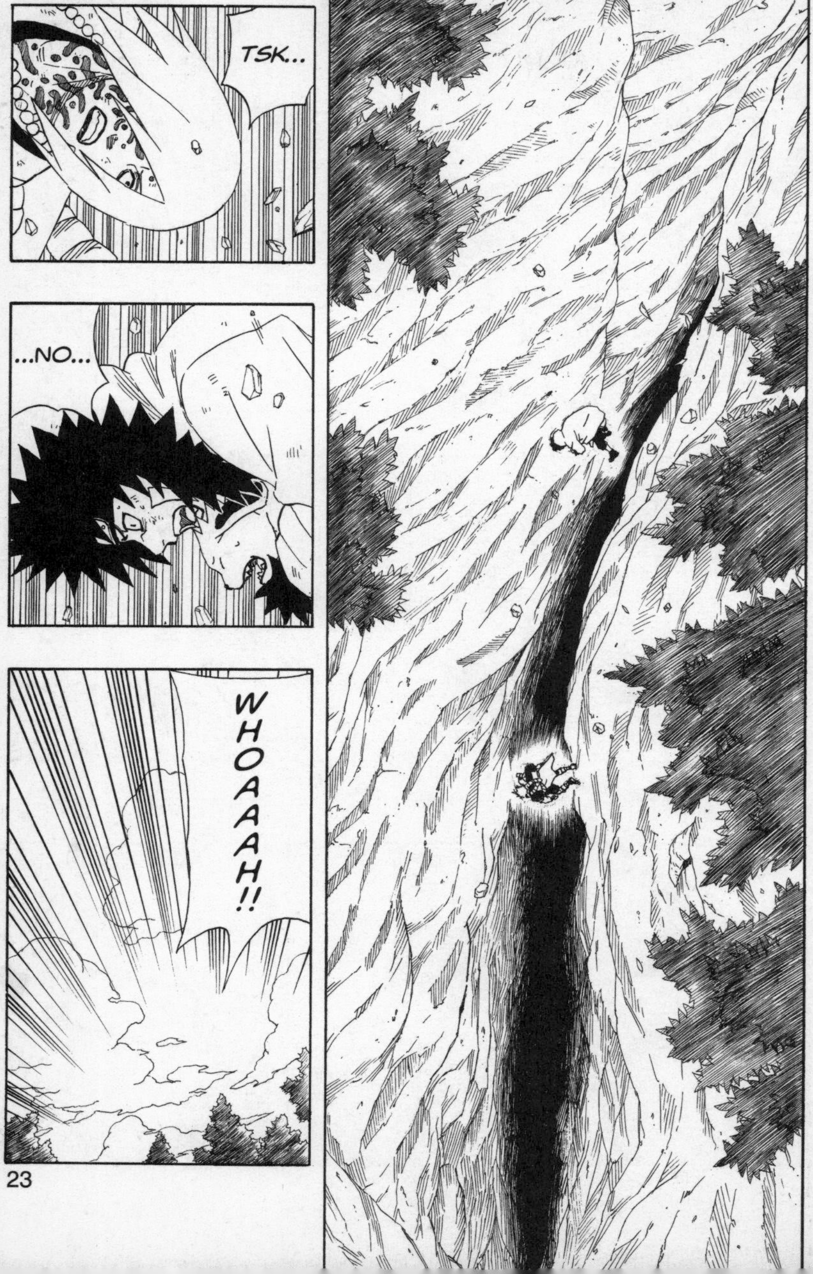
TSK...
...NO...
WHOAAAAH!!

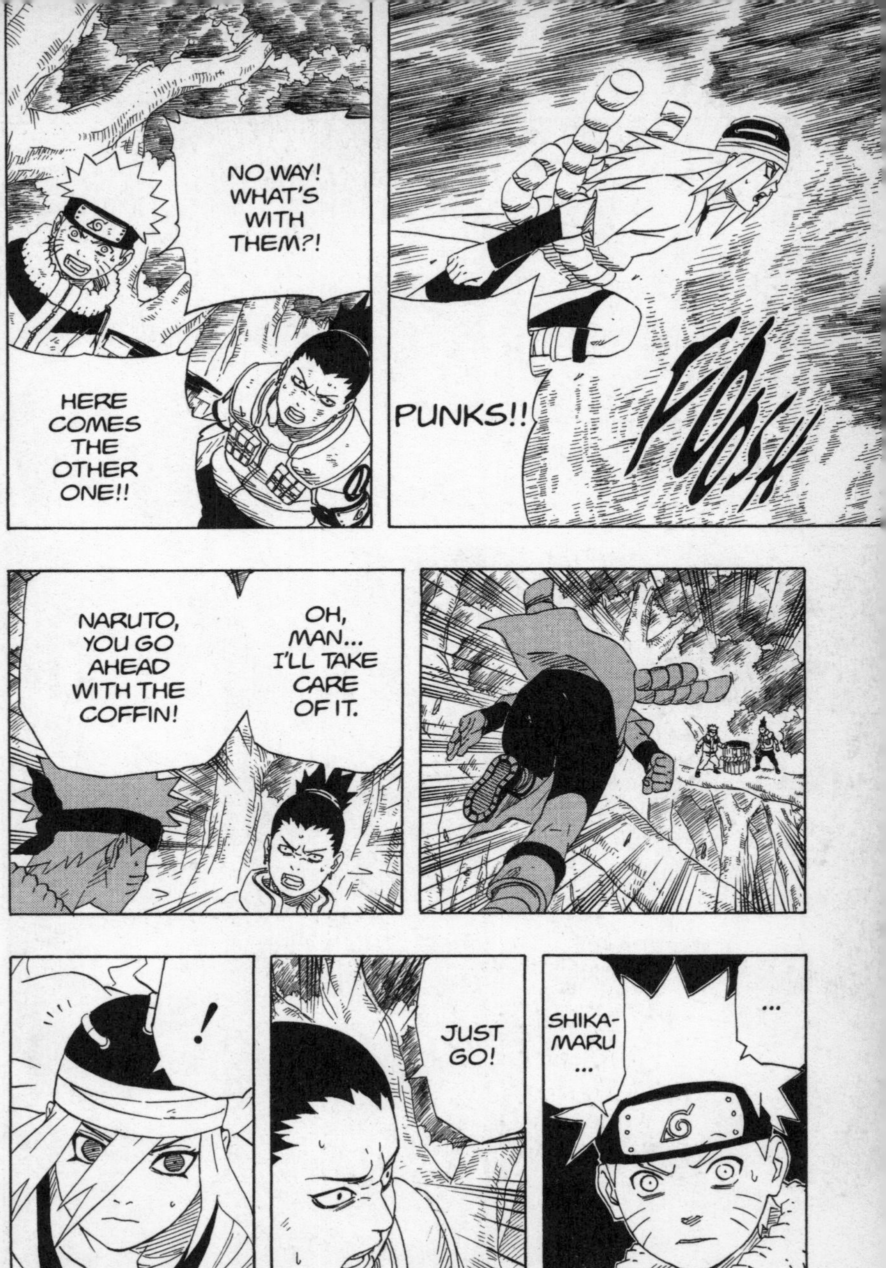
PUNKS!!
FOOSH
NO WAY! WHAT'S WITH THEM?!
HERE COMES THE OTHER ONE!!
OH, MAN... I'LL TAKE CARE OF IT.
NARUTO, YOU GO AHEAD WITH THE COFFIN!
...
SHIKA-MARU ...
JUST GO!
!

READ THIS WAY

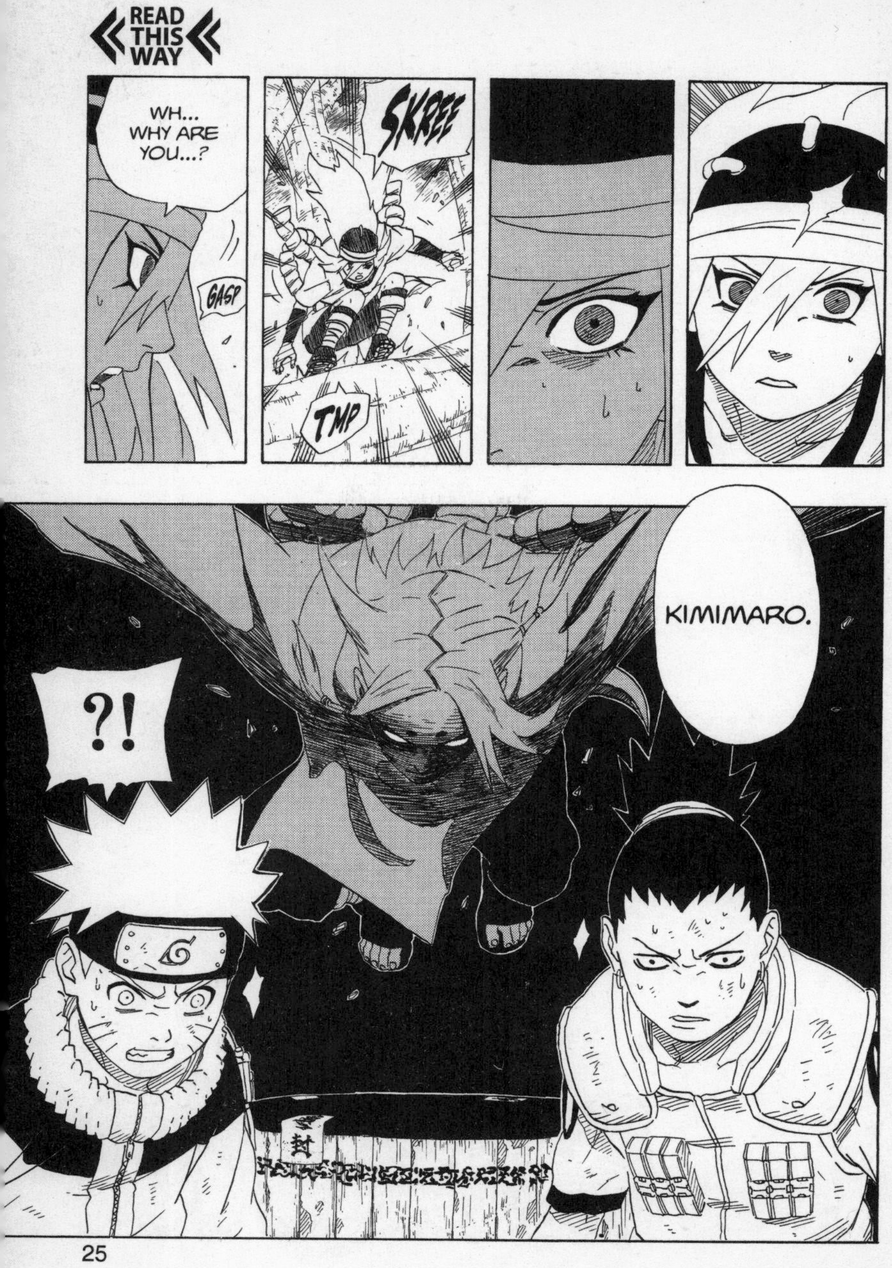
SKREE
TMP
WH... WHY ARE YOU...?
GASP
KIMIMARO.
?!

NARUTO™

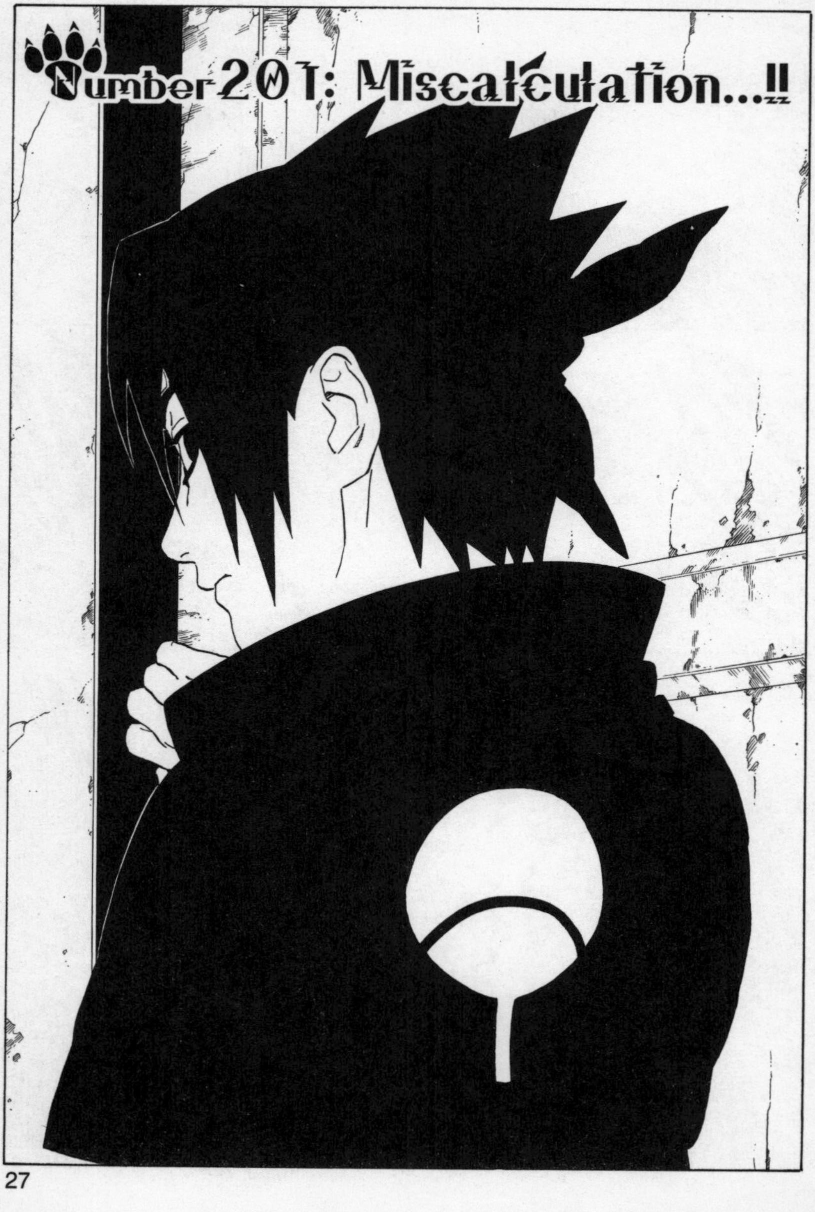
Number 201: Miscalculation...!!

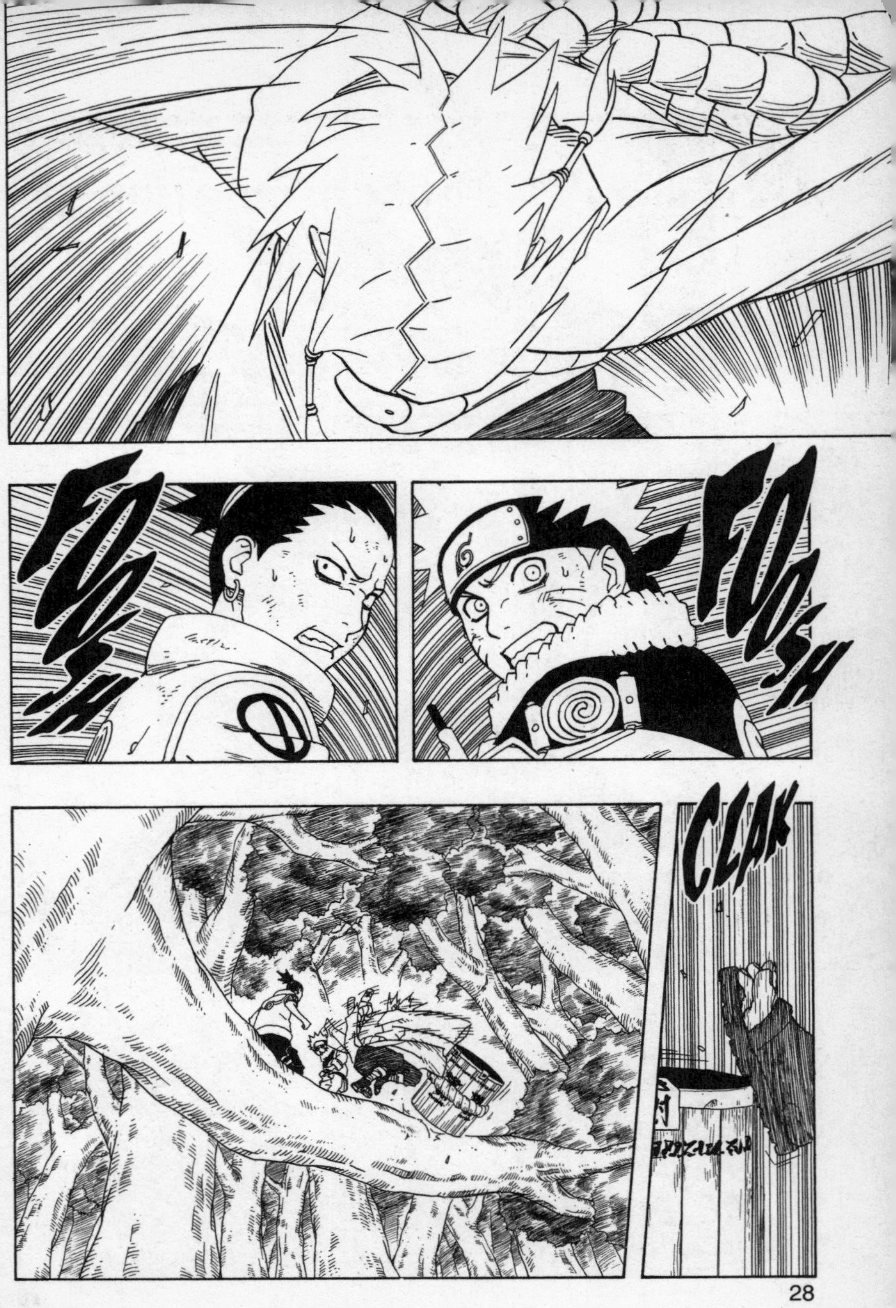
FWOSH
FWOSH
CLAK

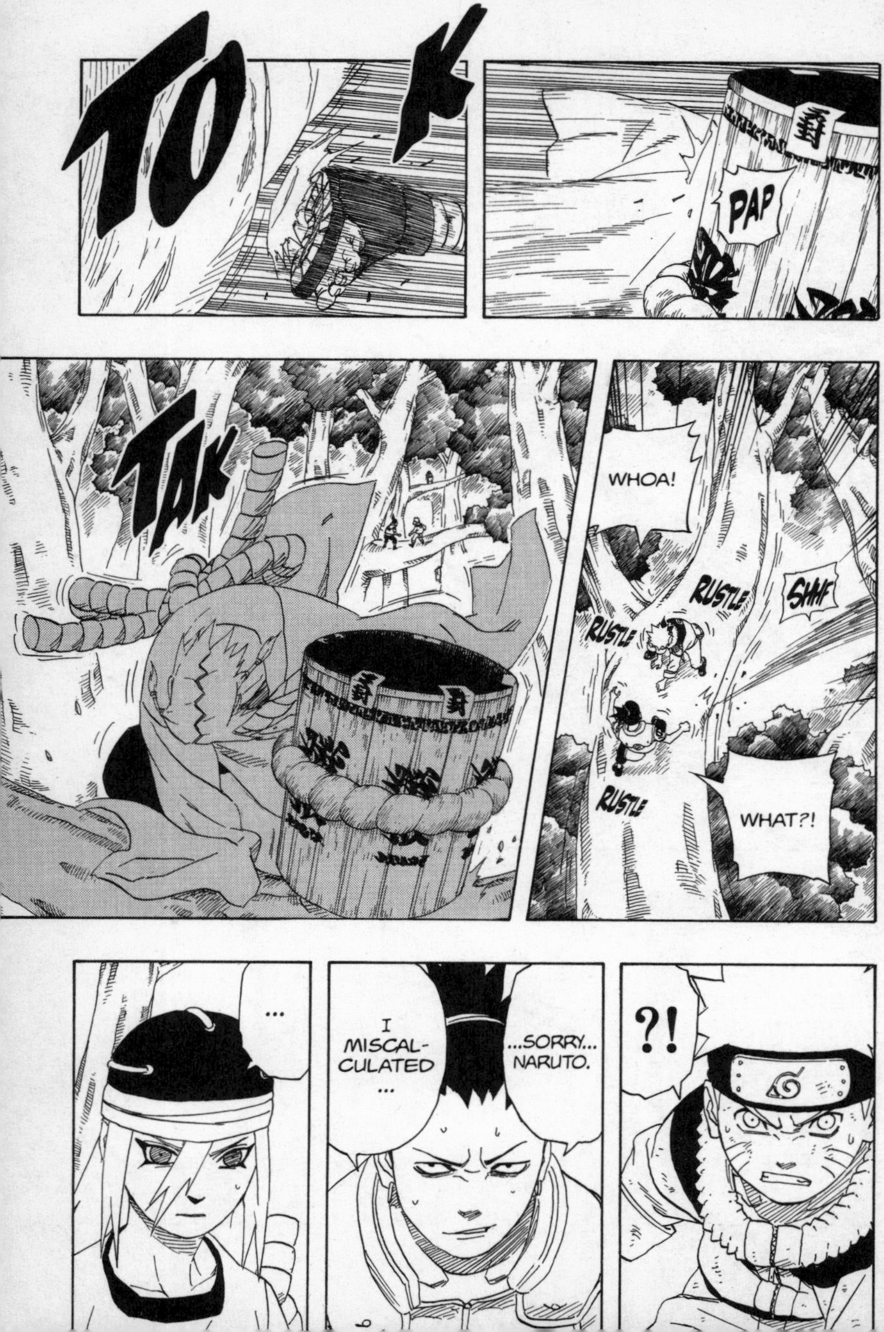
PAP
TOK
WHOA!
SHHF
RUSTLE
RUSTLE
RUSTLE
WHAT?!
TAK
?!
...SORRY... NARUTO.
I MISCAL-CULATED ...
...

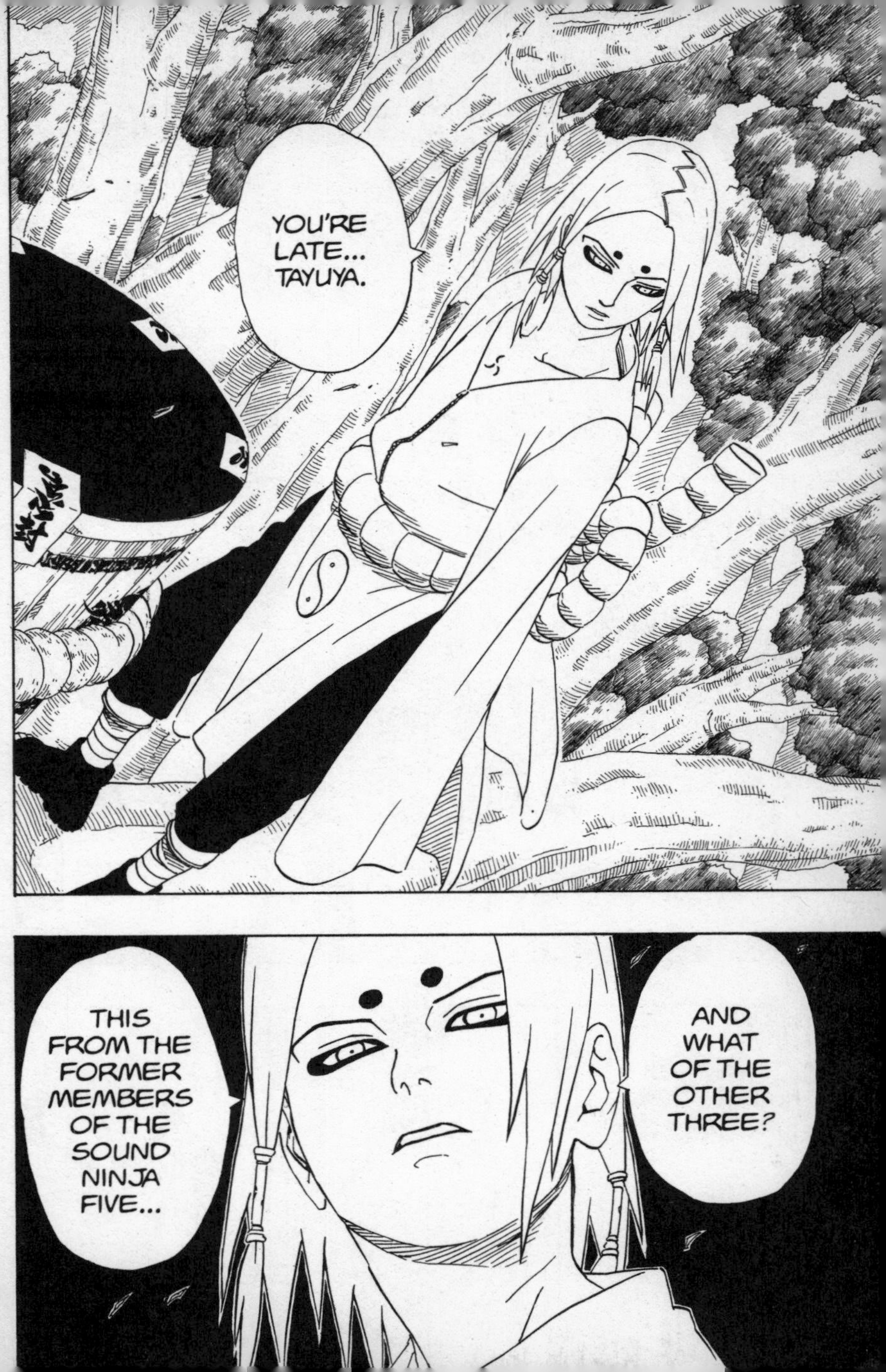
YOU'RE LATE... TAYUYA.
AND WHAT OF THE OTHER THREE?
THIS FROM THE FORMER MEMBERS OF THE SOUND NINJA FIVE...

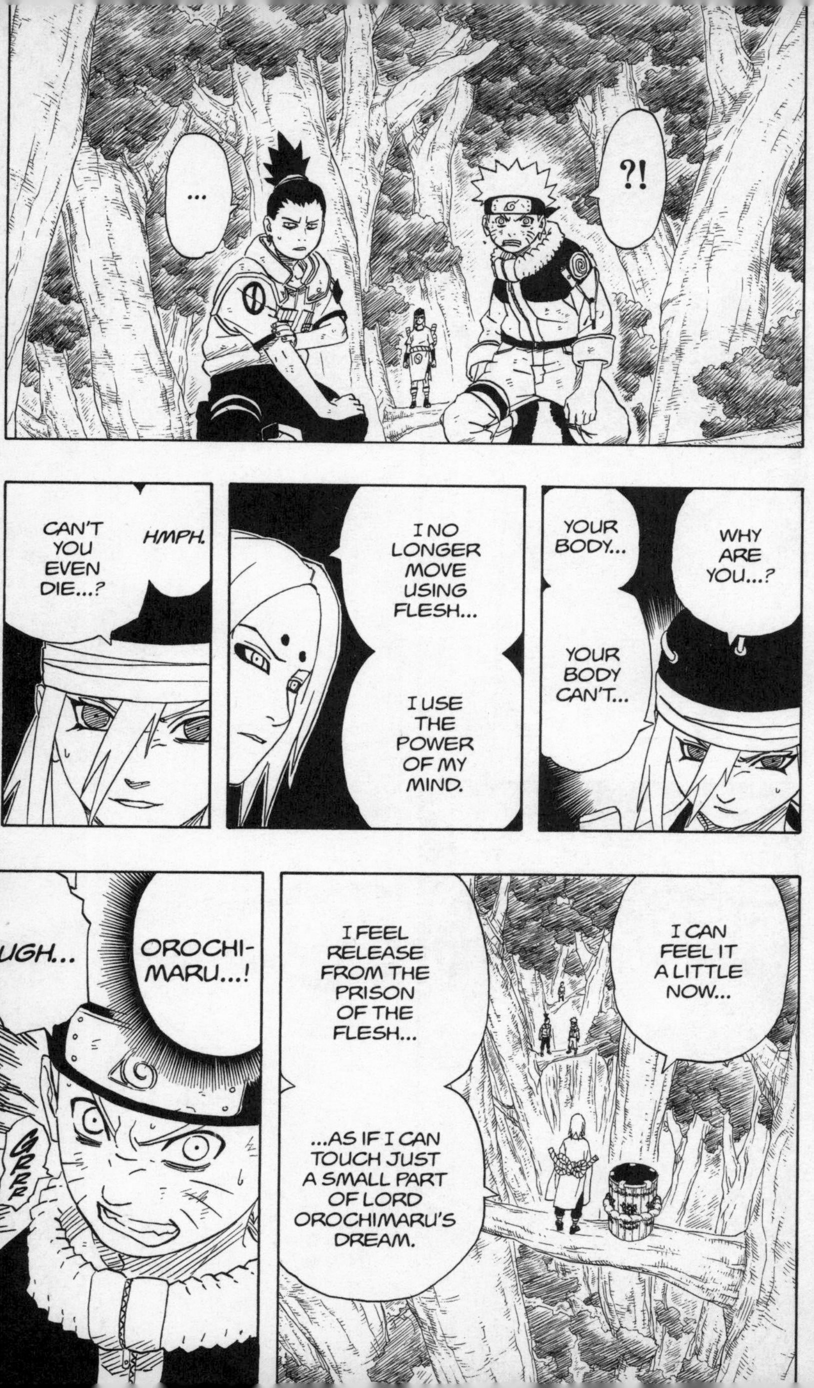
?!
...
WHY ARE YOU...?
YOUR BODY...
YOUR BODY CAN'T...
I NO LONGER MOVE USING FLESH...
I USE THE POWER OF MY MIND.
HMPH.
CAN'T YOU EVEN DIE...?
I CAN FEEL IT A LITTLE NOW...
I FEEL RELEASE FROM THE PRISON OF THE FLESH...
...AS IF I CAN TOUCH JUST A SMALL PART OF LORD OROCHIMARU'S DREAM.
OROCHI-MARU...!
UGH...
GRRR

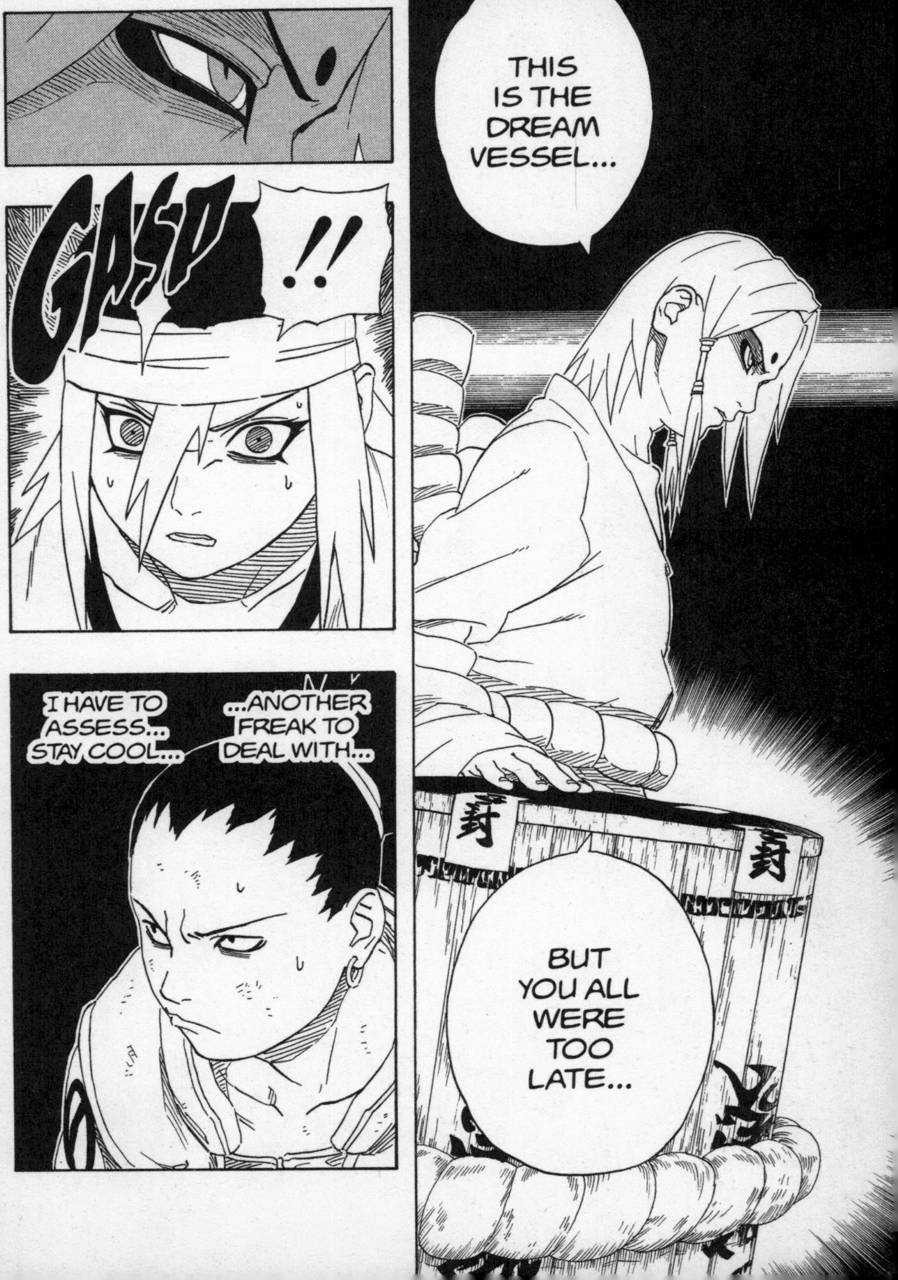
THIS IS THE DREAM VESSEL...
BUT YOU ALL WERE TOO LATE...
!!
GASP
...ANOTHER FREAK TO DEAL WITH...
I HAVE TO ASSESS... STAY COOL...

READ THIS WAY

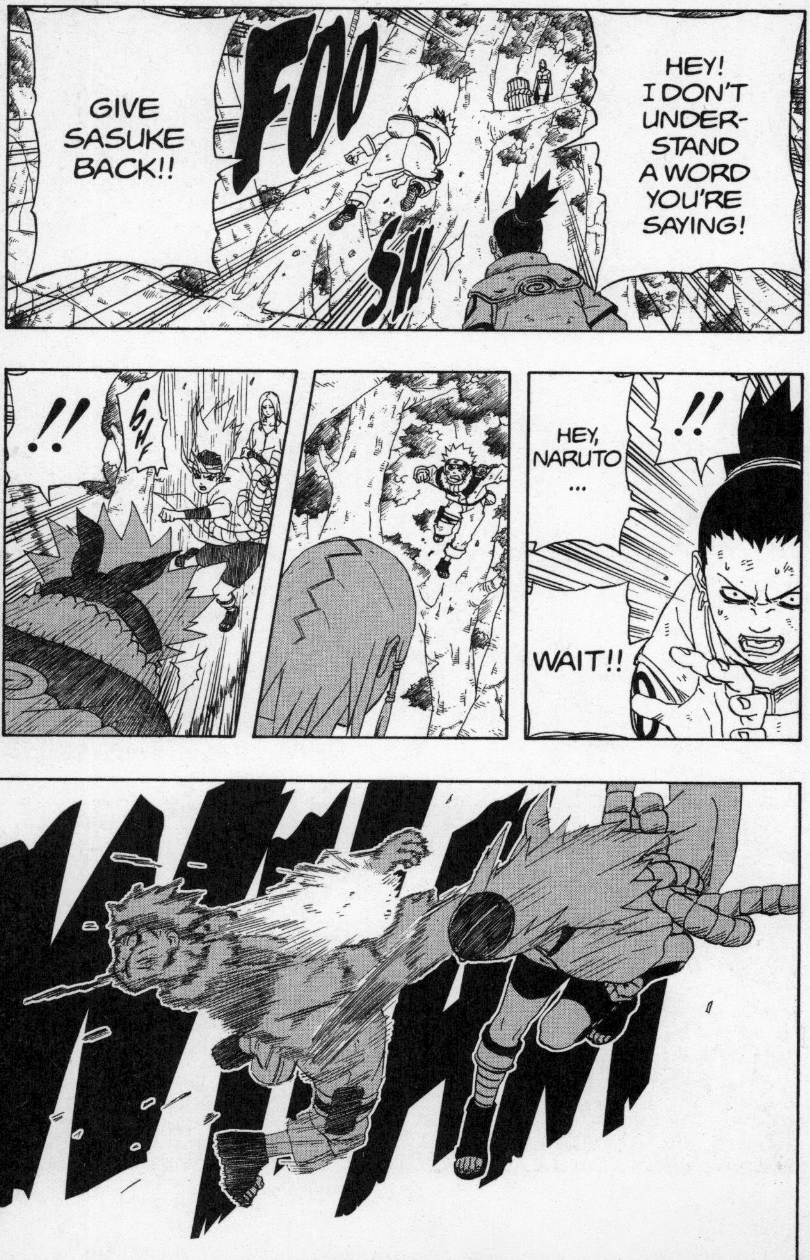
HEY! I DON'T UNDERSTAND A WORD YOU'RE SAYING!
FOOSH
GIVE SASUKE BACK!!
!!
HEY, NARUTO ...
WAIT!!
!!
SHF

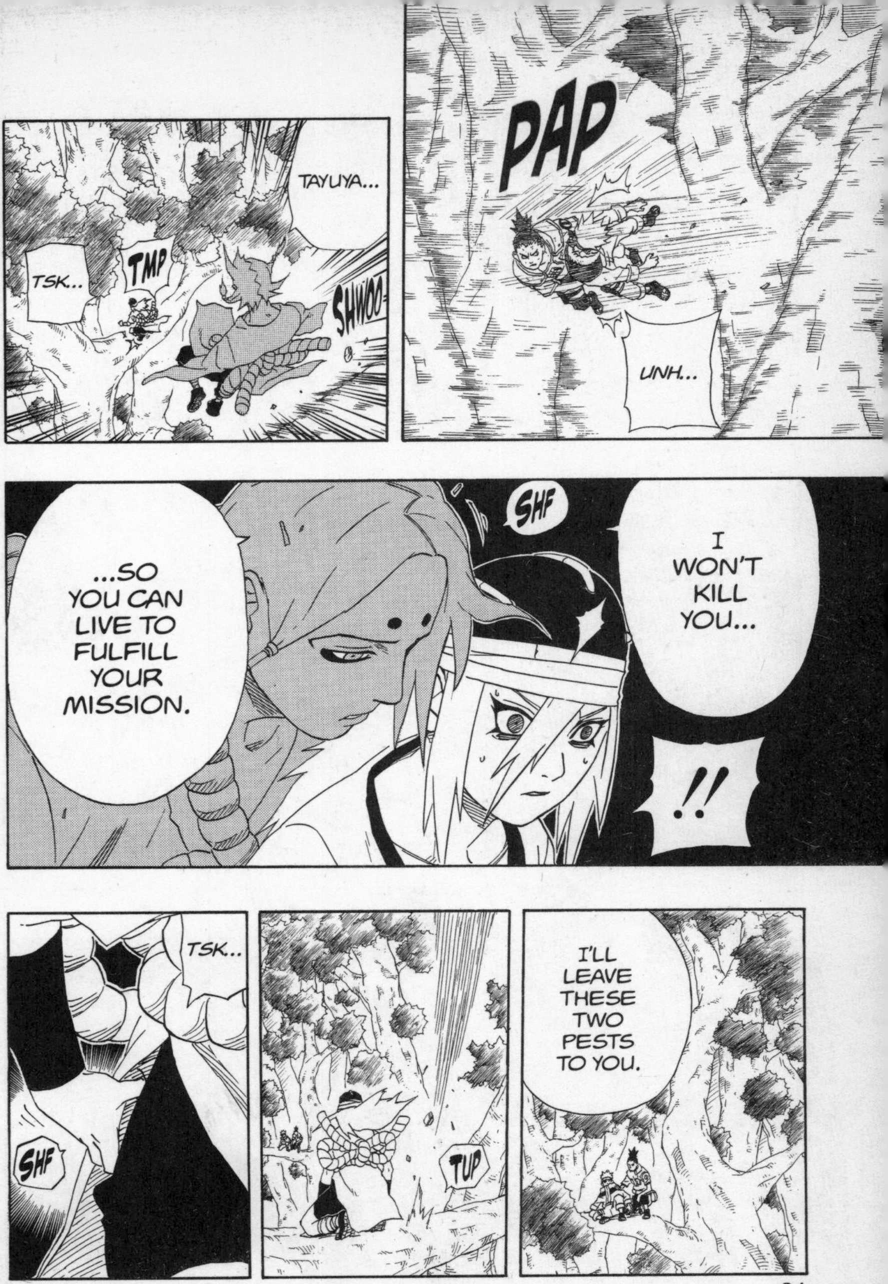
PAP
UNH...
TAYUYA...
SHWOO
TMP
TSK...
I WON'T KILL YOU...
SHF
!!
...SO YOU CAN LIVE TO FULFILL YOUR MISSION.
I'LL LEAVE THESE TWO PESTS TO YOU.
TUP
TSK...
SHF

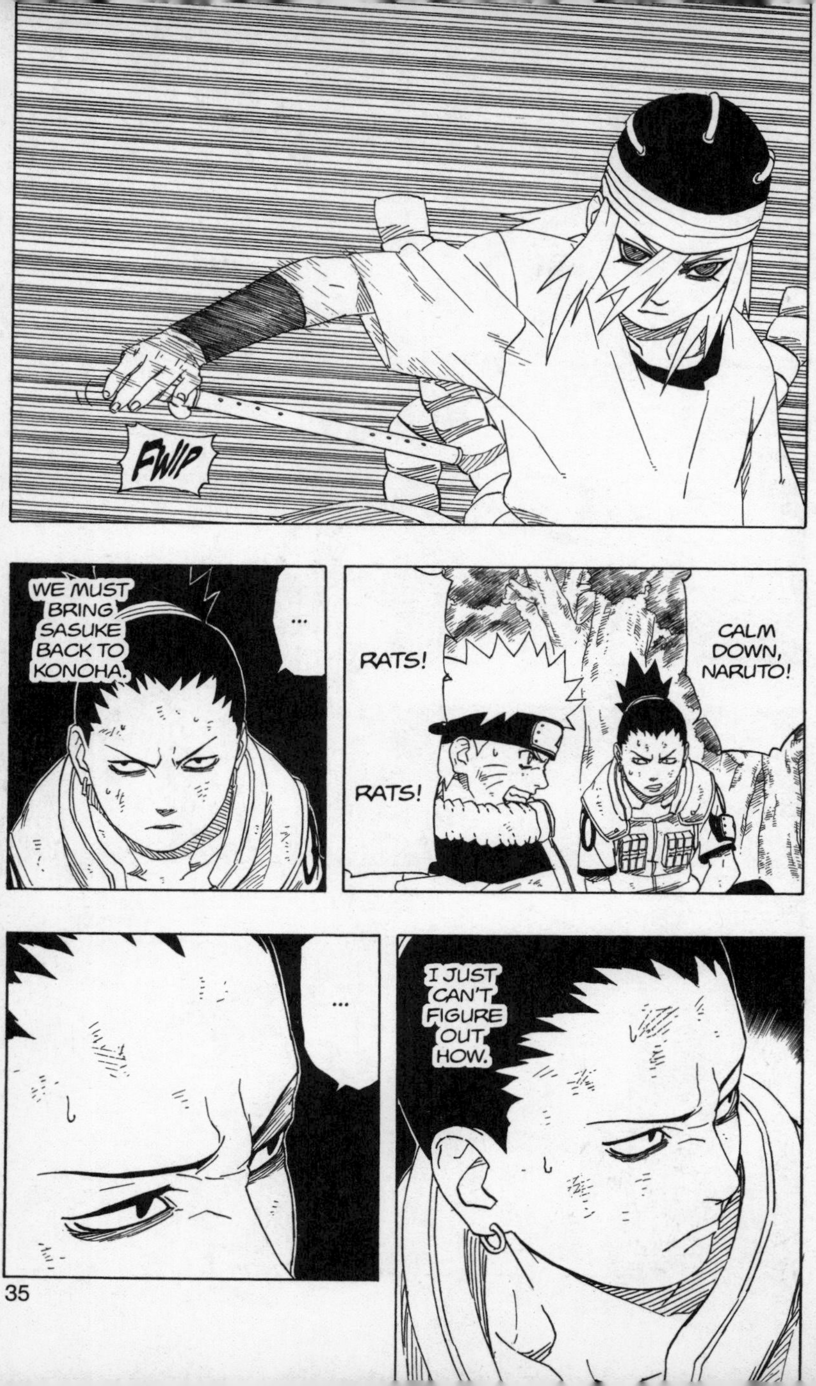
FWIP
CALM DOWN, NARUTO!
RATS!
RATS!
...
WE MUST BRING SASUKE BACK TO KONOHA.
I JUST CAN'T FIGURE OUT HOW.
...

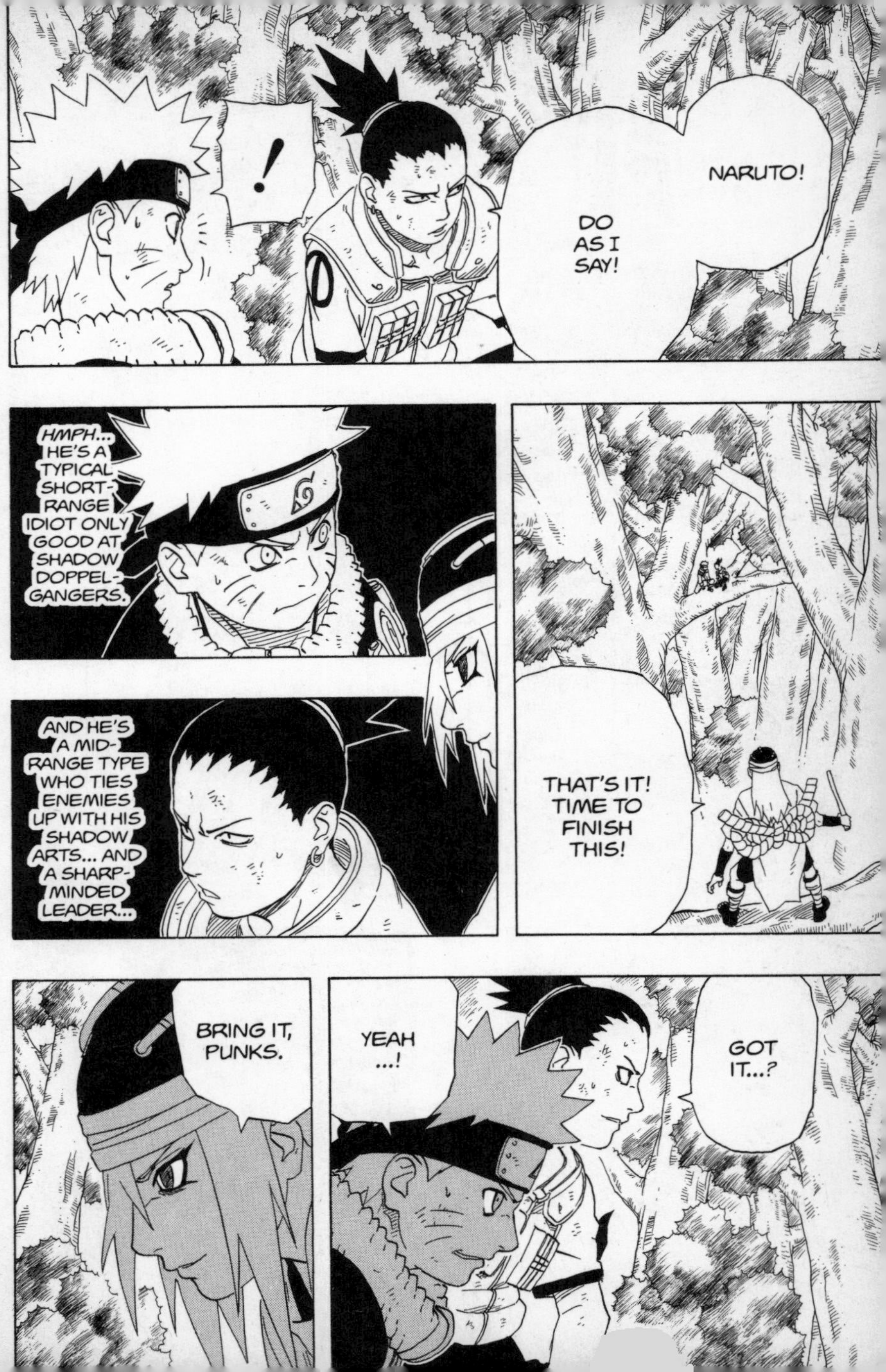
NARUTO! DO AS I SAY!
!
THAT'S IT! TIME TO FINISH THIS!
HMPH... HE'S A TYPICAL SHORT-RANGE IDIOT ONLY GOOD AT SHADOW DOPPEL-GANGERS.
AND HE'S A MID-RANGE TYPE WHO TIES ENEMIES UP WITH HIS SHADOW ARTS... AND A SHARP-MINDED LEADER...
GOT IT...?
YEAH ...!
BRING IT, PUNKS.

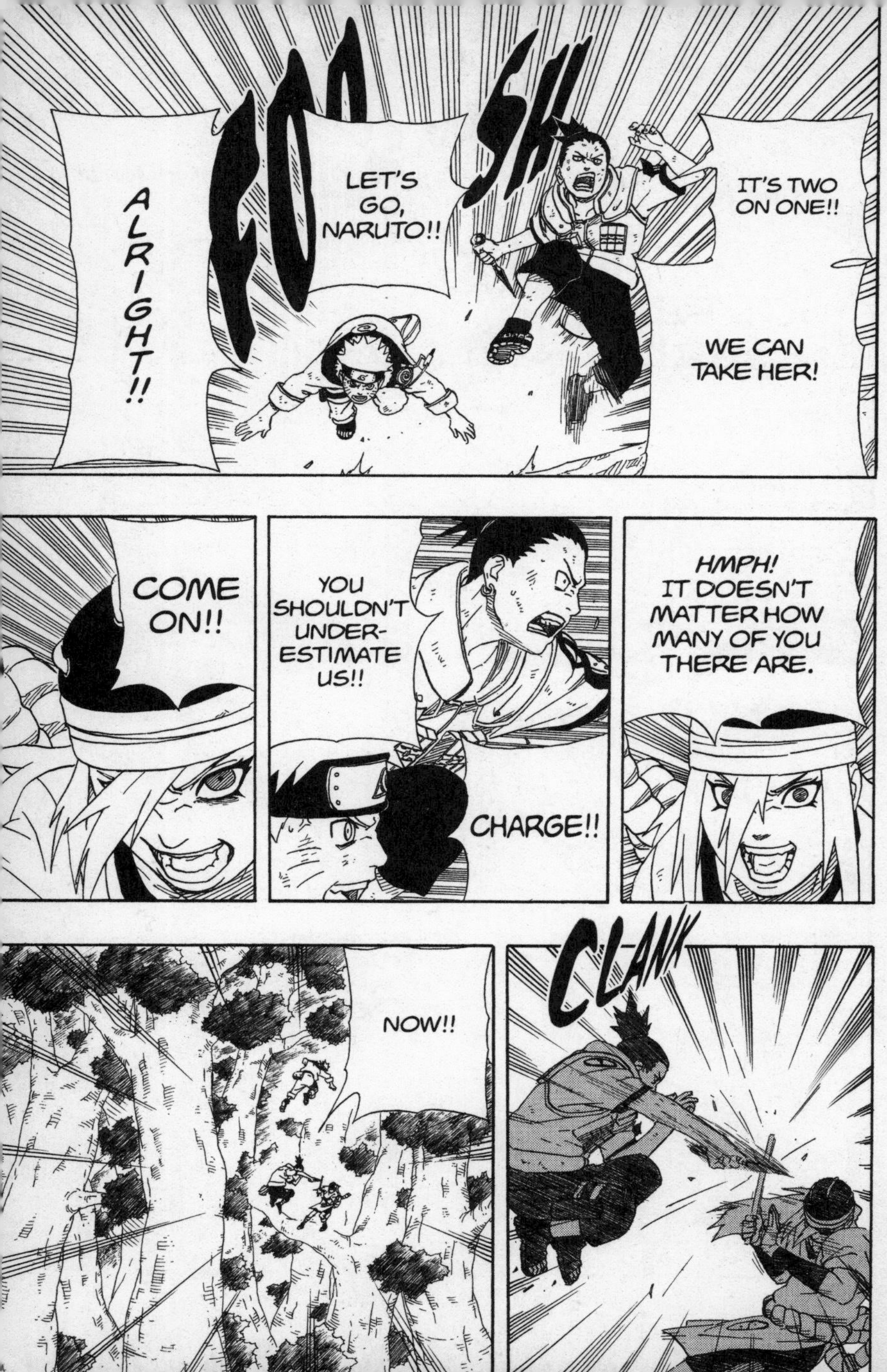
IT'S TWO ON ONE!!
WE CAN TAKE HER!
FOOSH
LET'S GO, NARUTO!!
ALRIGHT!!
HMPH! IT DOESN'T MATTER HOW MANY OF YOU THERE ARE.
YOU SHOULDN'T UNDER-ESTIMATE US!!
CHARGE!!
COME ON!!
CLANK
NOW!!

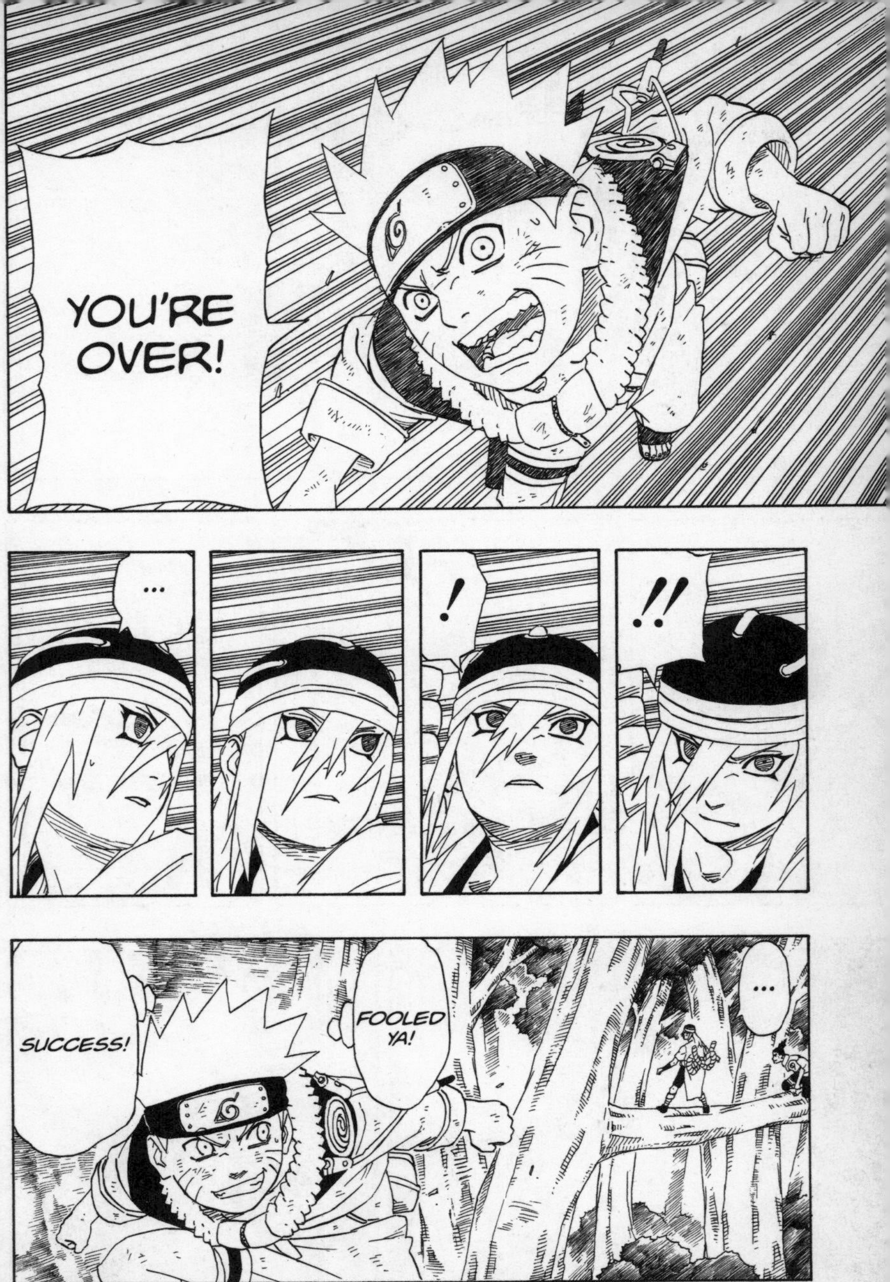
YOU'RE OVER!
!!
!
...
...
FOOLED YA!
SUCCESS!

READ THIS WAY

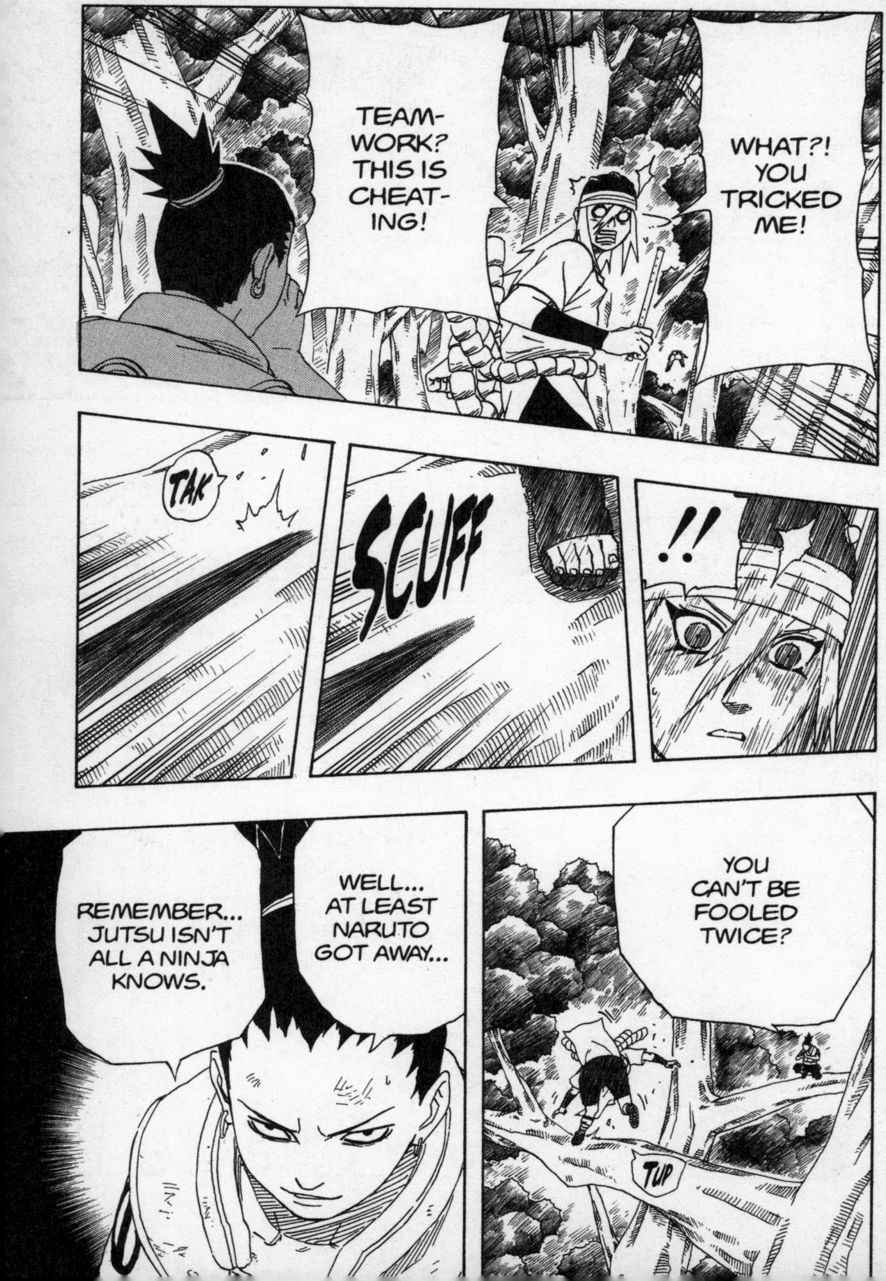
WHAT?! YOU TRICKED ME!
TEAM-WORK? THIS IS CHEAT-ING!
!!
SCUFF
TAK
YOU CAN'T BE FOOLED TWICE?
TUP
WELL... AT LEAST NARUTO GOT AWAY...
REMEMBER... JUTSU ISN'T ALL A NINJA KNOWS.

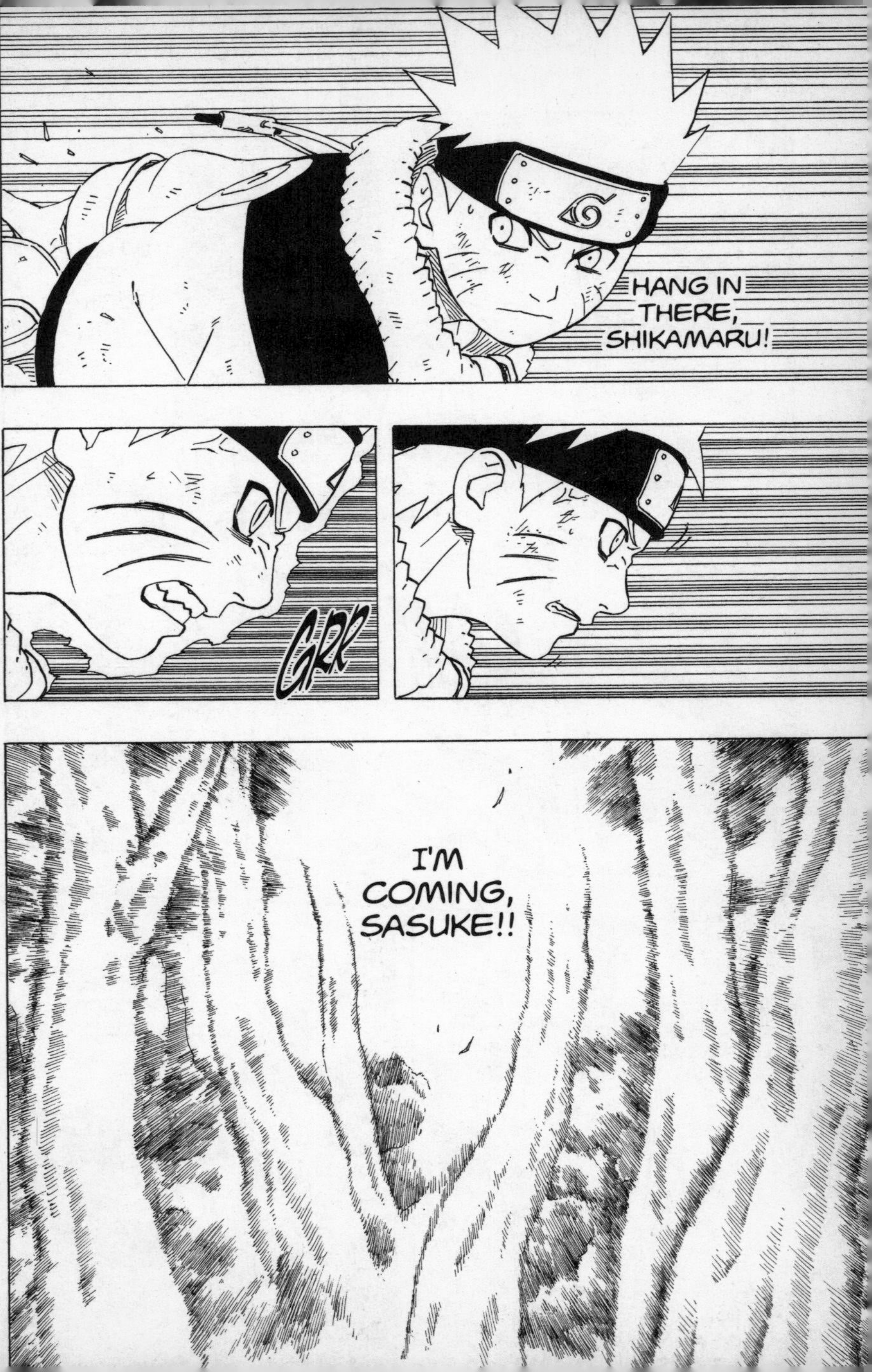
HANG IN THERE, SHIKAMARU!
GRR
I'M COMING, SASUKE!!

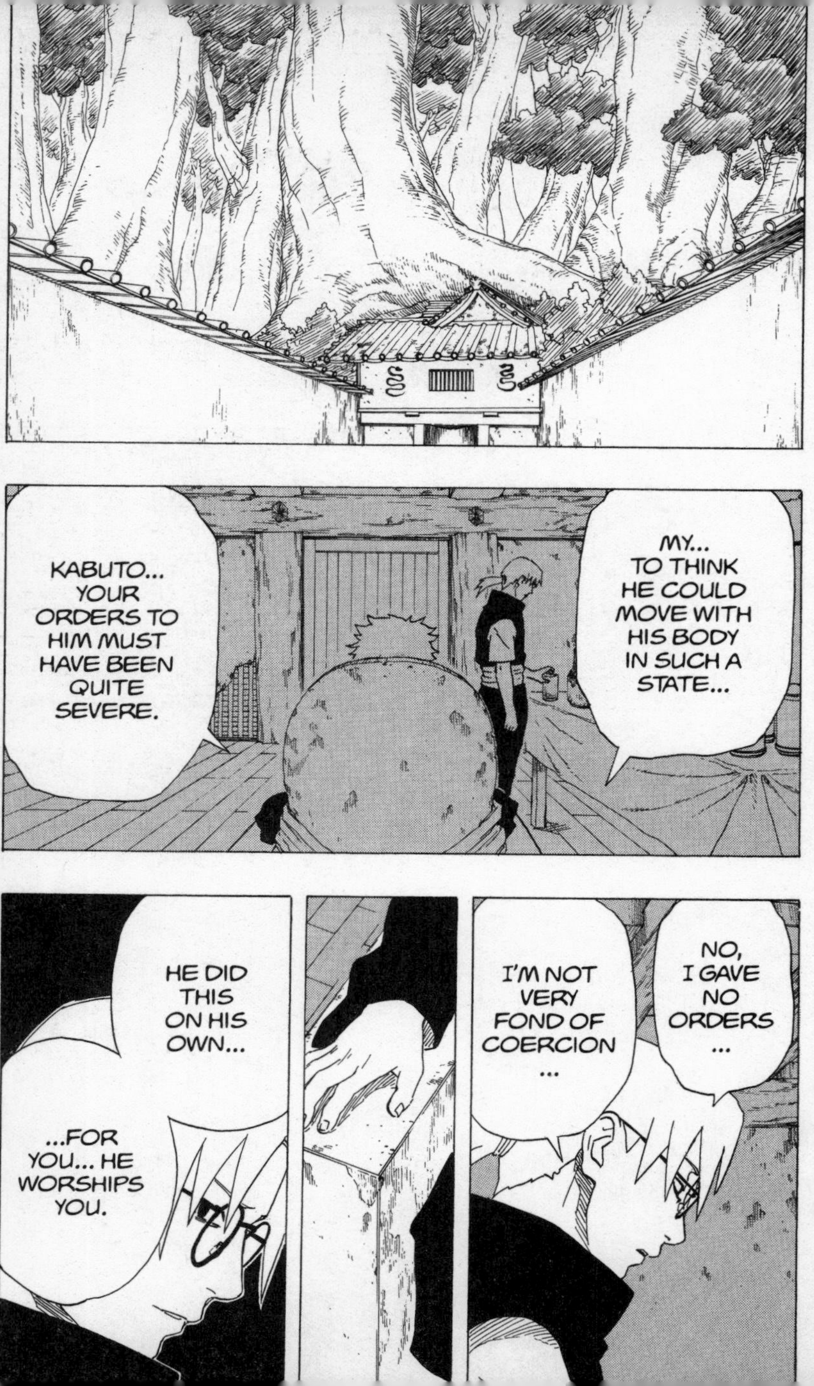
MY... TO THINK HE COULD MOVE WITH HIS BODY IN SUCH A STATE...
KABUTO... YOUR ORDERS TO HIM MUST HAVE BEEN QUITE SEVERE.
NO, I GAVE NO ORDERS ...
I'M NOT VERY FOND OF COERCION ...
HE DID THIS ON HIS OWN...
...FOR YOU... HE WORSHIPS YOU.

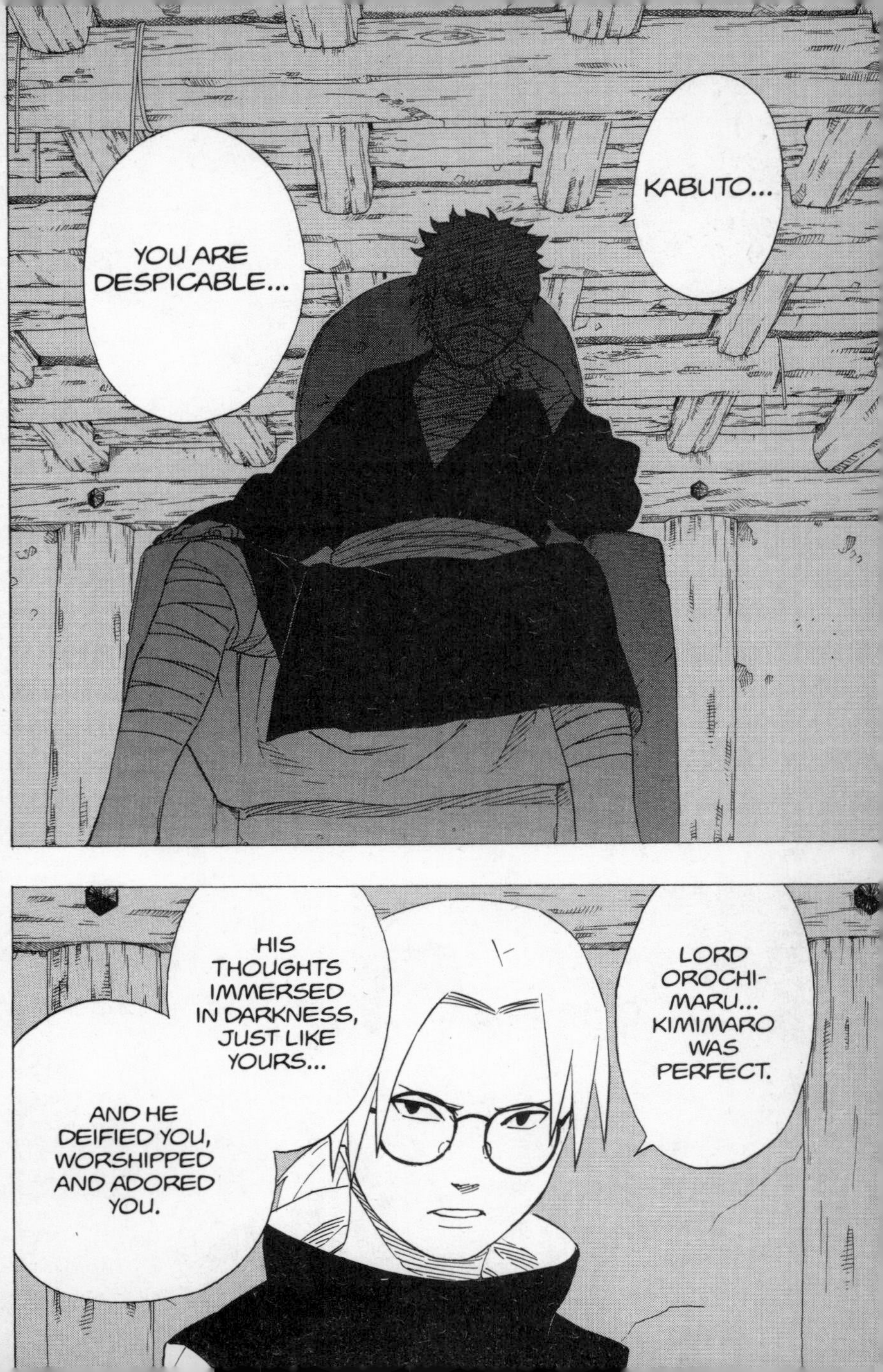
KABUTO...
YOU ARE DESPICABLE...
LORD OROCHI-MARU... KIMIMARO WAS PERFECT.
HIS THOUGHTS IMMERSED IN DARKNESS, JUST LIKE YOURS...
AND HE DEIFIED YOU, WORSHIPPED AND ADORED YOU.

READ THIS WAY

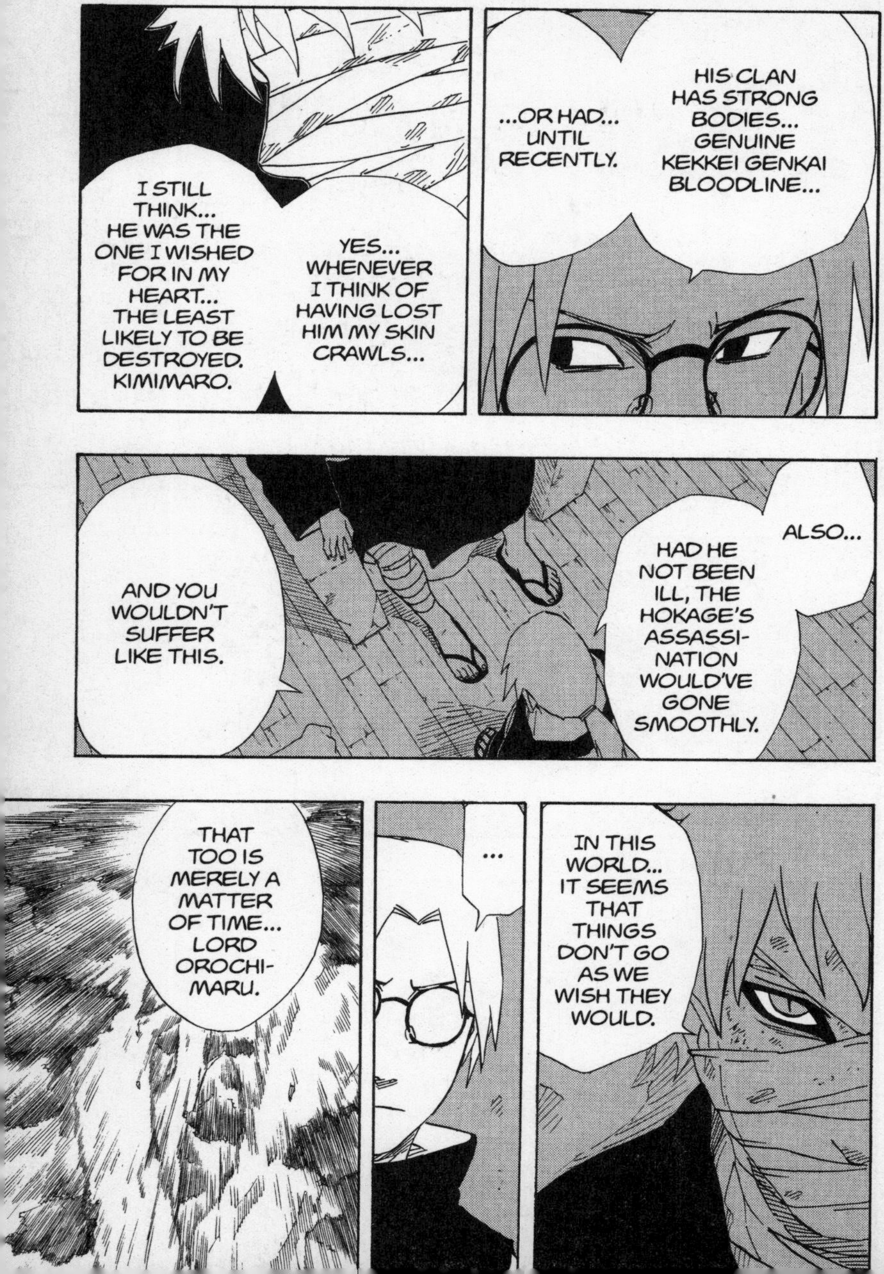

HIS CLAN HAS STRONG BODIES... GENUINE KEKKEI GENKAI BLOODLINE...
...OR HAD... UNTIL RECENTLY.
YES... WHENEVER I THINK OF HAVING LOST HIM MY SKIN CRAWLS...
I STILL THINK... HE WAS THE ONE I WISHED FOR IN MY HEART... THE LEAST LIKELY TO BE DESTROYED. KIMIMARO.
ALSO...
HAD HE NOT BEEN ILL, THE HOKAGE'S ASSASSI-NATION WOULD'VE GONE SMOOTHLY.
AND YOU WOULDN'T SUFFER LIKE THIS.
IN THIS WORLD... IT SEEMS THAT THINGS DON'T GO AS WE WISH THEY WOULD.
...
THAT TOO IS MERELY A MATTER OF TIME... LORD OROCHI-MARU.

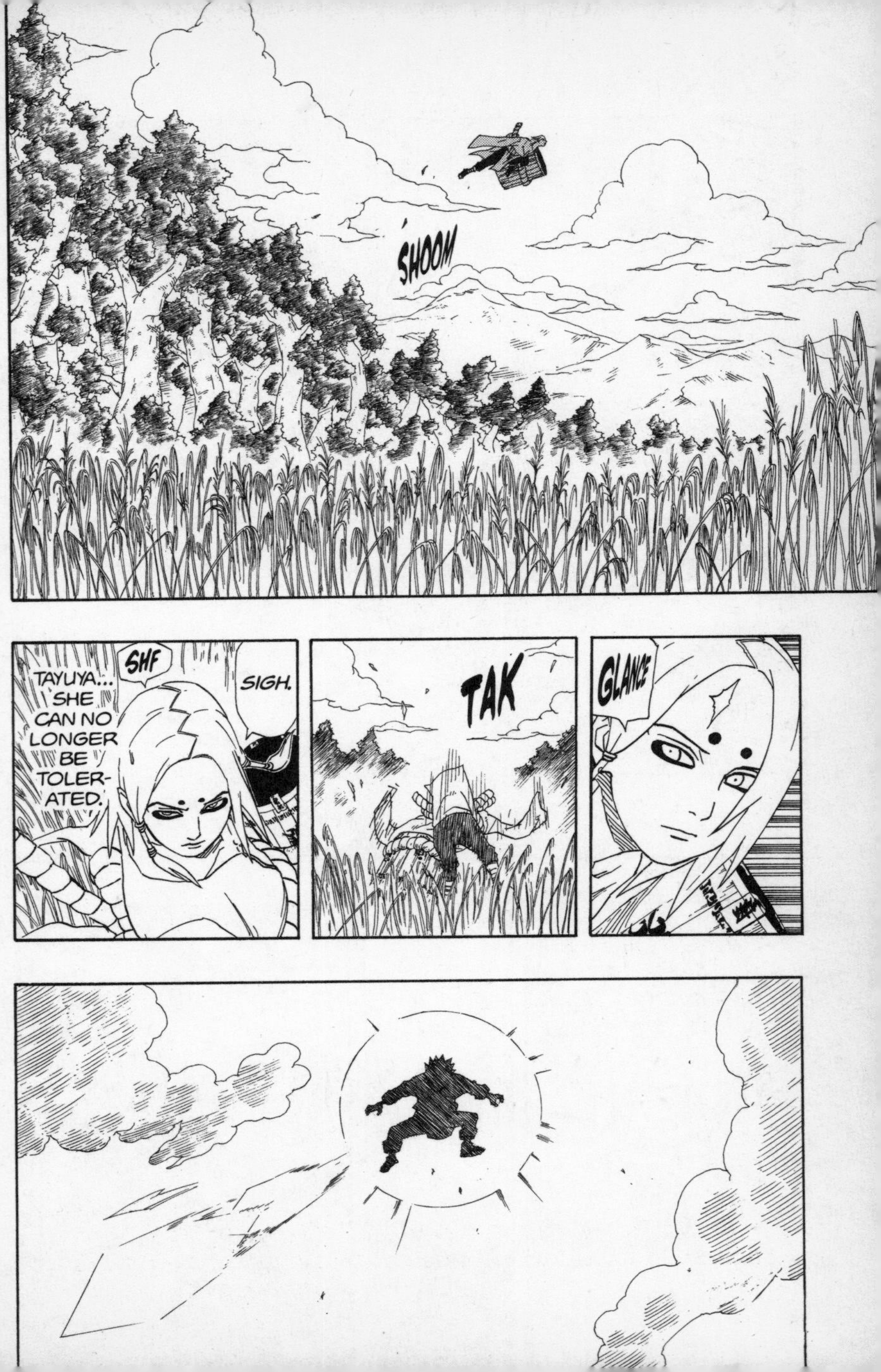
SHOOM
GLANCE
TAK
SIGH.
SHF
TAYUYA... SHE CAN NO LONGER BE TOLERATED.

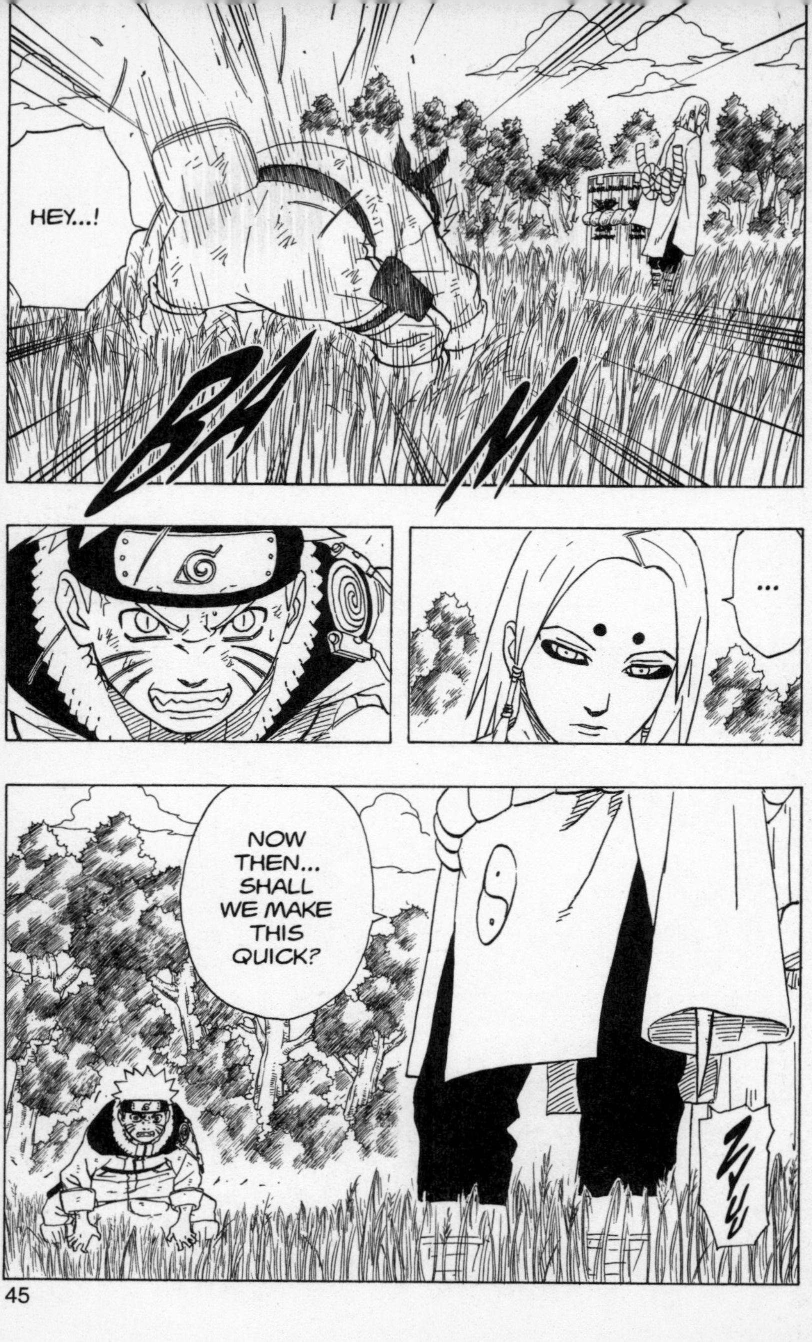
HEY...!
BAM
...
NOW THEN... SHALL WE MAKE THIS QUICK?

NARUTO™

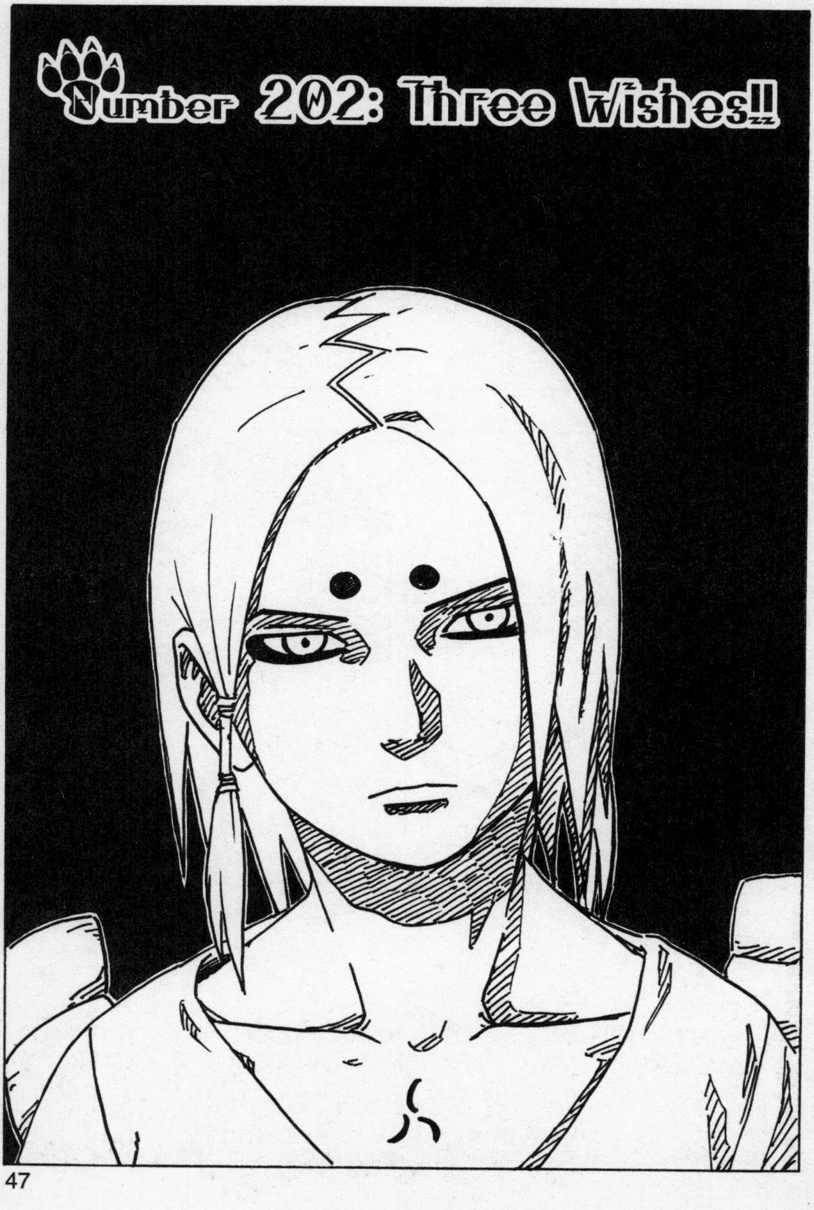
Number 202: Three Wishes!!

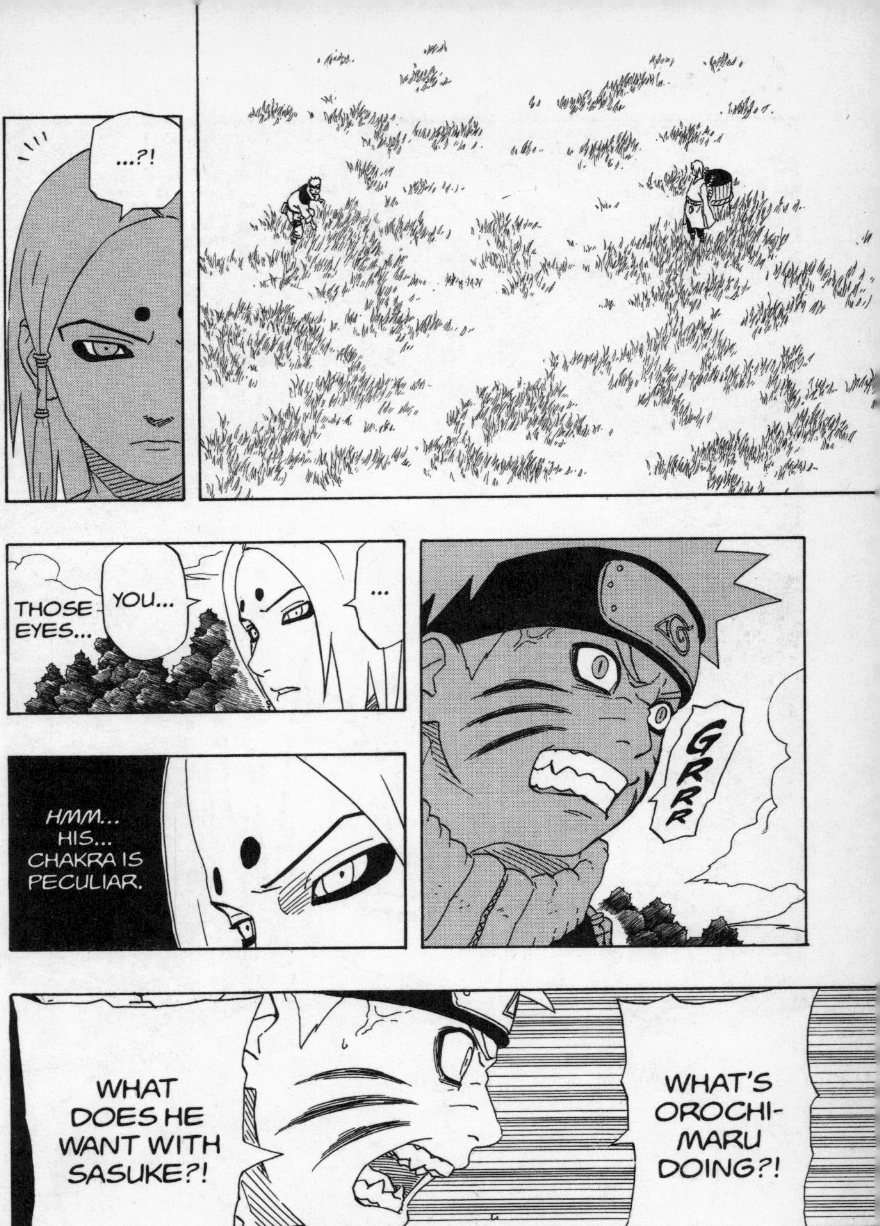
...?!
GRRR
...
YOU...
THOSE EYES...
HMM... HIS... CHAKRA IS PECULIAR.
WHAT'S OROCHIMARU DOING?!
WHAT DOES HE WANT WITH SASUKE?!

READ THIS WAY

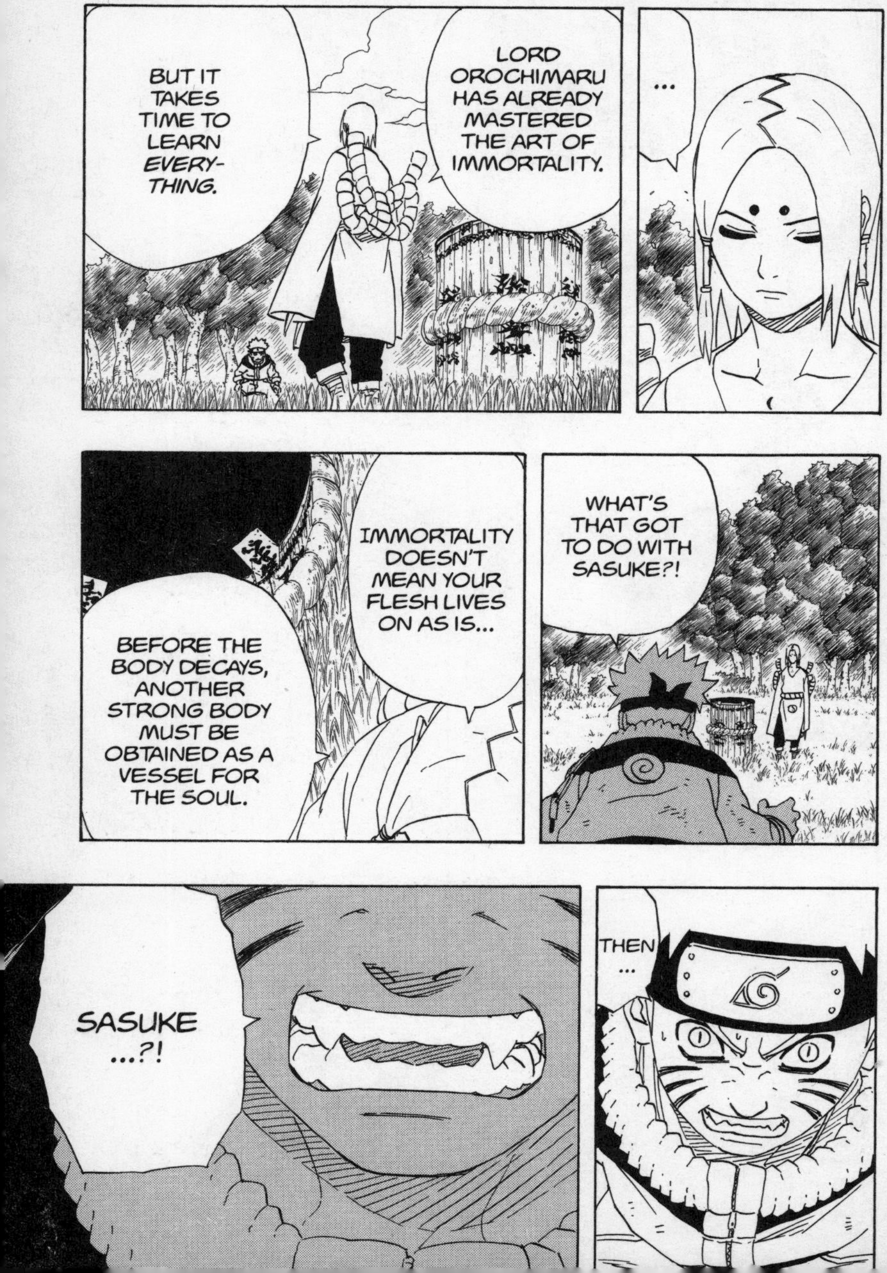
...
LORD OROCHIMARU HAS ALREADY MASTERED THE ART OF IMMORTALITY.
BUT IT TAKES TIME TO LEARN EVERY-THING.
WHAT'S THAT GOT TO DO WITH SASUKE?!
IMMORTALITY DOESN'T MEAN YOUR FLESH LIVES ON AS IS...
BEFORE THE BODY DECAYS, ANOTHER STRONG BODY MUST BE OBTAINED AS A VESSEL FOR THE SOUL.
THEN ...
SASUKE ...?!

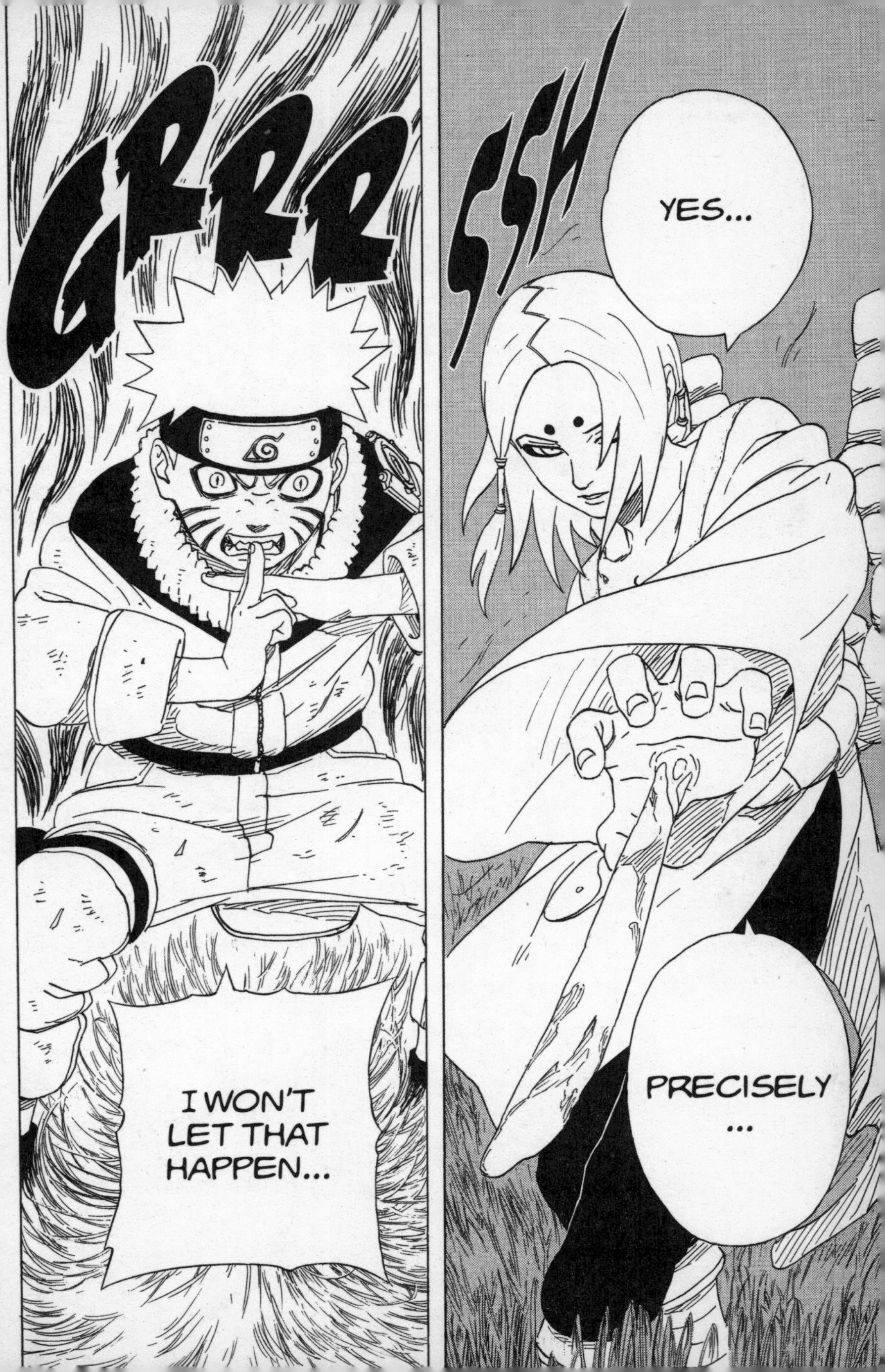
SSH
YES...
PRECISELY ...
GRRR
I WON'T LET THAT HAPPEN...

READ THIS WAY

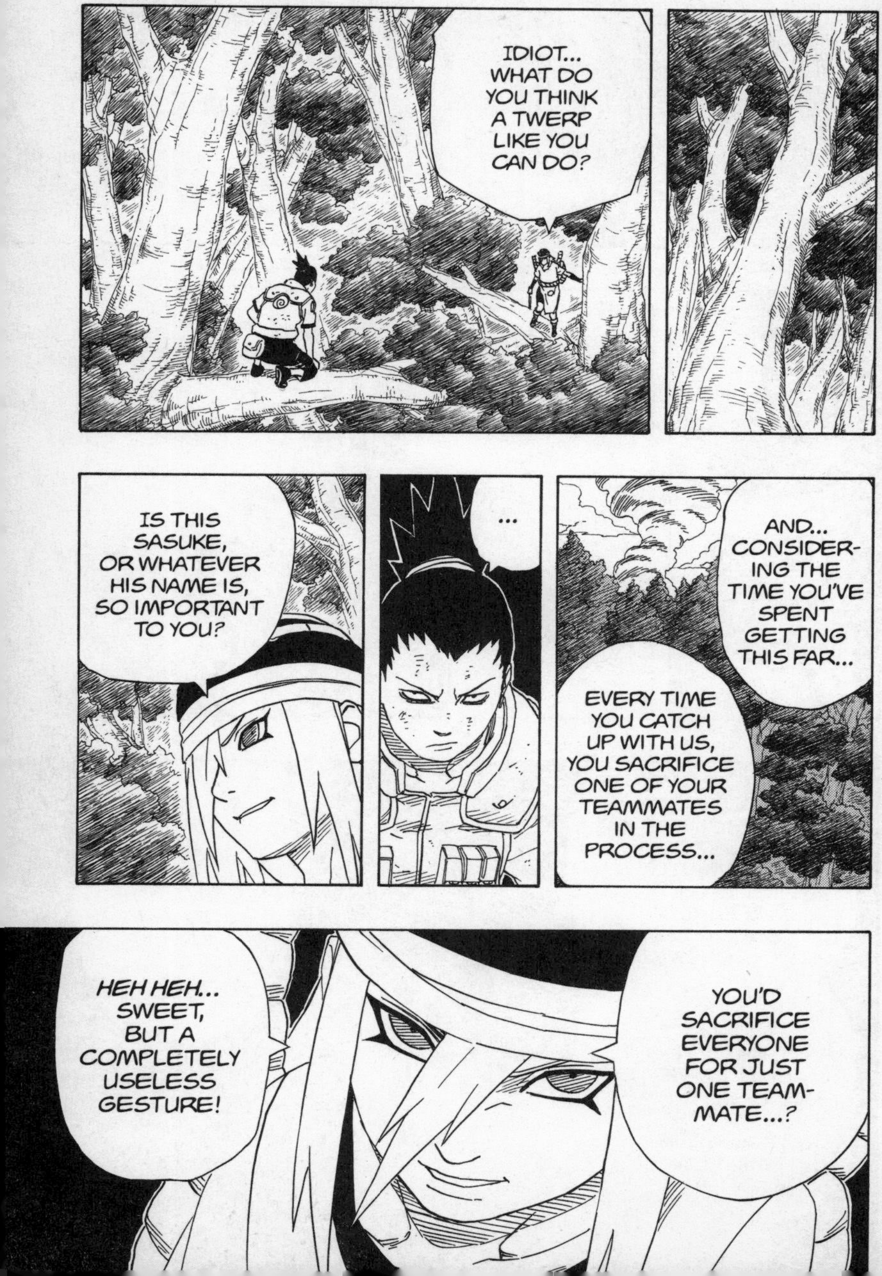
IDIOT... WHAT DO YOU THINK A TWERP LIKE YOU CAN DO?
AND... CONSIDER-ING THE TIME YOU'VE SPENT GETTING THIS FAR...
EVERY TIME YOU CATCH UP WITH US, YOU SACRIFICE ONE OF YOUR TEAMMATES IN THE PROCESS...
...
IS THIS SASUKE, OR WHATEVER HIS NAME IS, SO IMPORTANT TO YOU?
YOU'D SACRIFICE EVERYONE FOR JUST ONE TEAM-MATE...?
HEH HEH... SWEET, BUT A COMPLETELY USELESS GESTURE!

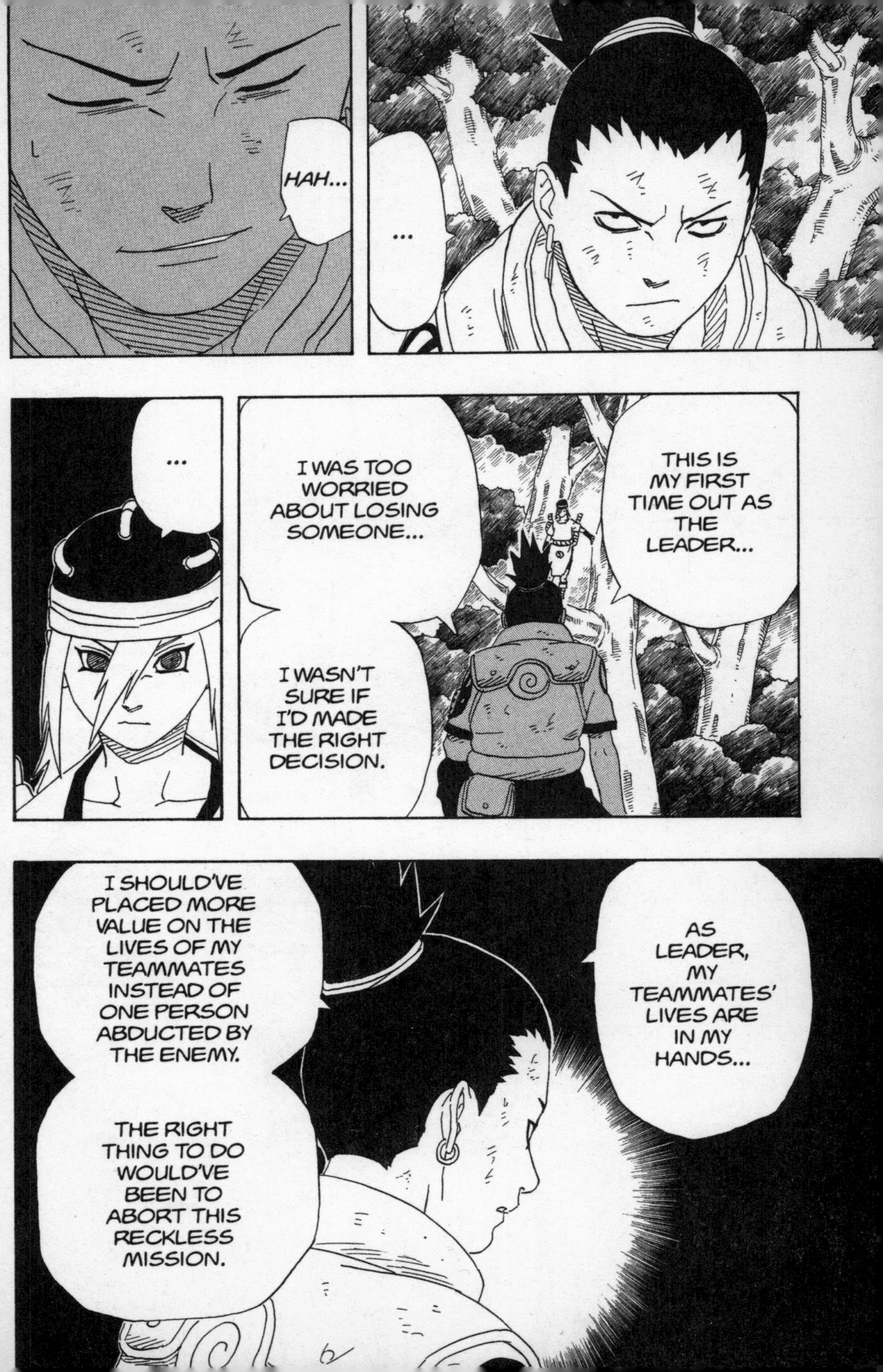
...
HAH...
THIS IS MY FIRST TIME OUT AS THE LEADER...
I WAS TOO WORRIED ABOUT LOSING SOMEONE...
I WASN'T SURE IF I'D MADE THE RIGHT DECISION.
...
AS LEADER, MY TEAMMATES' LIVES ARE IN MY HANDS...
I SHOULD'VE PLACED MORE VALUE ON THE LIVES OF MY TEAMMATES INSTEAD OF ONE PERSON ABDUCTED BY THE ENEMY.
THE RIGHT THING TO DO WOULD'VE BEEN TO ABORT THIS RECKLESS MISSION.

READ THIS WAY

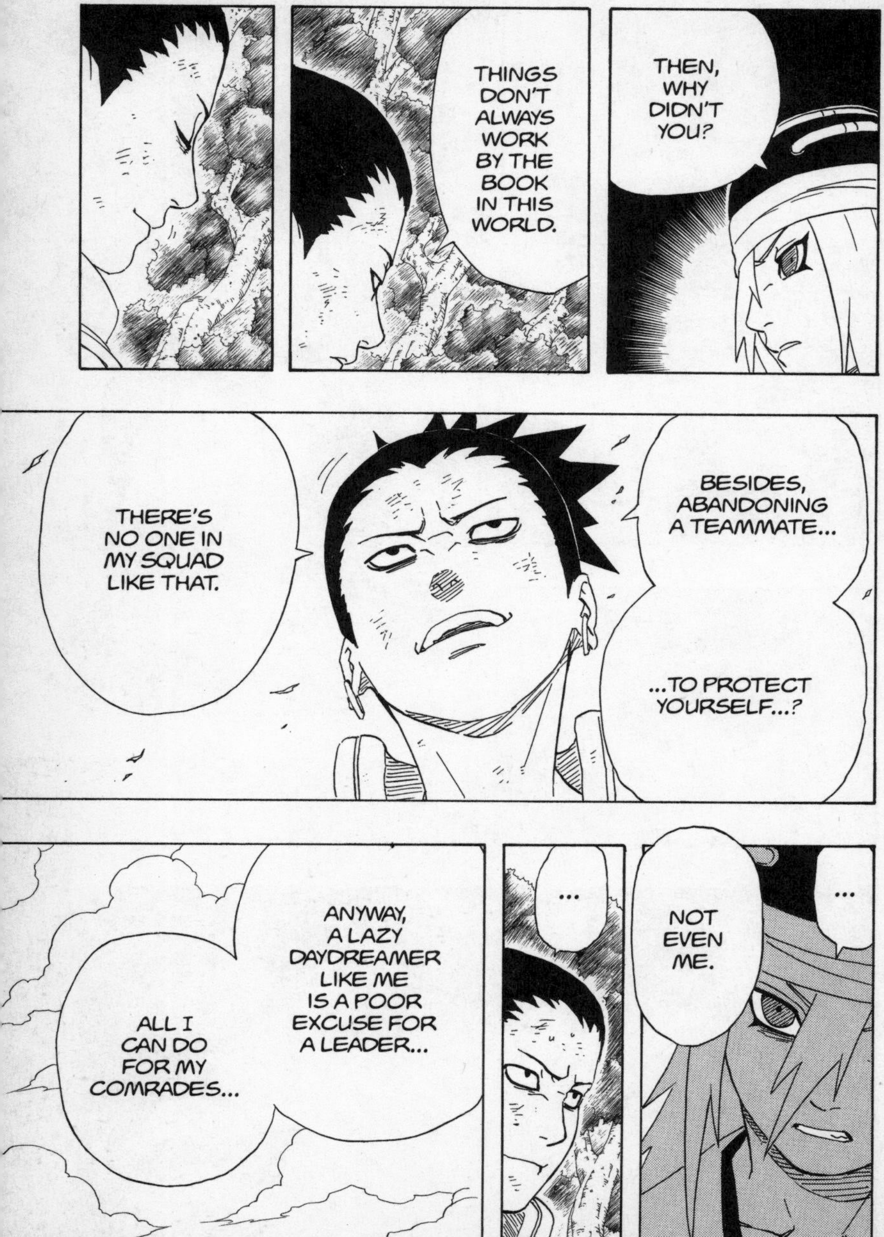
THEN, WHY DIDN'T YOU?
THINGS DON'T ALWAYS WORK BY THE BOOK IN THIS WORLD.
BESIDES, ABANDONING A TEAMMATE...
...TO PROTECT YOURSELF...?
THERE'S NO ONE IN MY SQUAD LIKE THAT.
...
NOT EVEN ME.
...
ANYWAY, A LAZY DAYDREAMER LIKE ME IS A POOR EXCUSE FOR A LEADER...
ALL I CAN DO FOR MY COMRADES...

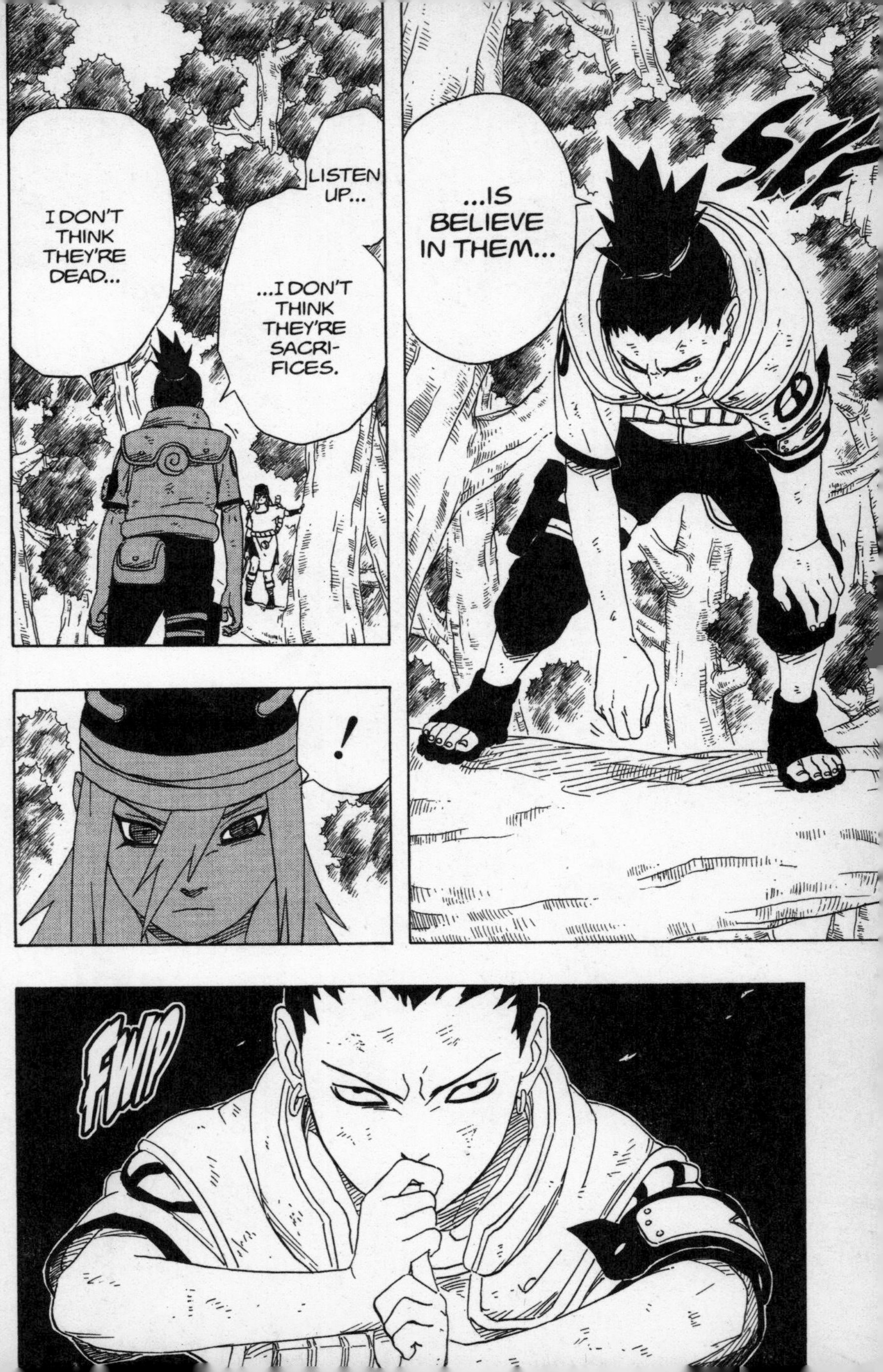
SKF
...IS BELIEVE IN THEM...
LISTEN UP...
...I DON'T THINK THEY'RE SACRIFICES.
I DON'T THINK THEY'RE DEAD...
!
FWIP

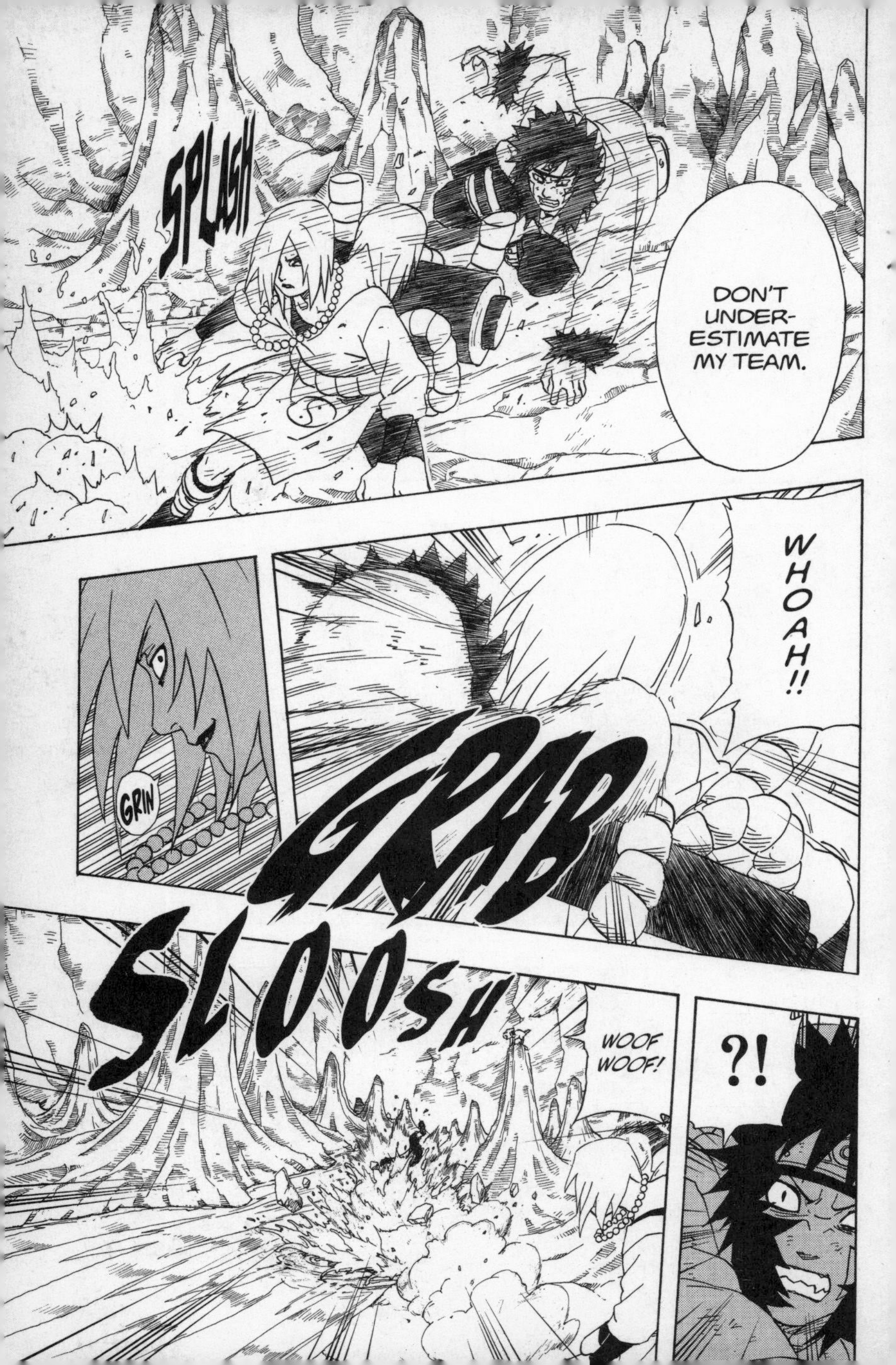
DON'T UNDER-ESTIMATE MY TEAM.
SPLASH
WHOAH!!
GRAB
GRIN
?!
WOOF WOOF!
SLOOSH

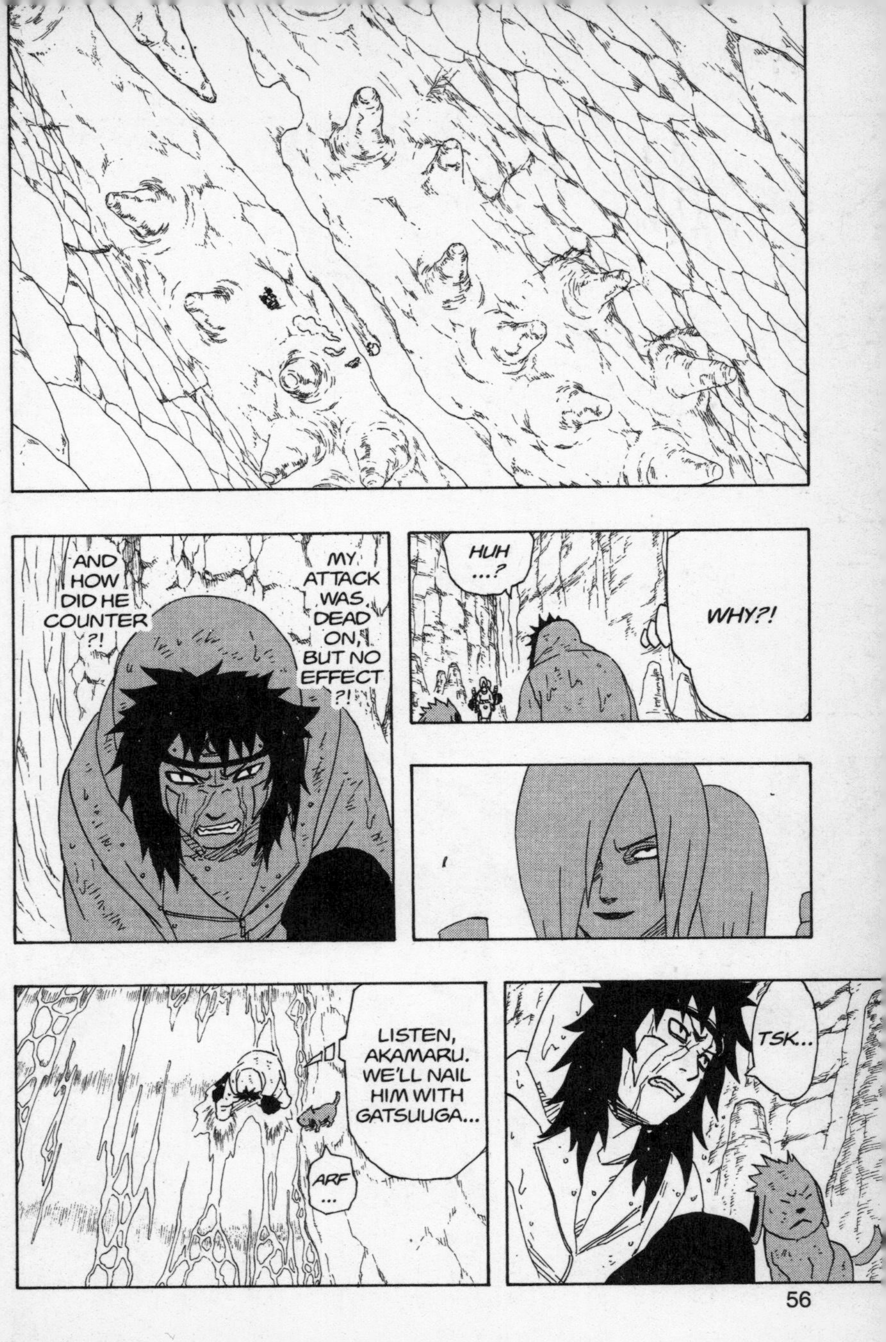
WHY?!
HUH ...?
MY ATTACK WAS DEAD ON, BUT NO EFFECT ?!
AND HOW DID HE COUNTER ?!
TSK...
LISTEN, AKAMARU. WE'LL NAIL HIM WITH GATSUUGA...
ARF ...

READ THIS WAY

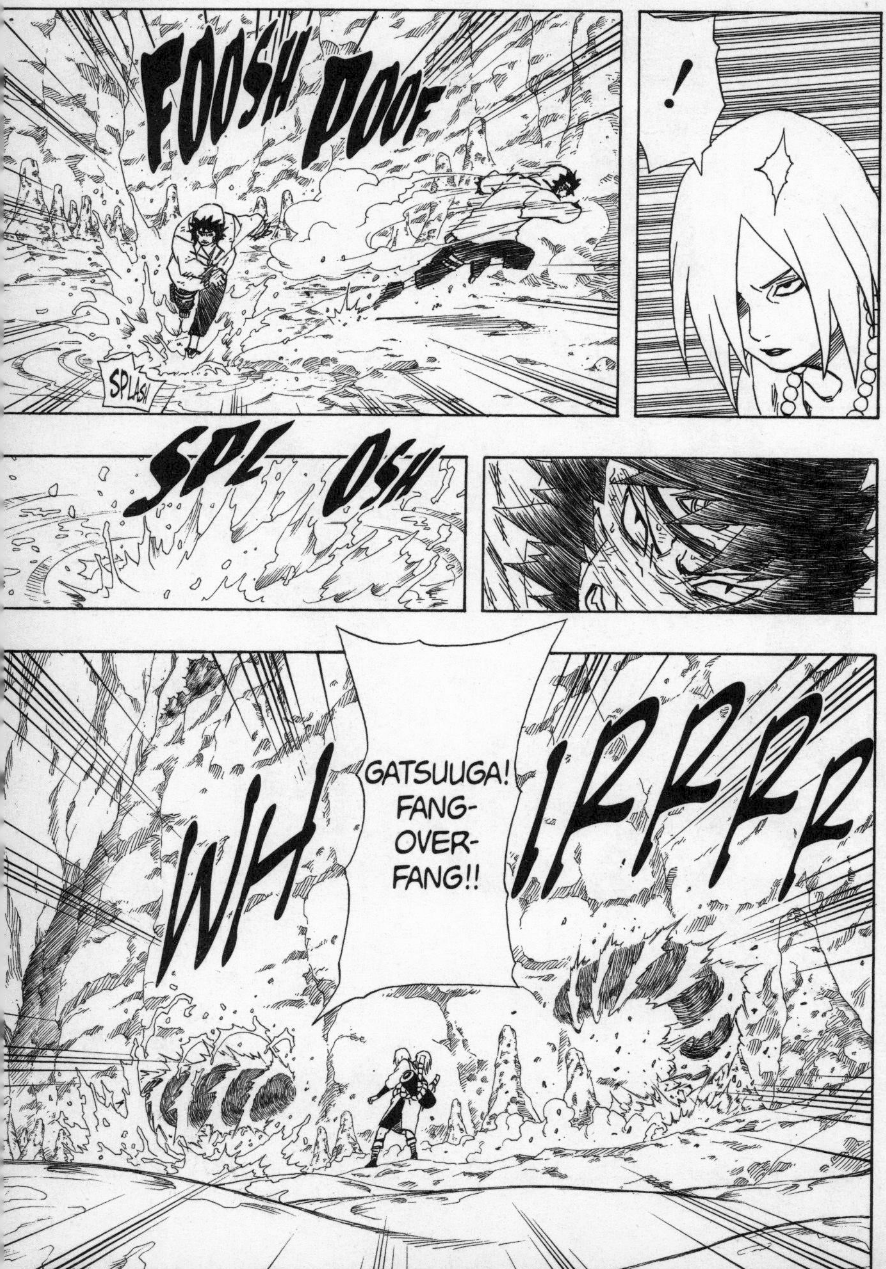
!
FOOSH
POOF
SPLASH
SPLOSH
GATSUUGA! FANG-OVER-FANG!!
WHIRRRR

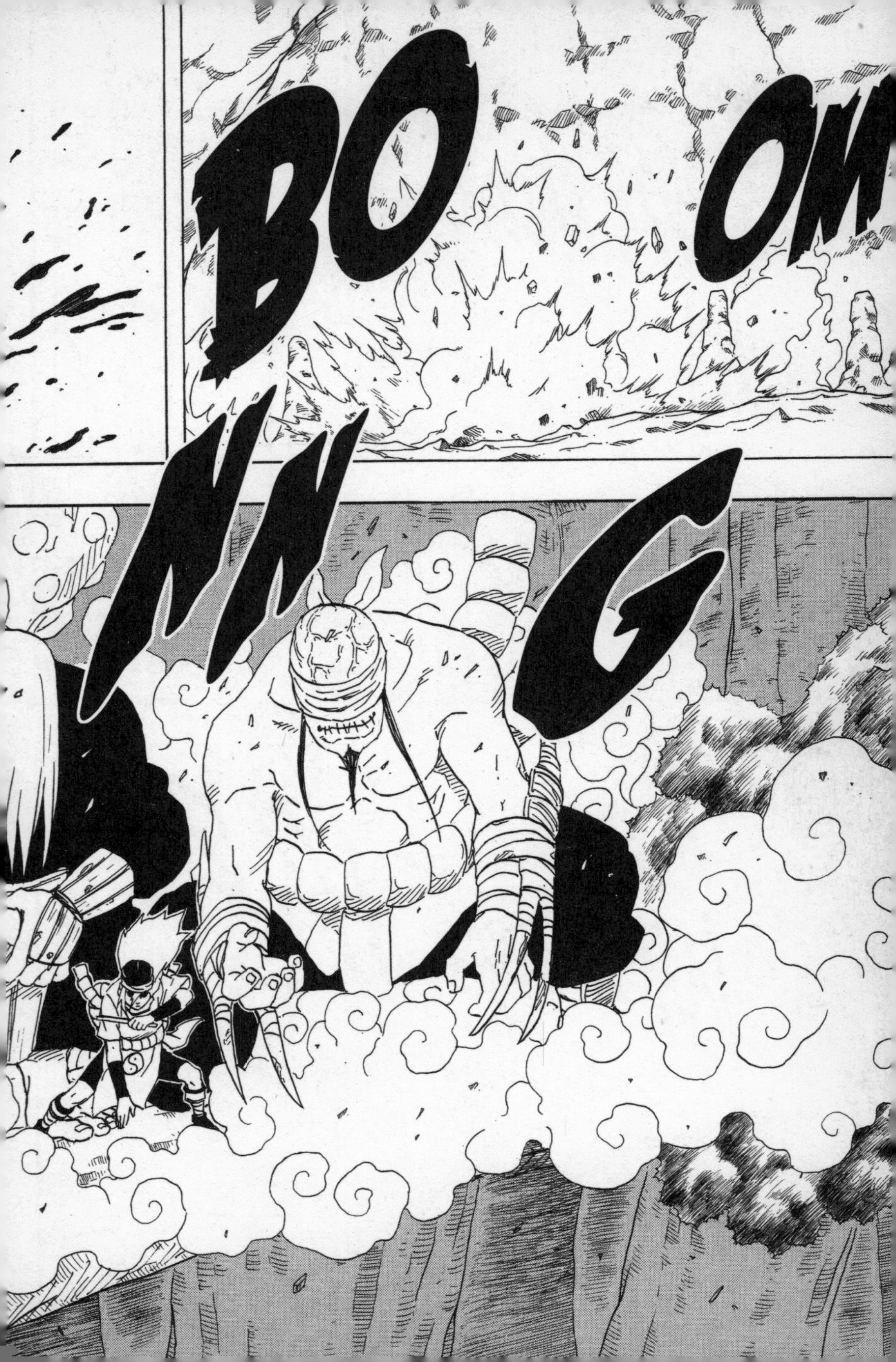
BOOM

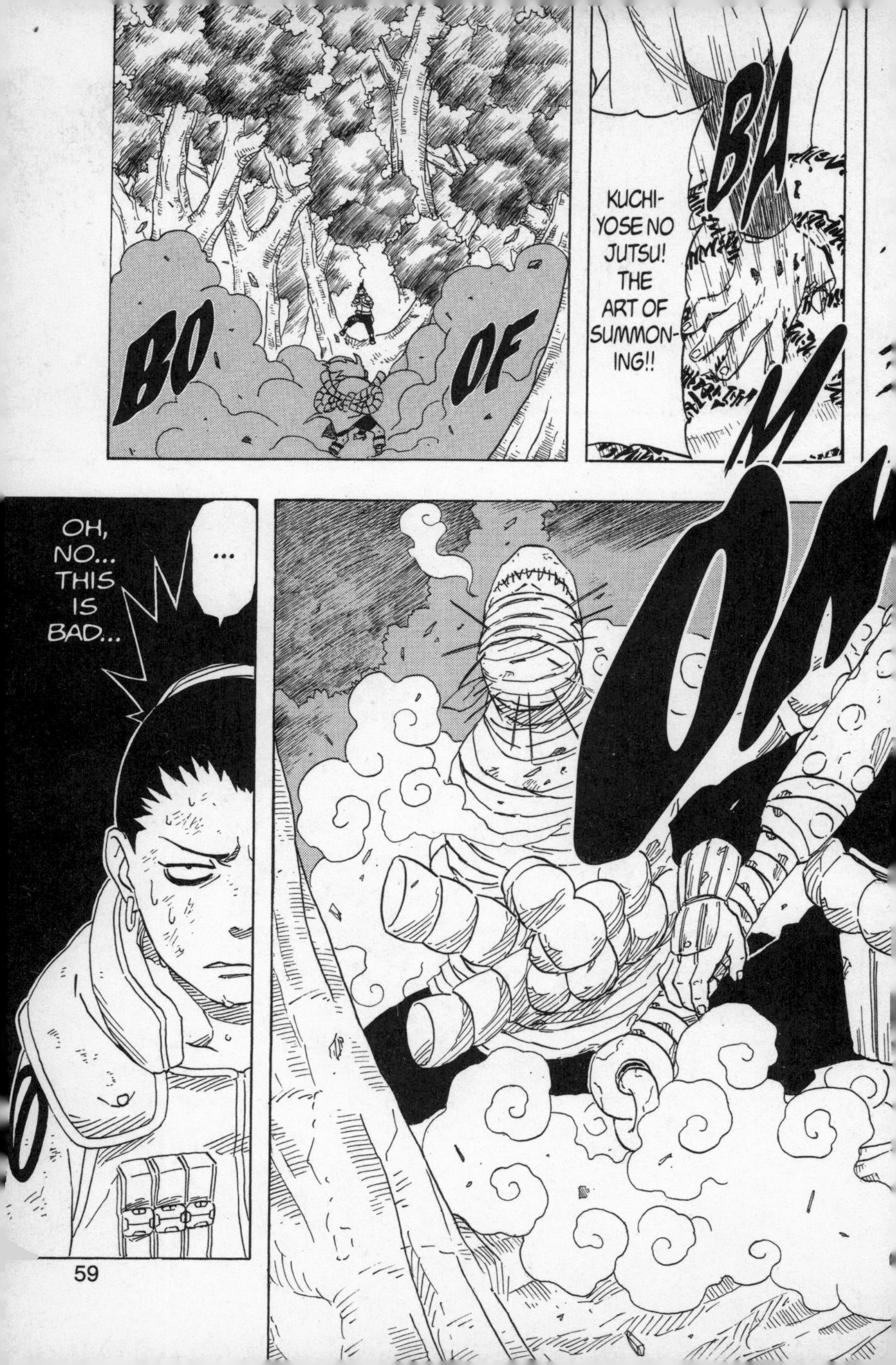
KUCHI-YOSE NO JUTSU! THE ART OF SUMMONING!!
BA
M
BO
OF
OO
OH, NO... THIS IS BAD...
...

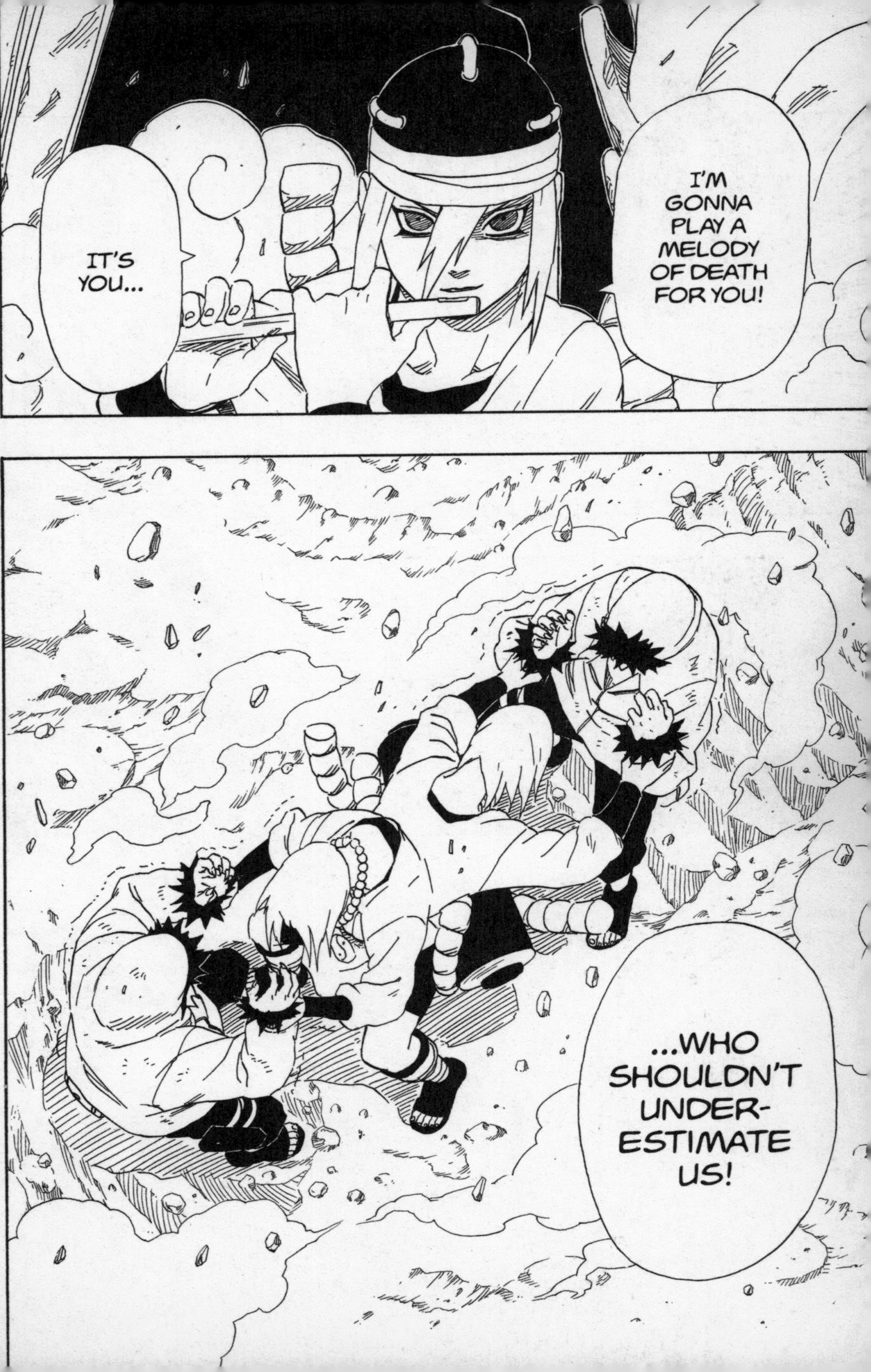
I'M GONNA PLAY A MELODY OF DEATH FOR YOU!
IT'S YOU...
...WHO SHOULDN'T UNDER-ESTIMATE US!

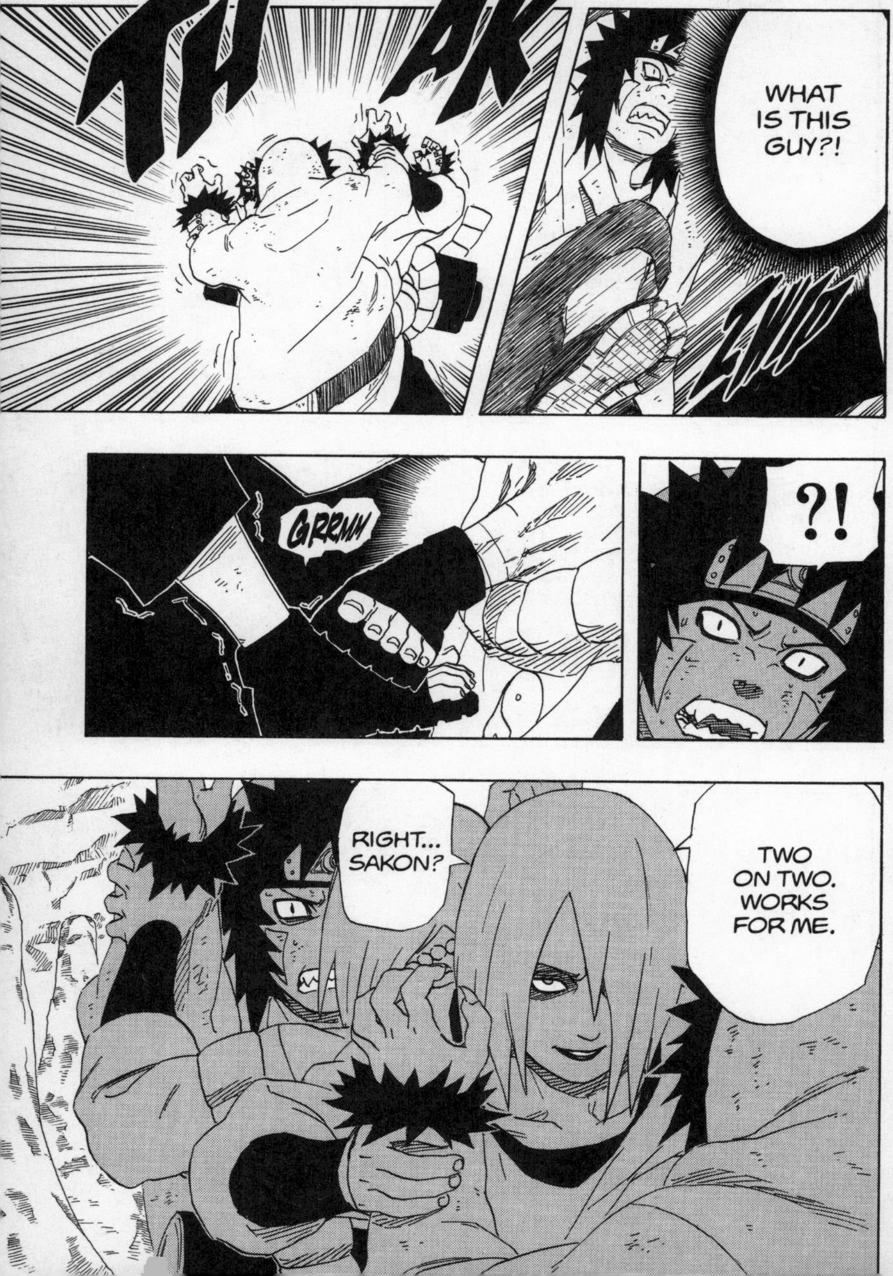
WHAT IS THIS GUY?!
THAK
?!
GRRMM
TWO ON TWO. WORKS FOR ME.
RIGHT... SAKON?

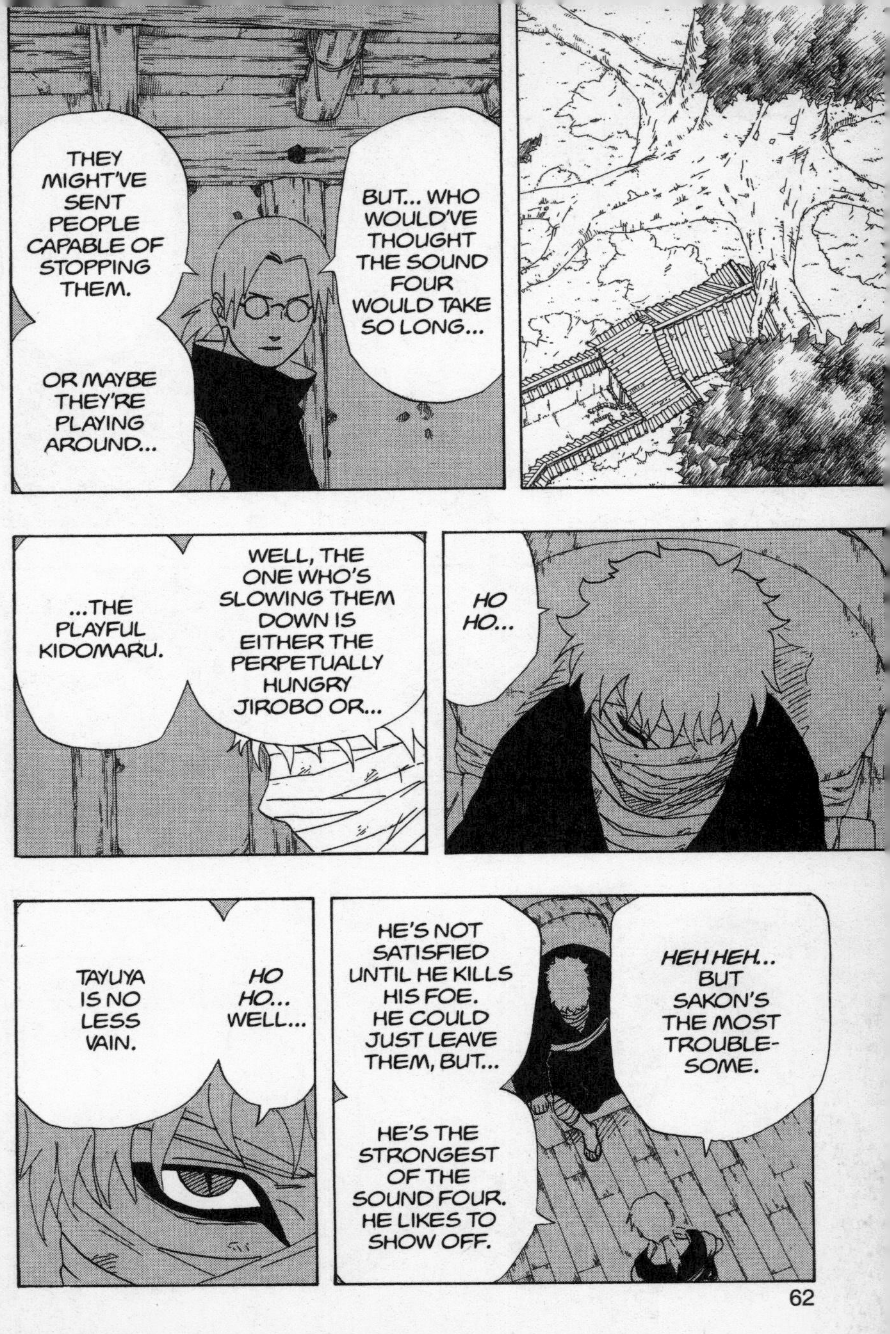

BUT... WHO WOULD'VE THOUGHT THE SOUND FOUR WOULD TAKE SO LONG...
THEY MIGHT'VE SENT PEOPLE CAPABLE OF STOPPING THEM.
OR MAYBE THEY'RE PLAYING AROUND...
HO HO...
WELL, THE ONE WHO'S SLOWING THEM DOWN IS EITHER THE PERPETUALLY HUNGRY JIROBO OR...
...THE PLAYFUL KIDOMARU.
HEH HEH... BUT SAKON'S THE MOST TROUBLE-SOME.
HE'S NOT SATISFIED UNTIL HE KILLS HIS FOE. HE COULD JUST LEAVE THEM, BUT...
HE'S THE STRONGEST OF THE SOUND FOUR. HE LIKES TO SHOW OFF.
HO HO... WELL...
TAYUYA IS NO LESS VAIN.

READ THIS WAY

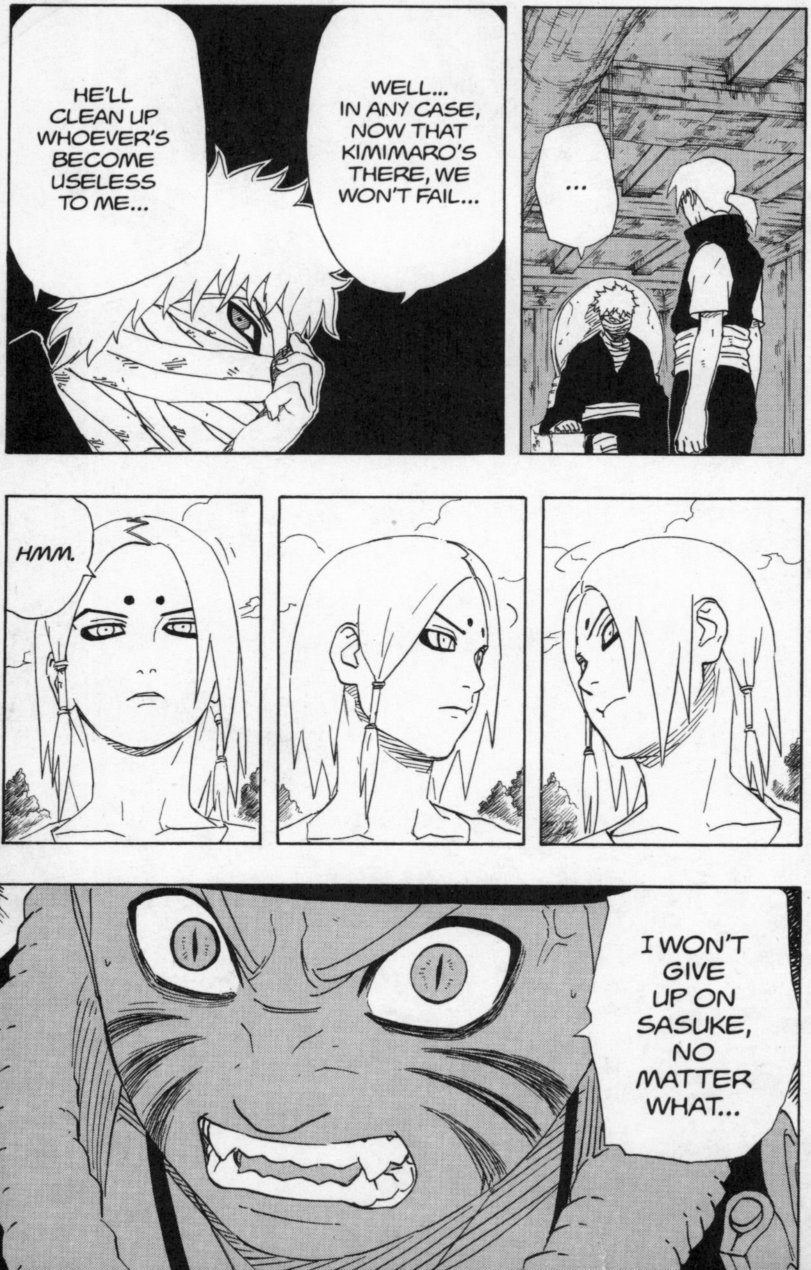
...
WELL... IN ANY CASE, NOW THAT KIMIMARO'S THERE, WE WON'T FAIL...
HE'LL CLEAN UP WHOEVER'S BECOME USELESS TO ME...
HMM.
I WON'T GIVE UP ON SASUKE, NO MATTER WHAT...

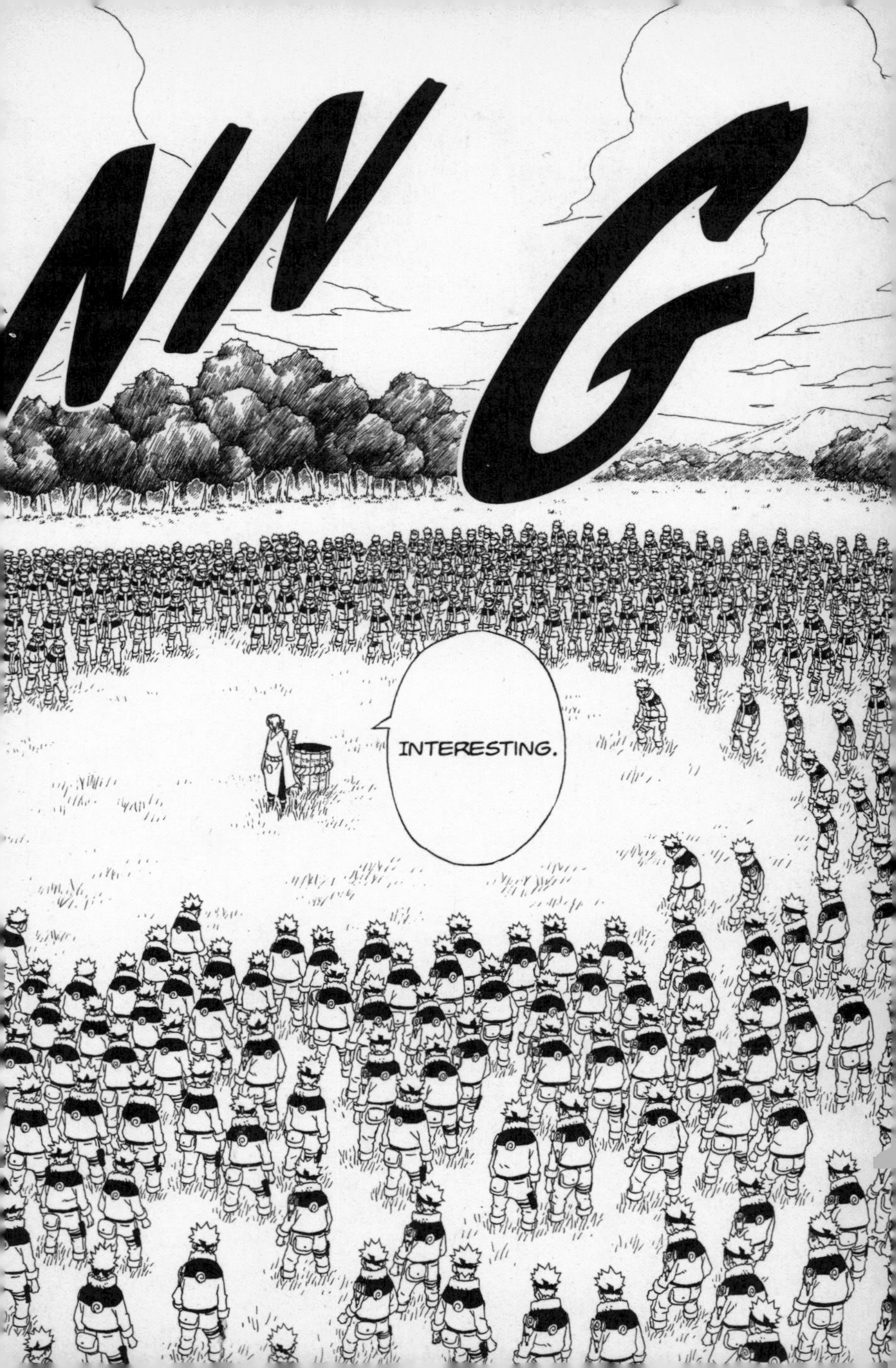
NNG
INTERESTING.

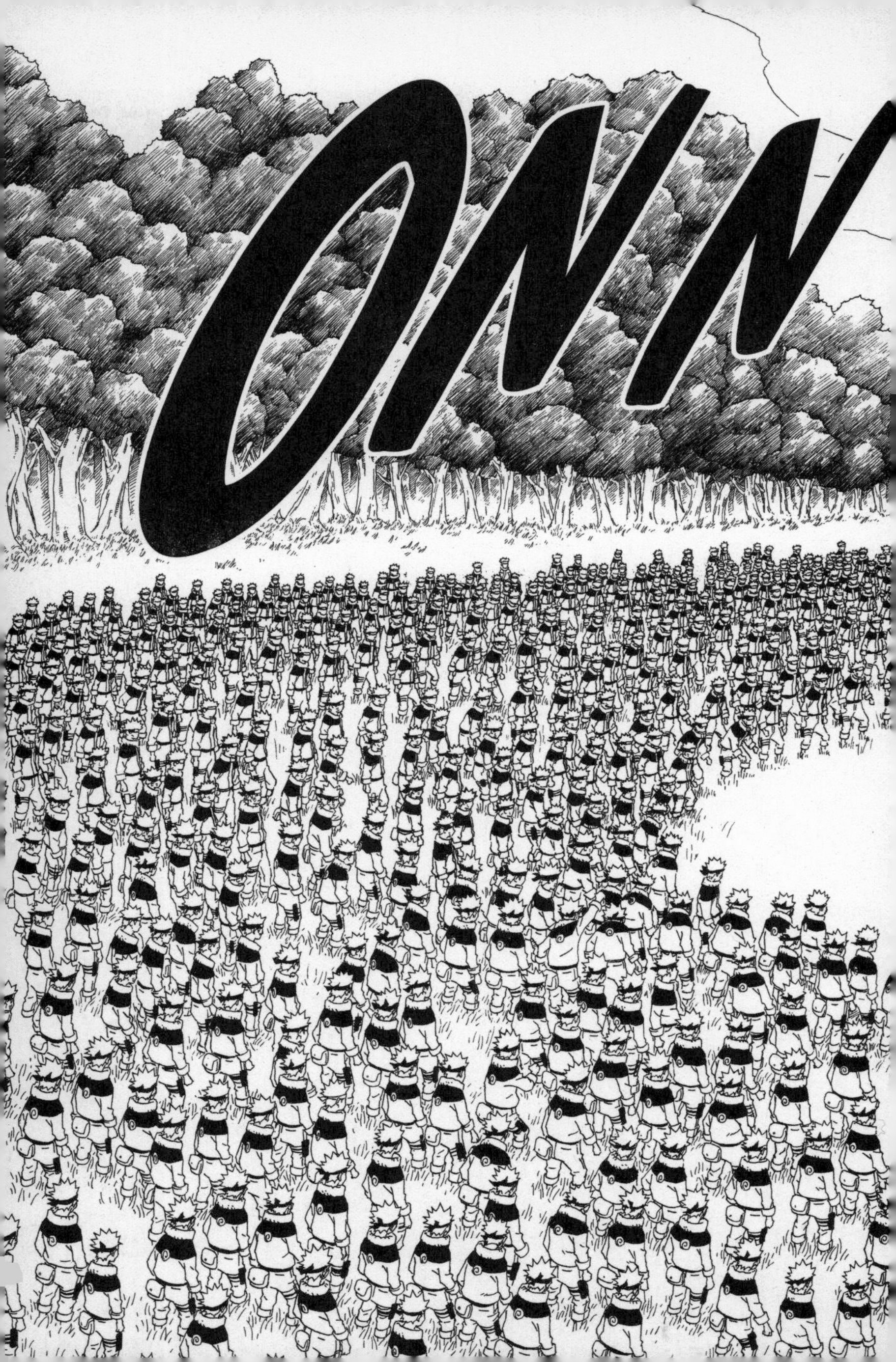
ONN

NARUTO™

Number 203: Sakon's Secret

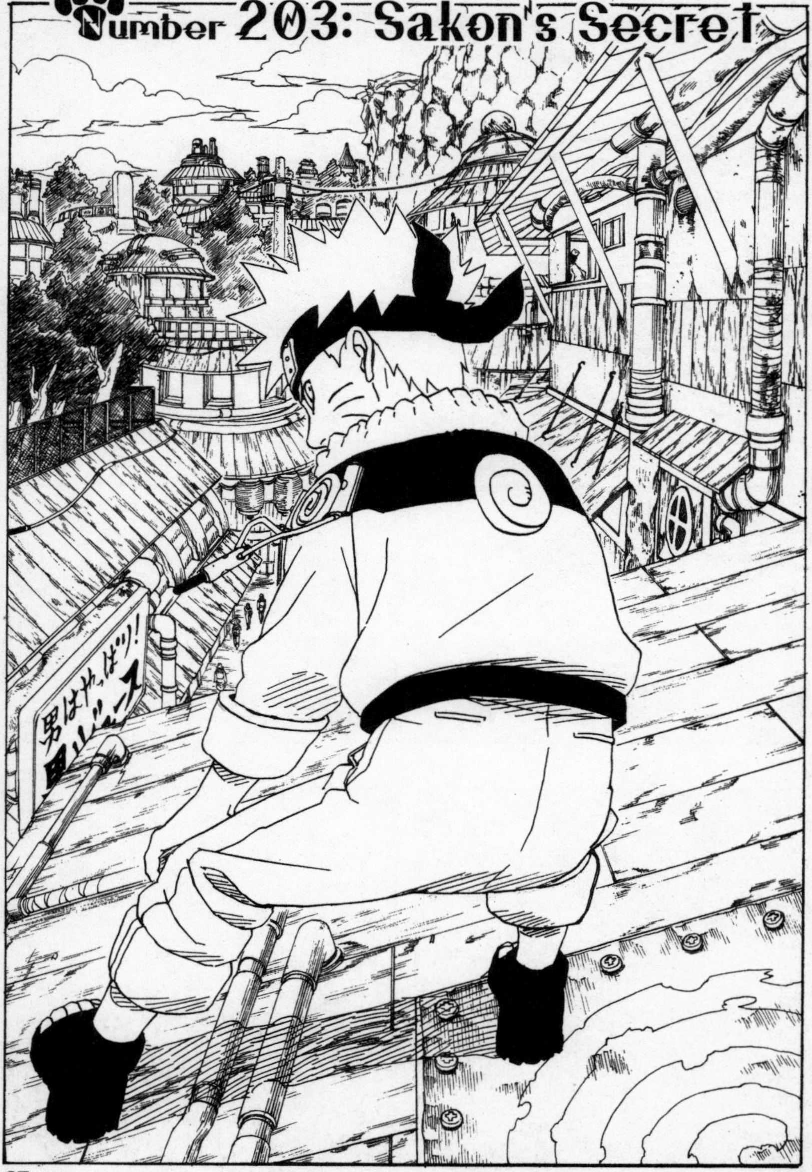
男はやっぱり!

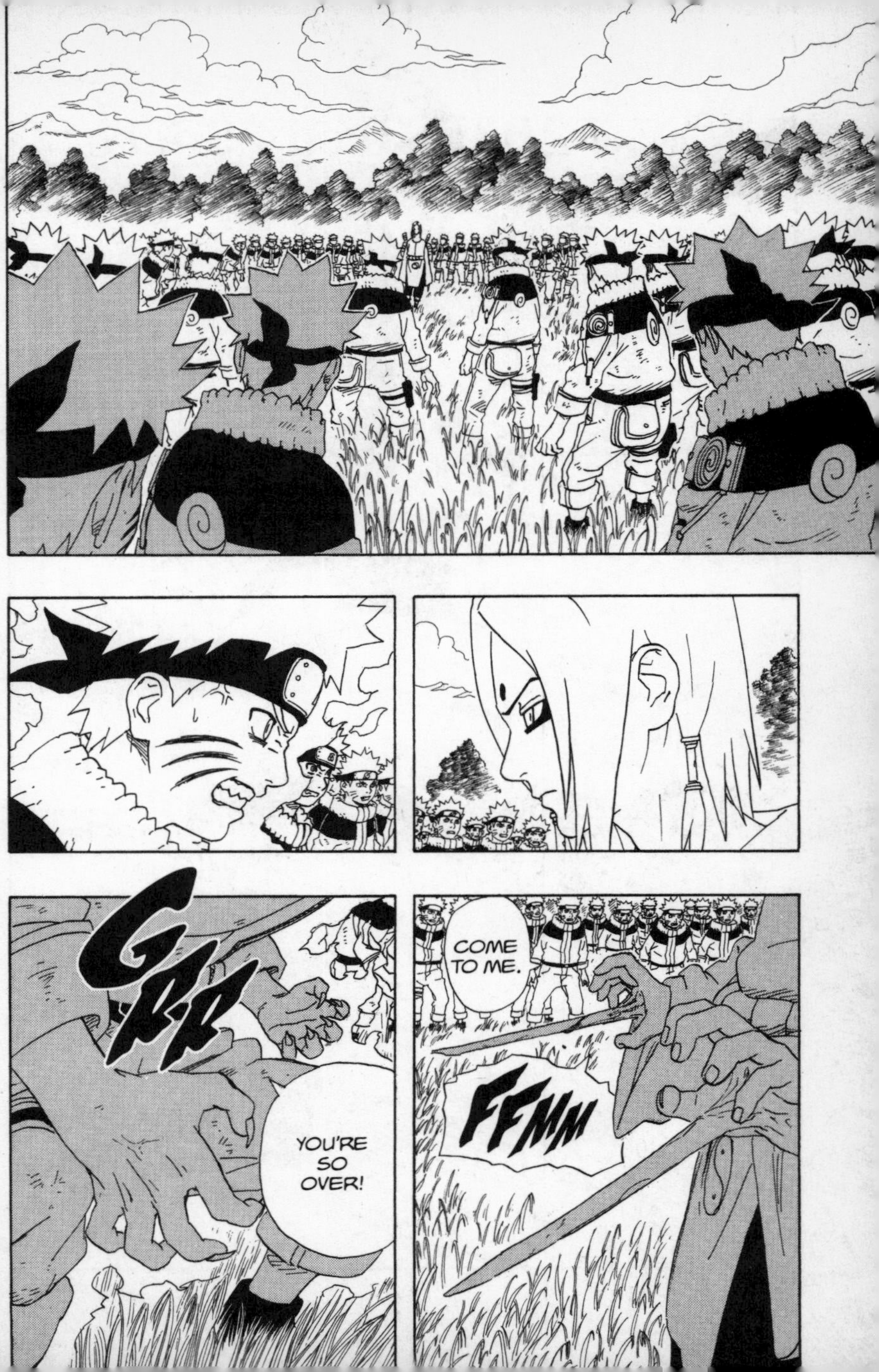
COME TO ME.
FFMM
GRR
YOU'RE SO OVER!

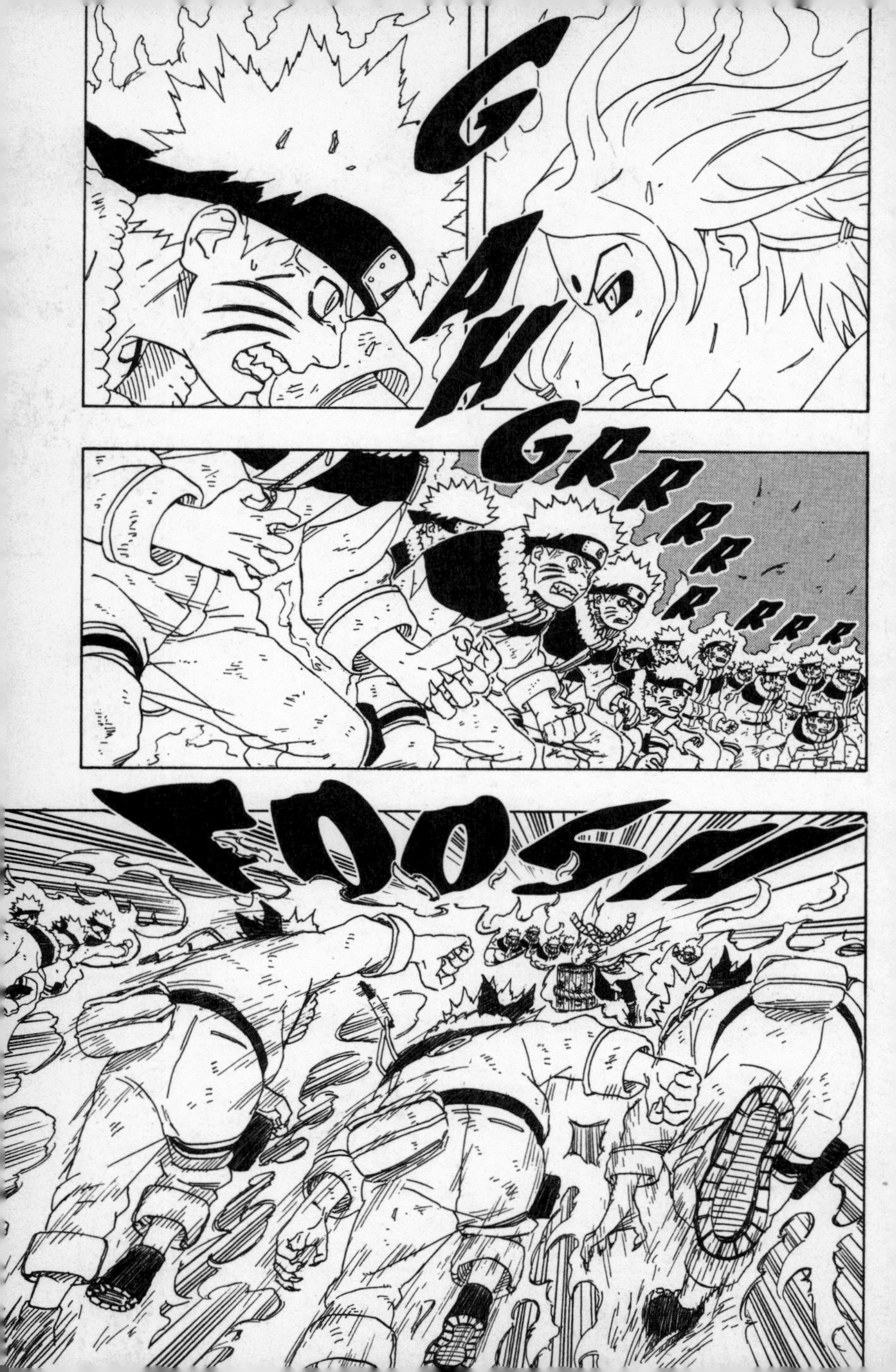
GAAHH
GRRRRRRRRRR
FOOSH

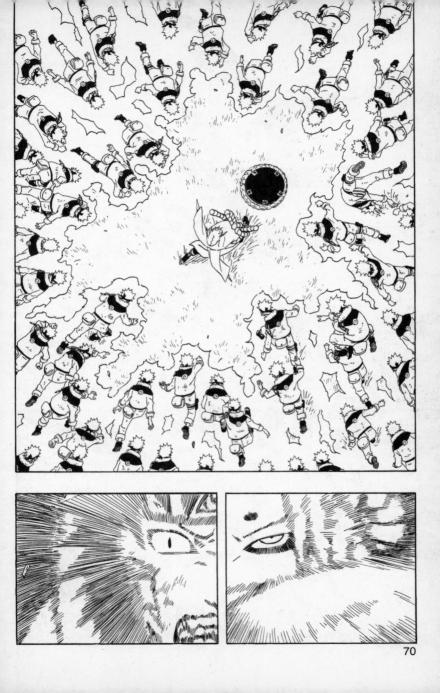

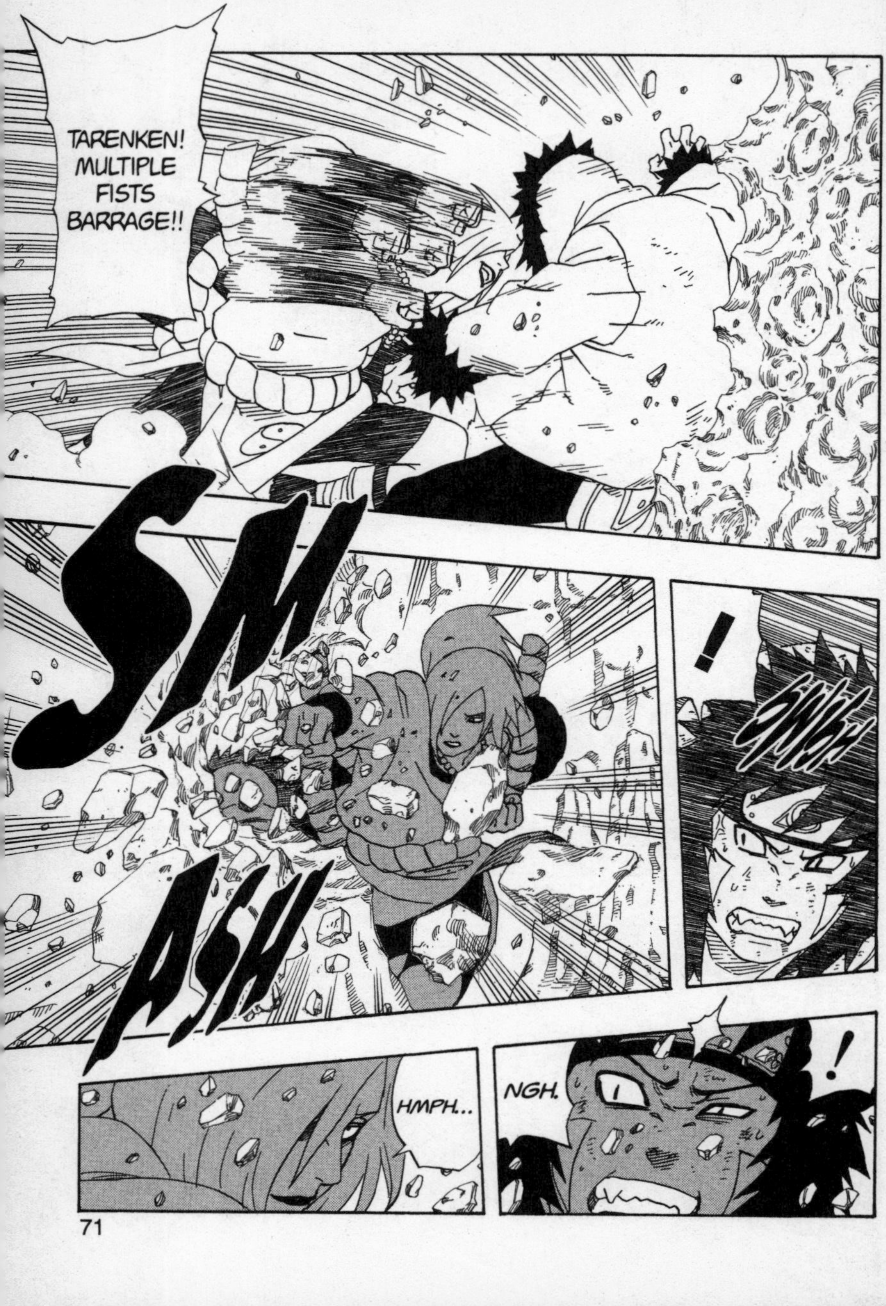
TARENKEN! MULTIPLE FISTS BARRAGE!!
!
SMASH
!
NGH.
HMPH...

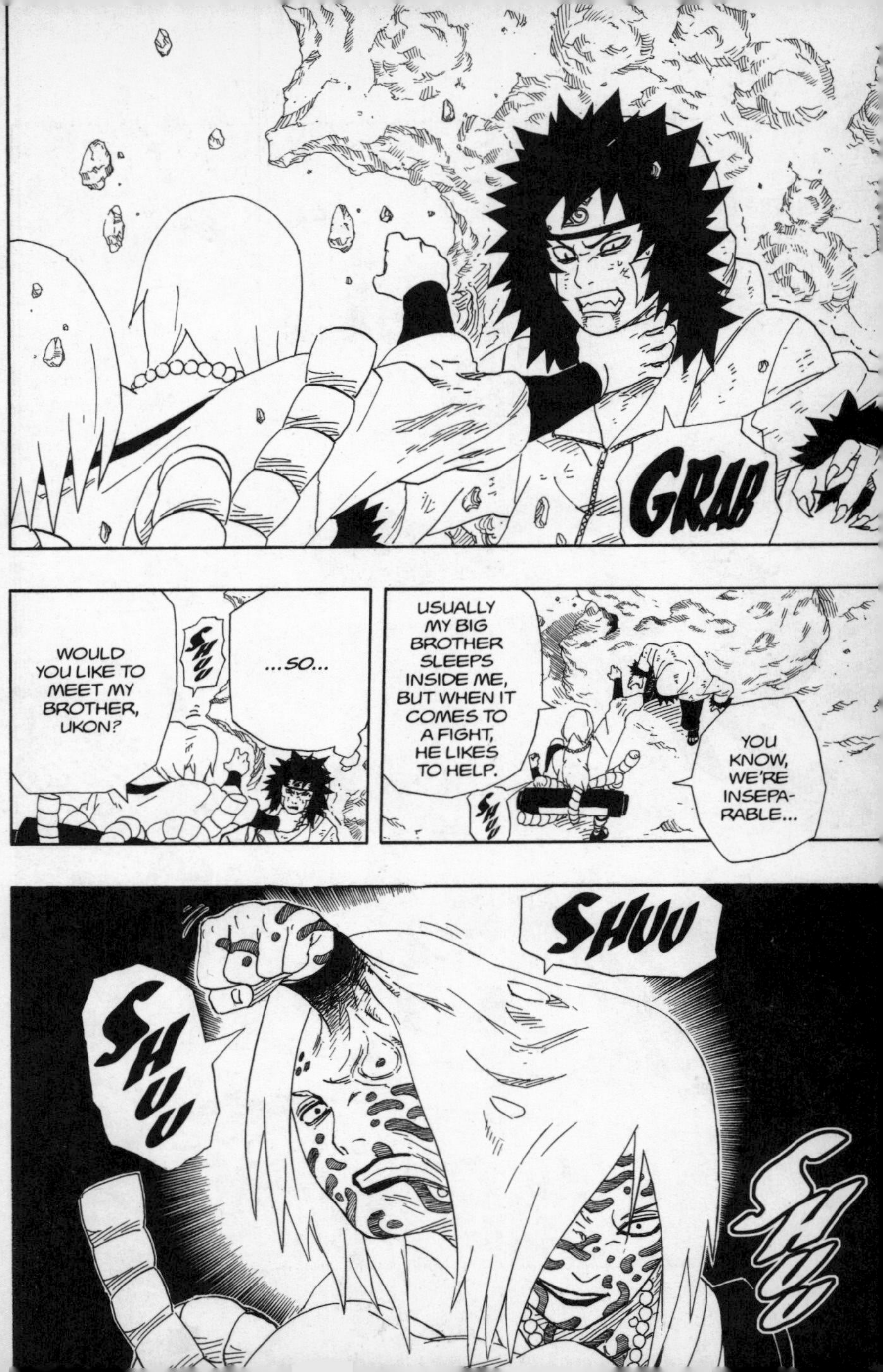

GRAB
YOU KNOW, WE'RE INSEPARABLE...
USUALLY MY BIG BROTHER SLEEPS INSIDE ME, BUT WHEN IT COMES TO A FIGHT, HE LIKES TO HELP.
SHUU
...SO...
SHUU
WOULD YOU LIKE TO MEET MY BROTHER, UKON?
SHUU
SHUU

READ THIS WAY

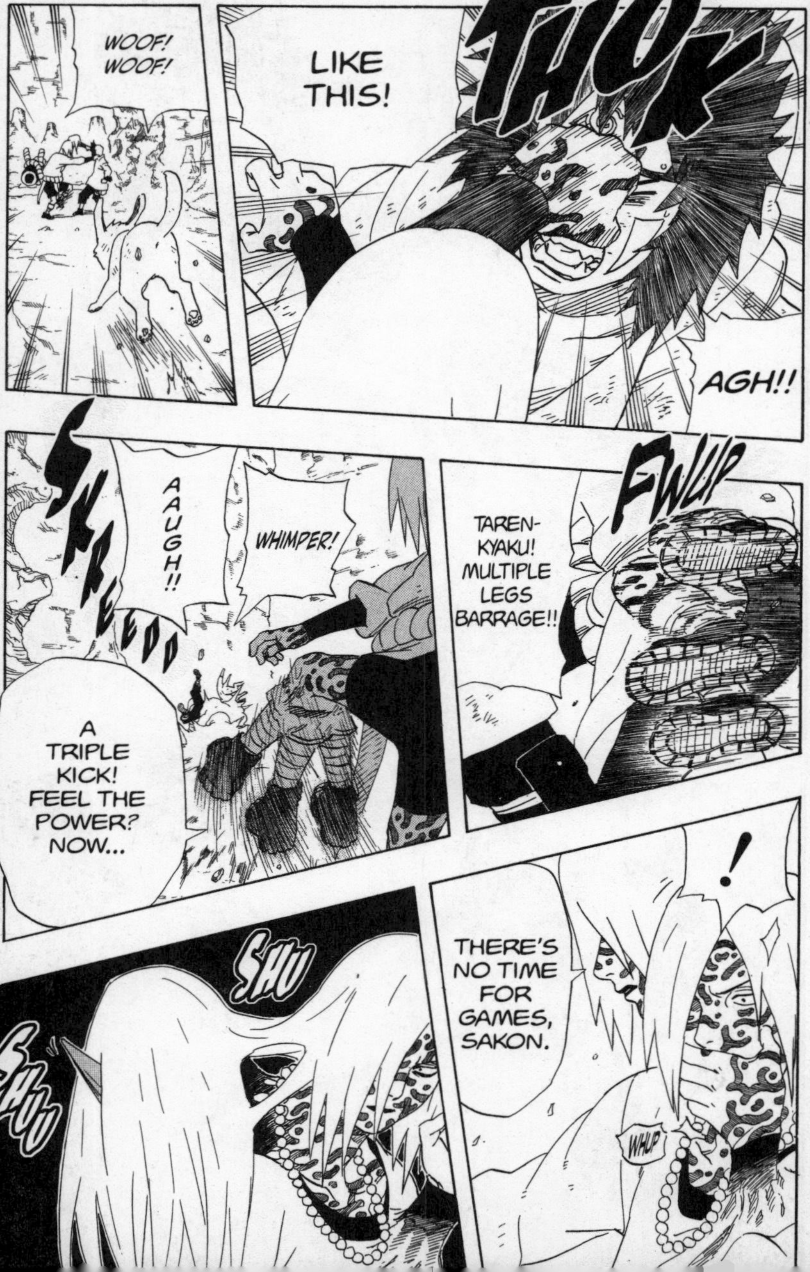

THOK
LIKE THIS!
AGH!!
WOOF! WOOF!
FWUP
TAREN-KYAKU! MULTIPLE LEGS BARRAGE!!
AAUGH!!
WHIMPER!
A TRIPLE KICK! FEEL THE POWER? NOW...
!
THERE'S NO TIME FOR GAMES, SAKON.
WHUP
SHU
SHUU

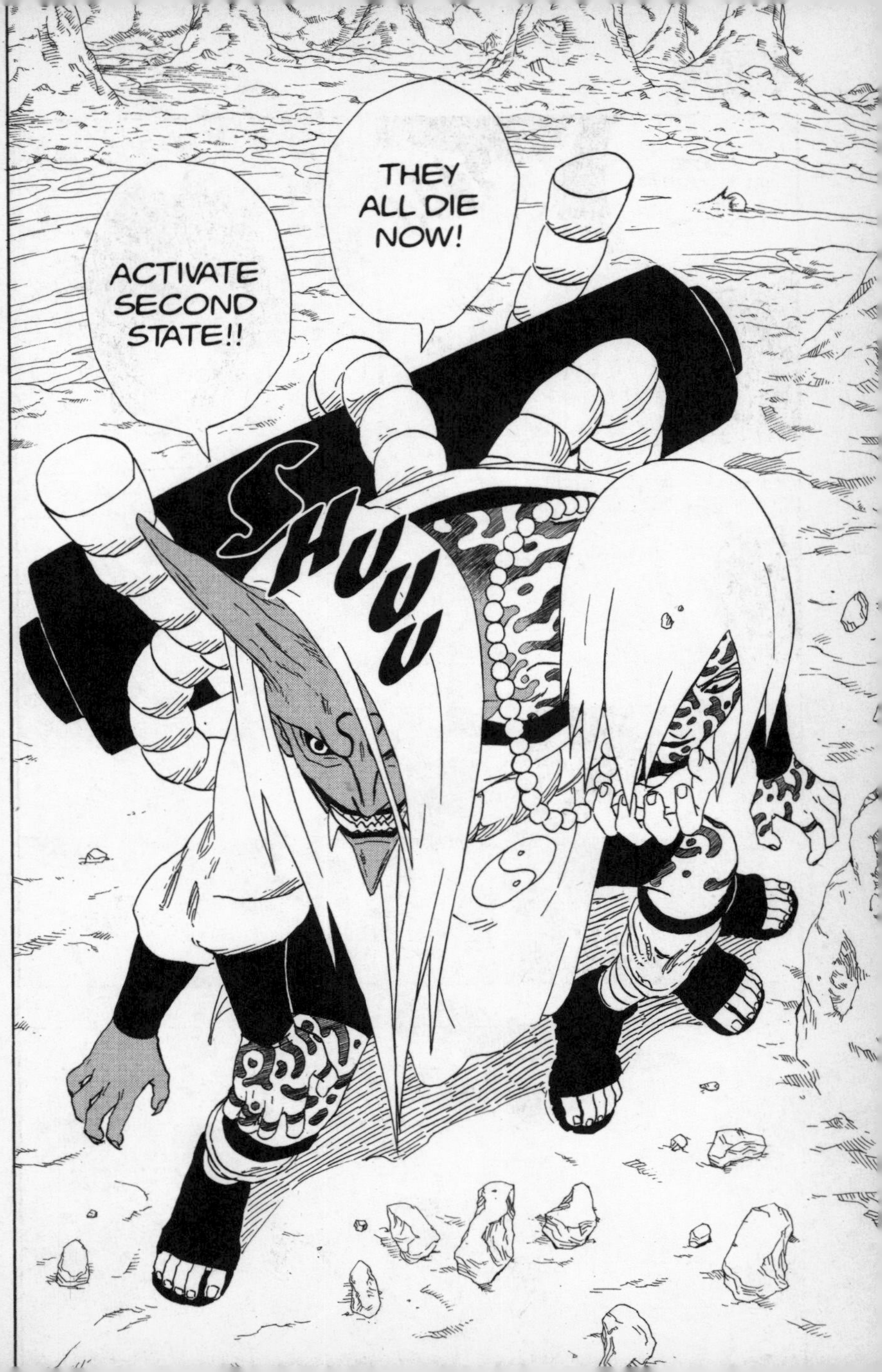
THEY ALL DIE NOW!
ACTIVATE SECOND STATE!!
SHUUU

READ THIS WAY

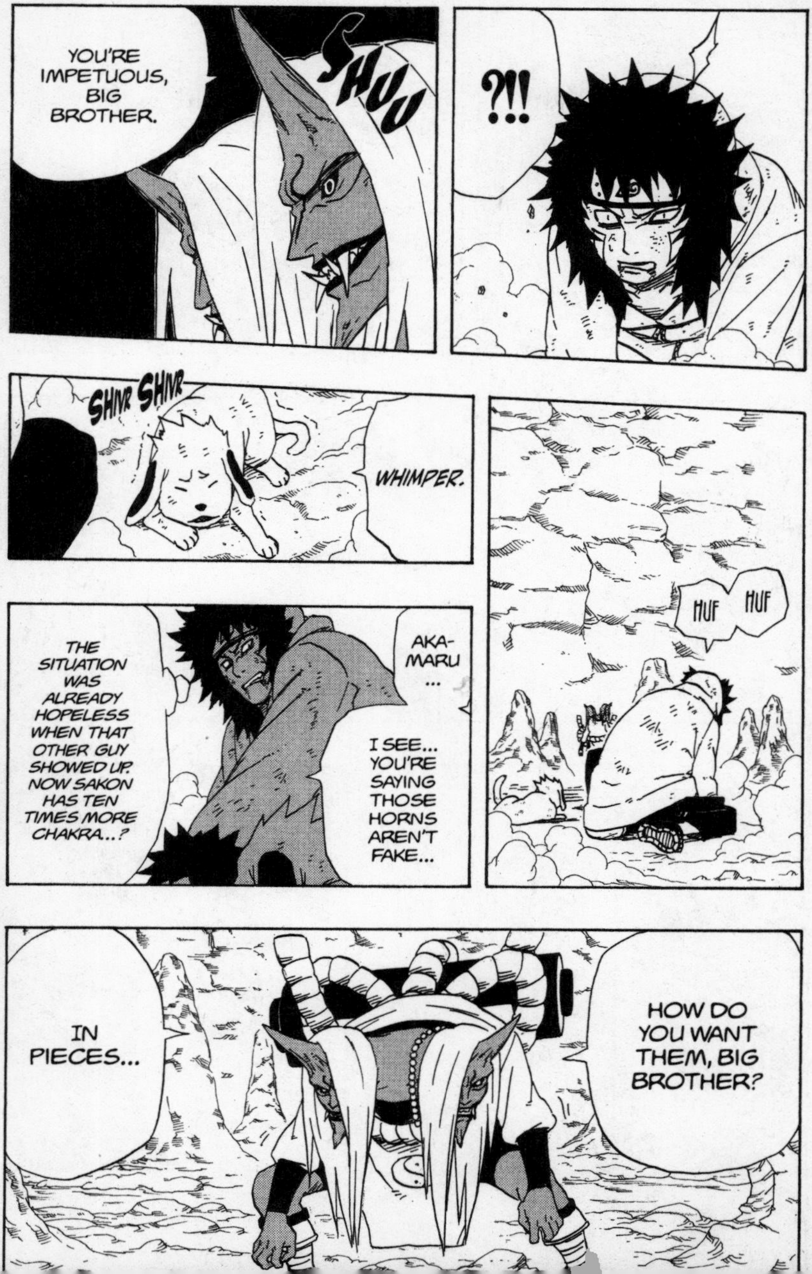
?!!
SHUU
YOU'RE IMPETUOUS, BIG BROTHER.
HUF
HUF
WHIMPER.
SHIVR SHIVR
AKA-MARU ...
I SEE... YOU'RE SAYING THOSE HORNS AREN'T FAKE...
THE SITUATION WAS ALREADY HOPELESS WHEN THAT OTHER GUY SHOWED UP. NOW SAKON HAS TEN TIMES MORE CHAKRA...?
HOW DO YOU WANT THEM, BIG BROTHER?
IN PIECES...

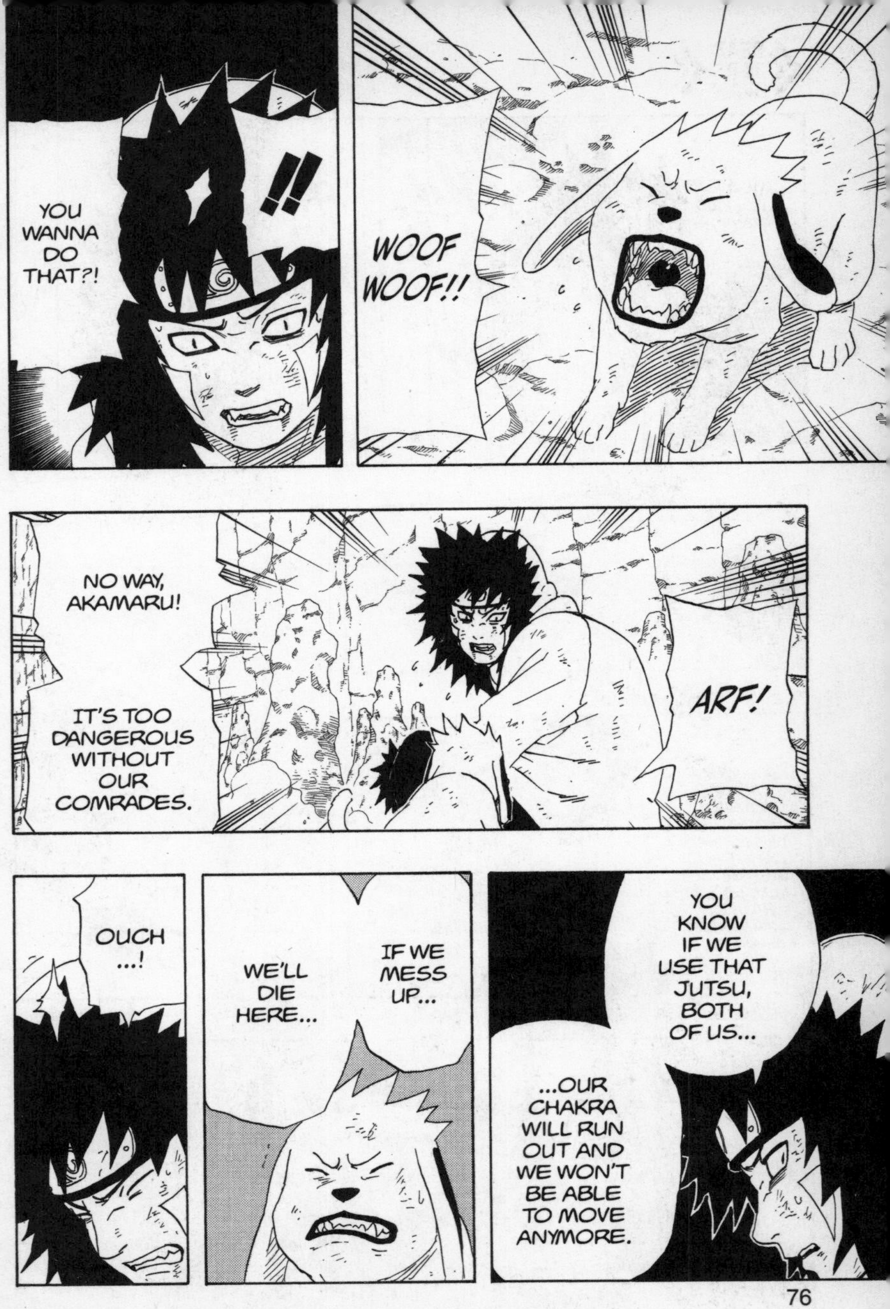
WOOF WOOF!!
!!
YOU WANNA DO THAT?!
NO WAY, AKAMARU!
IT'S TOO DANGEROUS WITHOUT OUR COMRADES.
ARF!
YOU KNOW IF WE USE THAT JUTSU, BOTH OF US...
...OUR CHAKRA WILL RUN OUT AND WE WON'T BE ABLE TO MOVE ANYMORE.
IF WE MESS UP...
WE'LL DIE HERE...
OUCH ...!

READ THIS WAY

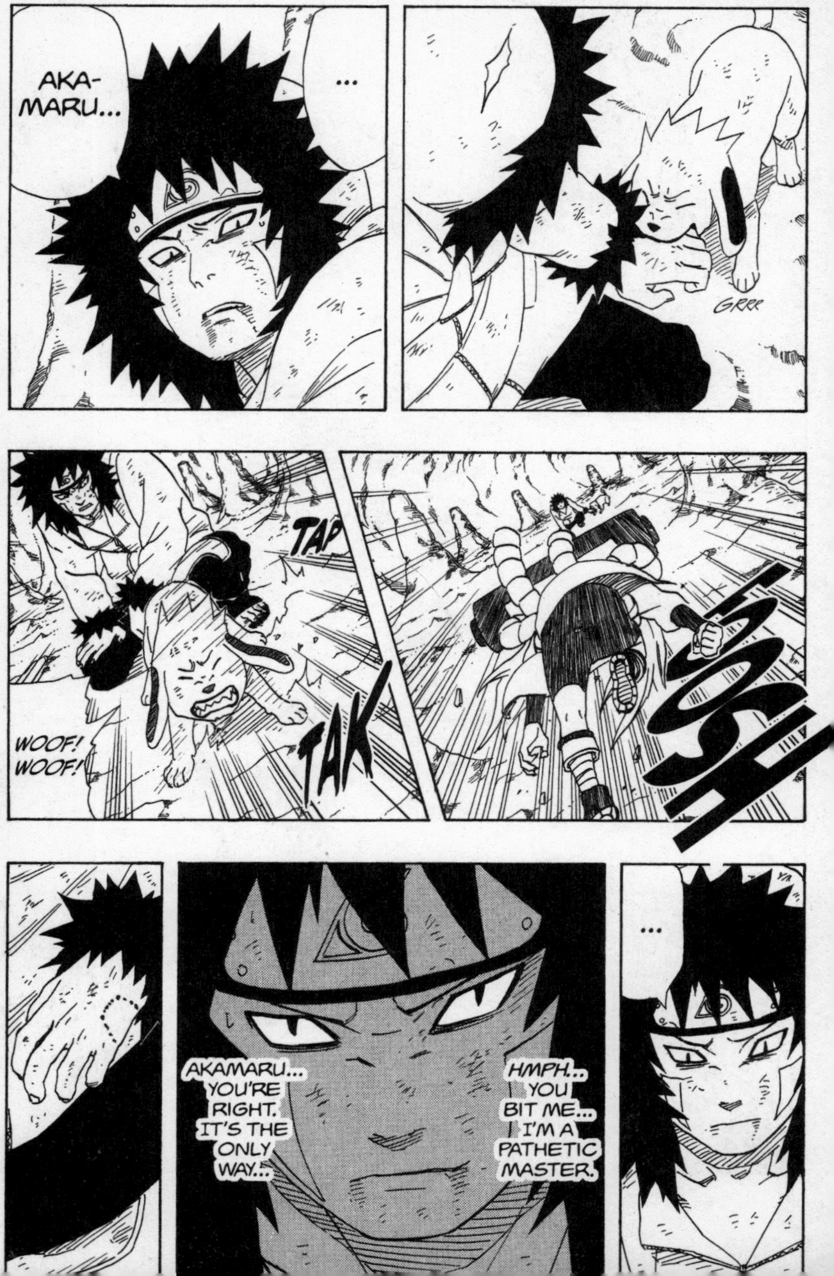
GRRR
...
AKA-MARU...
SSH
TAP
TAK
WOOF! WOOF!
...
HMPH... YOU BIT ME... I'M A PATHETIC MASTER.
AKAMARU... YOU'RE RIGHT. IT'S THE ONLY WAY...

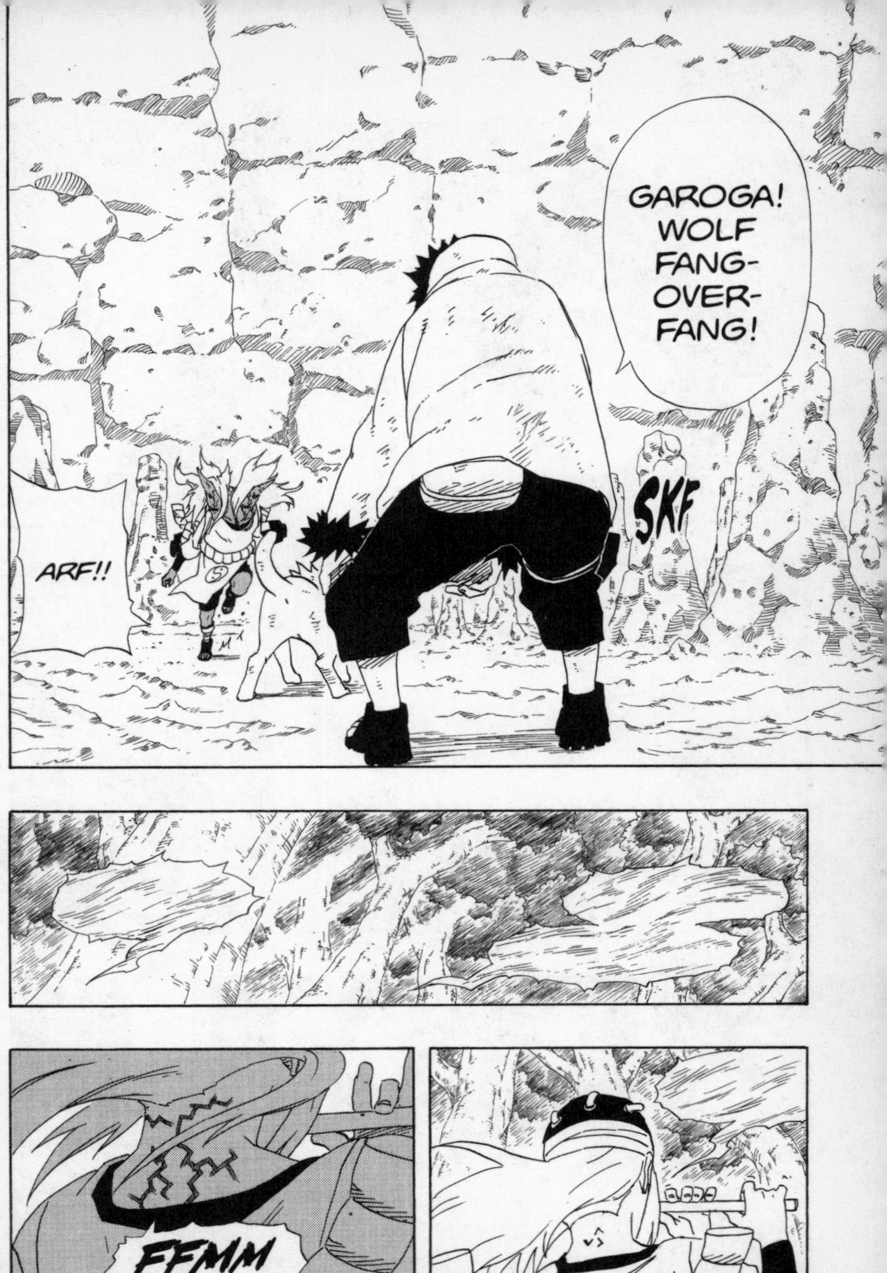
GAROGA! WOLF FANG-OVER-FANG!
SKF
ARF!!
FFMM

READ THIS WAY

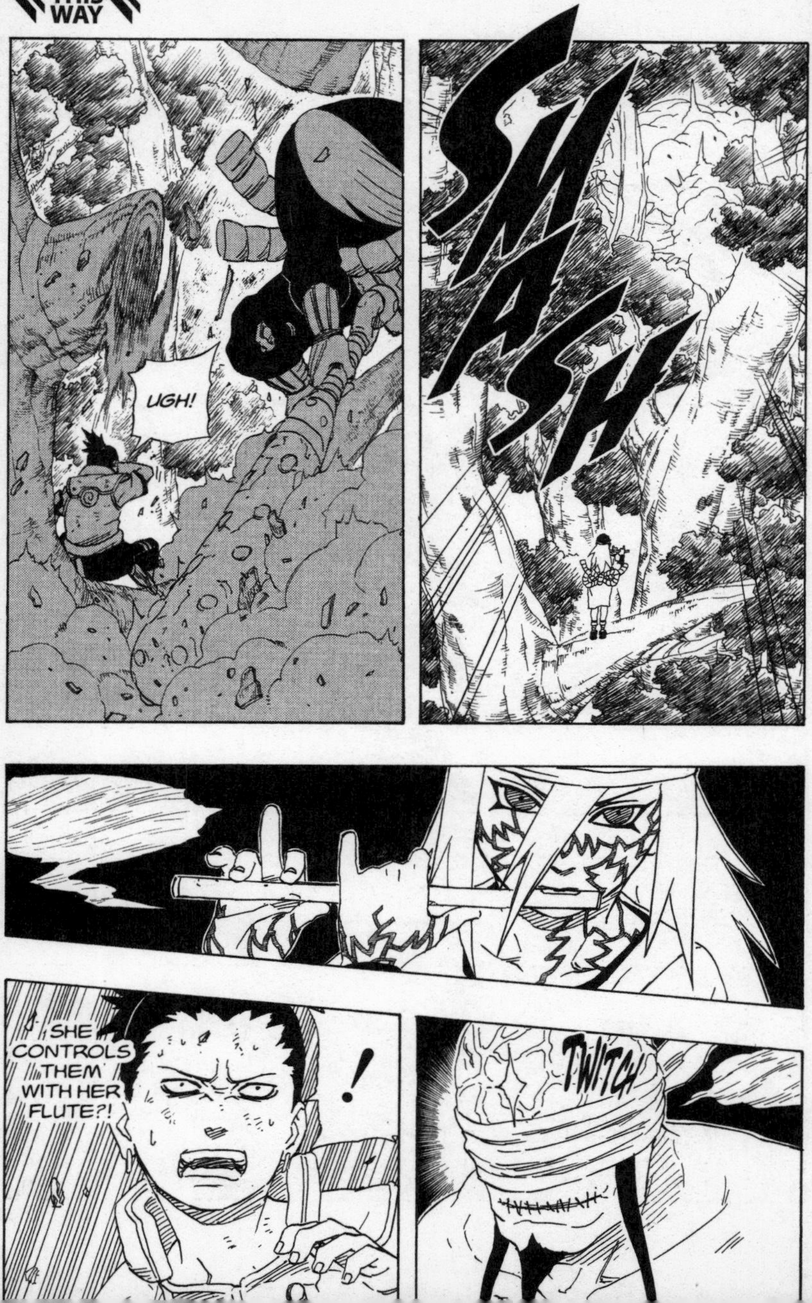
SMASH
UGH!
TWITCH
!
SHE CONTROLS THEM WITH HER FLUTE?!

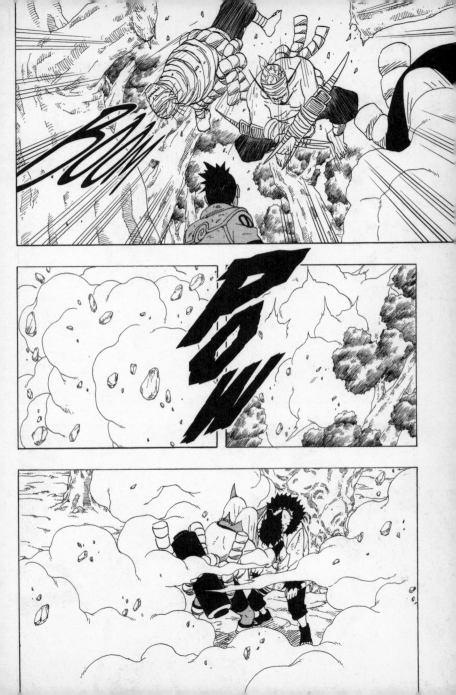

READ THIS WAY

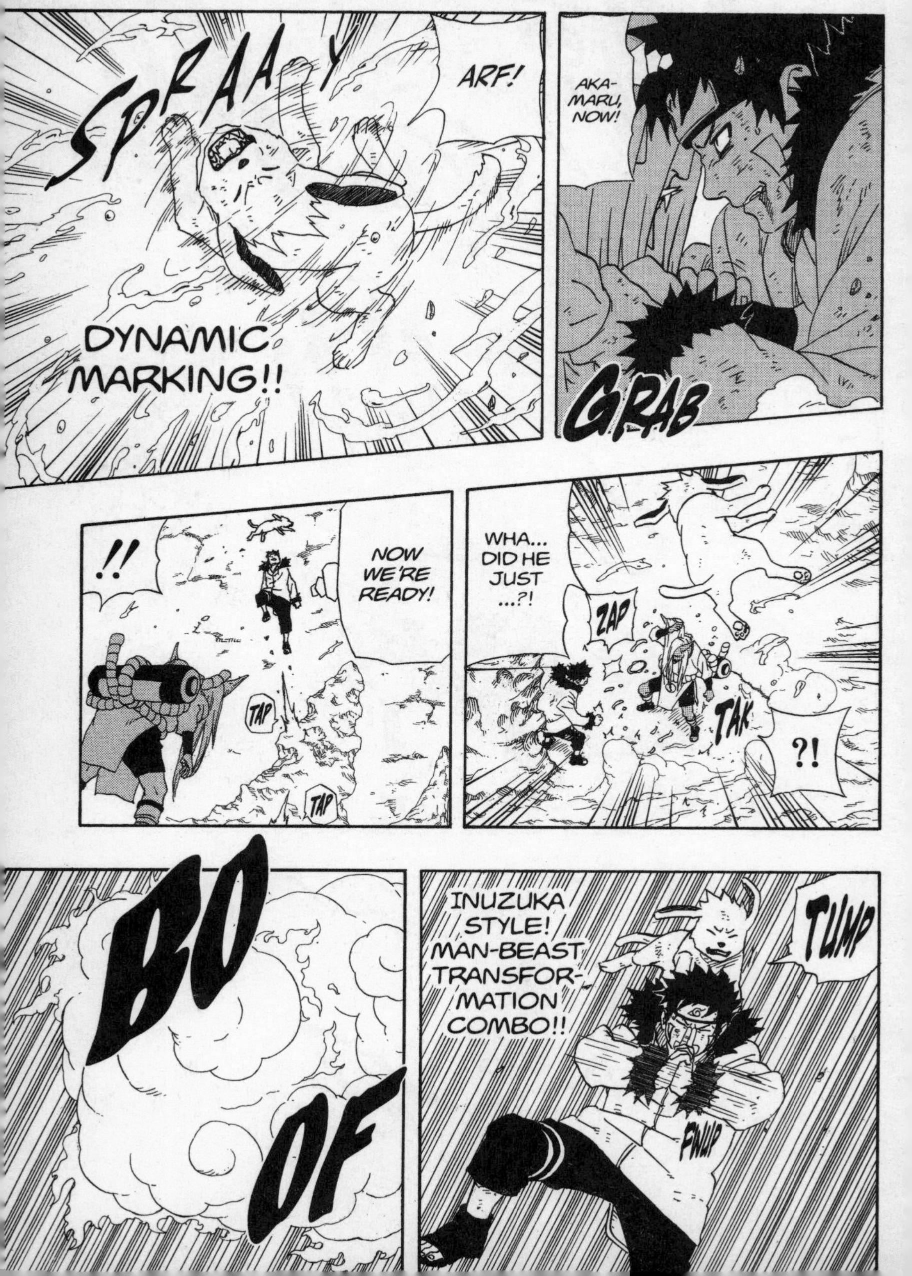
AKA-MARU, NOW!
GRAB
SPRAAAY
ARF!
DYNAMIC MARKING!!
WHA... DID HE JUST ...?!
ZAP
TAK
?!
NOW WE'RE READY!
!!
TAP
TAP
TUMP
INUZUKA STYLE! MAN-BEAST TRANSFORMATION COMBO!!
FWUP
BOOF

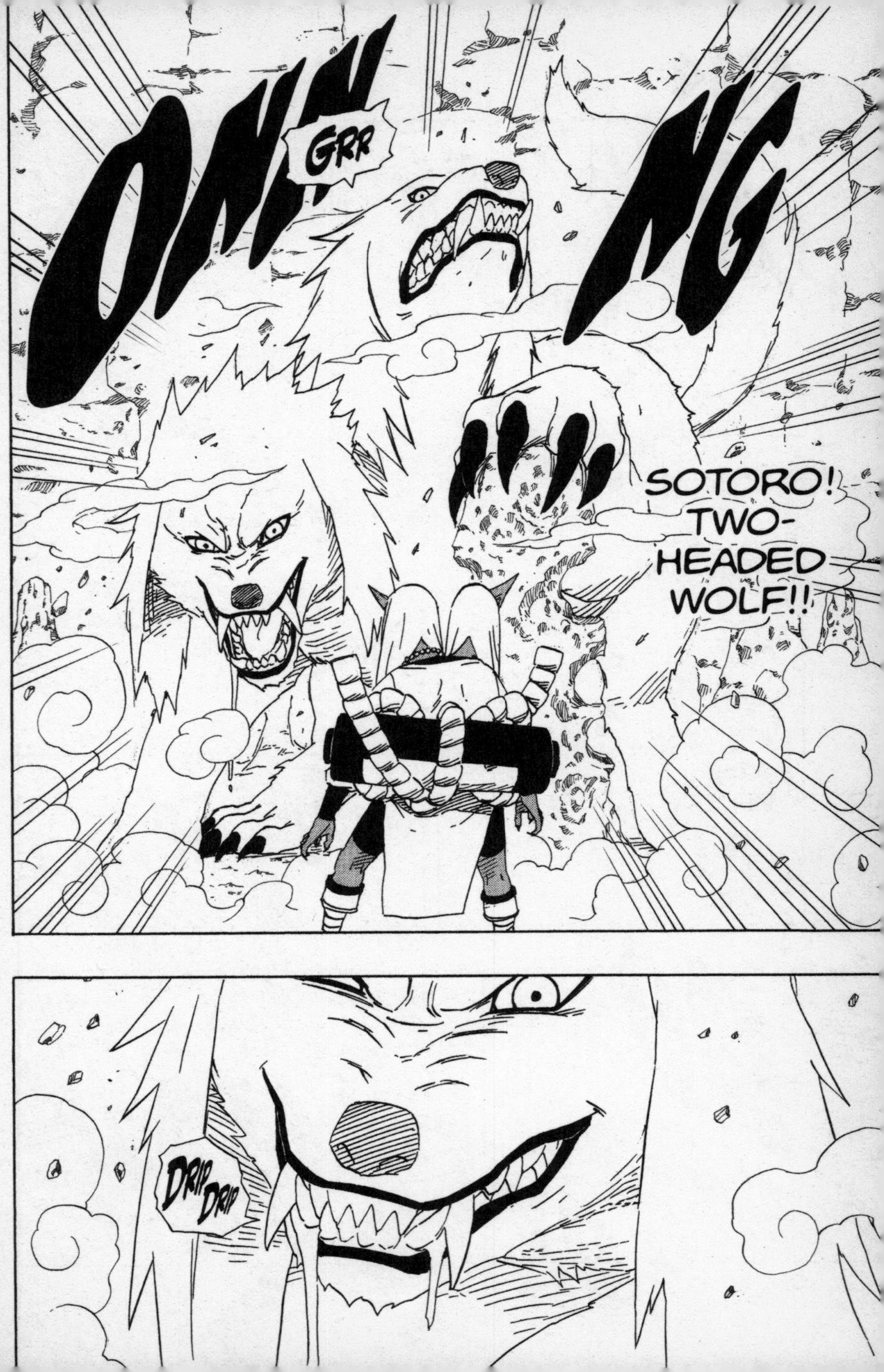
GRR
SOTORO! TWO-HEADED WOLF!!
DRIP DRIP

READ THIS WAY

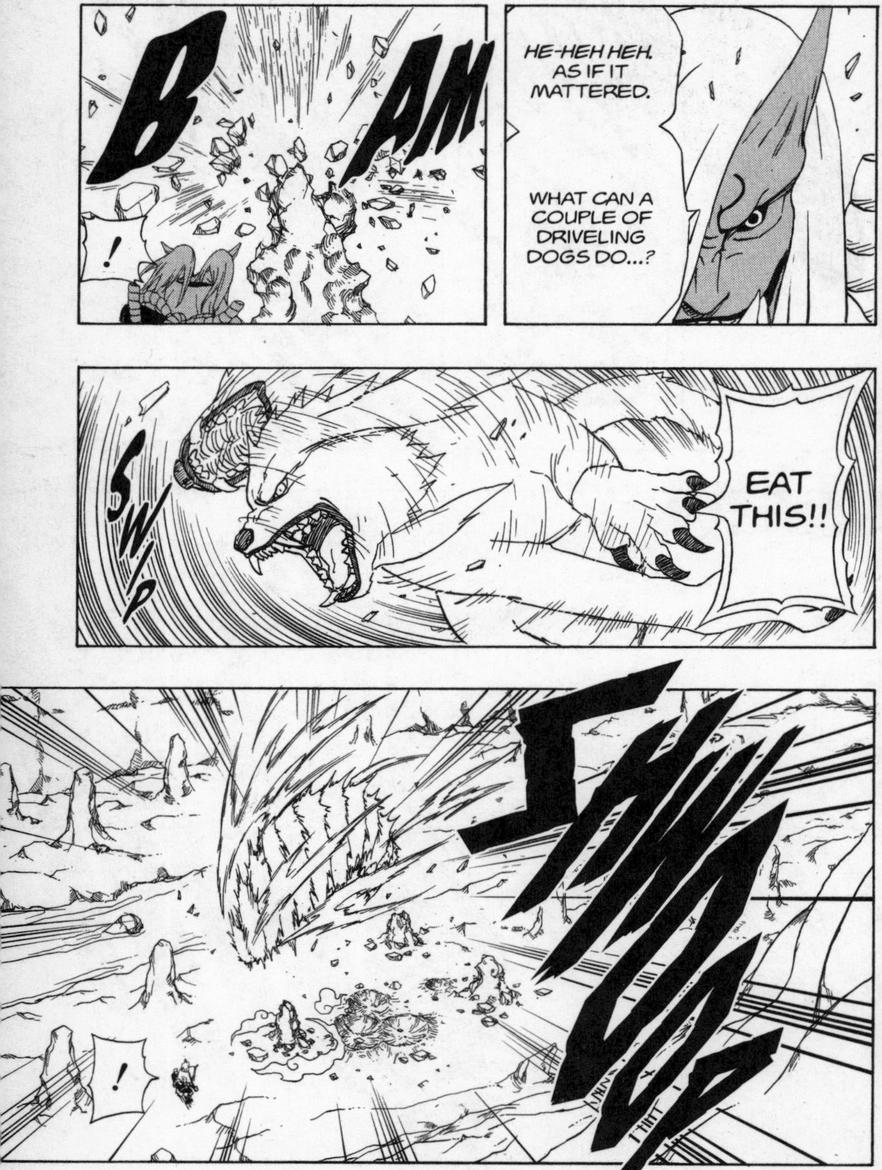
HE-HEH HEH. AS IF IT MATTERED.
WHAT CAN A COUPLE OF DRIVELING DOGS DO...?
BAM
!
EAT THIS!!
SWIP
!

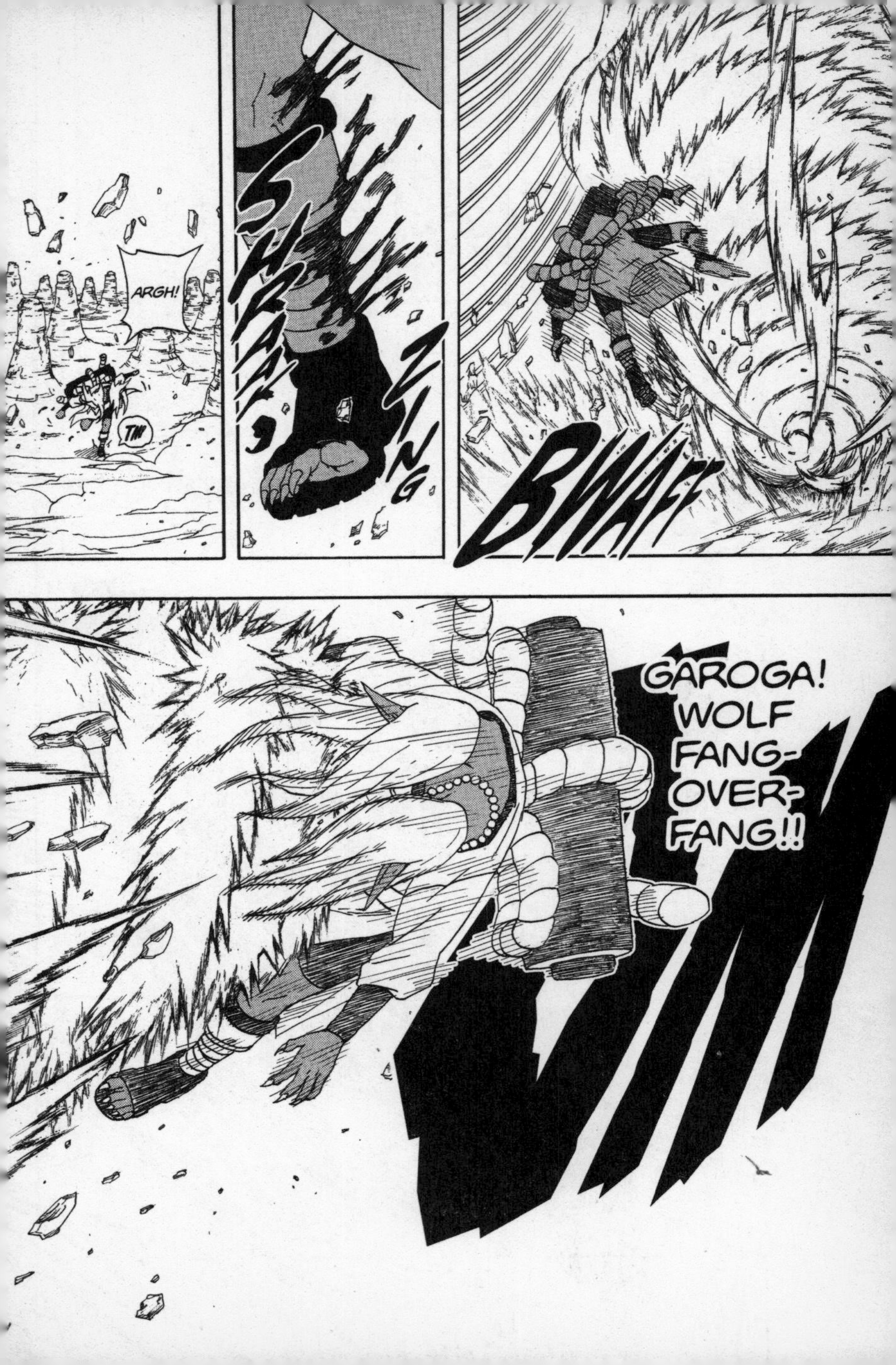
BWAFF
ZZING
ARGH!
GAROGA! WOLF FANG-OVER-FANG!!

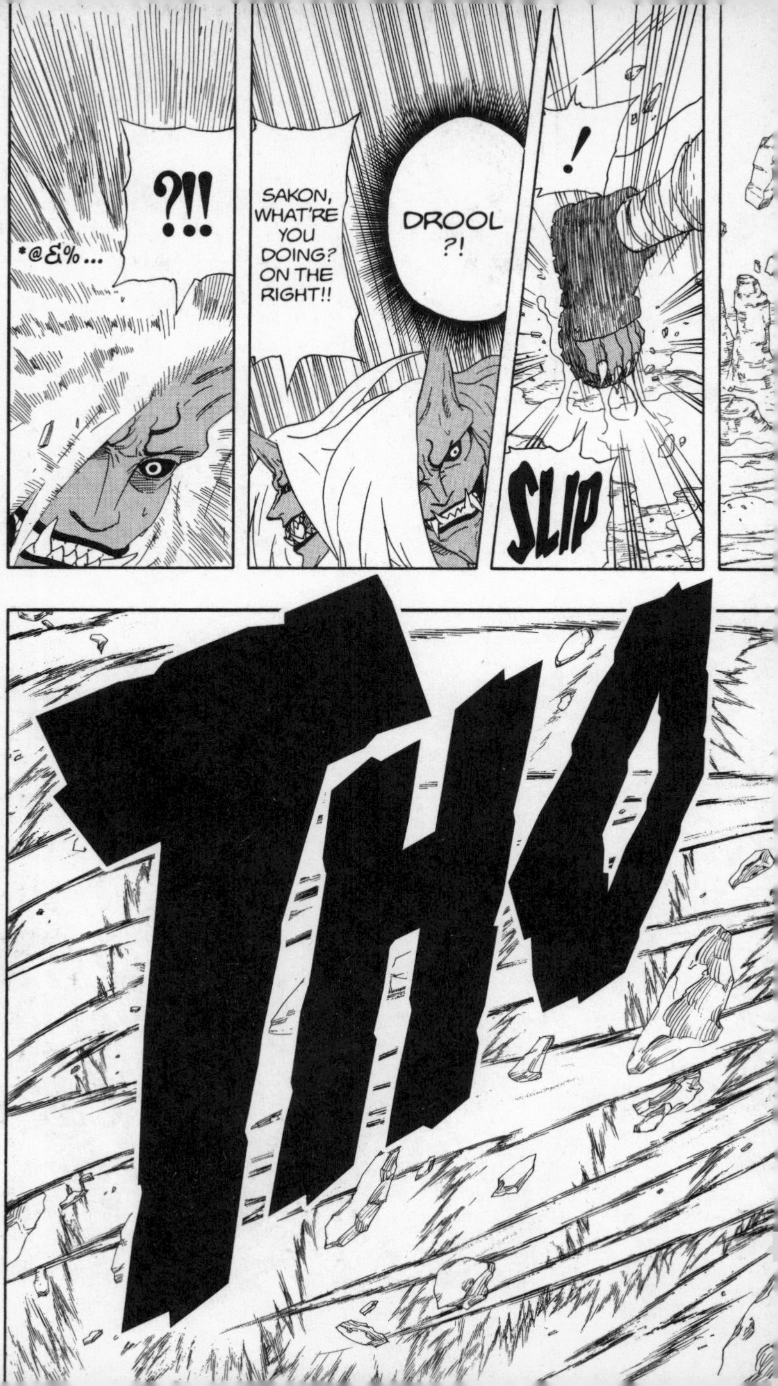
!
SLIP
DROOL ?!
SAKON, WHAT'RE YOU DOING? ON THE RIGHT!!
?!!
*@Ɛ%...
THD

NARUTO™

Number 204: Ukon's Prowess

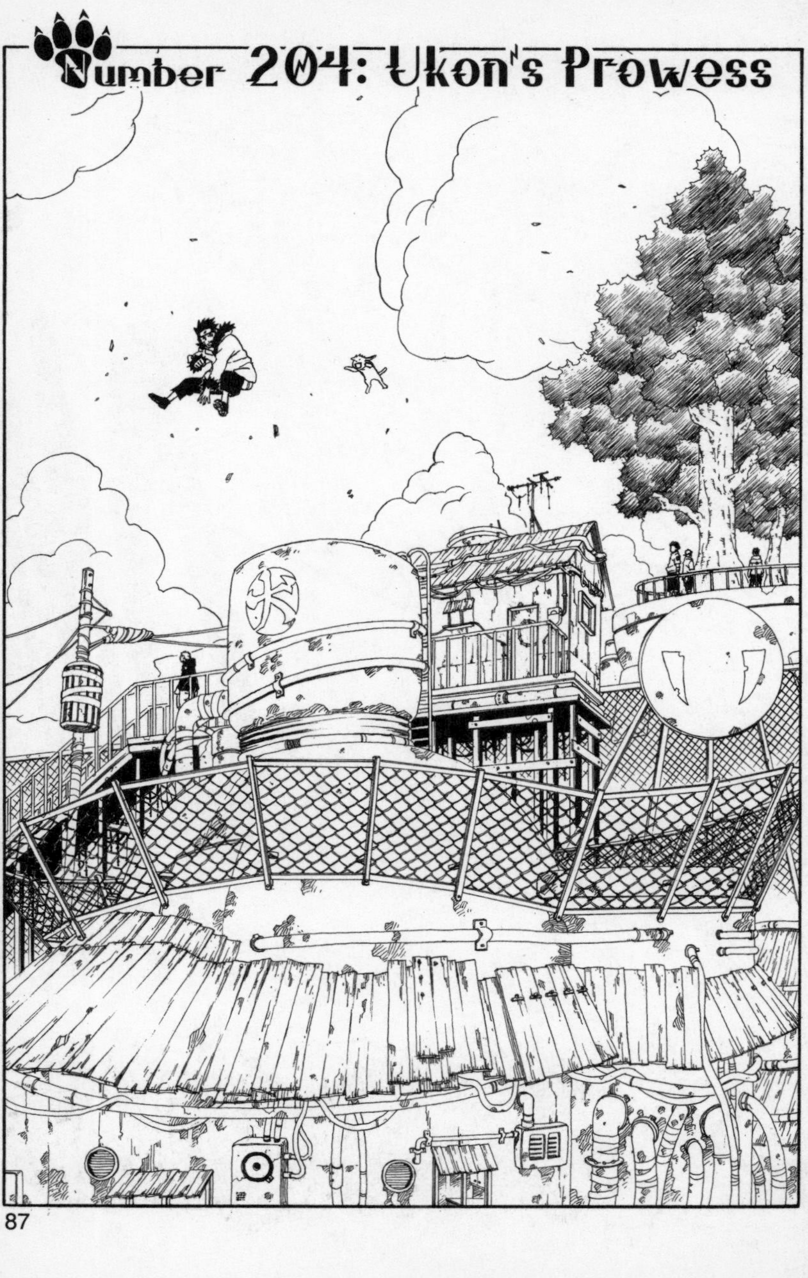

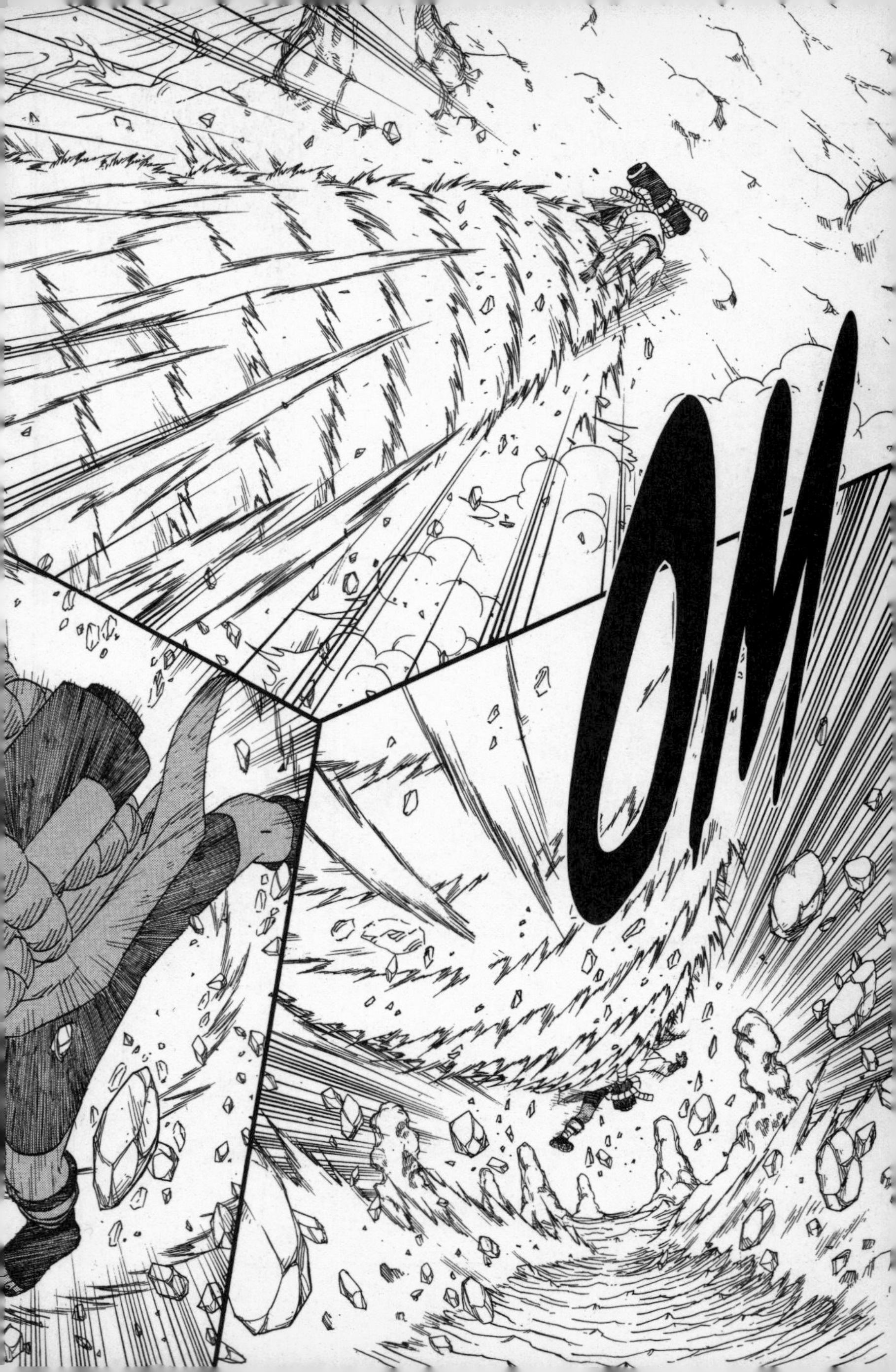
OM

READ THIS WAY

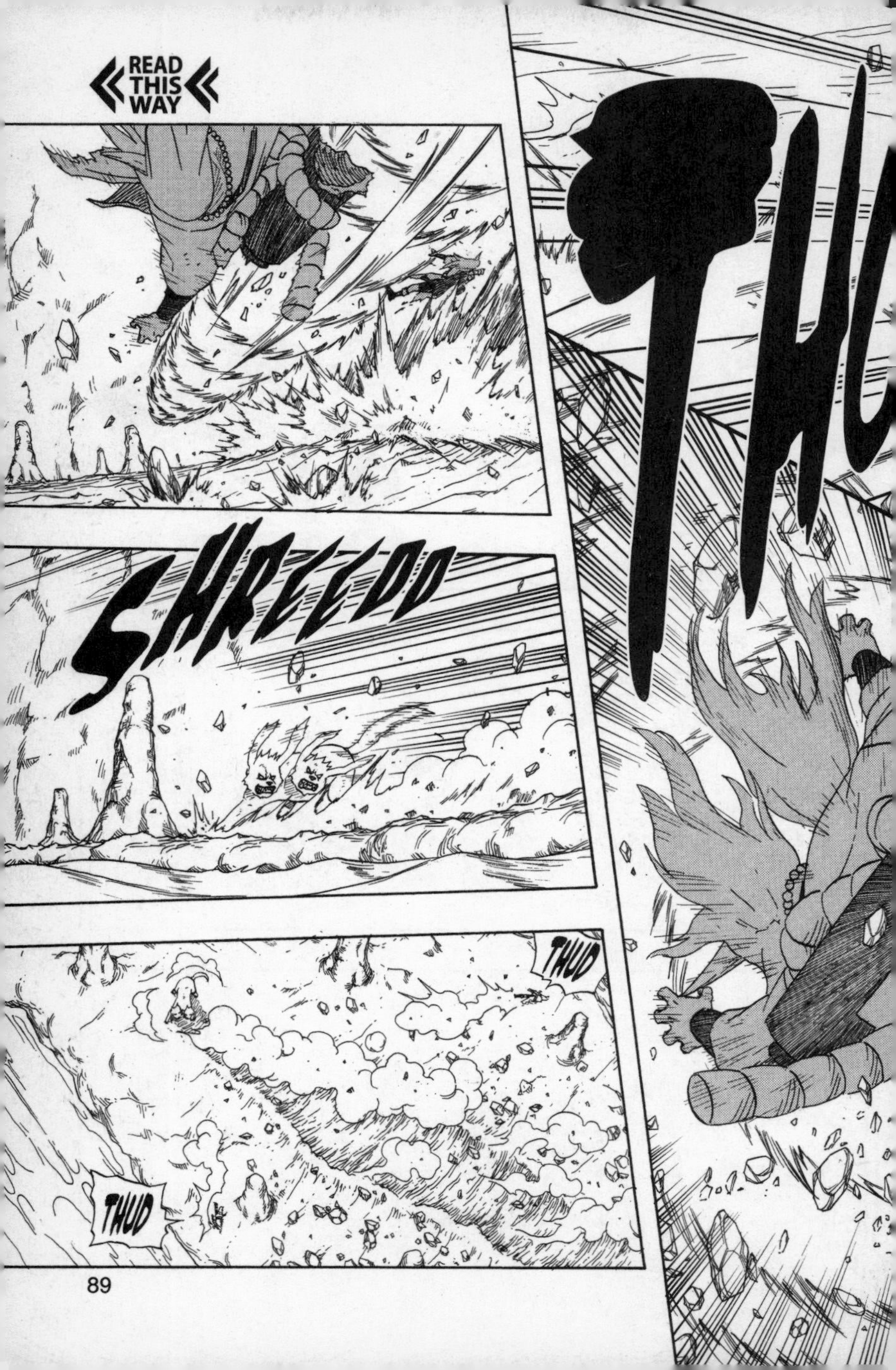
THU
SHREEDD
THUD
THUD

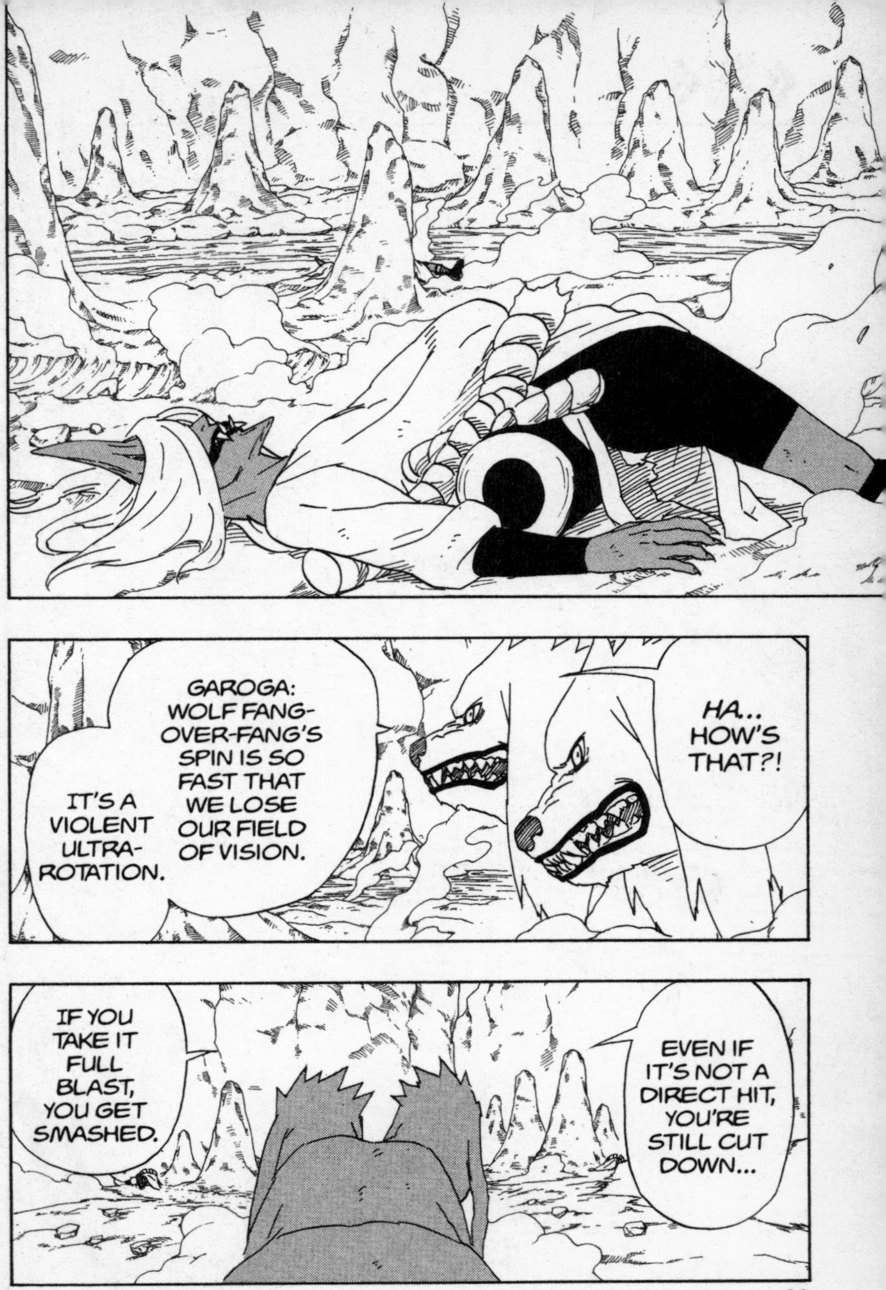
HA... HOW'S THAT?!
GAROGA: WOLF FANG-OVER-FANG'S SPIN IS SO FAST THAT WE LOSE OUR FIELD OF VISION.
IT'S A VIOLENT ULTRA-ROTATION.
EVEN IF IT'S NOT A DIRECT HIT, YOU'RE STILL CUT DOWN...
IF YOU TAKE IT FULL BLAST, YOU GET SMASHED.

READ THIS WAY

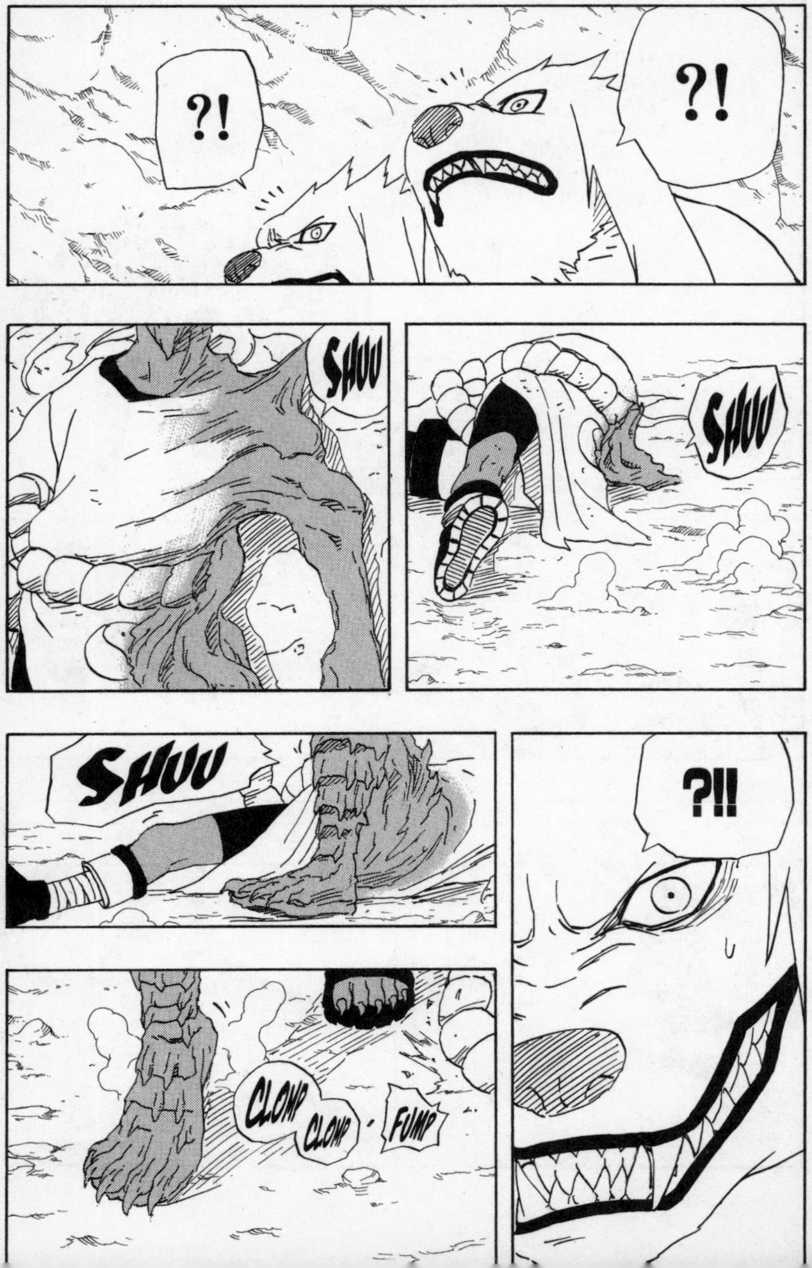
?!
?!
SHUU
SHUU
?!!
SHUU
CLOMP
CLOMP
FUMP

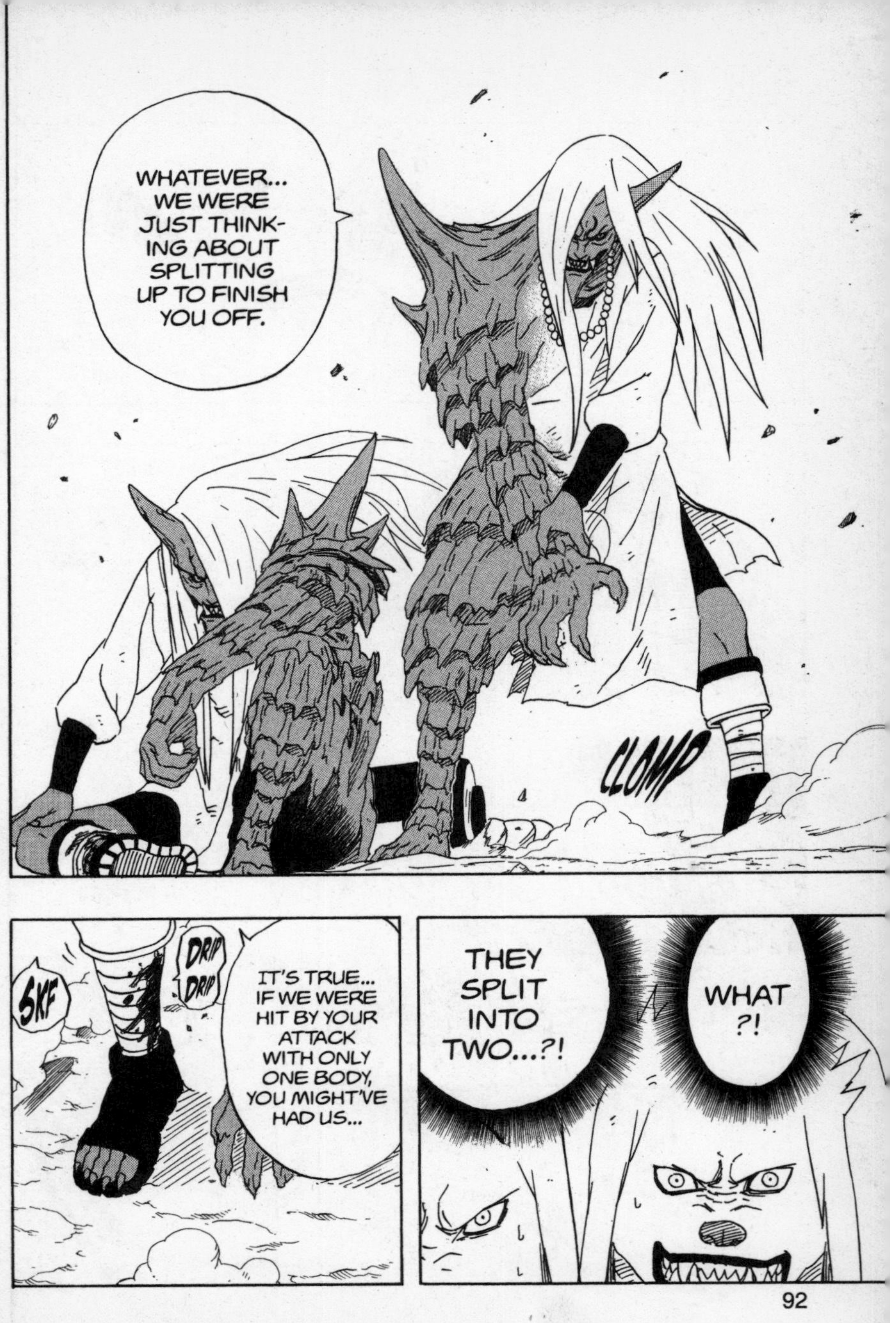
WHATEVER... WE WERE JUST THINKING ABOUT SPLITTING UP TO FINISH YOU OFF.
CLOMP
WHAT?!
THEY SPLIT INTO TWO...?!
DRIP DRIP
IT'S TRUE... IF WE WERE HIT BY YOUR ATTACK WITH ONLY ONE BODY, YOU MIGHT'VE HAD US...
SKF

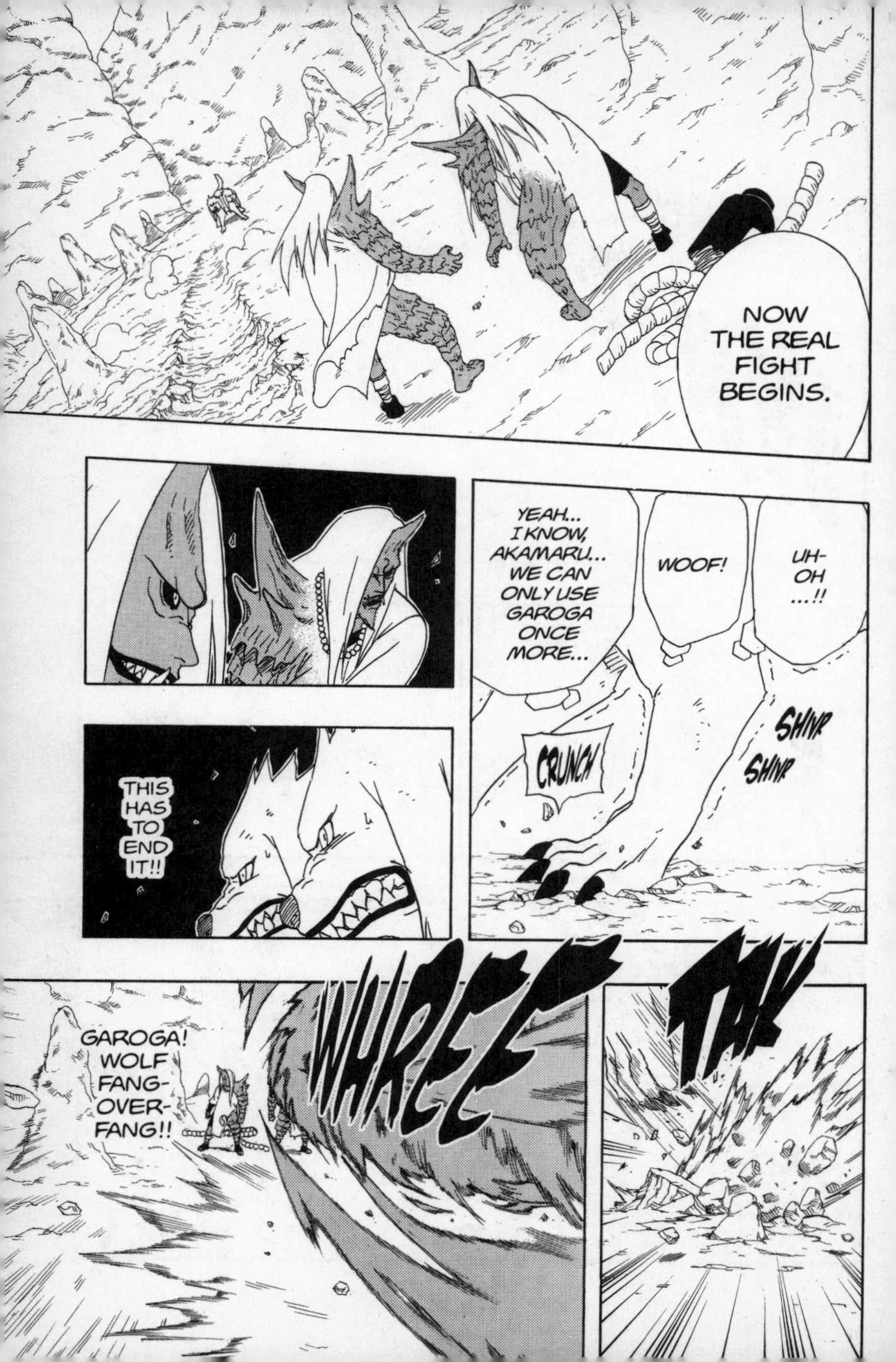
NOW THE REAL FIGHT BEGINS.
UH-OH ...!!
WOOF!
YEAH... I KNOW, AKAMARU... WE CAN ONLY USE GAROGA ONCE MORE...
CRUNCH
SHNK
SHNK
THIS HAS TO END IT!!
TAK
WHREEE
GAROGA! WOLF FANG-OVER-FANG!!

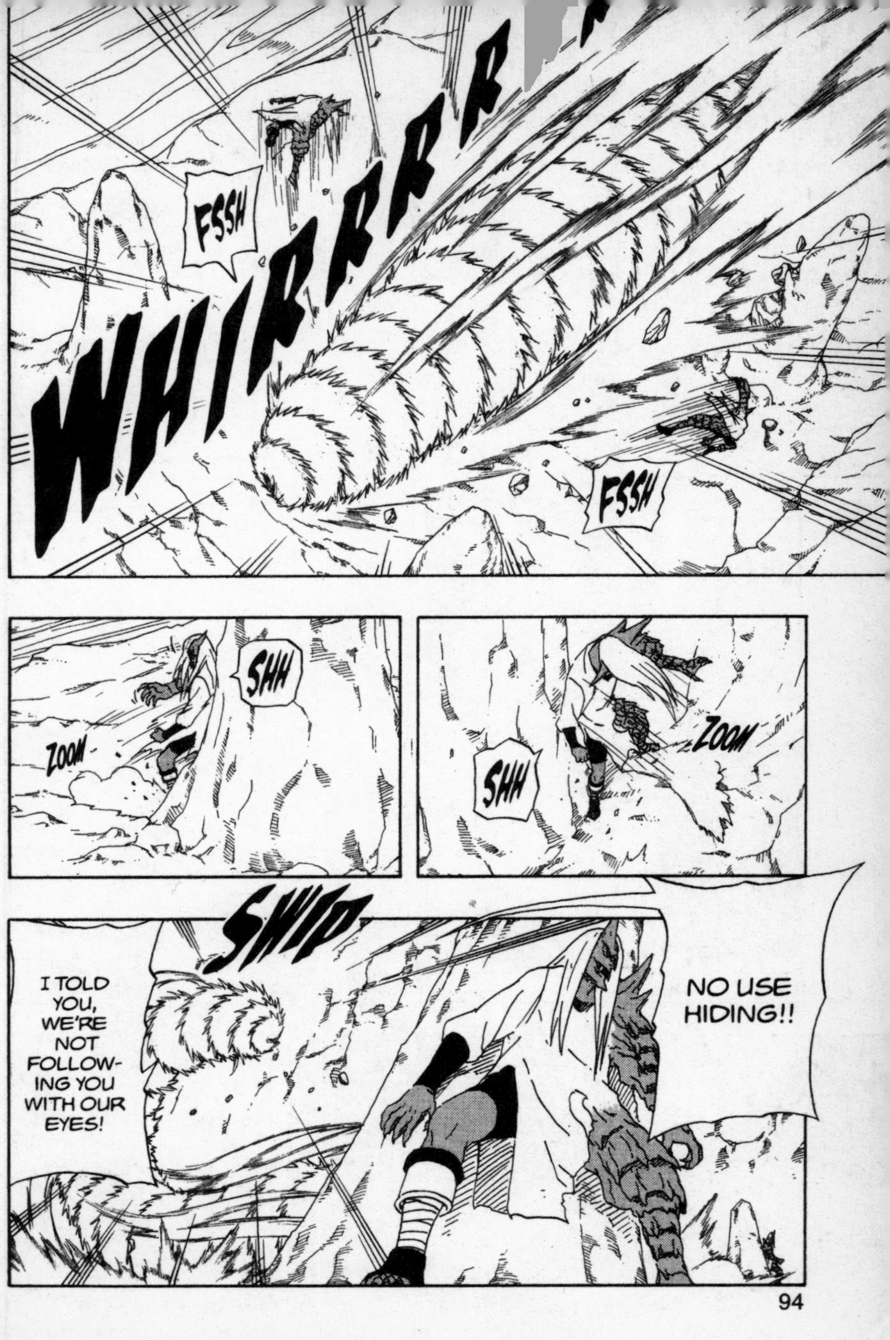
WHIRRRR
FSSH
FSSH
ZOOM
SHH
SHH
ZOOM
SWIP
NO USE HIDING!!
I TOLD YOU, WE'RE NOT FOLLOW-ING YOU WITH OUR EYES!

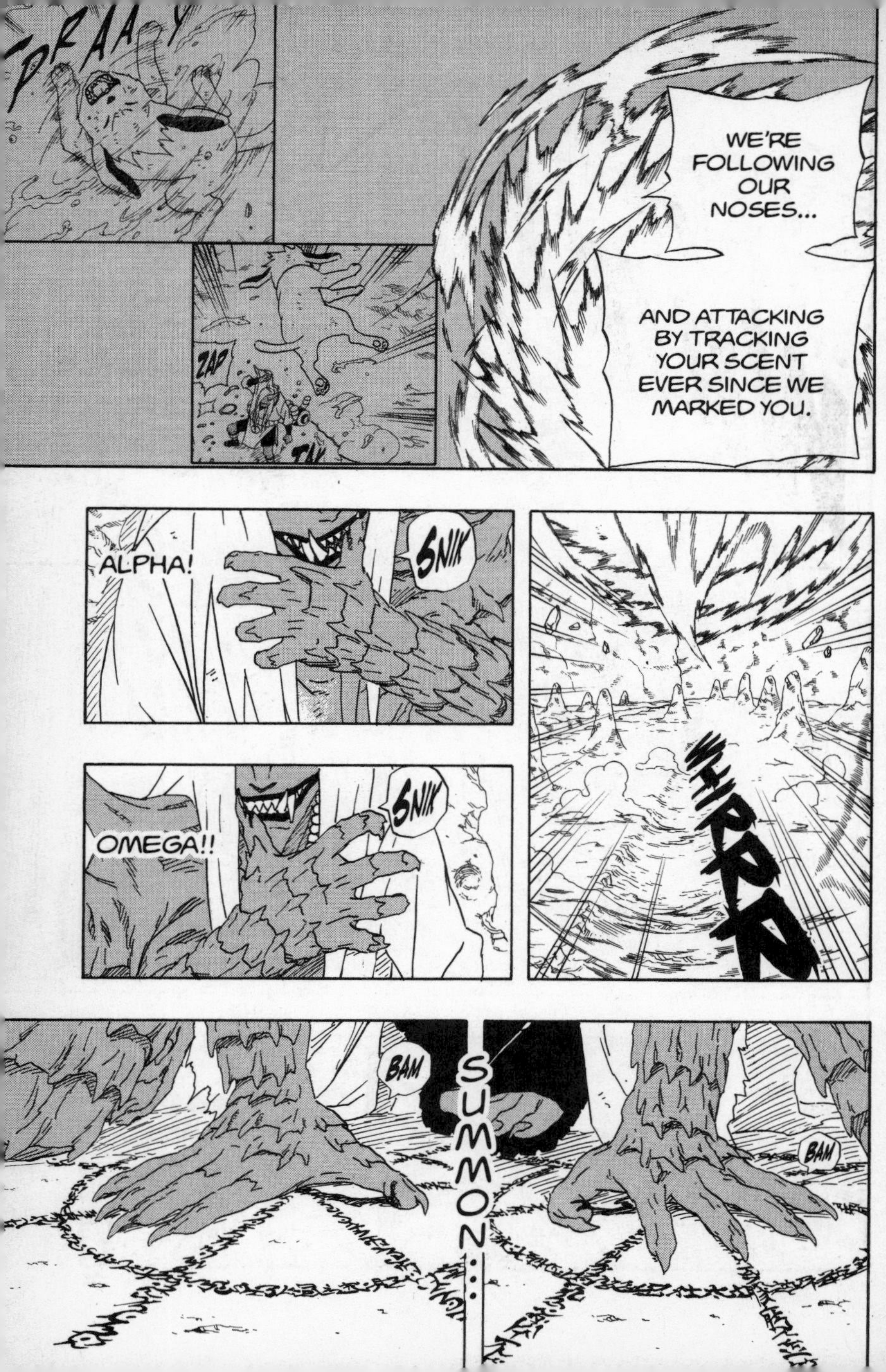

WE'RE FOLLOWING OUR NOSES...
AND ATTACKING BY TRACKING YOUR SCENT EVER SINCE WE MARKED YOU.
PRAAY
ZAP
TAK
WHIRRR
ALPHA!
SNIK
OMEGA!!
SNIK
BAM
SUMMON...
BAM

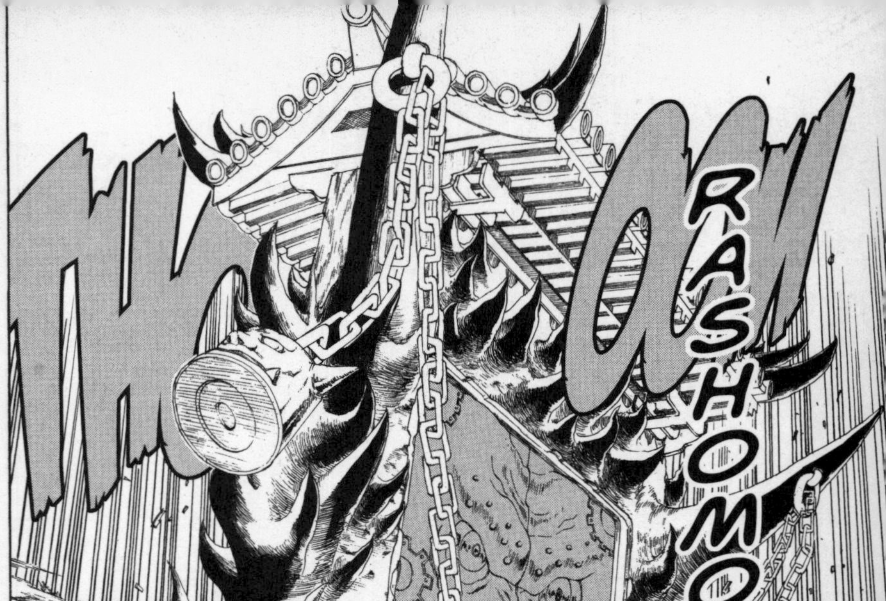
RASHOMON!!!
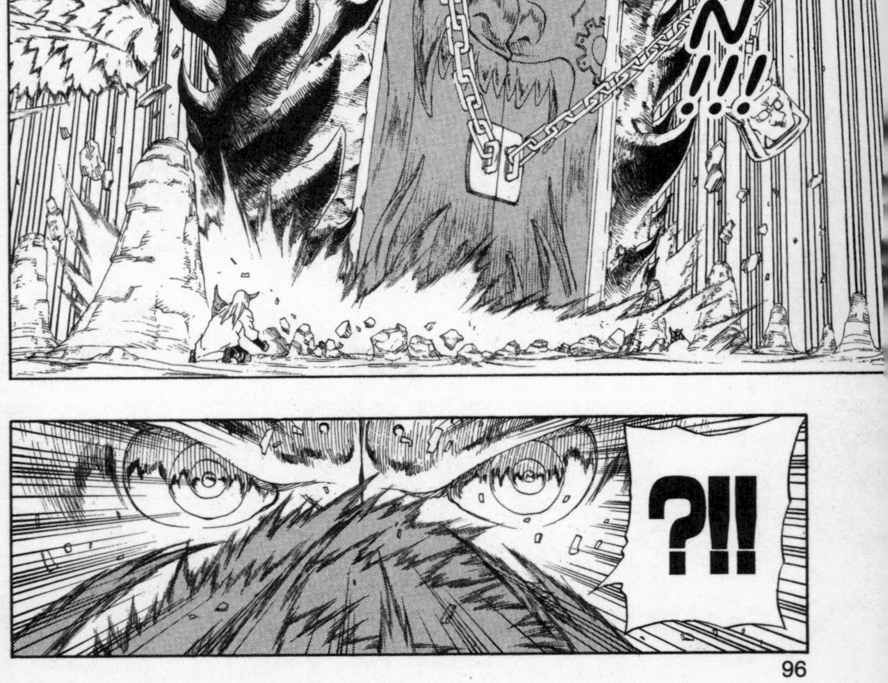
?!!

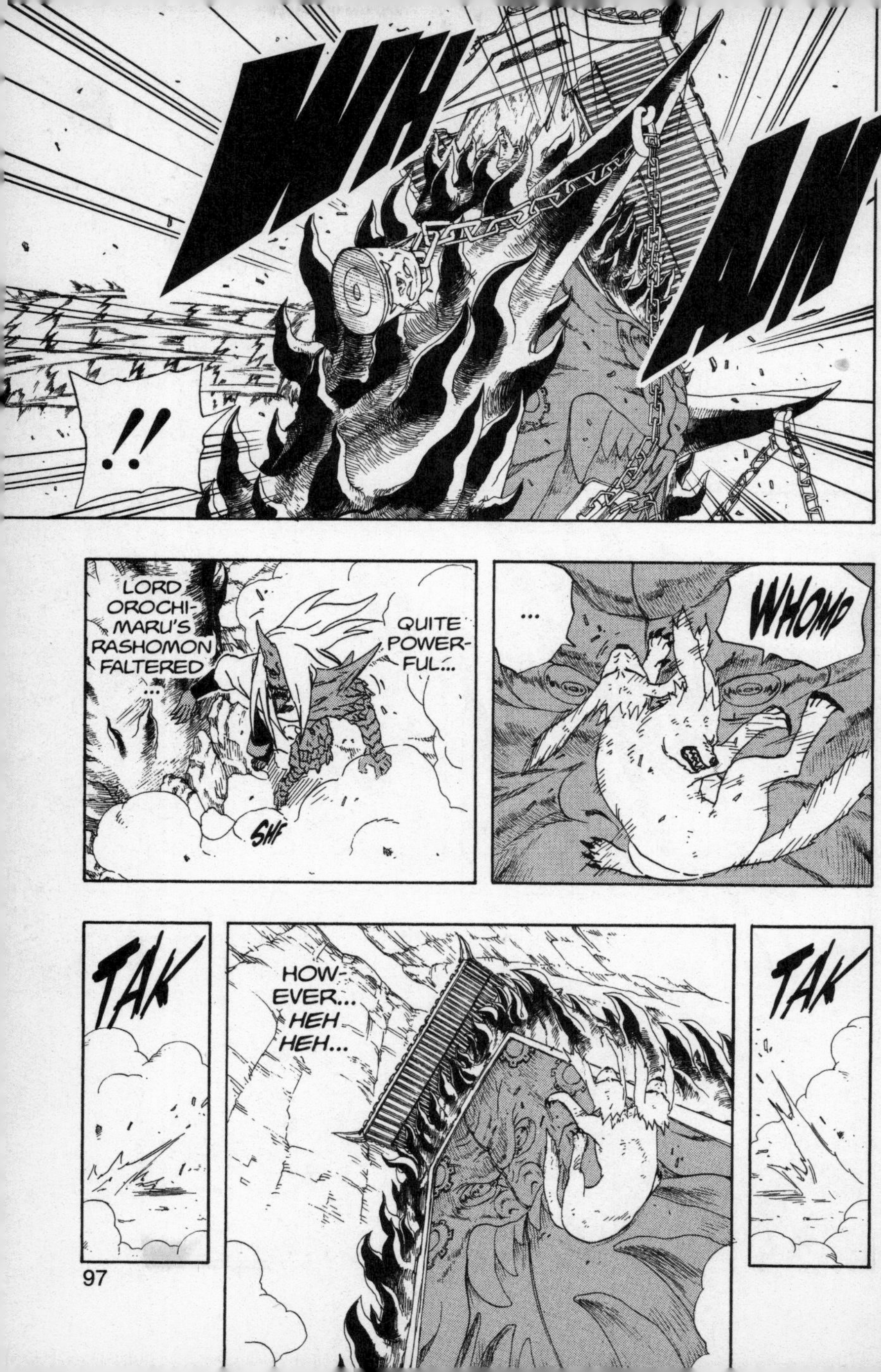
WHAM
!!
...
WHOMP
QUITE POWERFUL...
LORD OROCHIMARU'S RASHOMON FALTERED...
SHF
TAK
HOWEVER... HEH HEH...
TAK

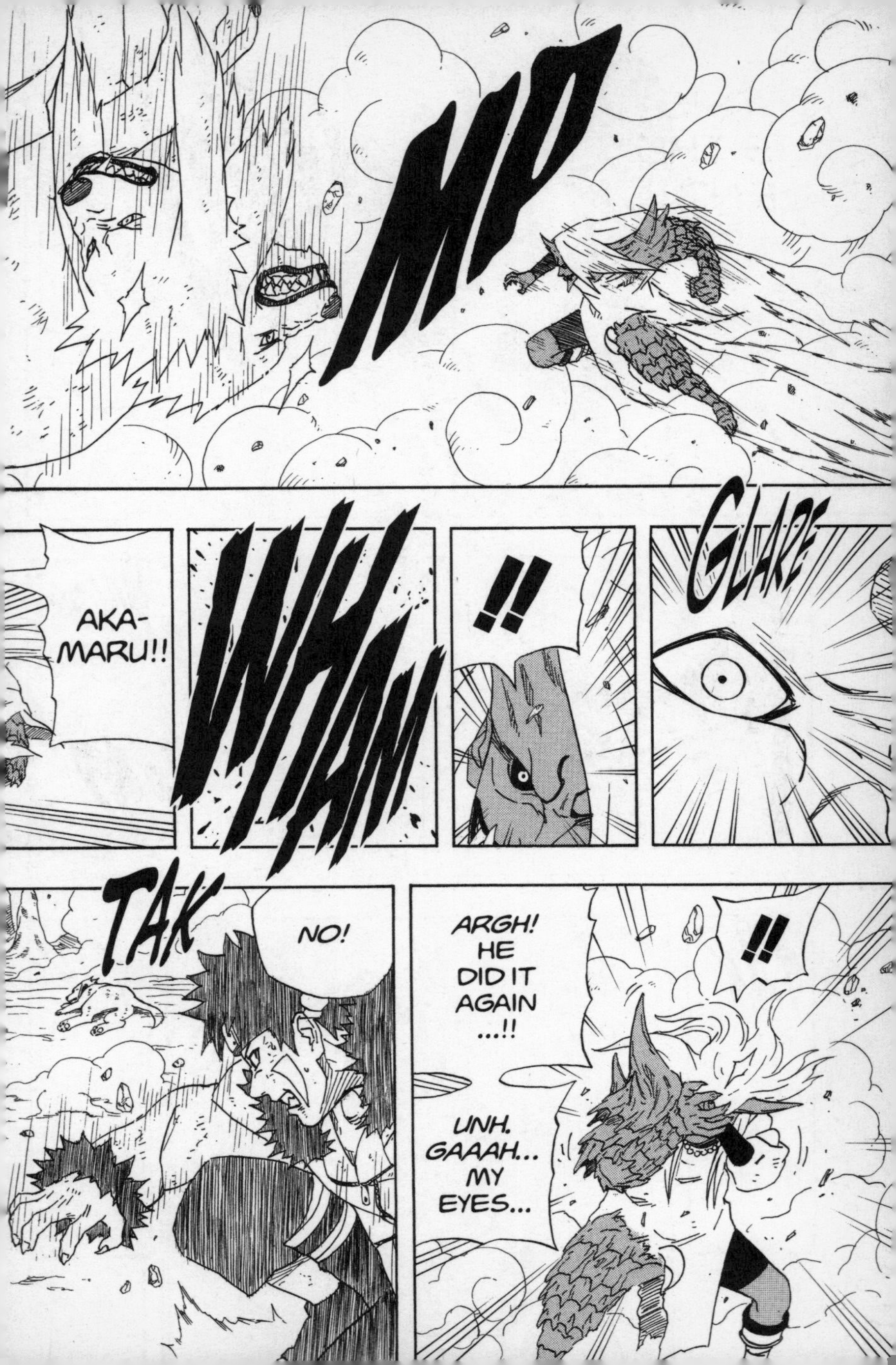
GLARE
!!
WHAM
AKA-MARU!!
!!
ARGH! HE DID IT AGAIN ...!!
UNH. GAAAH... MY EYES...
TAK
NO!

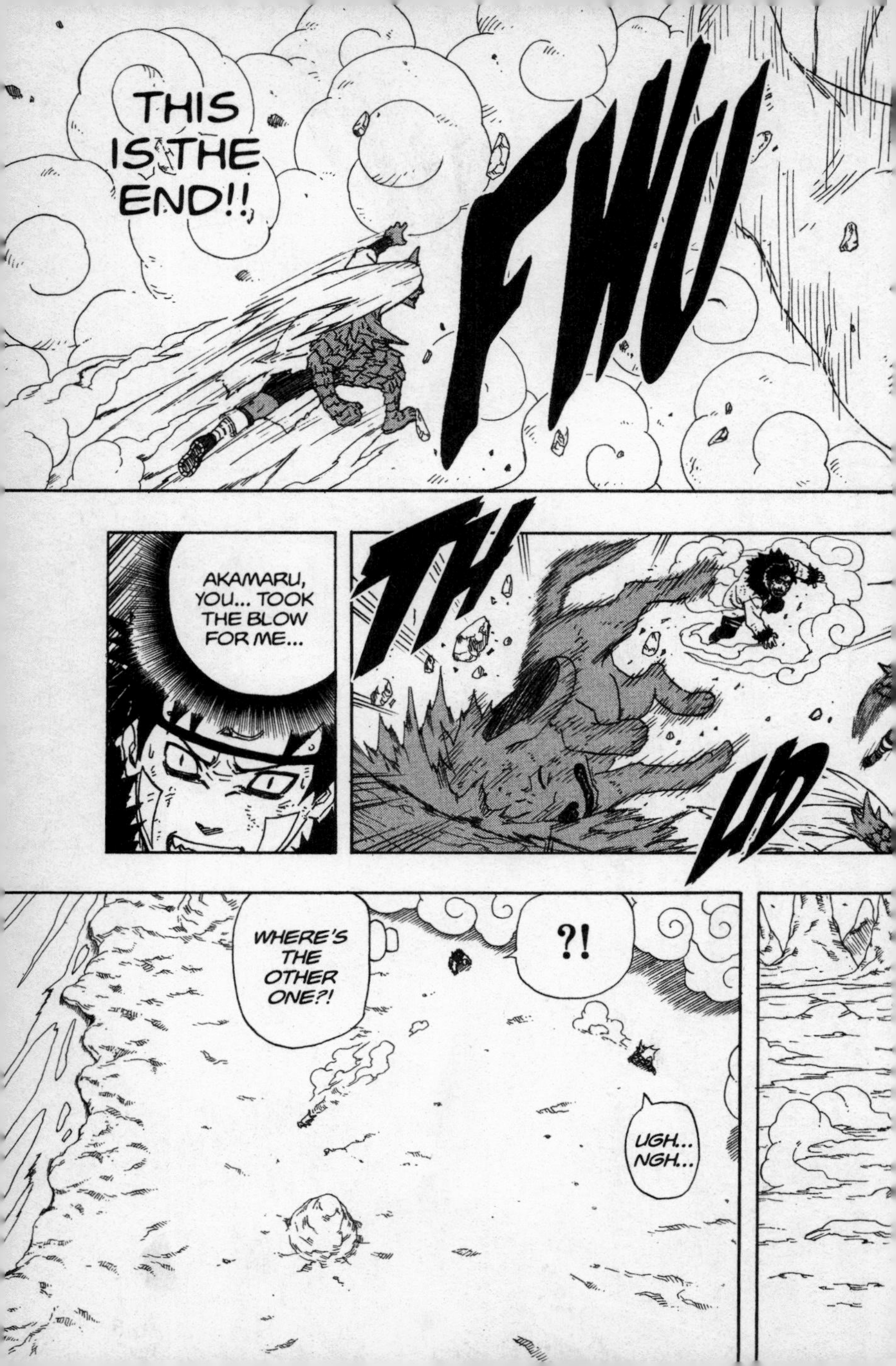
THIS IS THE END!!
FWU
TH
UD
AKAMARU, YOU... TOOK THE BLOW FOR ME...
?!
WHERE'S THE OTHER ONE?!
UGH... NGH...

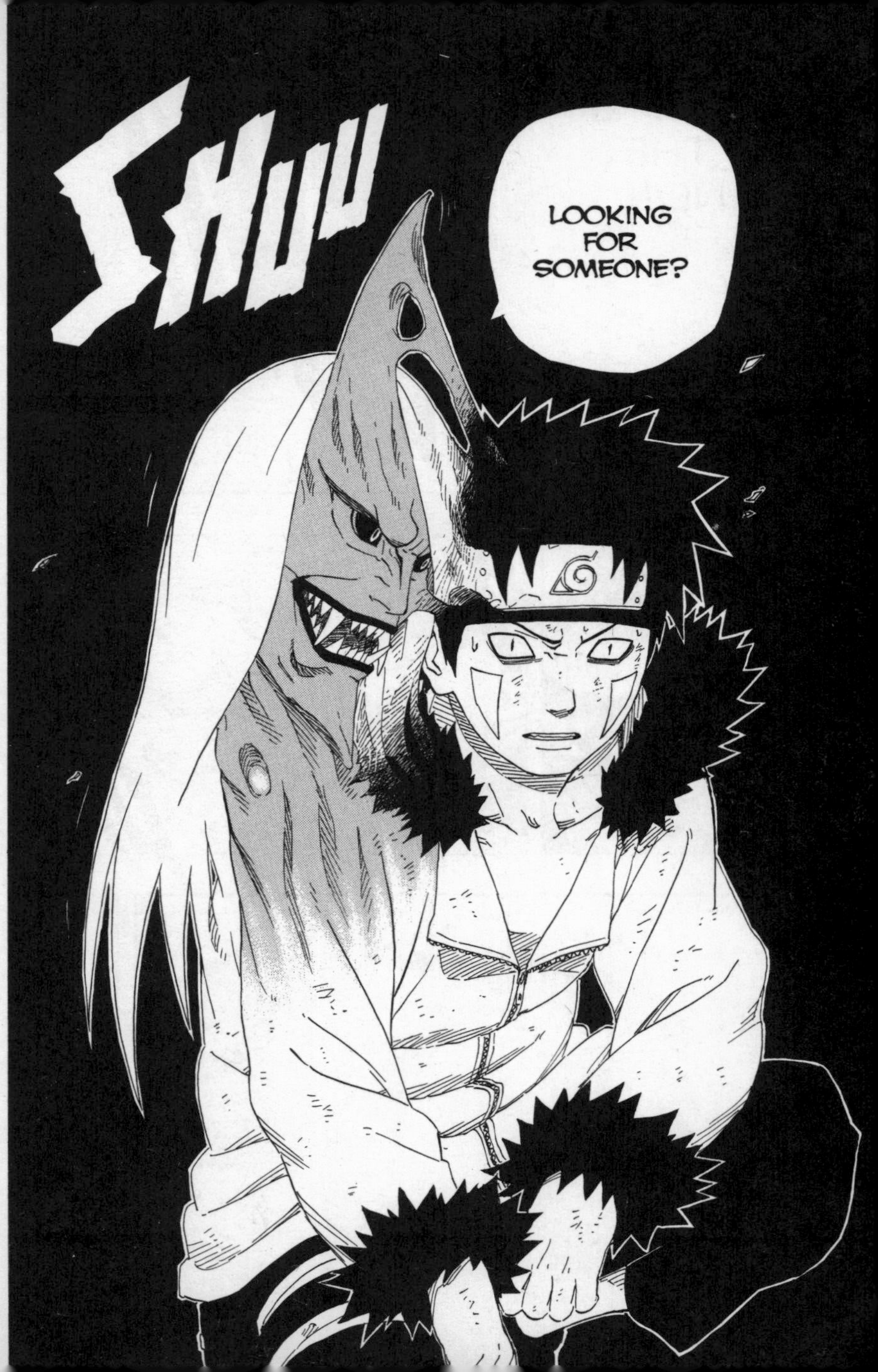
SHUU
LOOKING FOR SOMEONE?

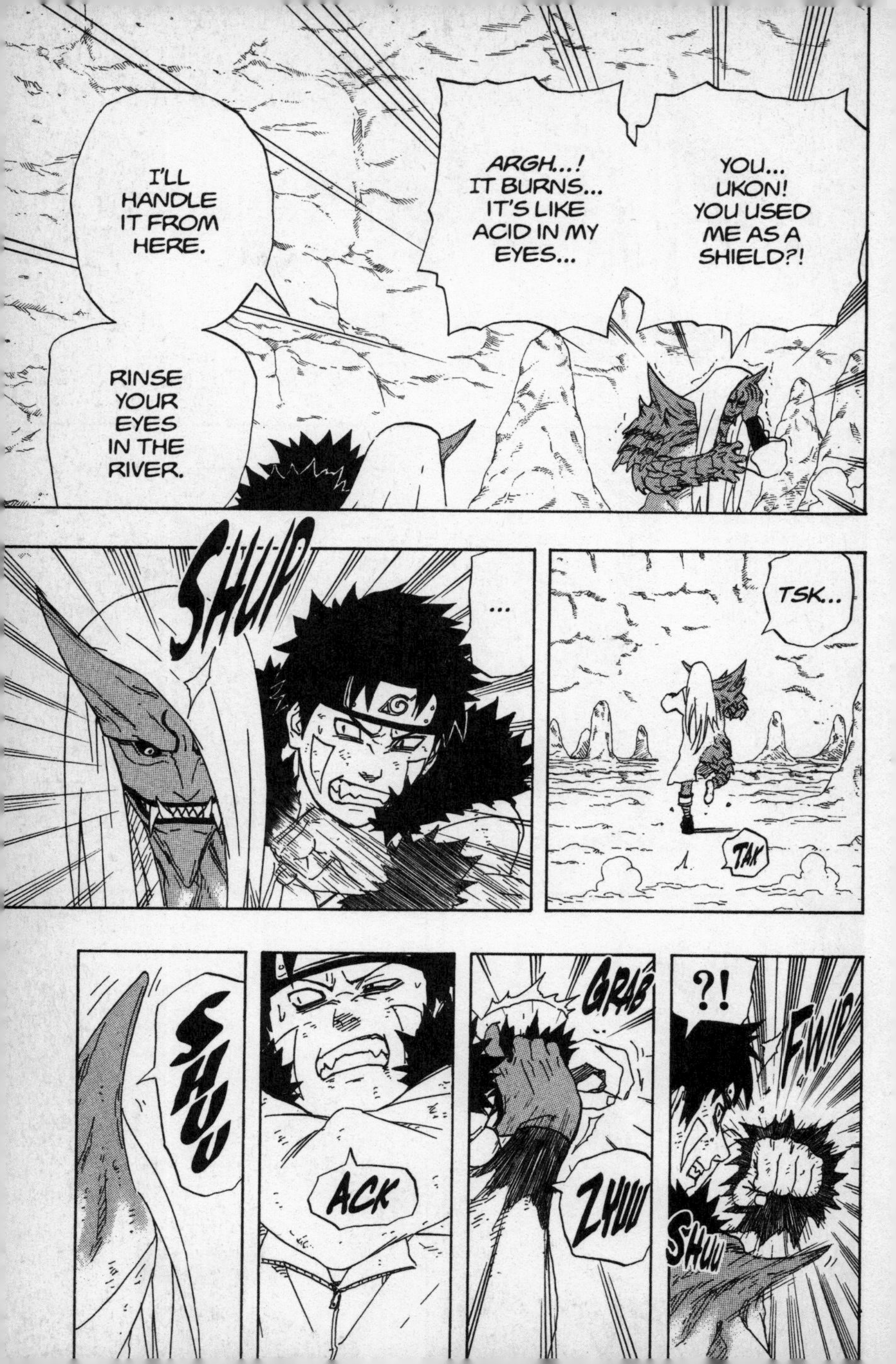
YOU... UKON! YOU USED ME AS A SHIELD?!
ARGH...! IT BURNS... IT'S LIKE ACID IN MY EYES...
I'LL HANDLE IT FROM HERE.
RINSE YOUR EYES IN THE RIVER.
TSK...
TAK
SHUP
...
?!
FWIP
SHUU
GRAB
ZHUU
ACK
SHUU

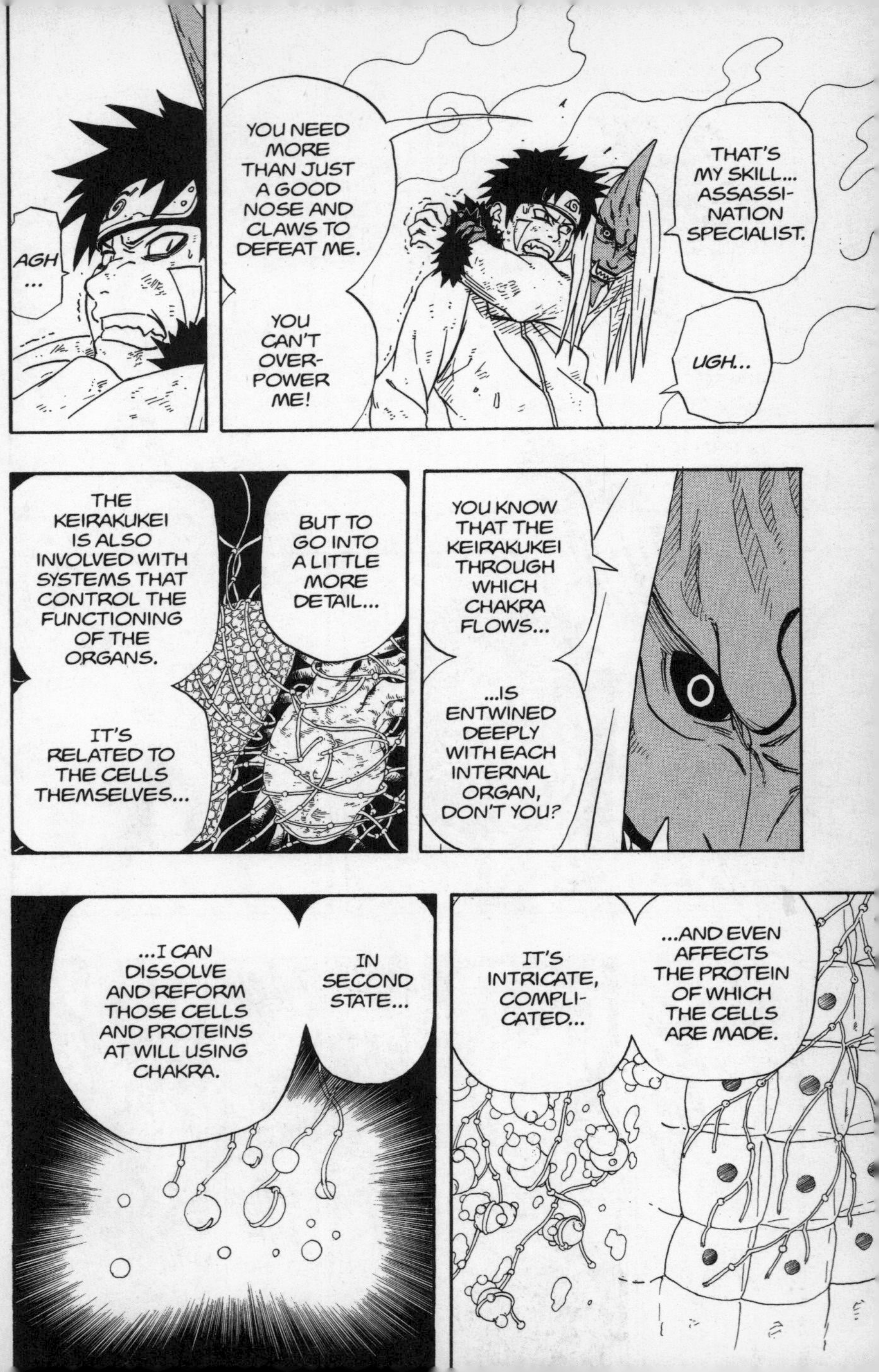
THAT'S MY SKILL... ASSASSI-NATION SPECIALIST.
UGH...
YOU NEED MORE THAN JUST A GOOD NOSE AND CLAWS TO DEFEAT ME.
YOU CAN'T OVER-POWER ME!
AGH...
YOU KNOW THAT THE KEIRAKUKEI THROUGH WHICH CHAKRA FLOWS...
...IS ENTWINED DEEPLY WITH EACH INTERNAL ORGAN, DON'T YOU?
BUT TO GO INTO A LITTLE MORE DETAIL...
THE KEIRAKUKEI IS ALSO INVOLVED WITH SYSTEMS THAT CONTROL THE FUNCTIONING OF THE ORGANS.
IT'S RELATED TO THE CELLS THEMSELVES...
...AND EVEN AFFECTS THE PROTEIN OF WHICH THE CELLS ARE MADE.
IT'S INTRICATE, COMPLI-CATED...
IN SECOND STATE...
...I CAN DISSOLVE AND REFORM THOSE CELLS AND PROTEINS AT WILL USING CHAKRA.

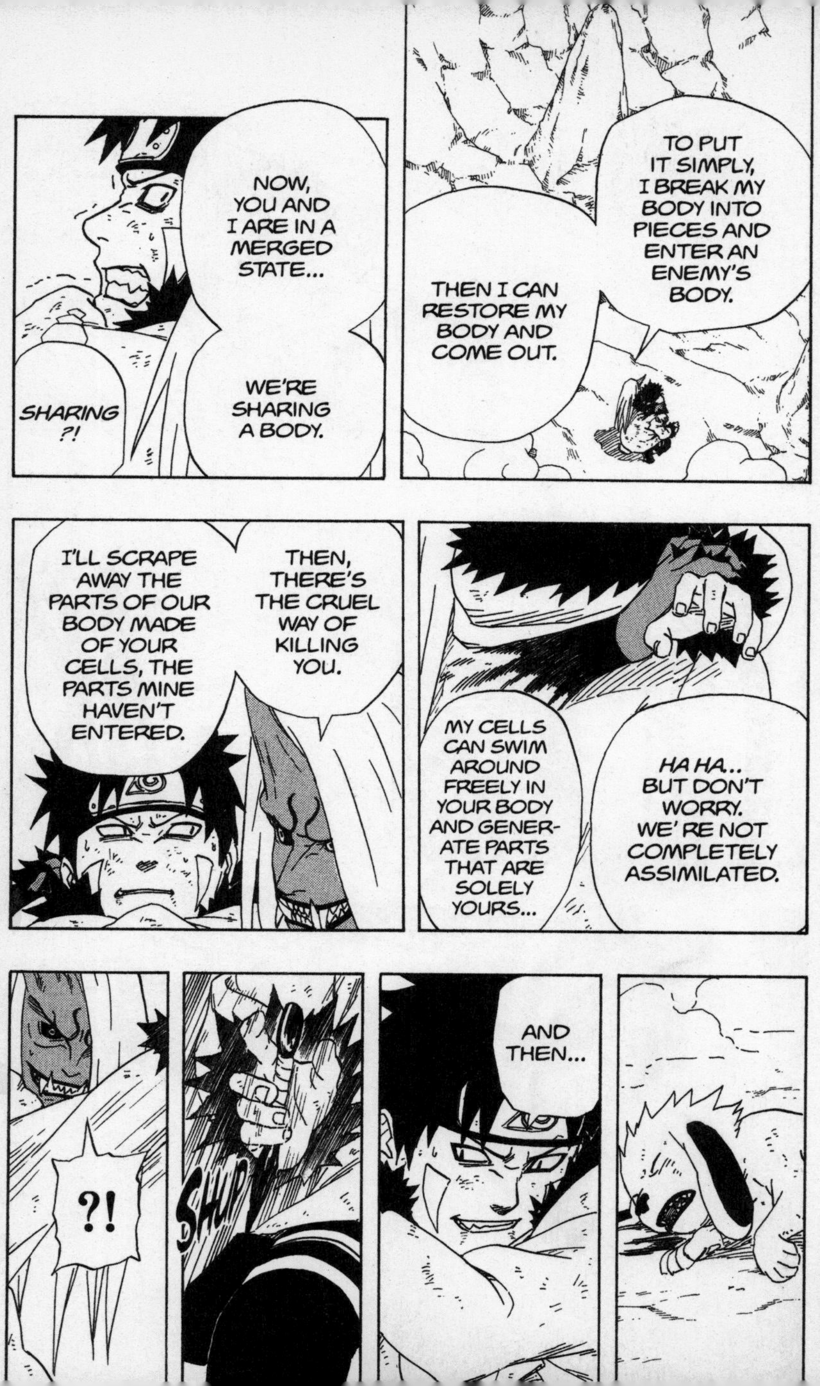

TO PUT IT SIMPLY, I BREAK MY BODY INTO PIECES AND ENTER AN ENEMY'S BODY.
THEN I CAN RESTORE MY BODY AND COME OUT.
NOW, YOU AND I ARE IN A MERGED STATE...
WE'RE SHARING A BODY.
SHARING ?!
HA HA... BUT DON'T WORRY. WE' RE NOT COMPLETELY ASSIMILATED.
MY CELLS CAN SWIM AROUND FREELY IN YOUR BODY AND GENER-ATE PARTS THAT ARE SOLELY YOURS...
THEN, THERE'S THE CRUEL WAY OF KILLING YOU.
I'LL SCRAPE AWAY THE PARTS OF OUR BODY MADE OF YOUR CELLS, THE PARTS MINE HAVEN'T ENTERED.
AND THEN...
SHUP
?!

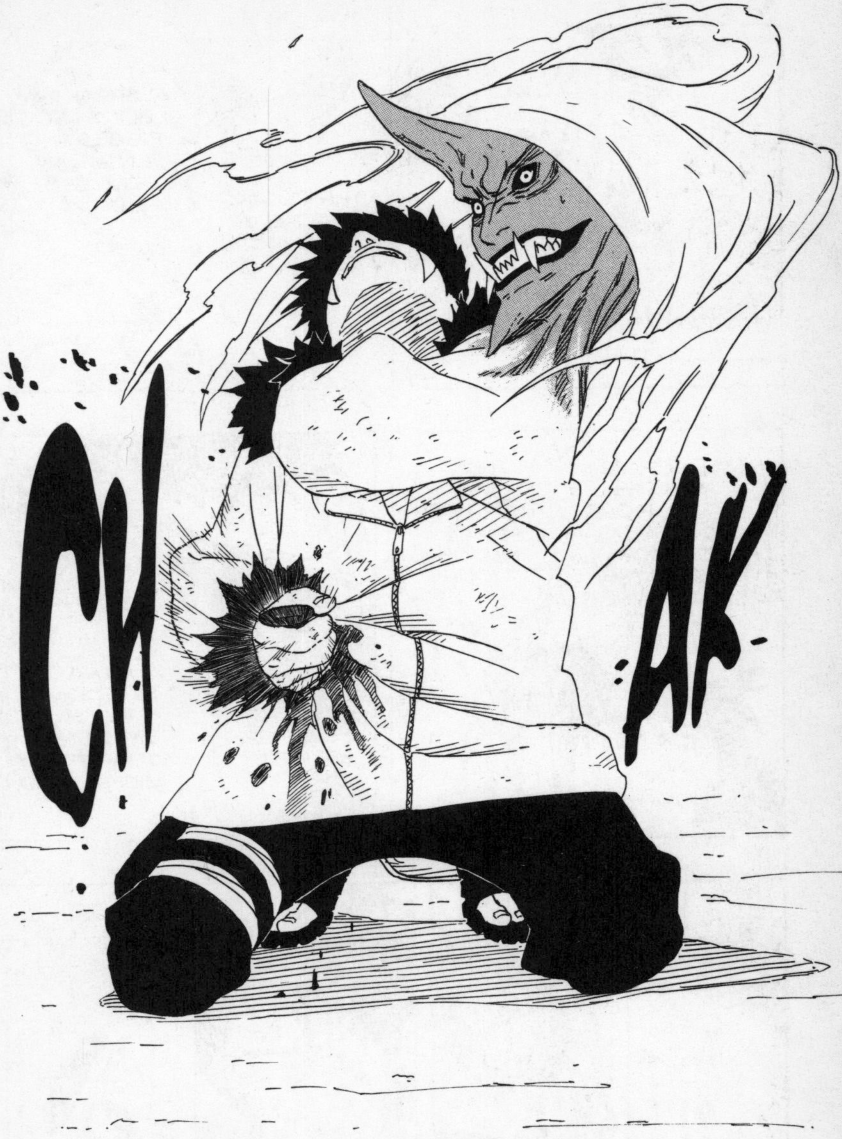
CHAK

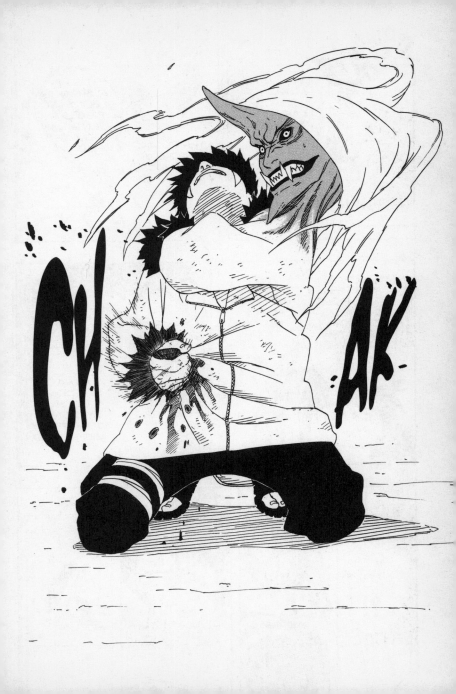

READ THIS WAY

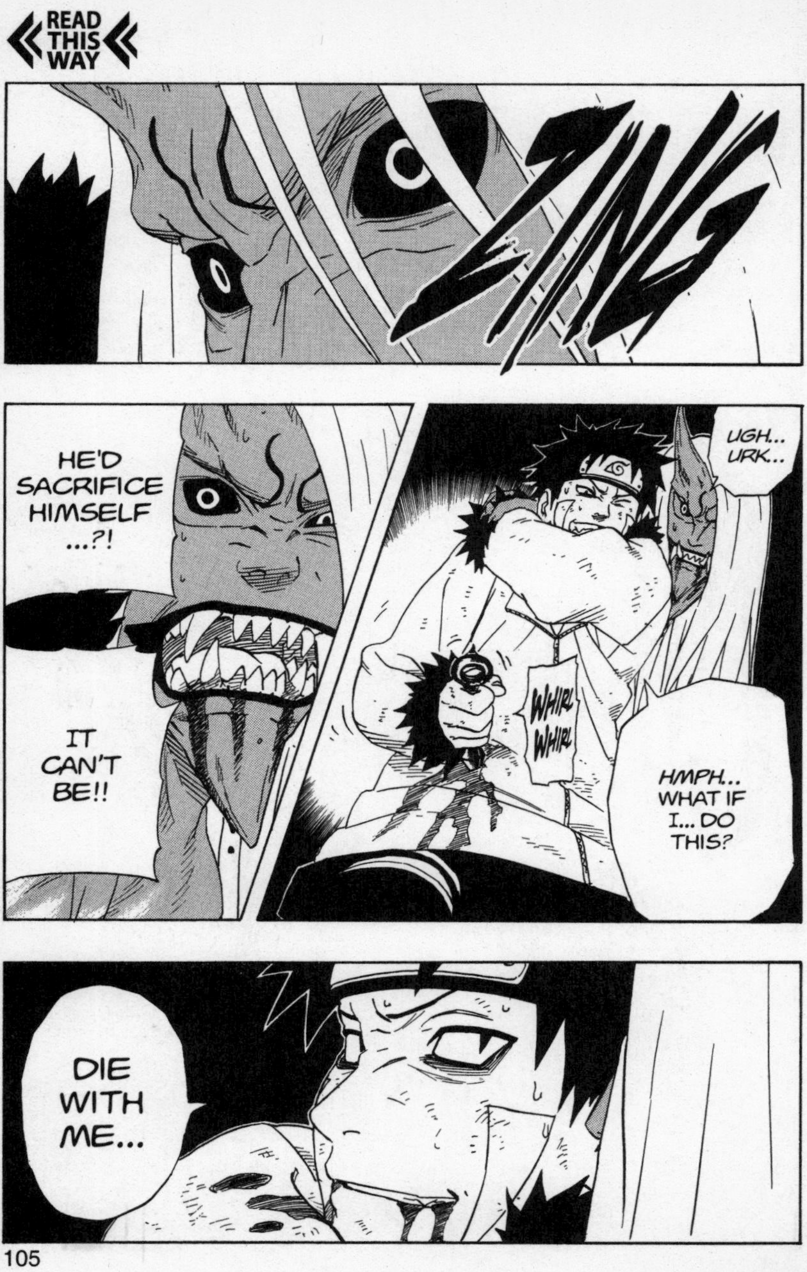
ZING
UGH... URK...
WHIRL WHIRL
HMPH... WHAT IF I... DO THIS?
HE'D SACRIFICE HIMSELF ...?!
IT CAN'T BE!!
DIE WITH ME...

NARUTO™

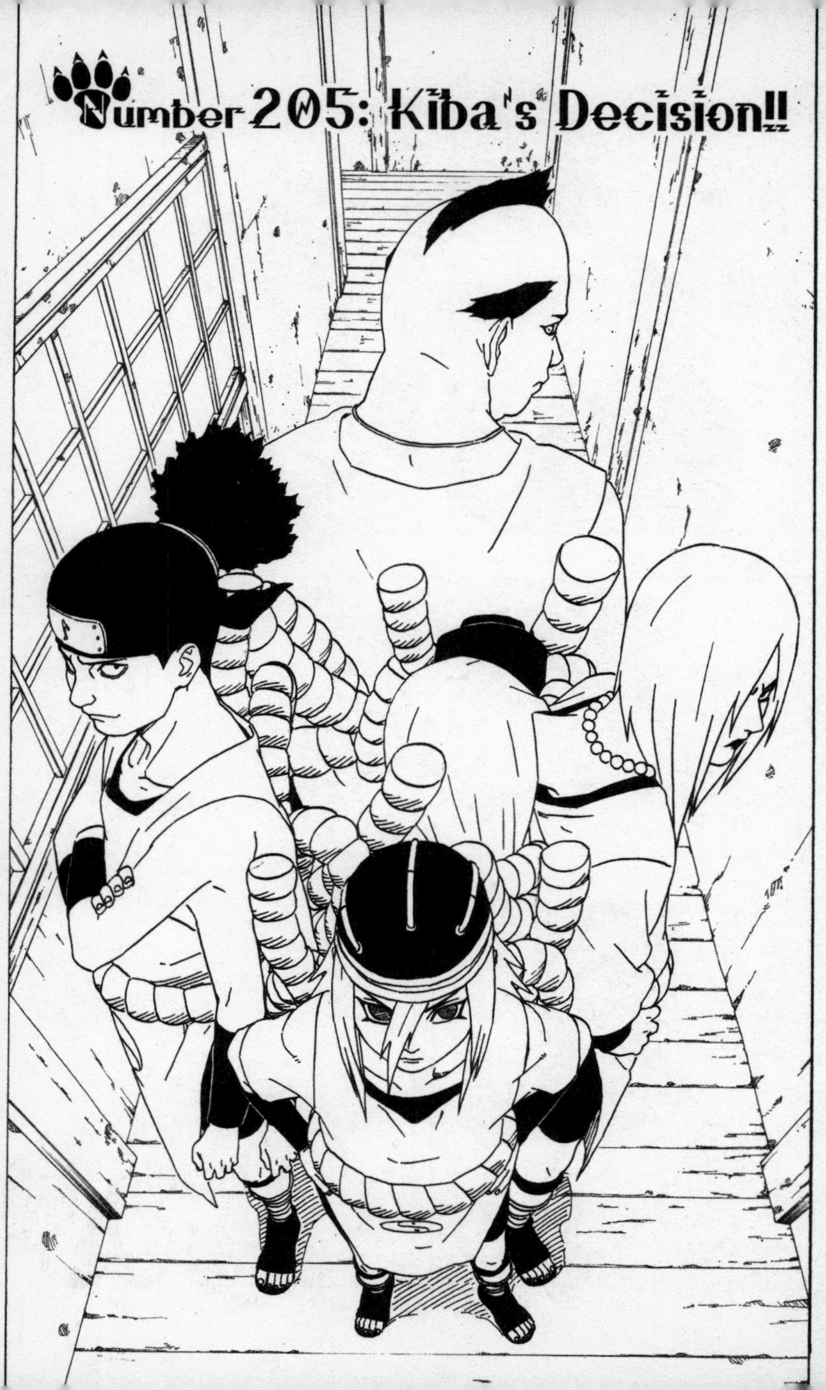
Number 205: Kiba's Decision!!

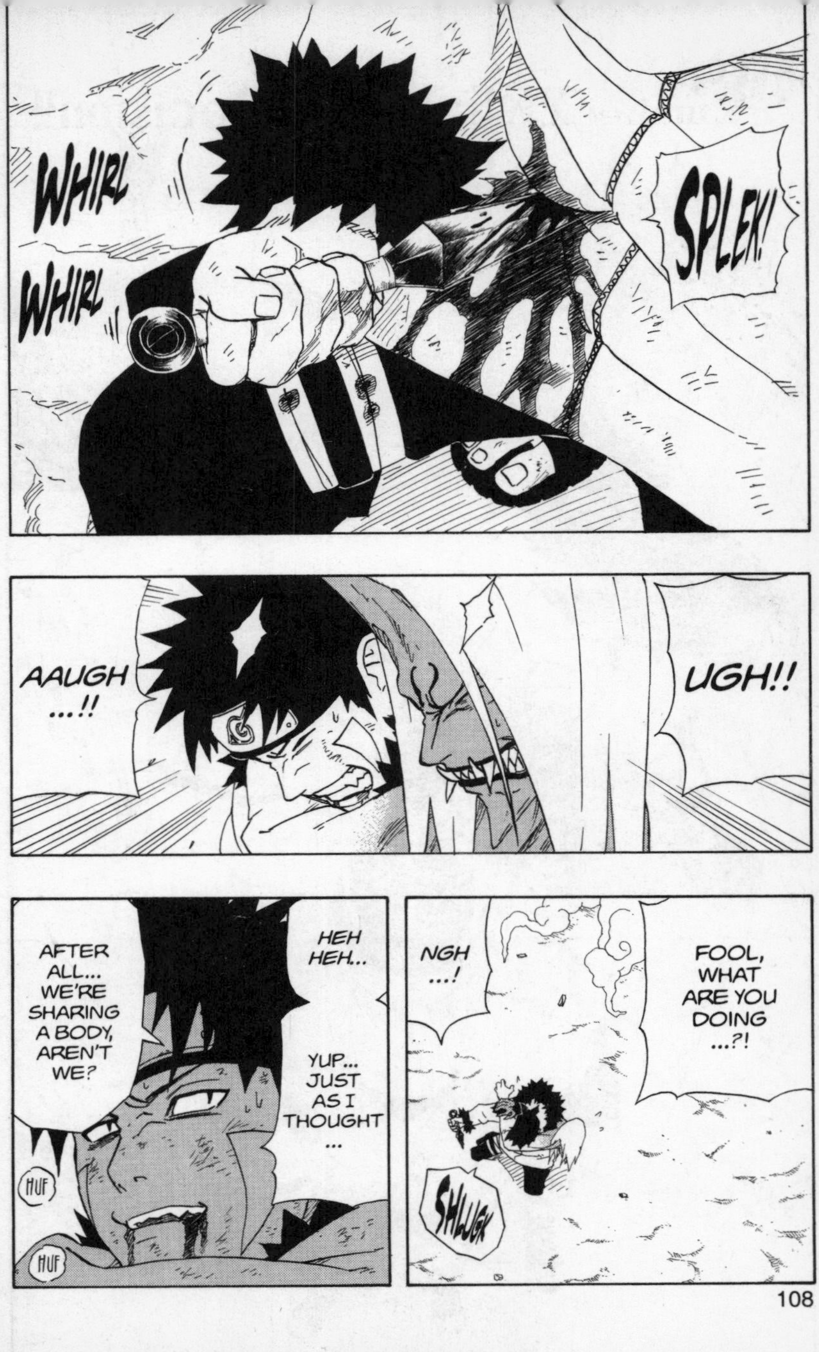
SPLEK!
WHIRL
WHIRL
UGH!!
AAUGH ...!!
FOOL, WHAT ARE YOU DOING ...?!
NGH ...!
SHLUGK
HEH HEH...
YUP... JUST AS I THOUGHT ...
AFTER ALL... WE'RE SHARING A BODY, AREN'T WE?
HUF
HUF

READ THIS WAY

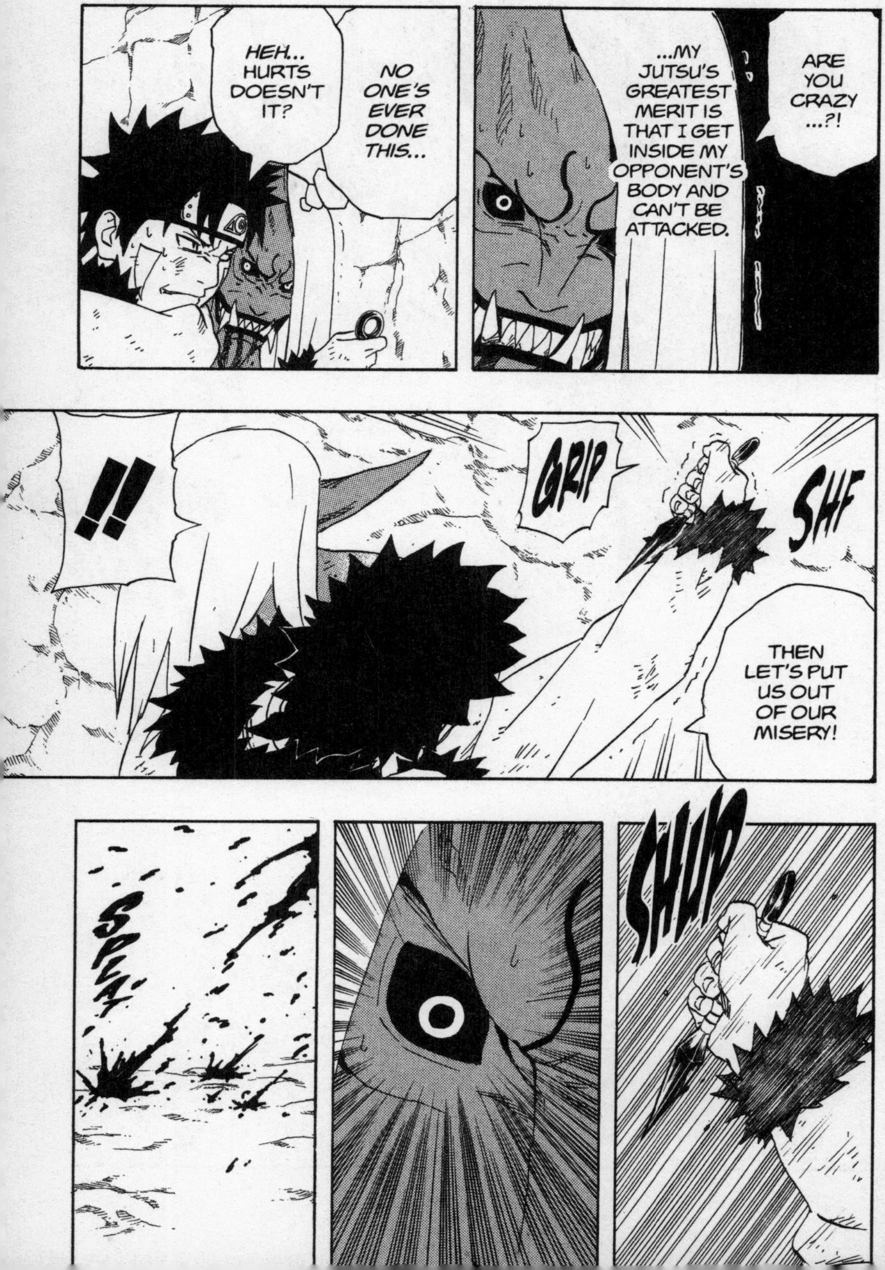
ARE YOU CRAZY ...?!
...MY JUTSU'S GREATEST MERIT IS THAT I GET INSIDE MY OPPONENT'S BODY AND CAN'T BE ATTACKED.
NO ONE'S EVER DONE THIS...
HEH... HURTS DOESN'T IT?
SHF
GRIP
!!
THEN LET'S PUT US OUT OF OUR MISERY!
SHUP
SPLAT

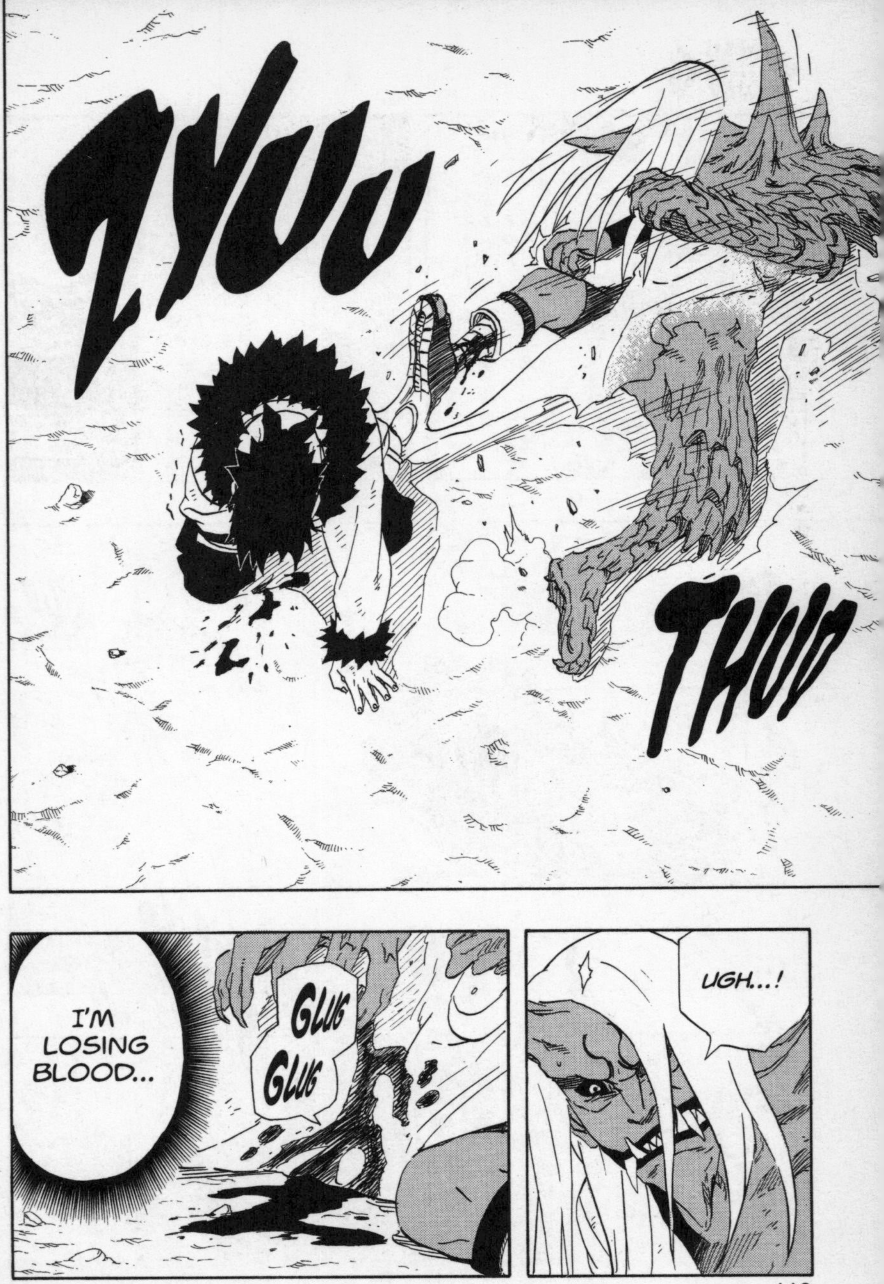
ZYUU
THUD
UGH...!
GLUG GLUG
I'M LOSING BLOOD...

READ THIS WAY

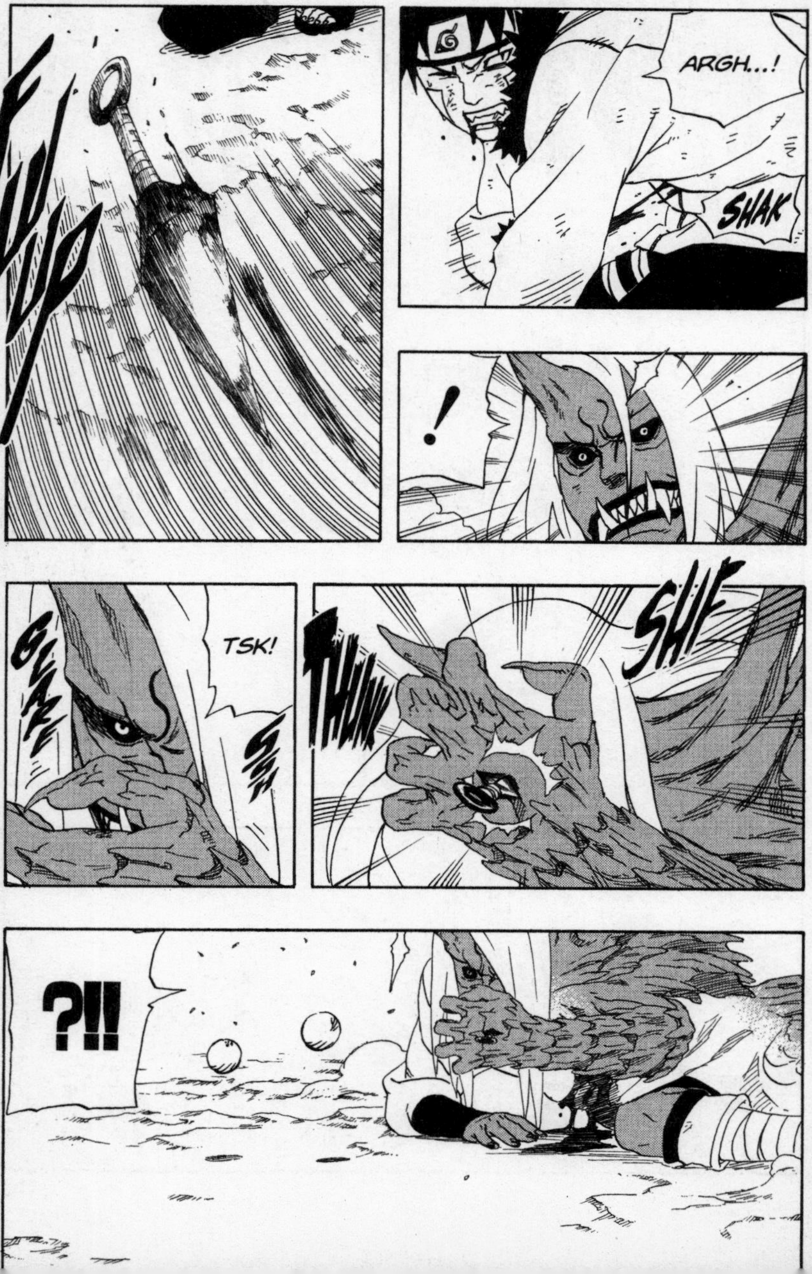
ARGH...!
SHAK
!
FWUP
SHF
THUNK
TSK!
?!!

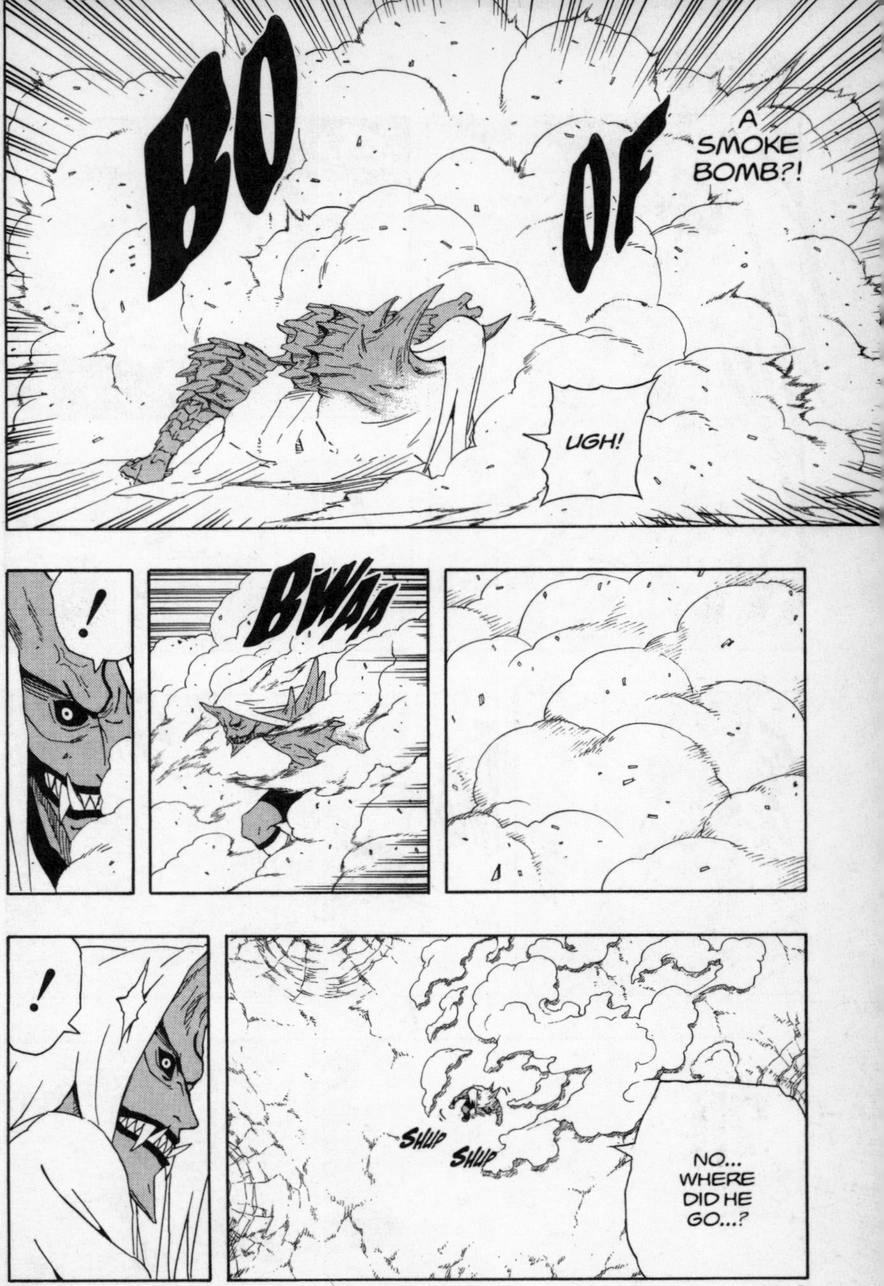
A SMOKE BOMB?!
BOOF
UGH!
BWAP
!
NO... WHERE DID HE GO...?
SHUP SHUP
!

READ THIS WAY

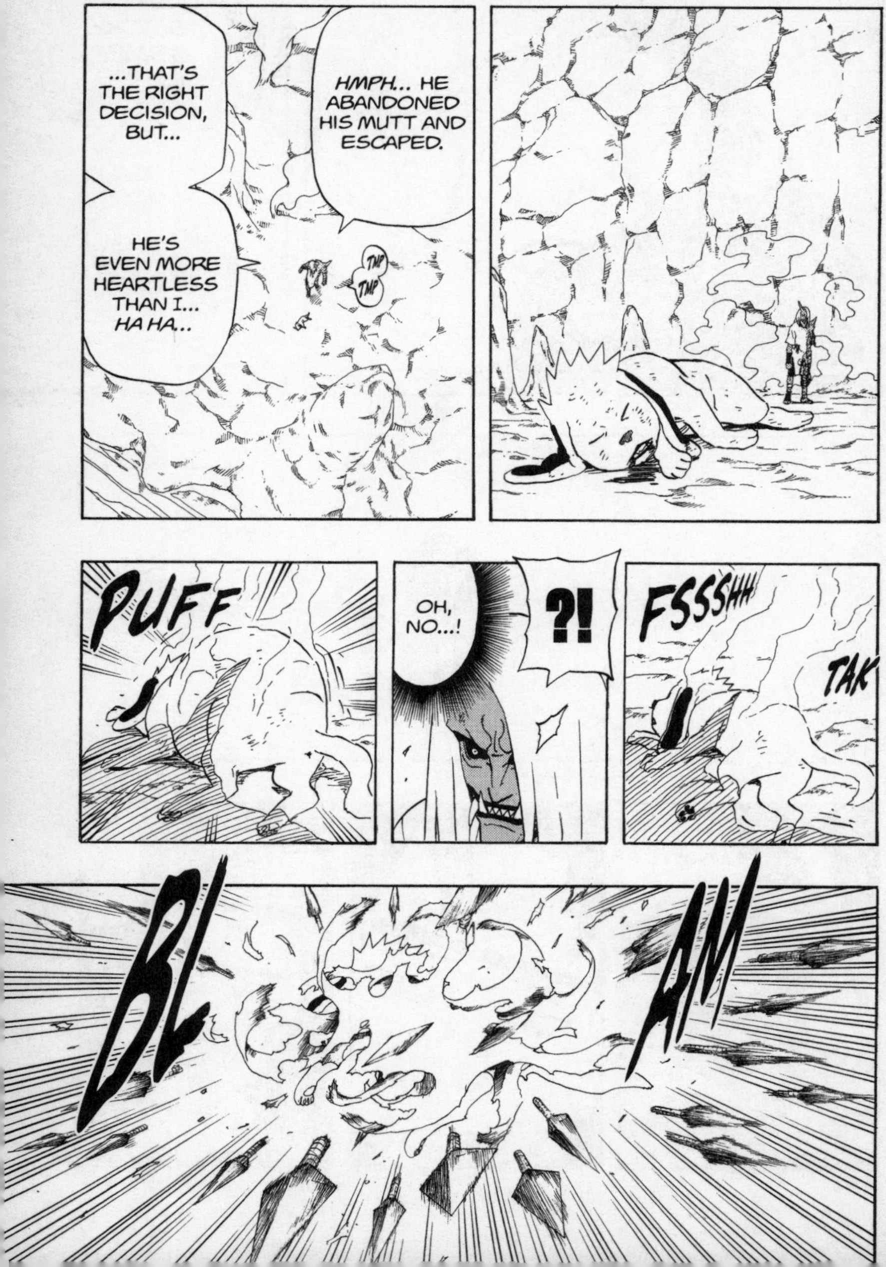
HMPH... HE ABANDONED HIS MUTT AND ESCAPED.
...THAT'S THE RIGHT DECISION, BUT...
HE'S EVEN MORE HEARTLESS THAN I... HA HA...
TMP TMP
FSSSHH
TAK
?!
OH, NO...!
PUFF
BLAM

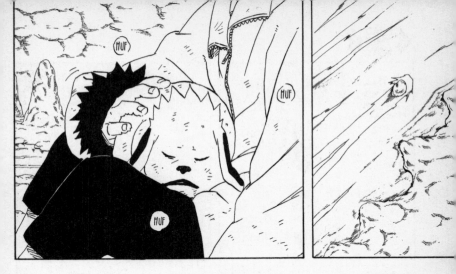

(HUF) (HUF)

(HUF)

(HUF)

GOOD... HE'S STILL BREATHING.

UNGH...!

THANK GOOD- NESS...

...

READ THIS WAY

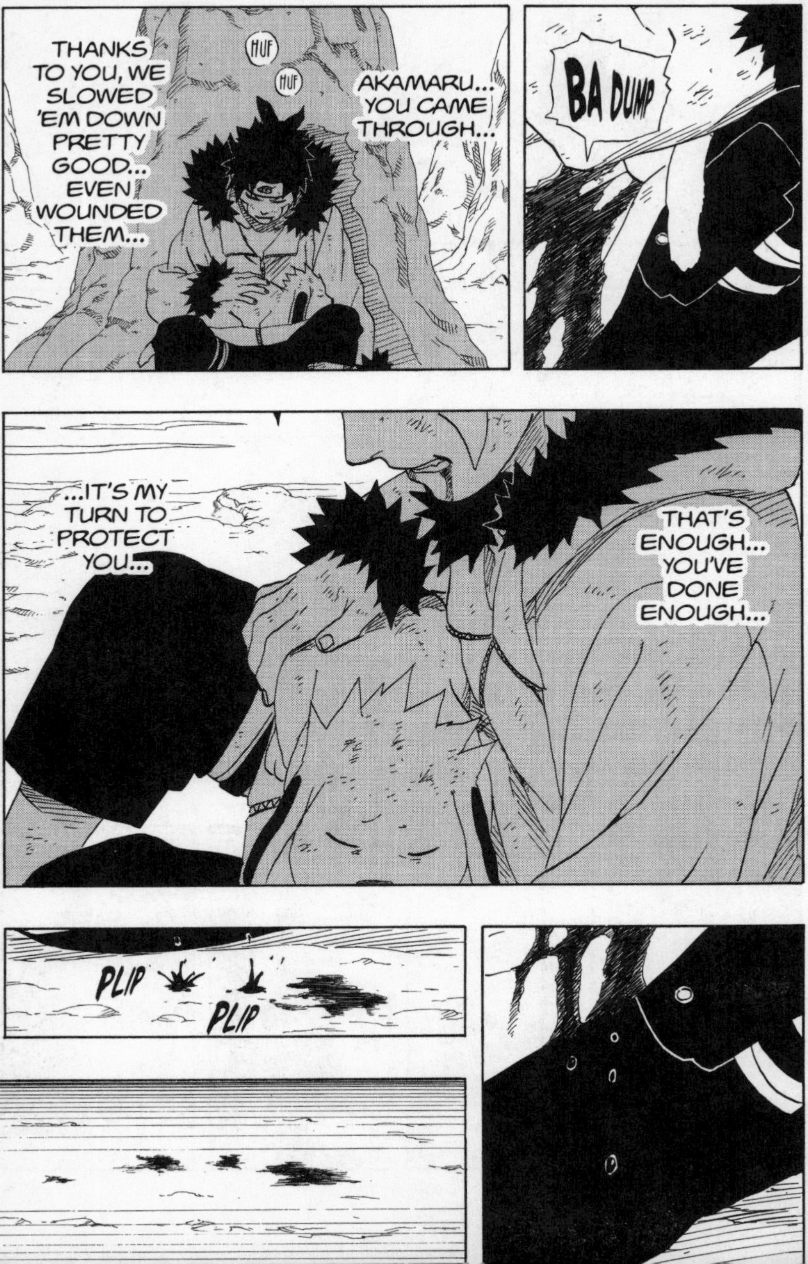

BA DUMP
HUF
HUF
AKAMARU... YOU CAME THROUGH...
THANKS TO YOU, WE SLOWED 'EM DOWN PRETTY GOOD... EVEN WOUNDED THEM...
THAT'S ENOUGH... YOU'VE DONE ENOUGH...
...IT'S MY TURN TO PROTECT YOU...
PLIP
PLIP

THEY SET A TRAP...

SNEAKY RATS...

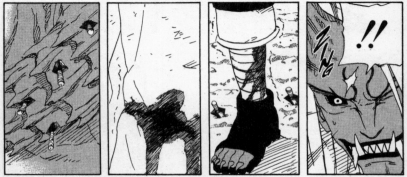

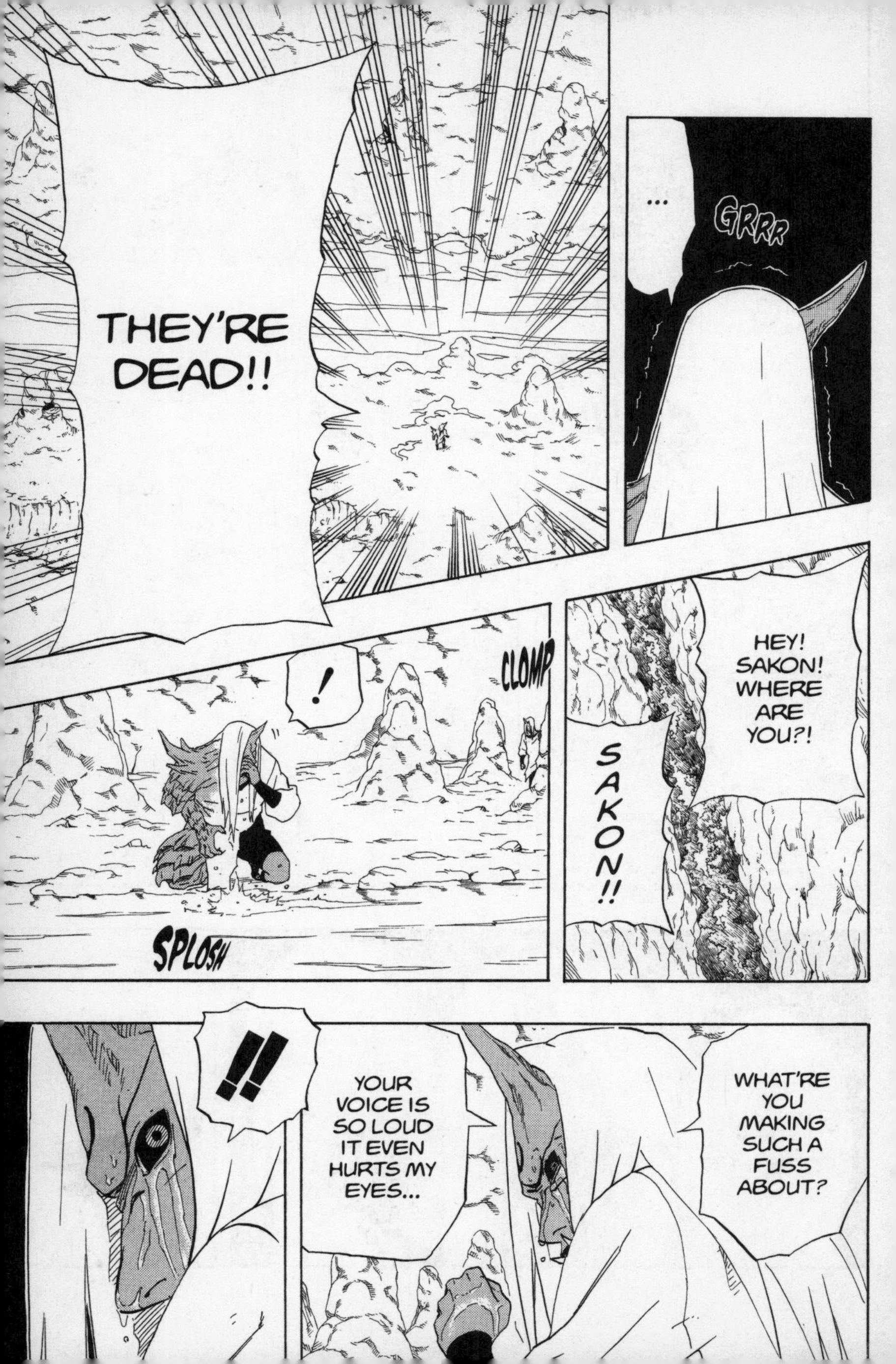
...
GRRR
THEY'RE DEAD!!
HEY! SAKON! WHERE ARE YOU?!
SAKON!!
CLOMP
!
SPLOSH
WHAT'RE YOU MAKING SUCH A FUSS ABOUT?
YOUR VOICE IS SO LOUD IT EVEN HURTS MY EYES...
!!

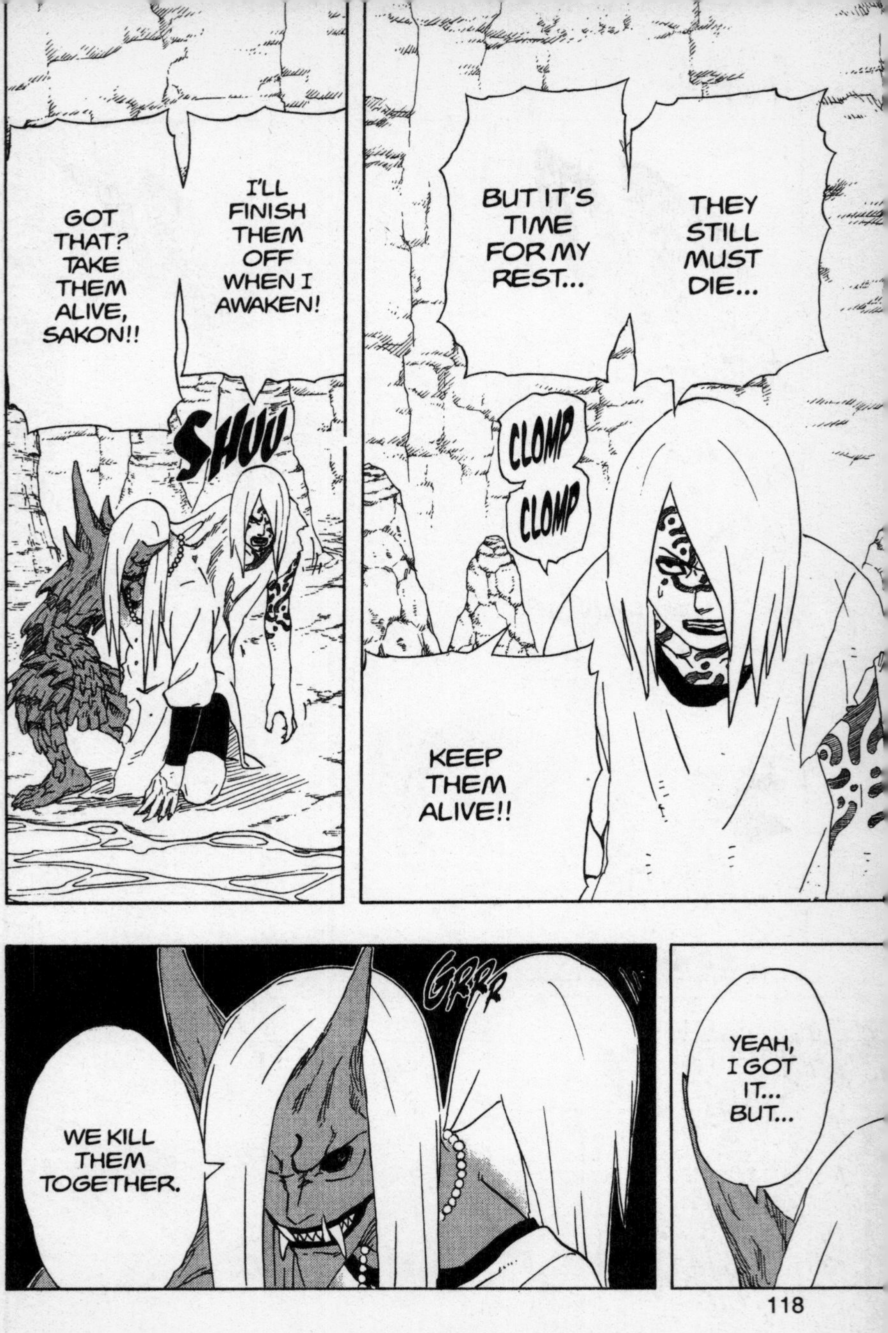
THEY STILL MUST DIE...
BUT IT'S TIME FOR MY REST...
CLOMP CLOMP
KEEP THEM ALIVE!!
I'LL FINISH THEM OFF WHEN I AWAKEN!
GOT THAT? TAKE THEM ALIVE, SAKON!!
SHUU
YEAH, I GOT IT... BUT...
GRRR
WE KILL THEM TOGETHER.

READ THIS WAY

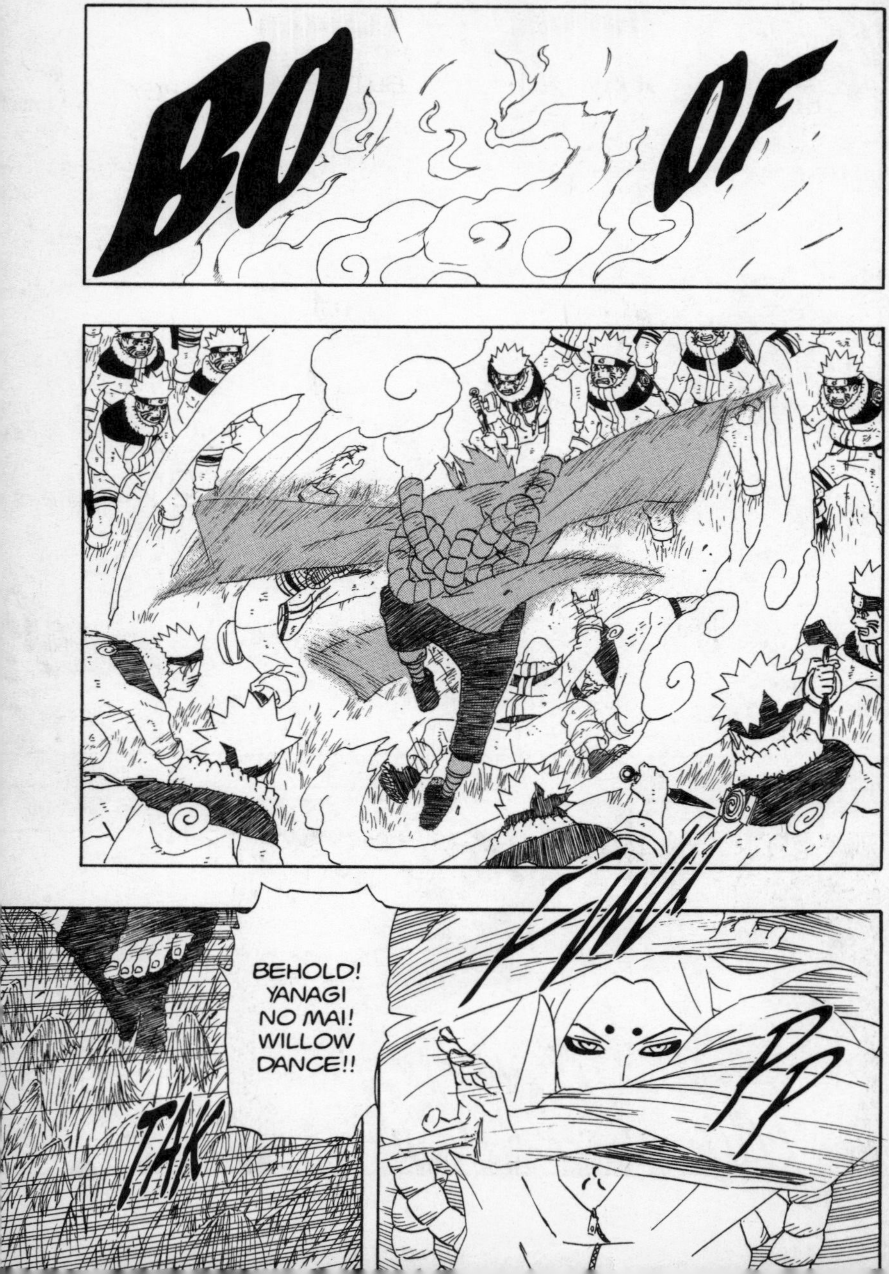
BOOF
BEHOLD! YANAGI NO MAI! WILLOW DANCE!!
TAK

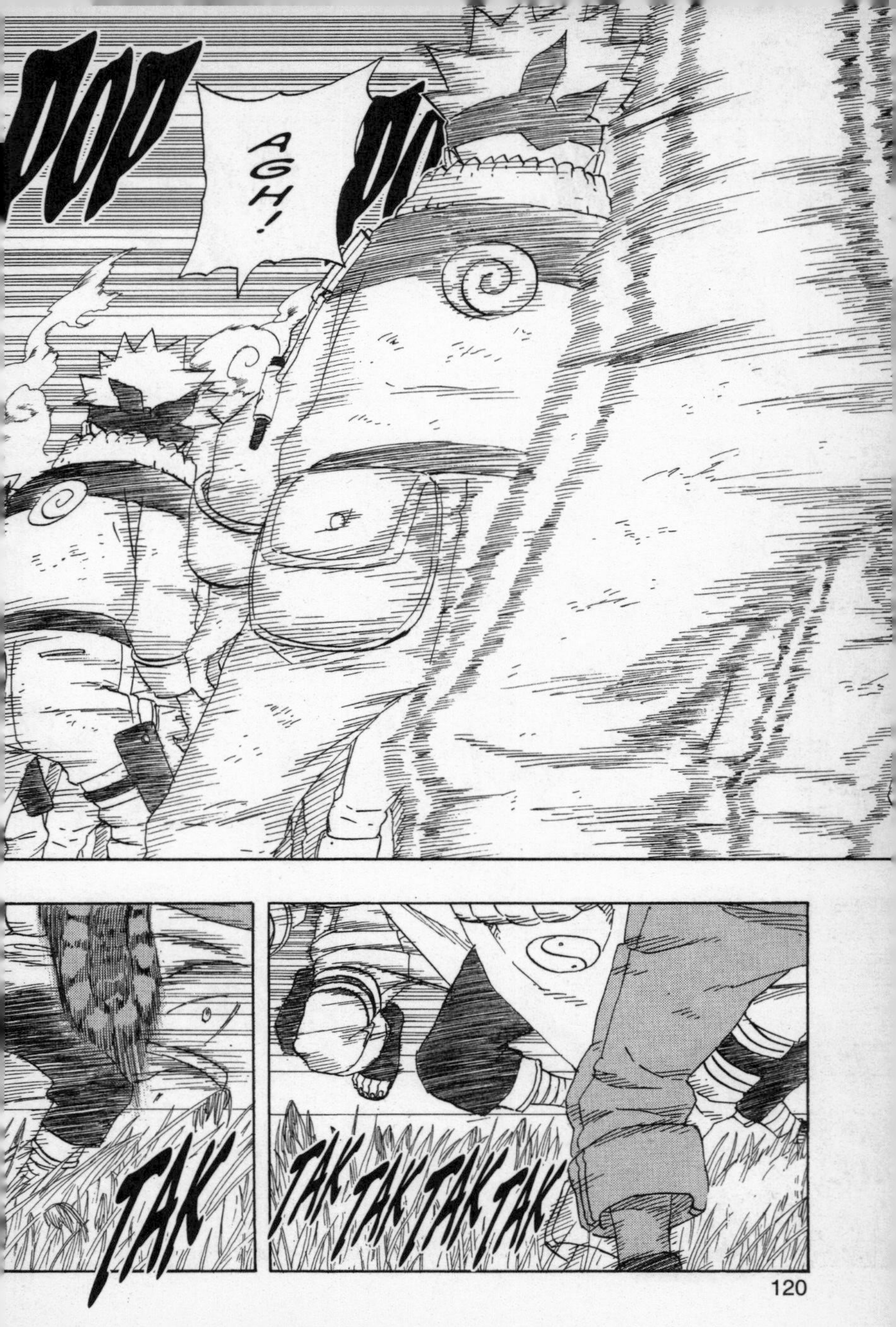
DO
AGH!
DOO
TAK TAK TAK TAK
TAK

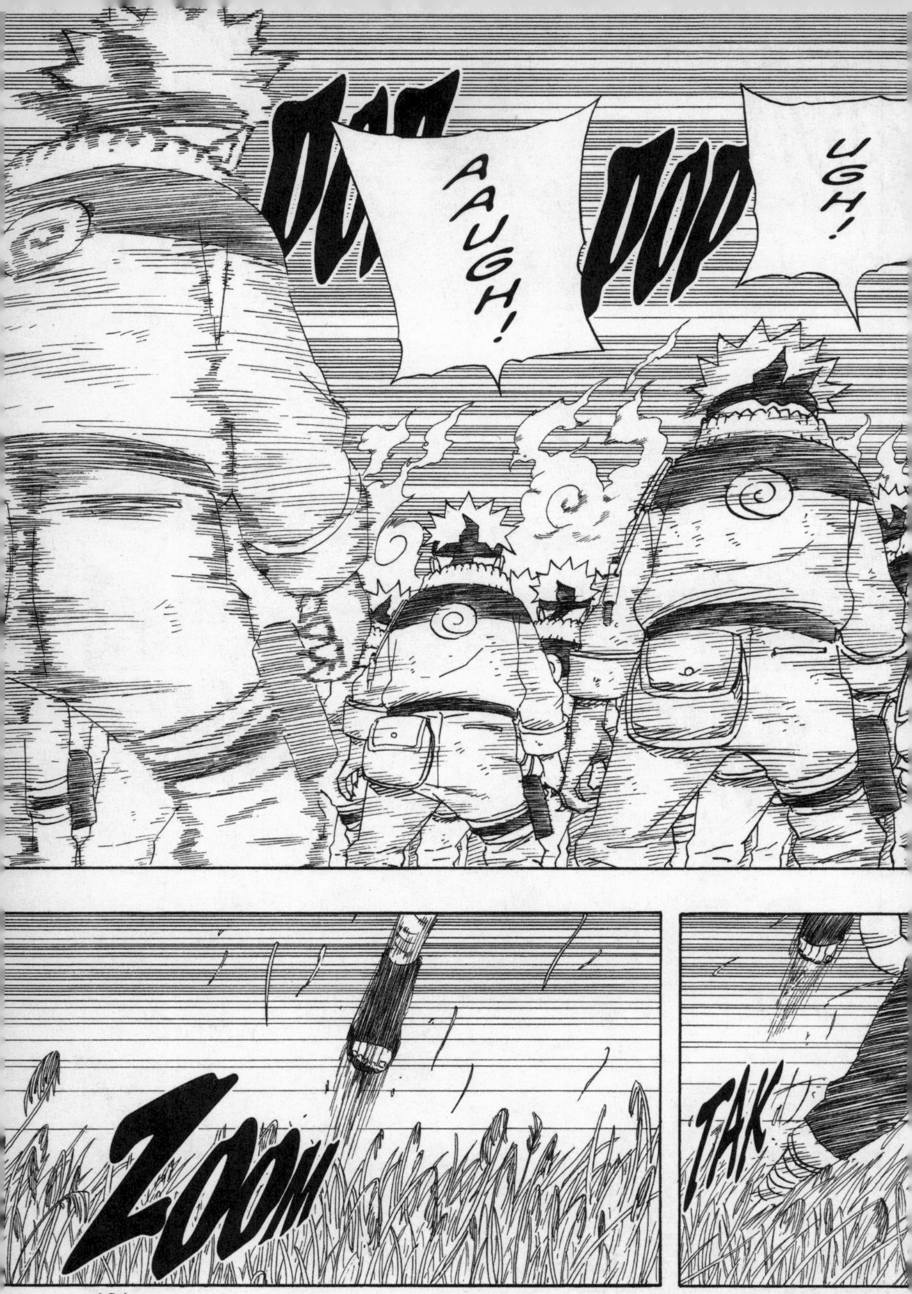
UGH!
AAUGH!
TAK
ZOOM

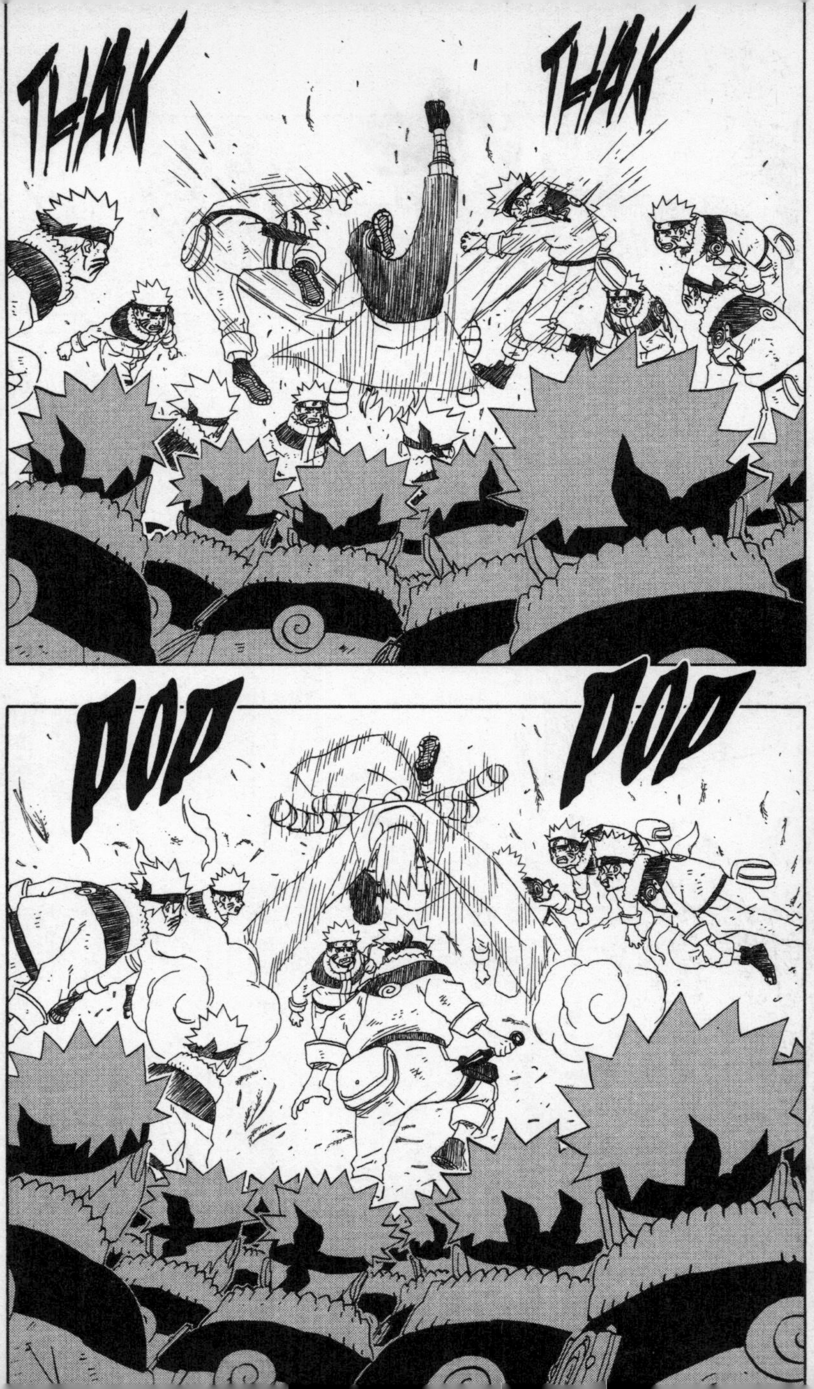
THAK
THAK
POP
POP

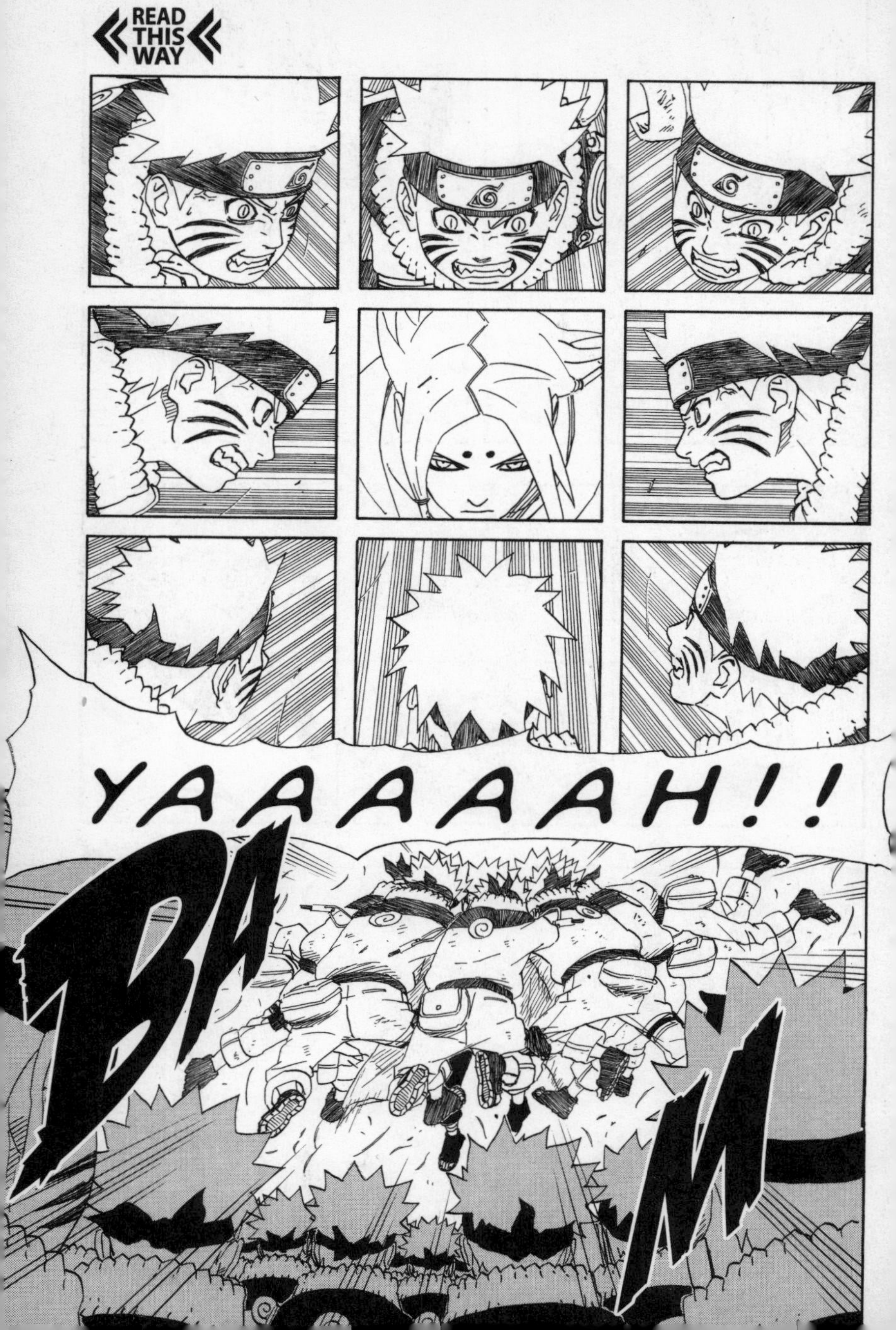
READ THIS WAY
YAAAAAH!!
BAM

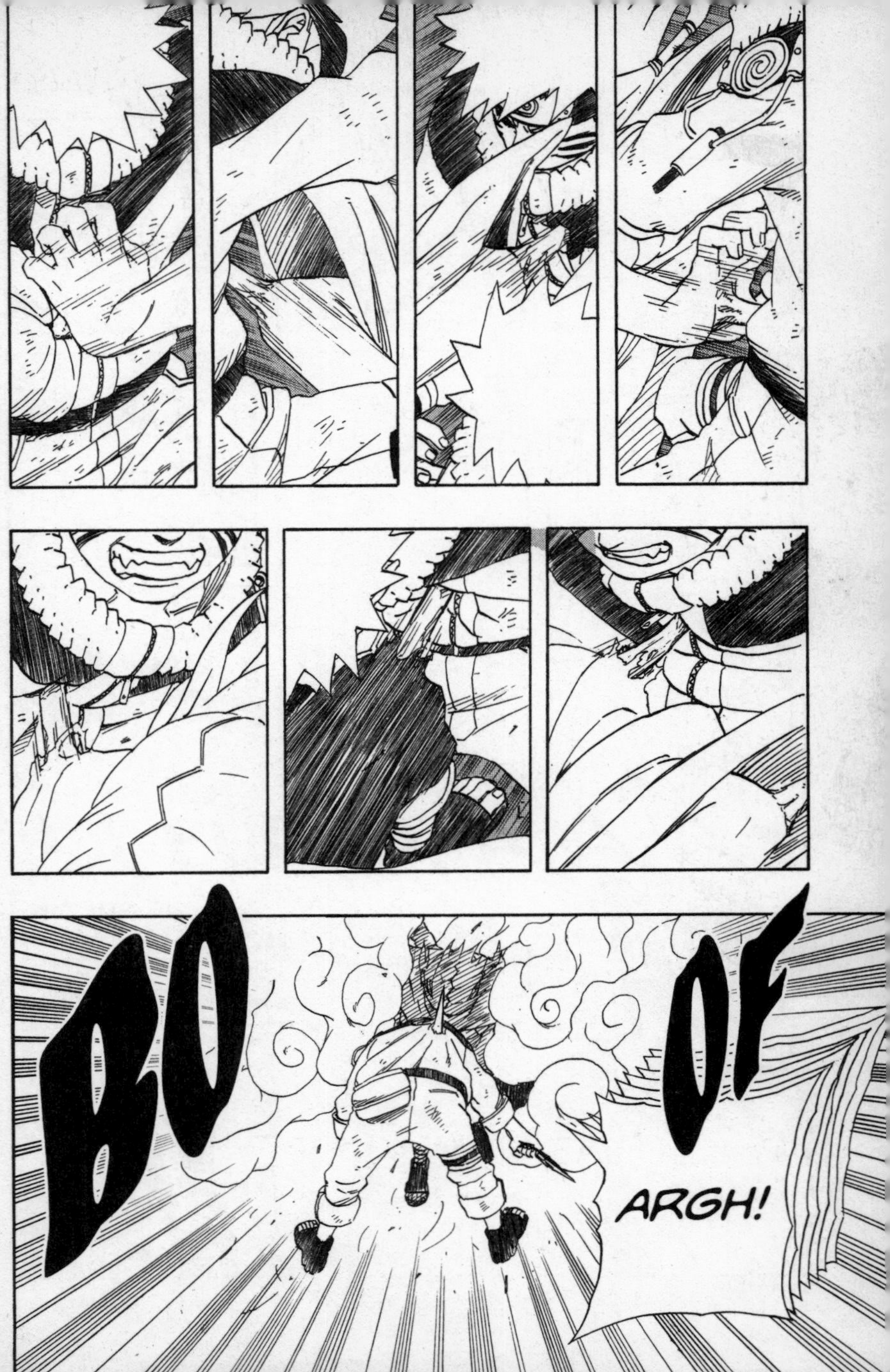
BOOF
ARGH!

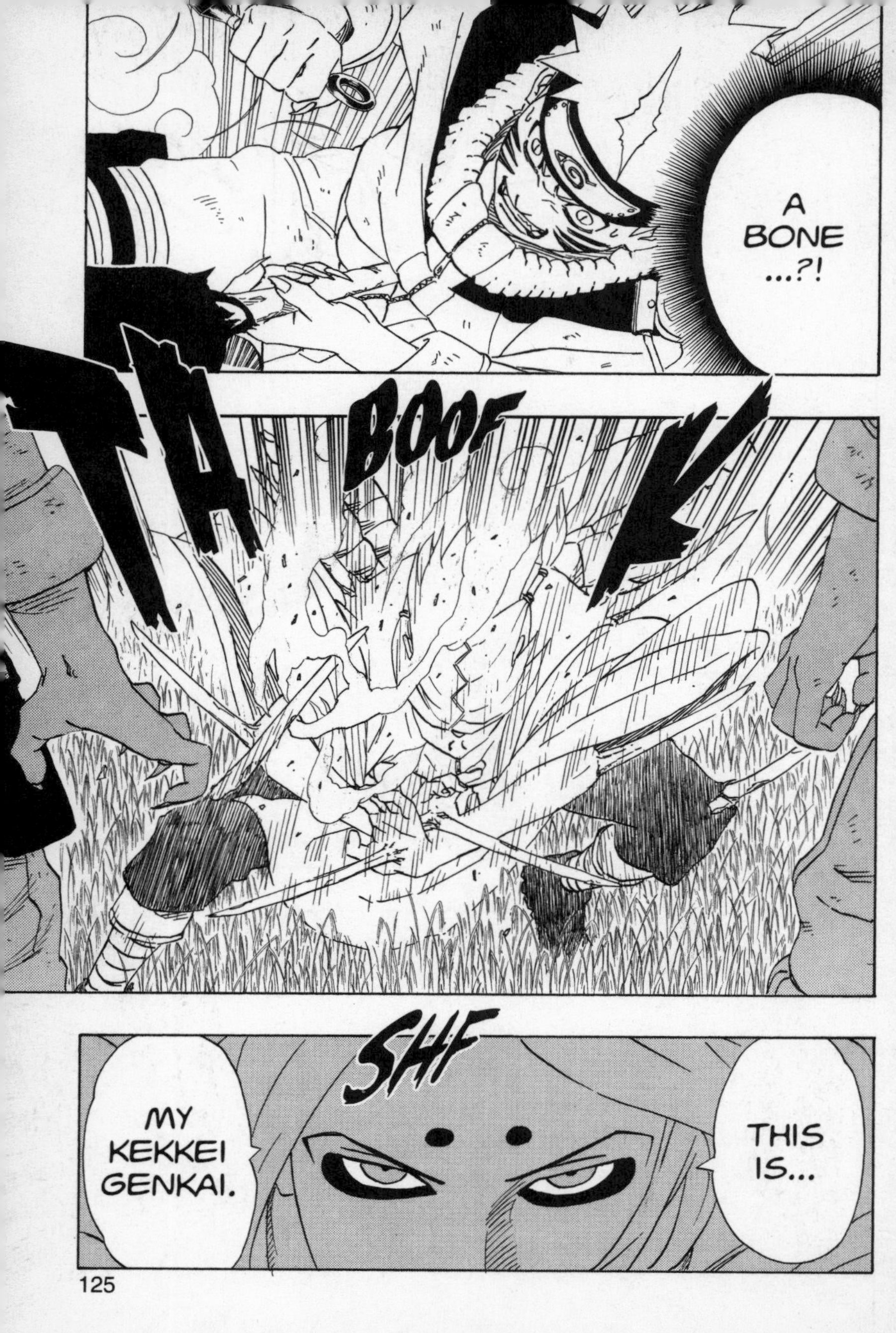
A BONE ...?!
THA
BOOF
K
SHF
THIS IS...
MY KEKKEI GENKAI.

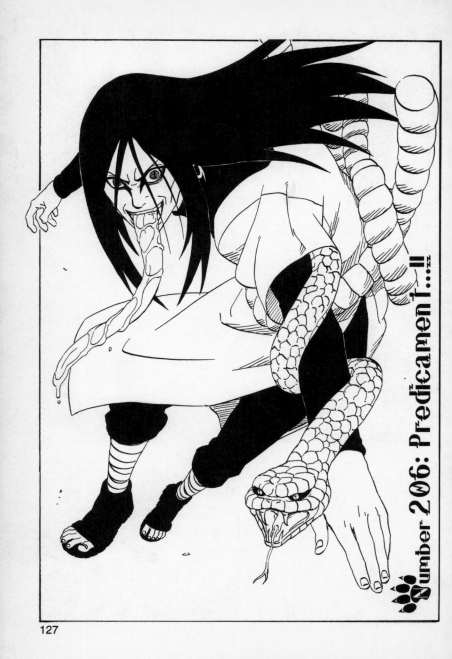

Number 206: Predicament!...zz

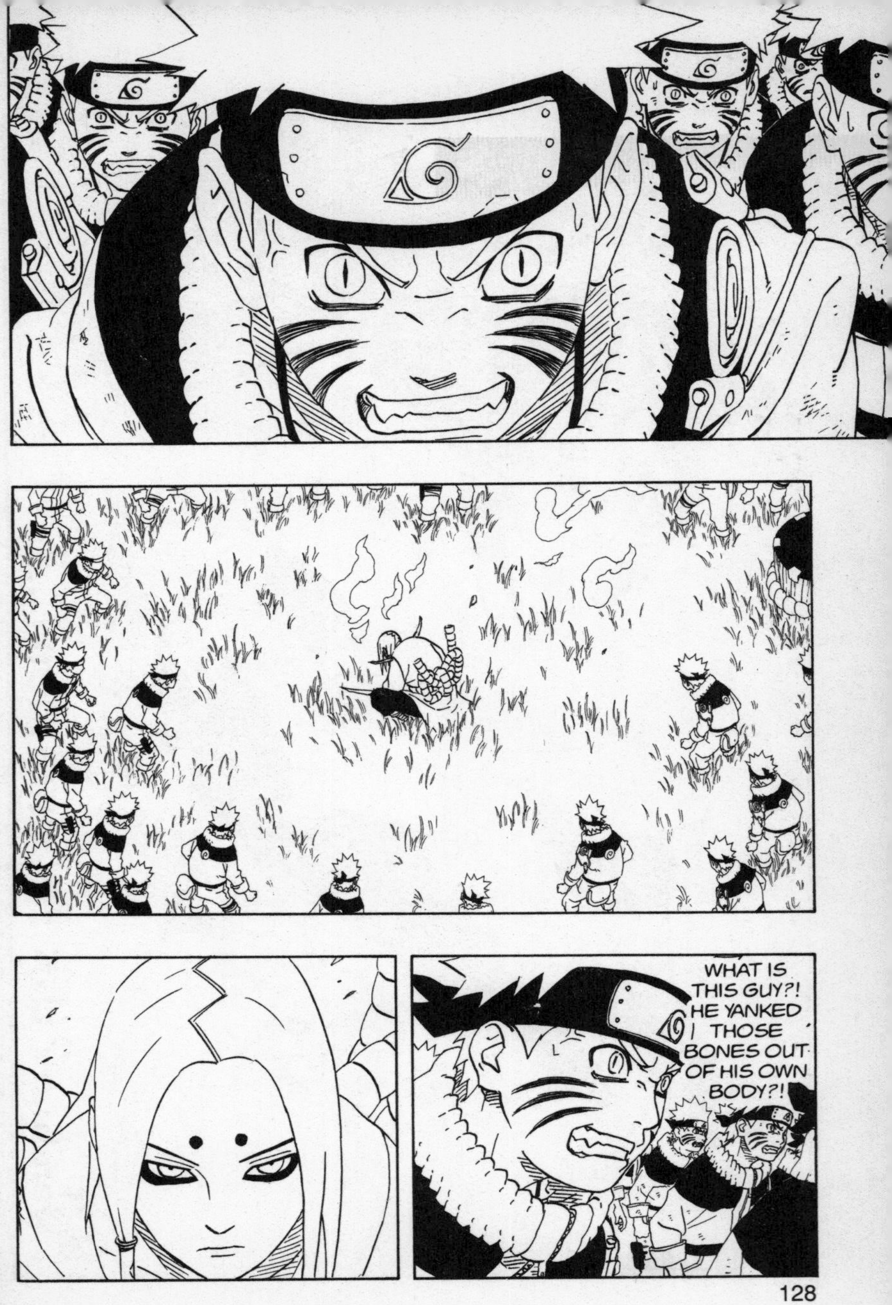
WHAT IS THIS GUY?! HE YANKED THOSE BONES OUT OF HIS OWN BODY?!

READ THIS WAY

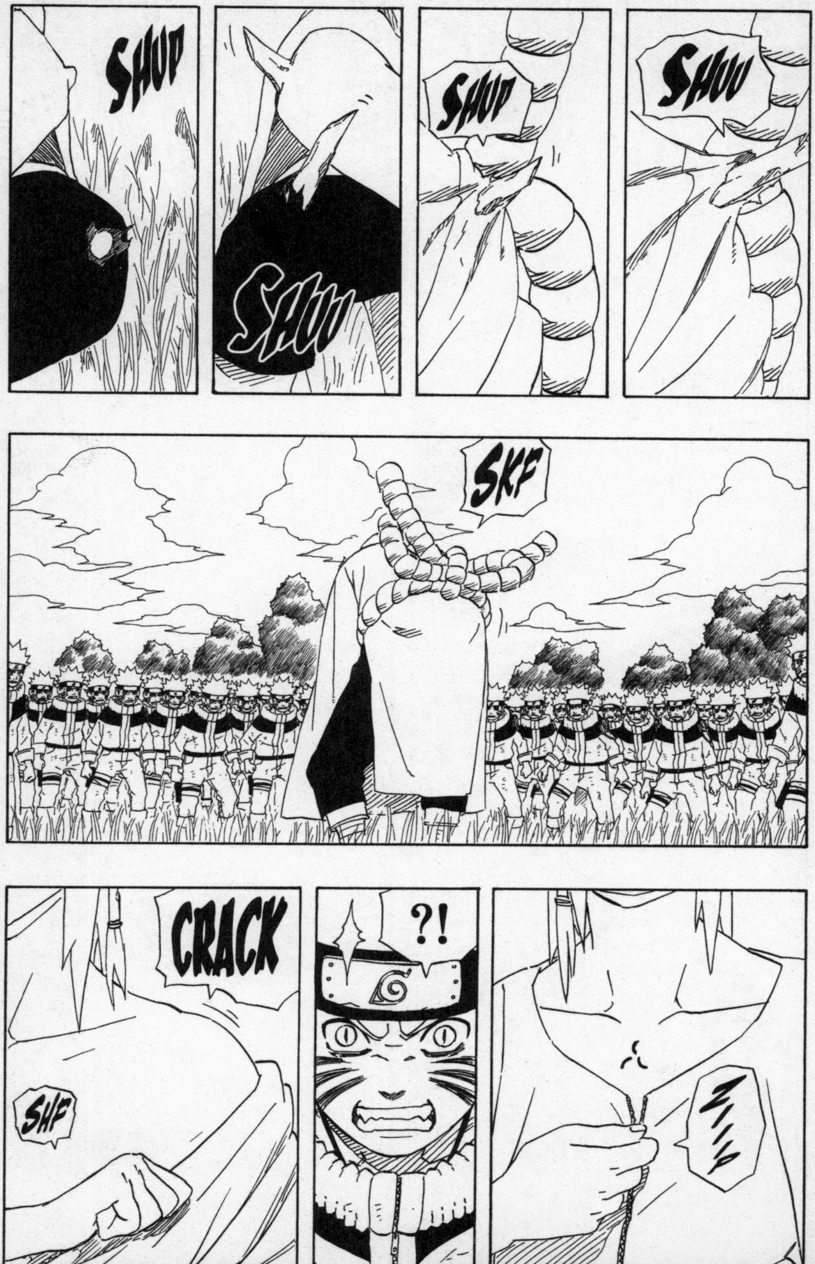
SHUU
SHUP
SHUU
SHUP
SKF
ZIIP
?!
CRACK
SHF

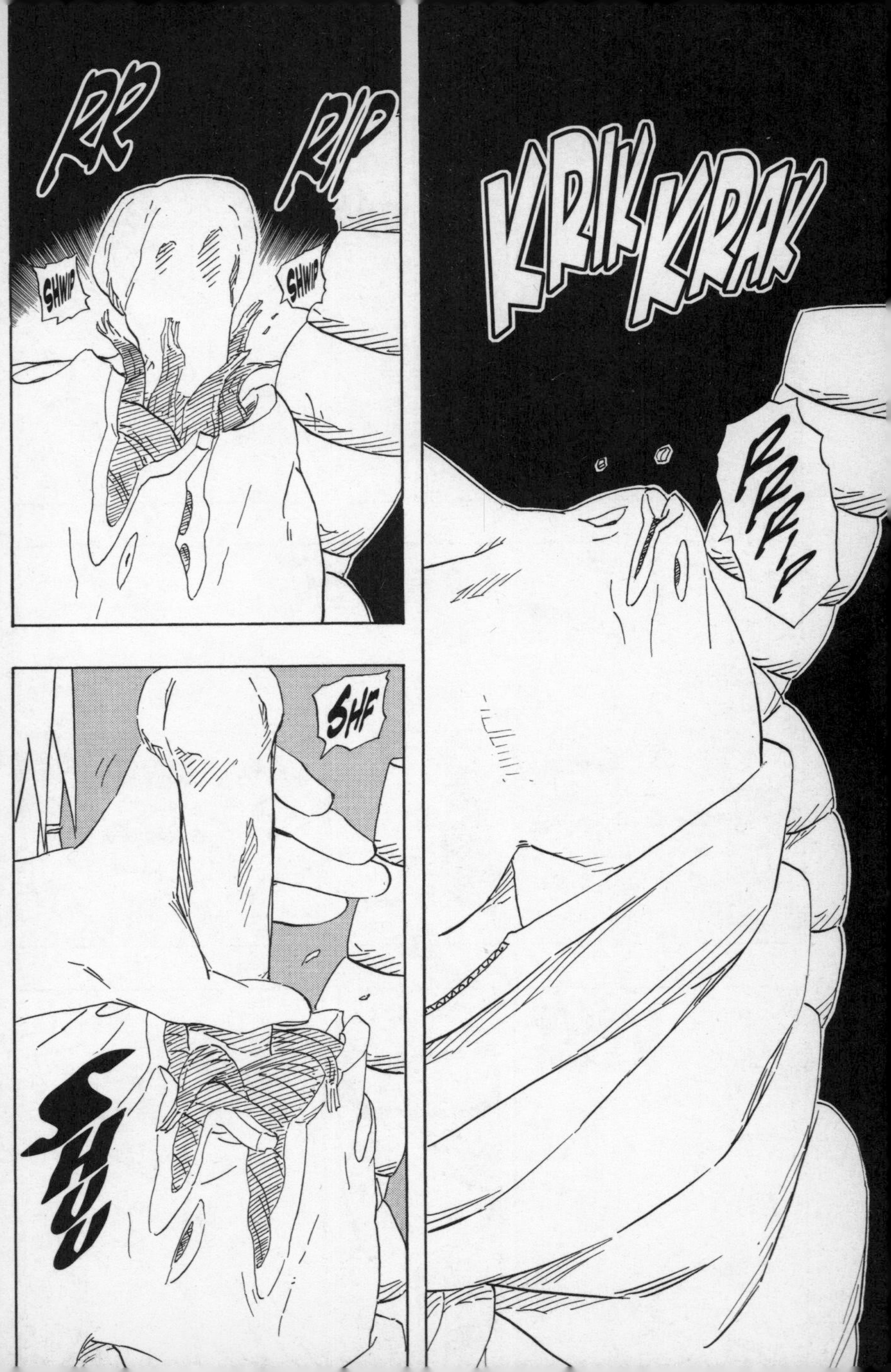
KRIK KRAK
RIP
SHWIP
RIP
SHWIP
SHF
SHUU

READ THIS WAY

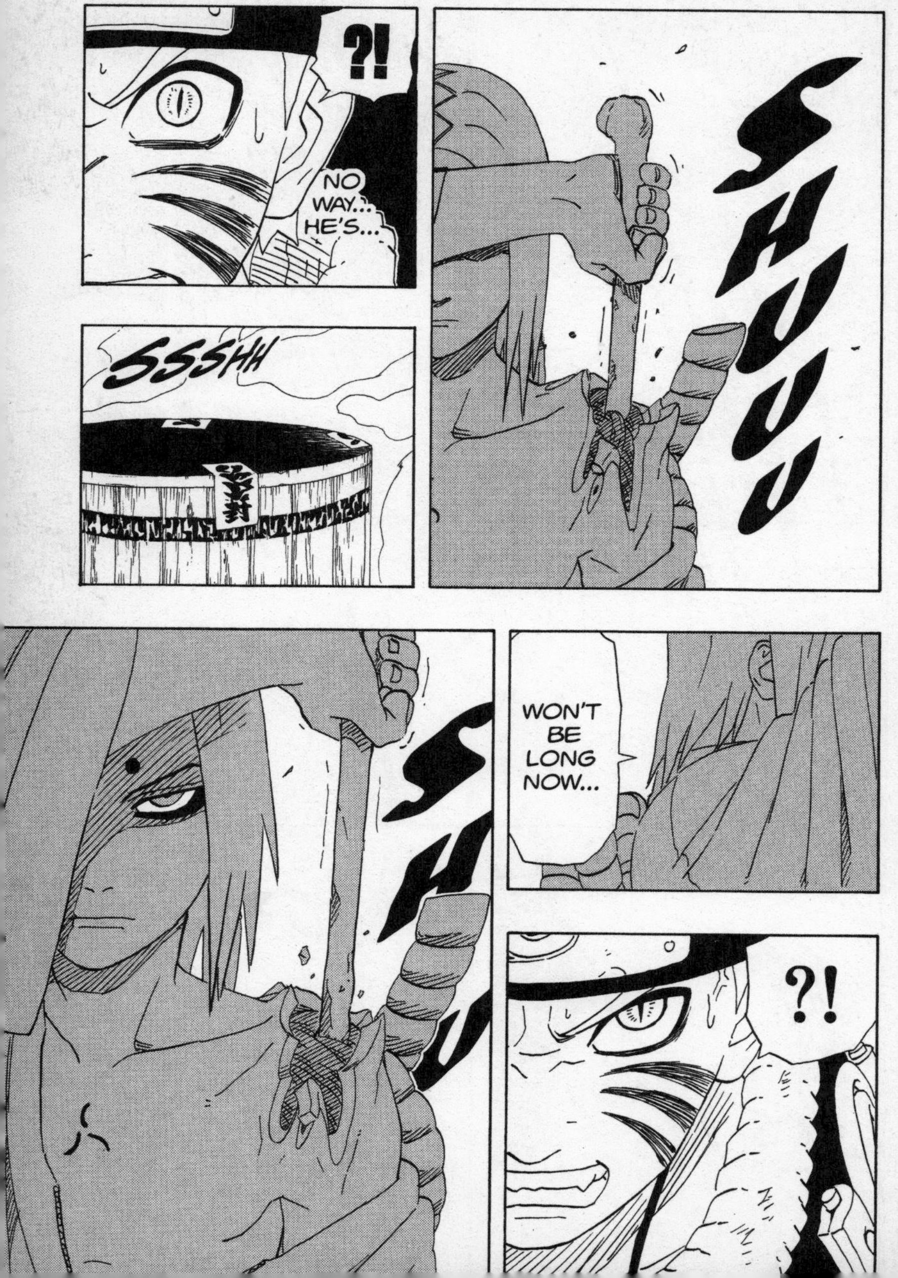
SHUUUU
?!
NO WAY... HE'S...
SSSHH
WON'T BE LONG NOW...
?!
SHU

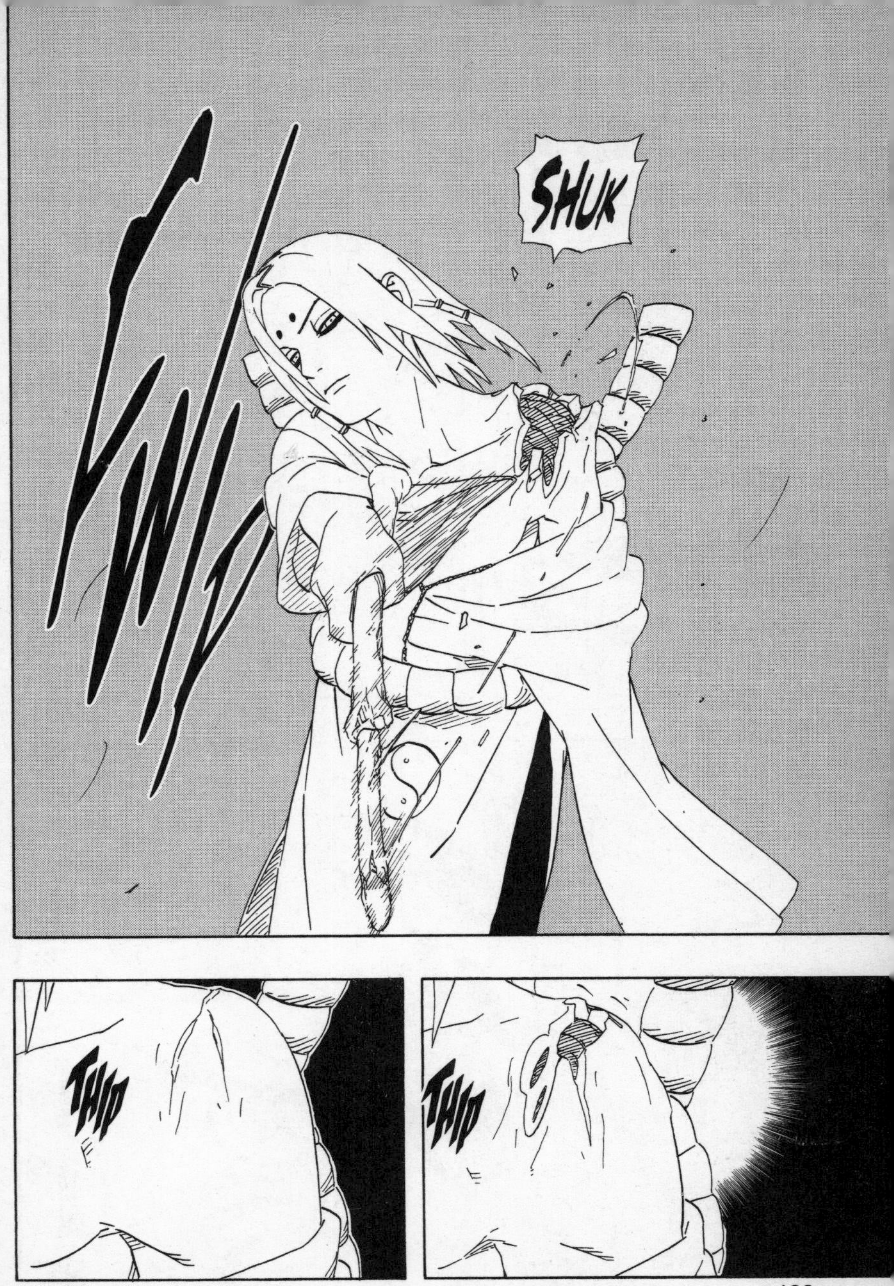
SHUK
THIP
THIP

READ THIS WAY

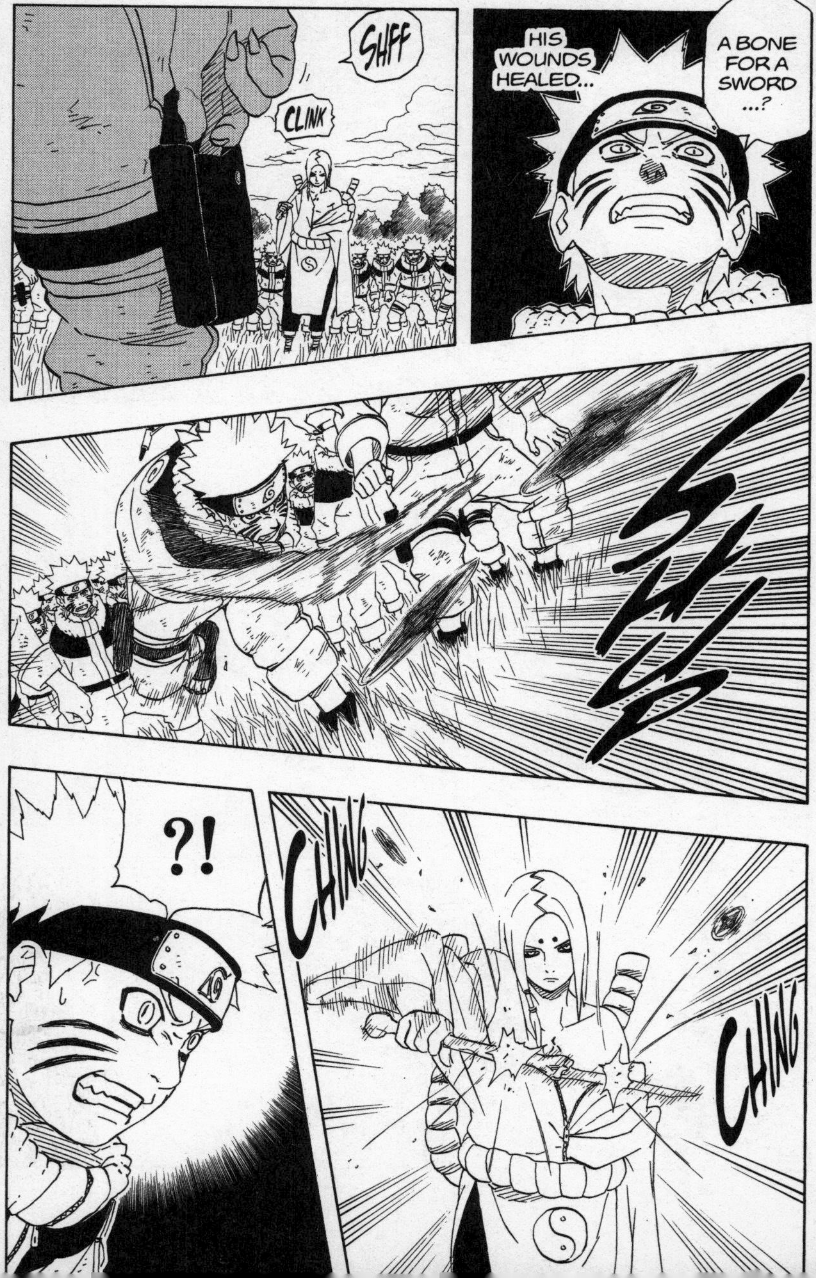

A BONE FOR A SWORD ...?
HIS WOUNDS HEALED...
SHFF
CLINK
CHING
CHING
?!

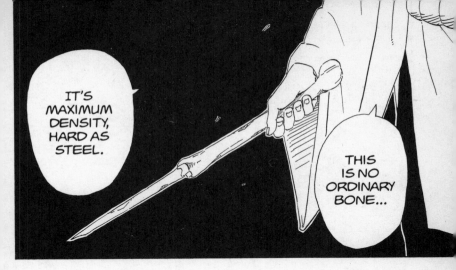

THIS IS NO ORDINARY BONE...
IT'S MAXIMUM DENSITY, HARD AS STEEL.
...YEAH, SO?
I'M GONNA SMASH IT...
I HAVE FIVE DANCES.
DON'T EVEN THINK THAT YOU UNDER-STAND THAT POWER.
SSSHH

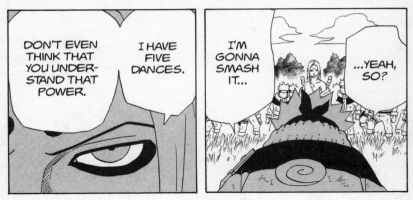

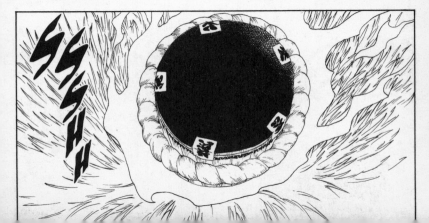

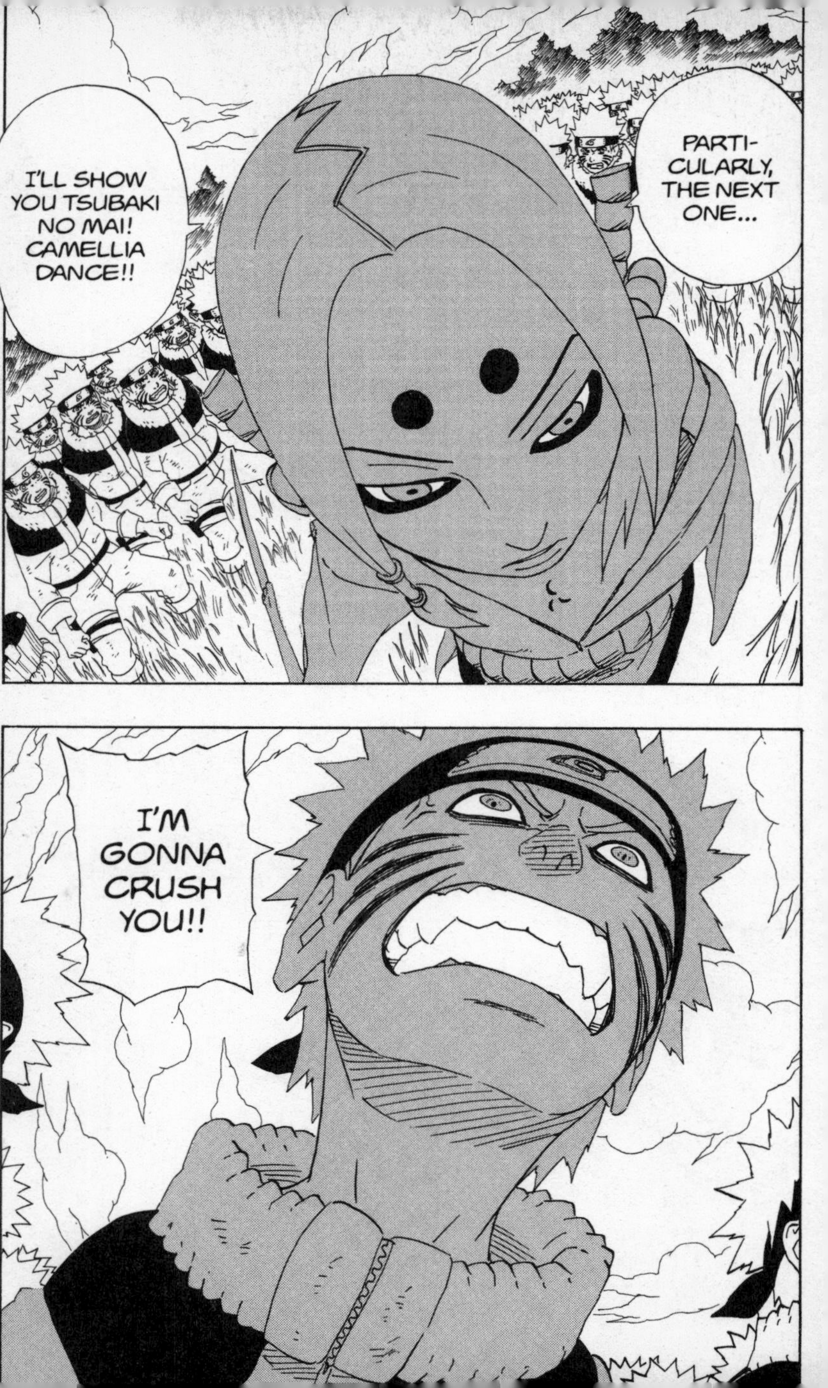
PARTI-CULARLY, THE NEXT ONE...
I'LL SHOW YOU TSUBAKI NO MAI! CAMELLIA DANCE!!
I'M GONNA CRUSH YOU!!

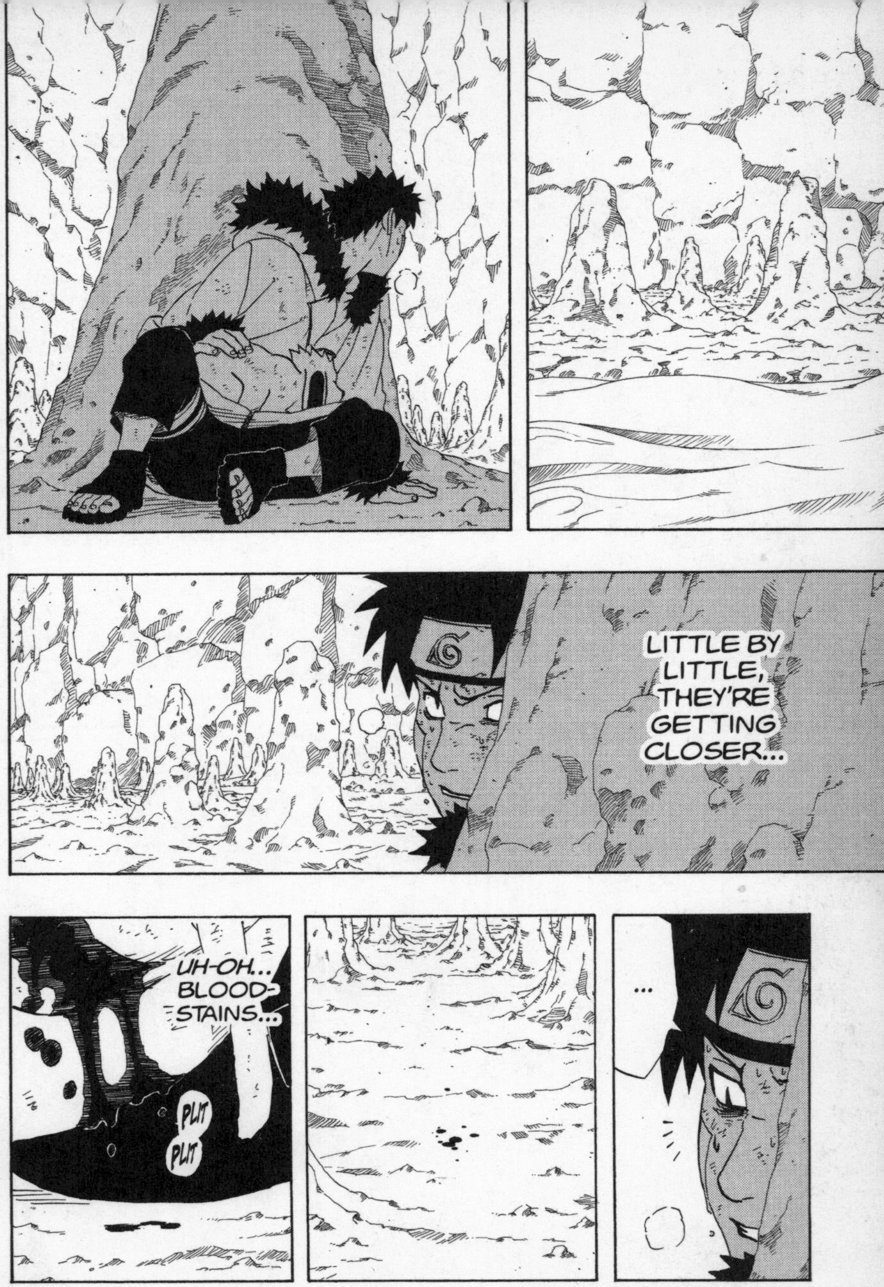
LITTLE BY LITTLE, THEY'RE GETTING CLOSER...
...
UH-OH... BLOOD-STAINS...
PLIT PLIT

READ THIS WAY

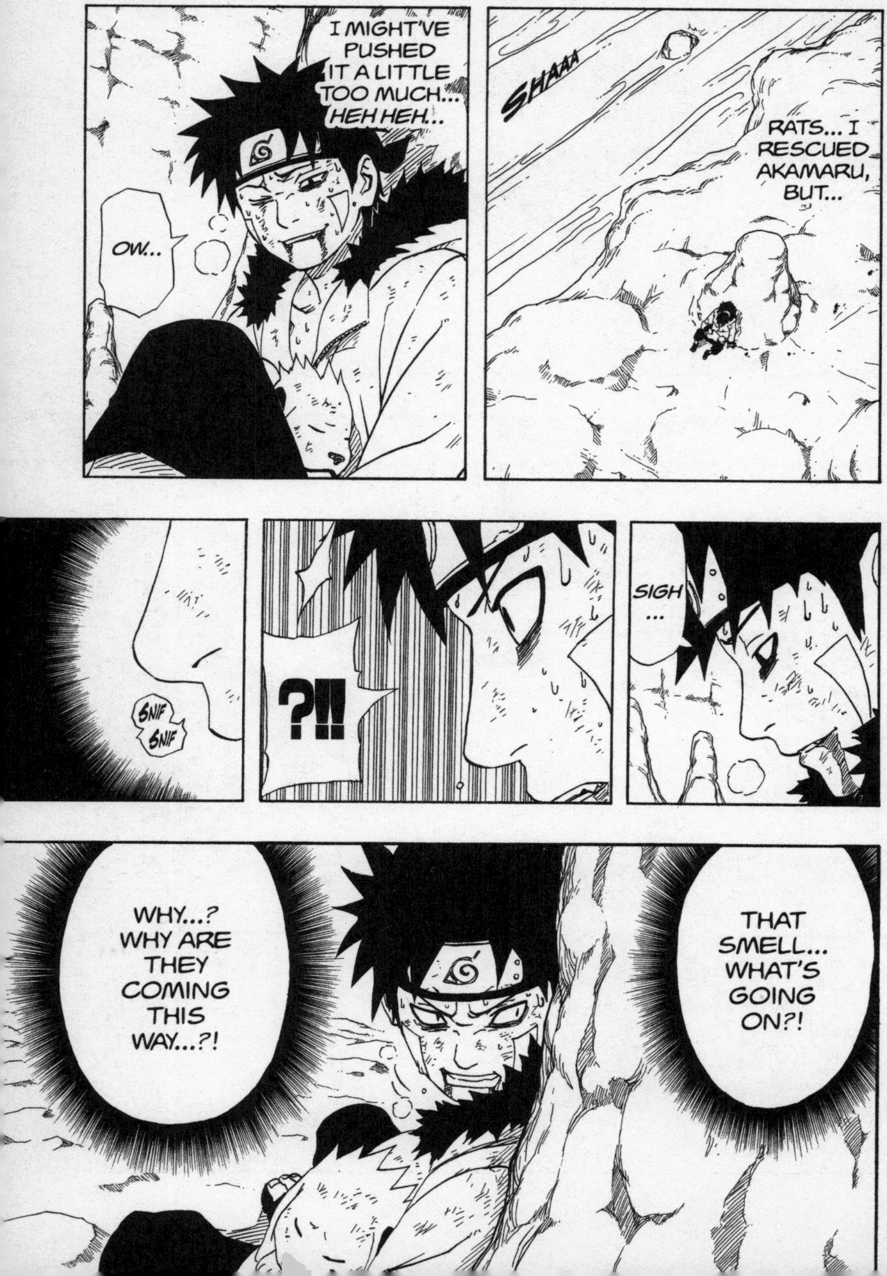

SHAAA
RATS... I RESCUED AKAMARU, BUT...
I MIGHT'VE PUSHED IT A LITTLE TOO MUCH... HEH HEH...
OW...
SIGH ...
?!!
SNIF SNIF
THAT SMELL... WHAT'S GOING ON?!
WHY...? WHY ARE THEY COMING THIS WAY...?!

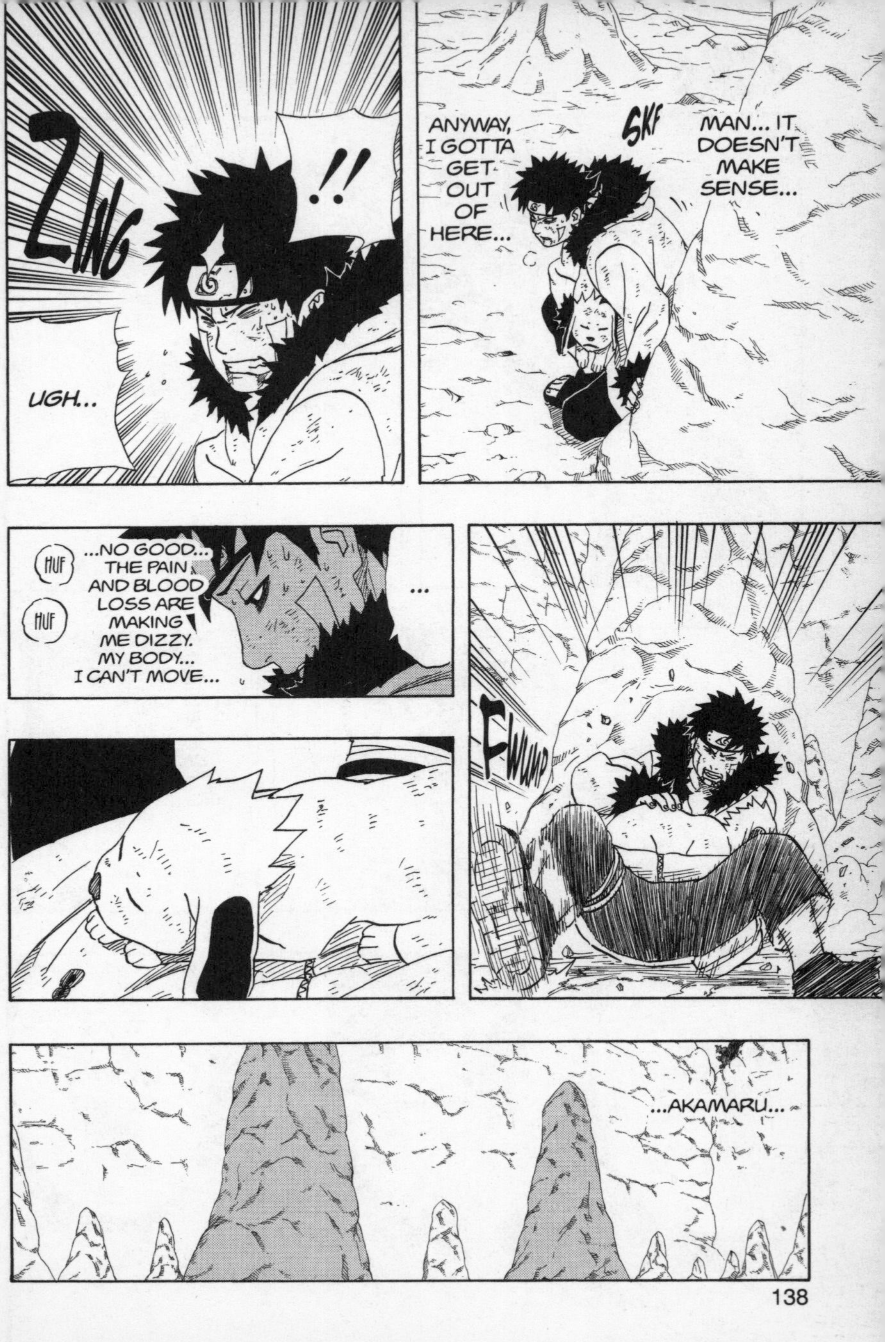
MAN... IT DOESN'T MAKE SENSE...
SKF
ANYWAY, I GOTTA GET OUT OF HERE...
!!
ZING
UGH...
FWUMP
...
...NO GOOD... THE PAIN AND BLOOD LOSS ARE MAKING ME DIZZY. MY BODY... I CAN'T MOVE...
HUF
HUF
...AKAMARU...

READ THIS WAY

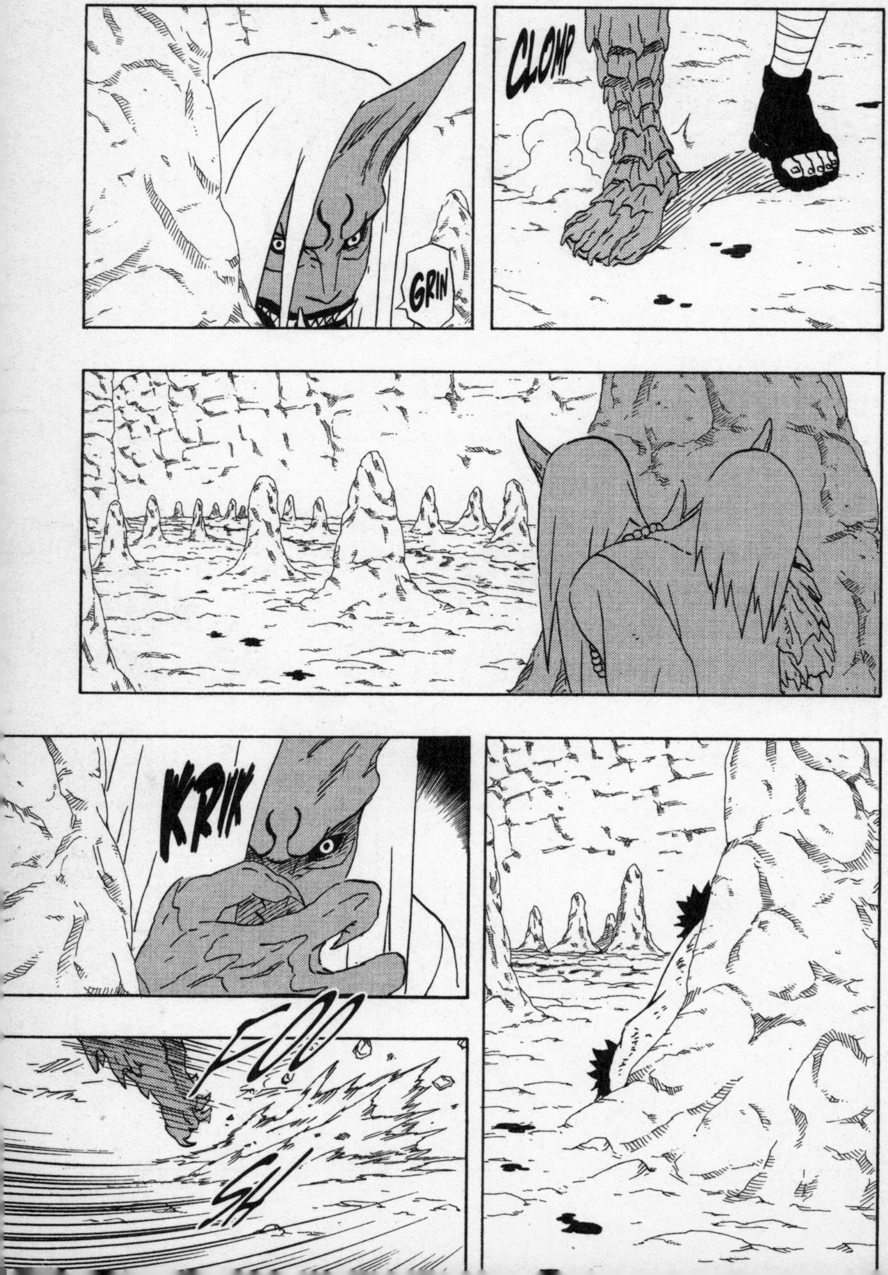
CLOMP
GRIN
KRIK
FOO
SH

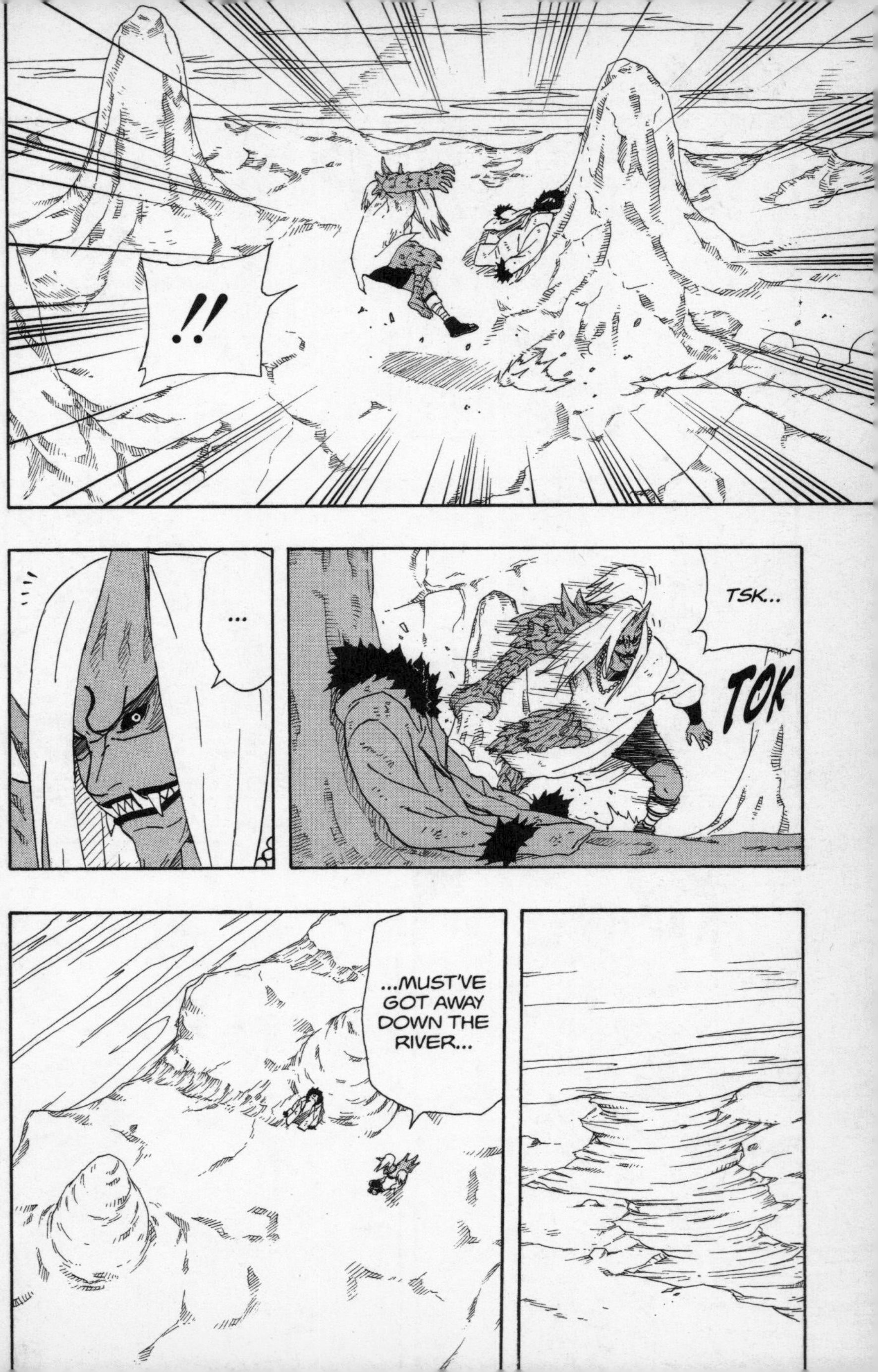
!!
TSK...
TOK
...
...MUST'VE GOT AWAY DOWN THE RIVER...

READ THIS WAY

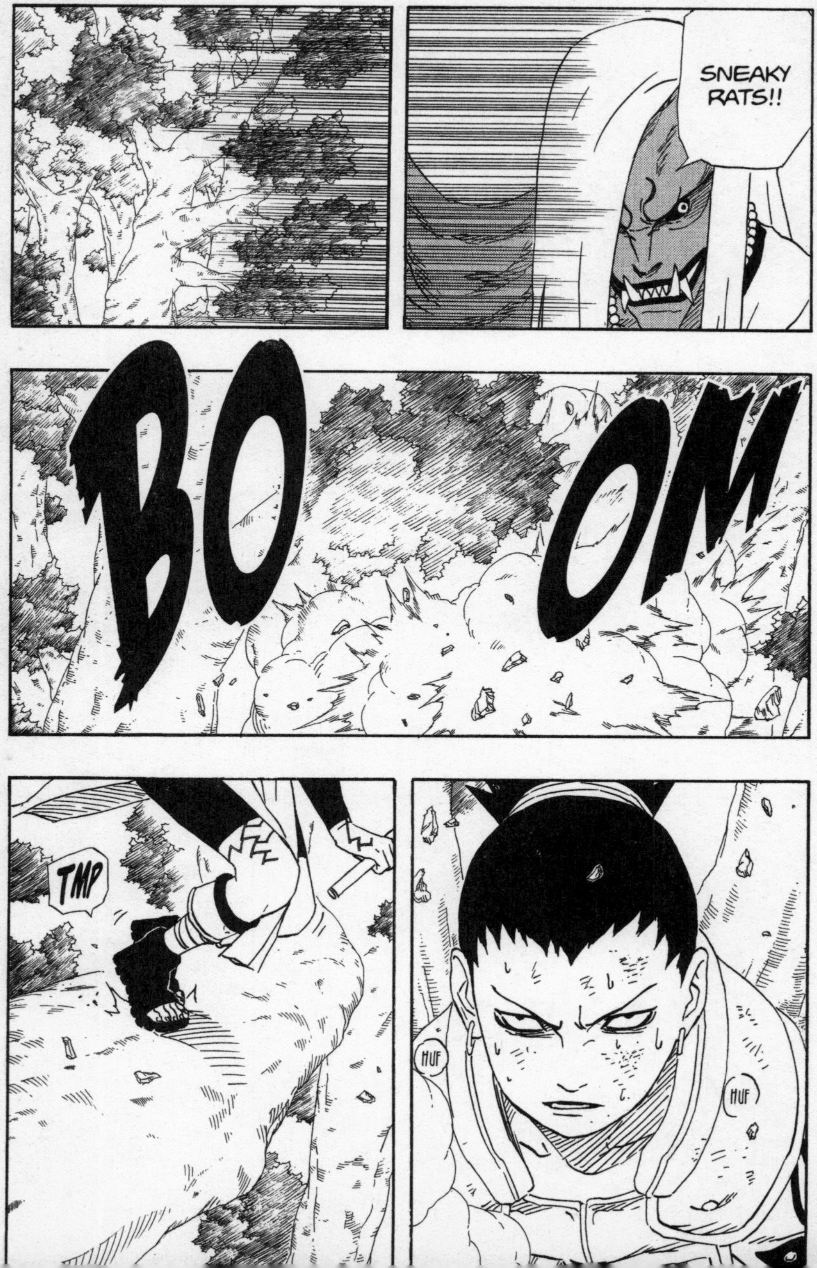
SNEAKY RATS!!
BOOOM
HUF
HUF
TMP

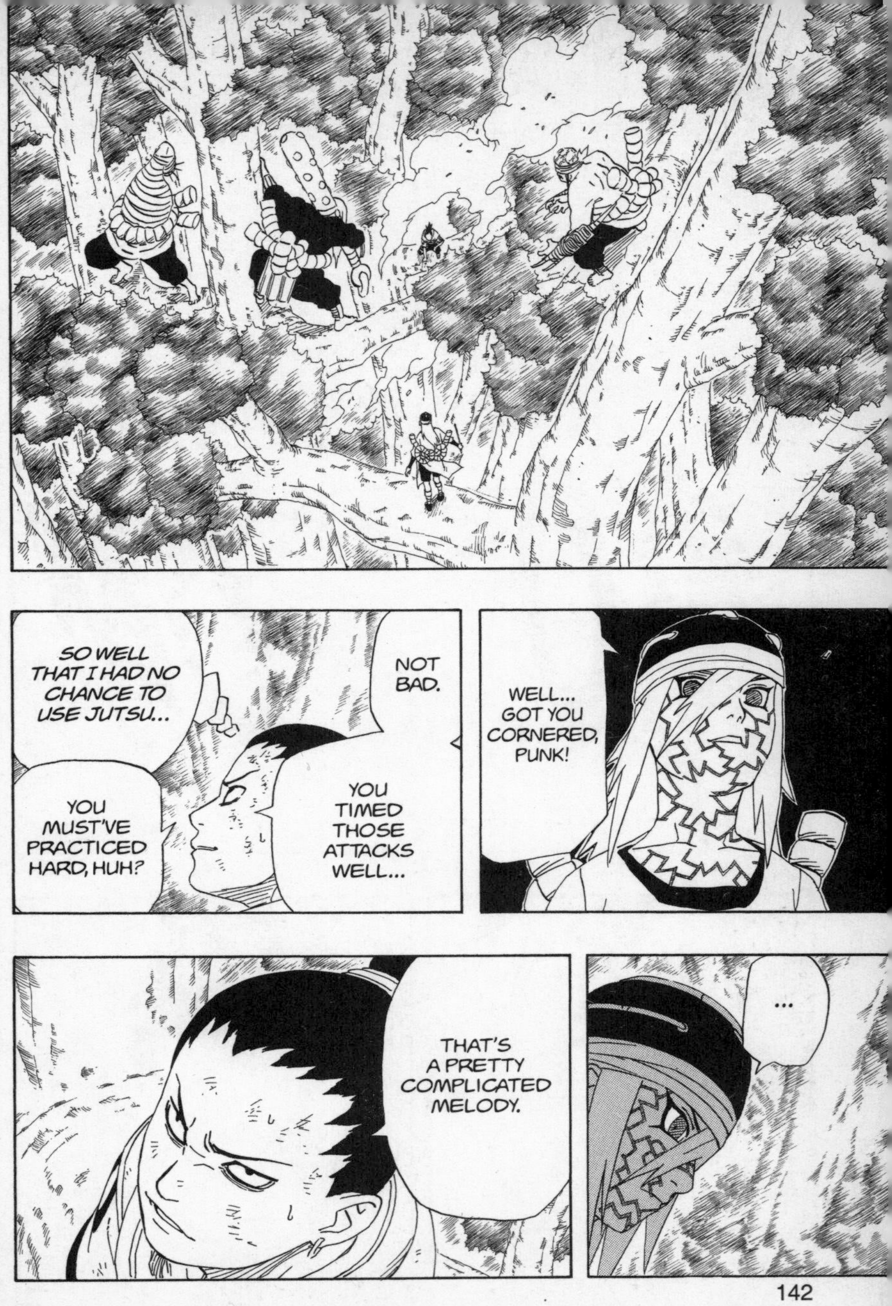
WELL... GOT YOU CORNERED, PUNK!
NOT BAD.
YOU TIMED THOSE ATTACKS WELL...
SO WELL THAT I HAD NO CHANCE TO USE JUTSU...
YOU MUST'VE PRACTICED HARD, HUH?
...
THAT'S A PRETTY COMPLICATED MELODY.

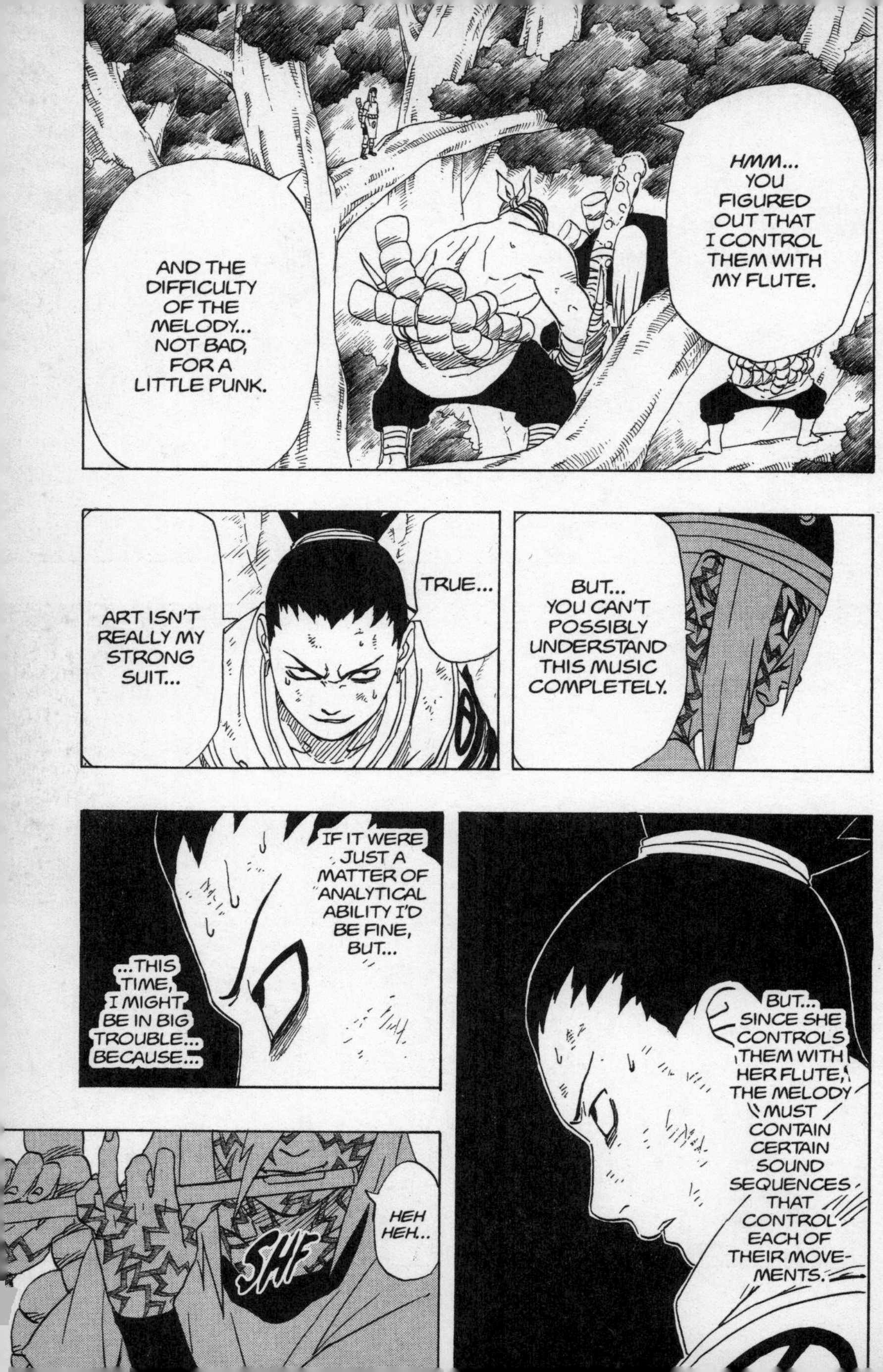
HMM... YOU FIGURED OUT THAT I CONTROL THEM WITH MY FLUTE.
AND THE DIFFICULTY OF THE MELODY... NOT BAD, FOR A LITTLE PUNK.
BUT... YOU CAN'T POSSIBLY UNDERSTAND THIS MUSIC COMPLETELY.
TRUE...
ART ISN'T REALLY MY STRONG SUIT...
BUT... SINCE SHE CONTROLS THEM WITH HER FLUTE, THE MELODY MUST CONTAIN CERTAIN SOUND SEQUENCES THAT CONTROL EACH OF THEIR MOVE-MENTS.
IF IT WERE JUST A MATTER OF ANALYTICAL ABILITY I'D BE FINE, BUT...
...THIS TIME, I MIGHT BE IN BIG TROUBLE... BECAUSE...
HEH HEH...
SHF

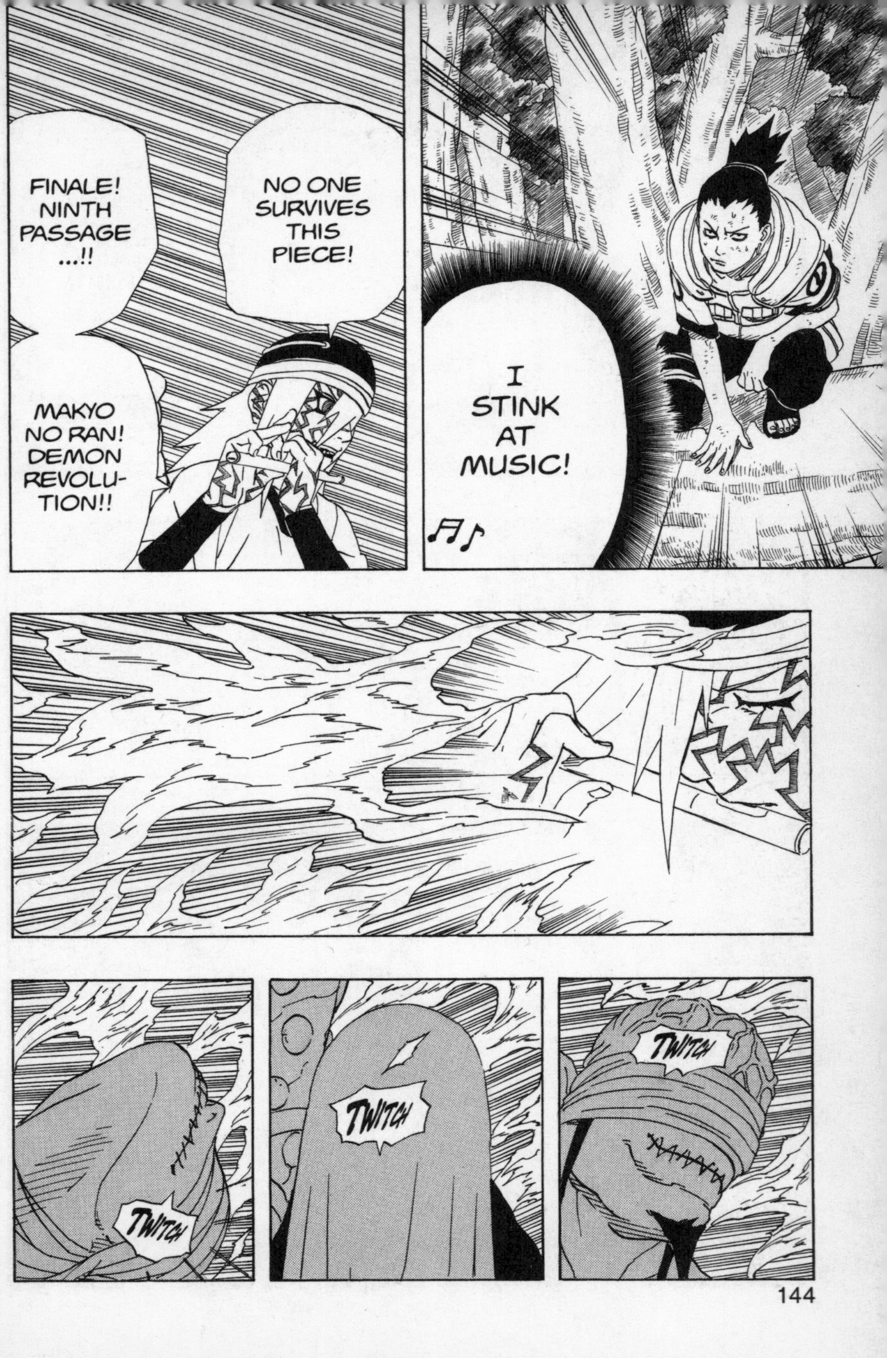
♬♪
I STINK AT MUSIC!
NO ONE SURVIVES THIS PIECE!
FINALE! NINTH PASSAGE ...!!
MAKYO NO RAN! DEMON REVOLUTION!!
TWITCH
TWITCH
TWITCH

READ THIS WAY

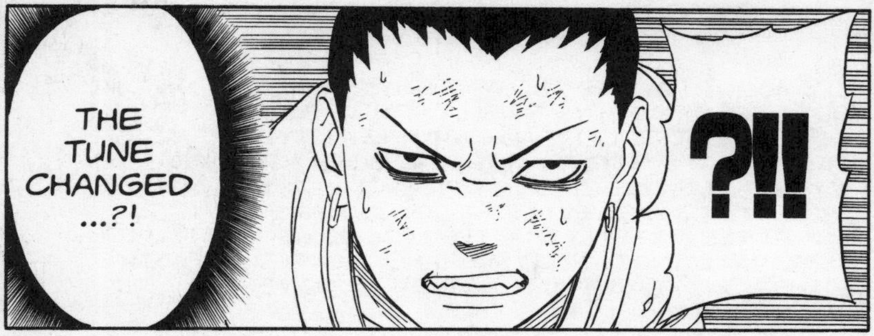
?!!
THE TUNE CHANGED ...?!

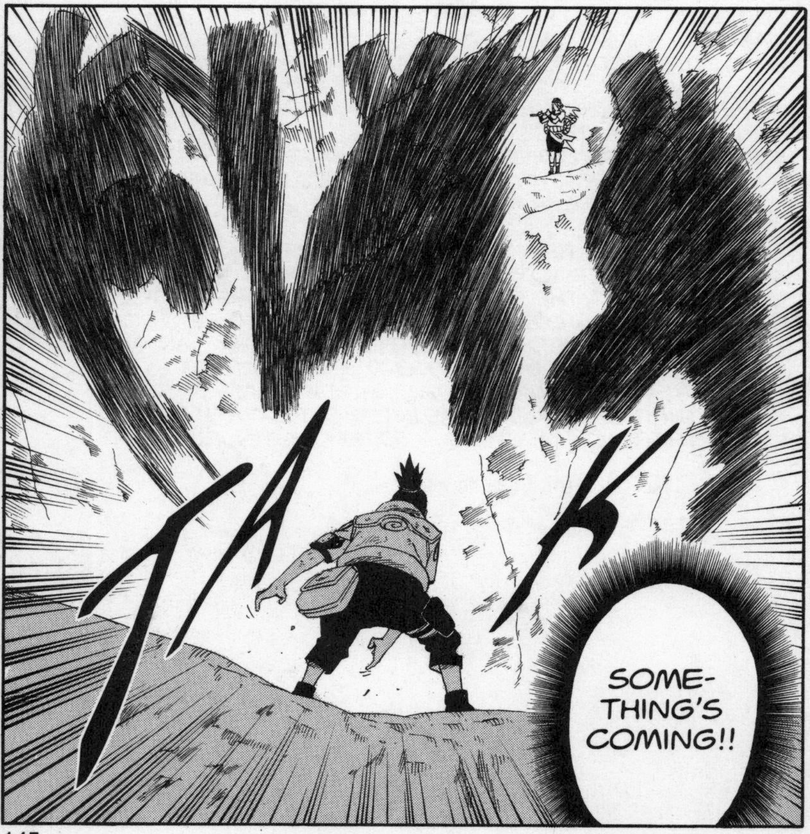
TAK
SOME-THING'S COMING!!

THE WORLD OF KISHIMOTO MASASHI
MY PERSONAL HISTORY: A STORY TOO EMBARRASSING
TO WRITE DOWN, PART 1

IT'S ABOUT TIME I ENDED WRITING MY PERSONAL HISTORY, BUT I'VE GOT NOTHING TO FILL OUT THIS BLANK PAGE WITH, SO I DECIDED TO CONTINUE WRITING A LITTLE BIT MORE. IT SEEMS THE MORE I WRITE, THE MORE I EMBARRASS MYSELF... BUT, I'M GOING TO WRITE AGAIN ANYWAY, AGAINST MY BETTER JUDGMENT. FIRST OF ALL, THIS STORY IS SO POINTLESS AND SILLY THAT I'VE AVOIDED WRITING IT UNTIL NOW, AND I'M NOT REALLY GUNG-HO ON WRITING IT NOW EITHER. BUT, AGAINST... MY...BETTER...JUDGMENT...

I THINK IT WAS WHEN I WAS IN THE FIRST GRADE. I WAS SO INTO THIS ONE SENTAI, SFX ACTION/ADVENTURE HERO SERIES. THE ONE I PLAYED MOST OFTEN AT THAT AGE WAS *TAIYO SENTAI SAN BARUKAN* (SOLAR SQUADRON SUN VULCAN). I USED TO PLAY SUN VULCAN FIGHTERS WITH MY FRIEND AND MY TWIN BROTHER A LOT. SUN VULCAN WAS A BIT DIFFERENT FROM THE OTHER SENTAI SERIES. WHILE MOST SENTAI SERIES HEROES WERE MADE UP OF A CELL OF FIVE, SUN VULCAN WAS BRAVE ENOUGH TO SAVE THE EARTH WITH A CELL OF THREE. THE CELL CONSISTED OF VULEAGLE, VULSHARK AND VULPANTHER.

I'VE NEVER LIKED BEING THE LEADER, EVER SINCE I WAS A KID. SO I DECIDED TO PLAY THE ROLES OF EITHER VULSHARK OR VULPANTHER, THE SECOND OR THIRD RANKED GUYS. BUT, BECAUSE VULSHARK'S POSE LOOKED LAME TO ME, EVEN AT THAT AGE, I DECIDED TO GO WITH VULPANTHER. ...ANYWAY... WELL... *UMM*... I REALLY GOT INTO THE VULPANTHER CHARACTER. OR, IT WAS MORE LIKE... I ALREADY WAS VULPANTHER. BASICALLY, I WAS INTOXICATED WITH VULPANTHER. HOW MUCH SO...? TO BE CONTINUED...

P.S. THE TRUTH SHALL BE REVEALED!

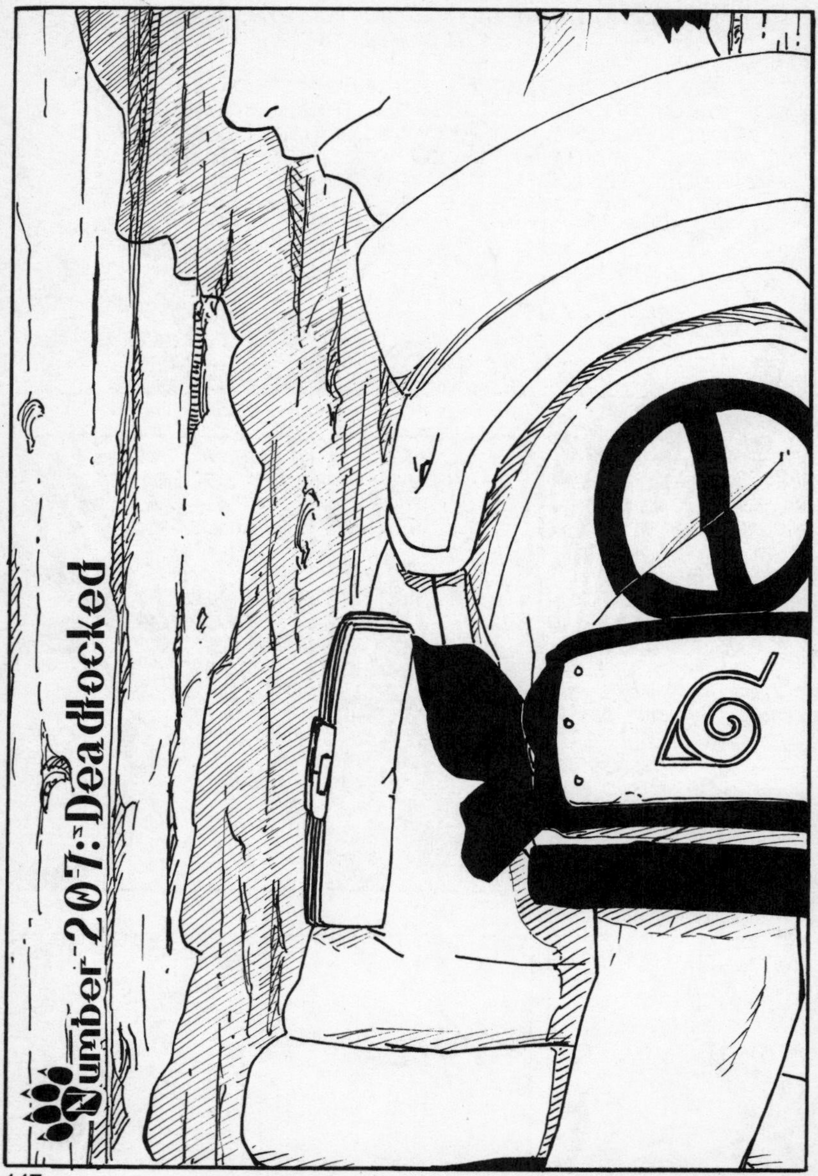
Number 207: Deadlocked

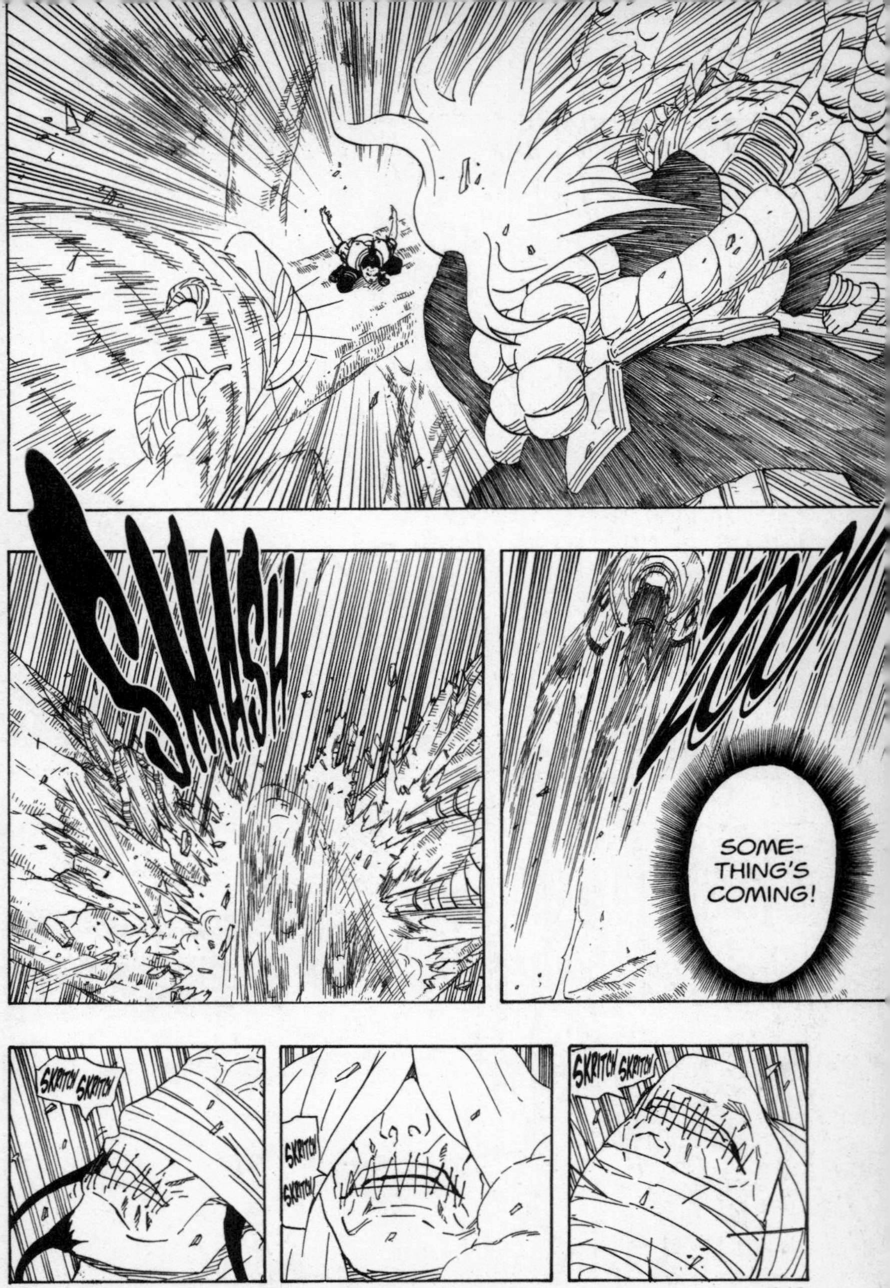

ZOOM
SOME-
THING'S
COMING!
SMASH
SKRITCH SKRITCH
SKRITCH
SKRITCH
SKRITCH SKRITCH

READ THIS WAY

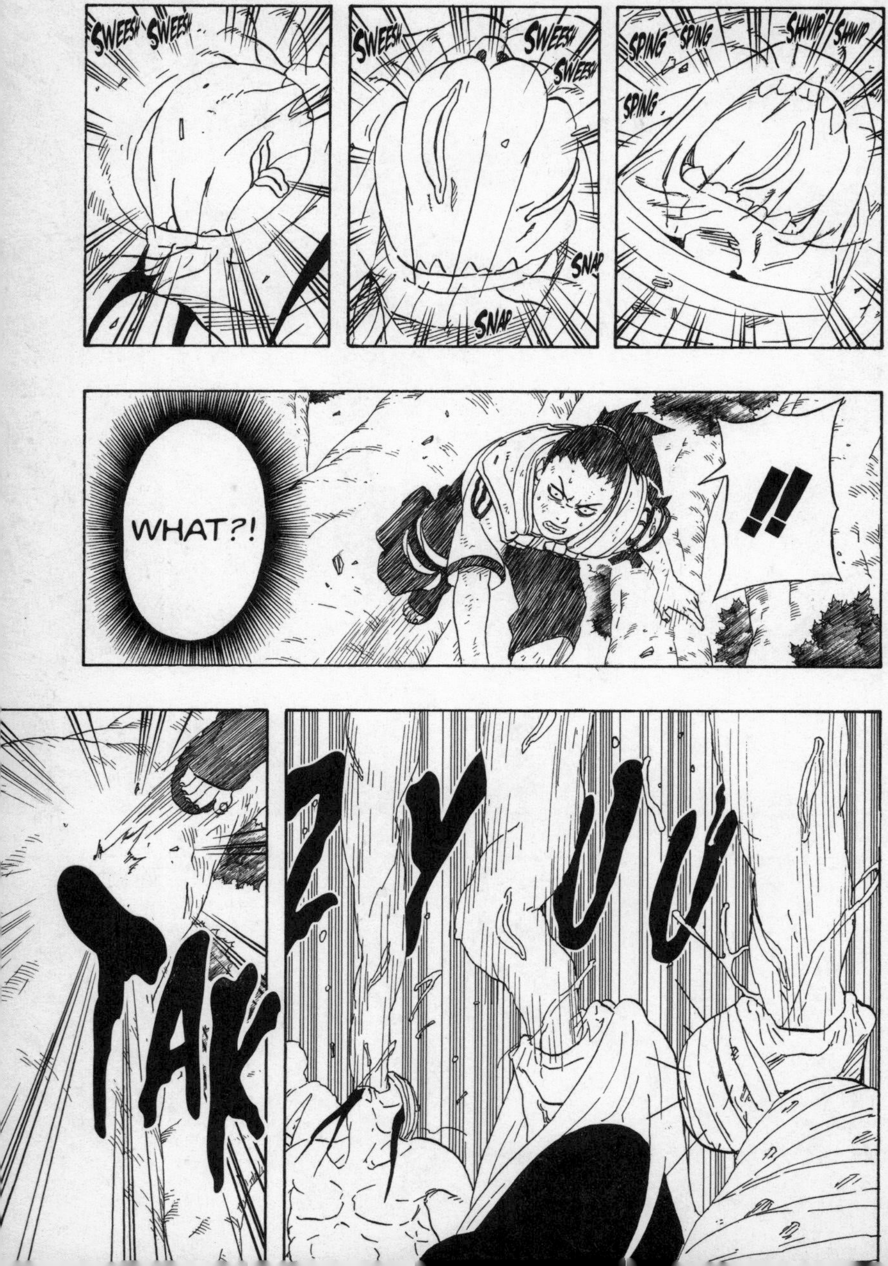
SPING SPING
SHWIP SHWIP
SPING
SWEESH
SWEESH
SWEESH
SNAP
SNAP
SWEESH SWEESH
!!
WHAT?!
ZYUU
TAK

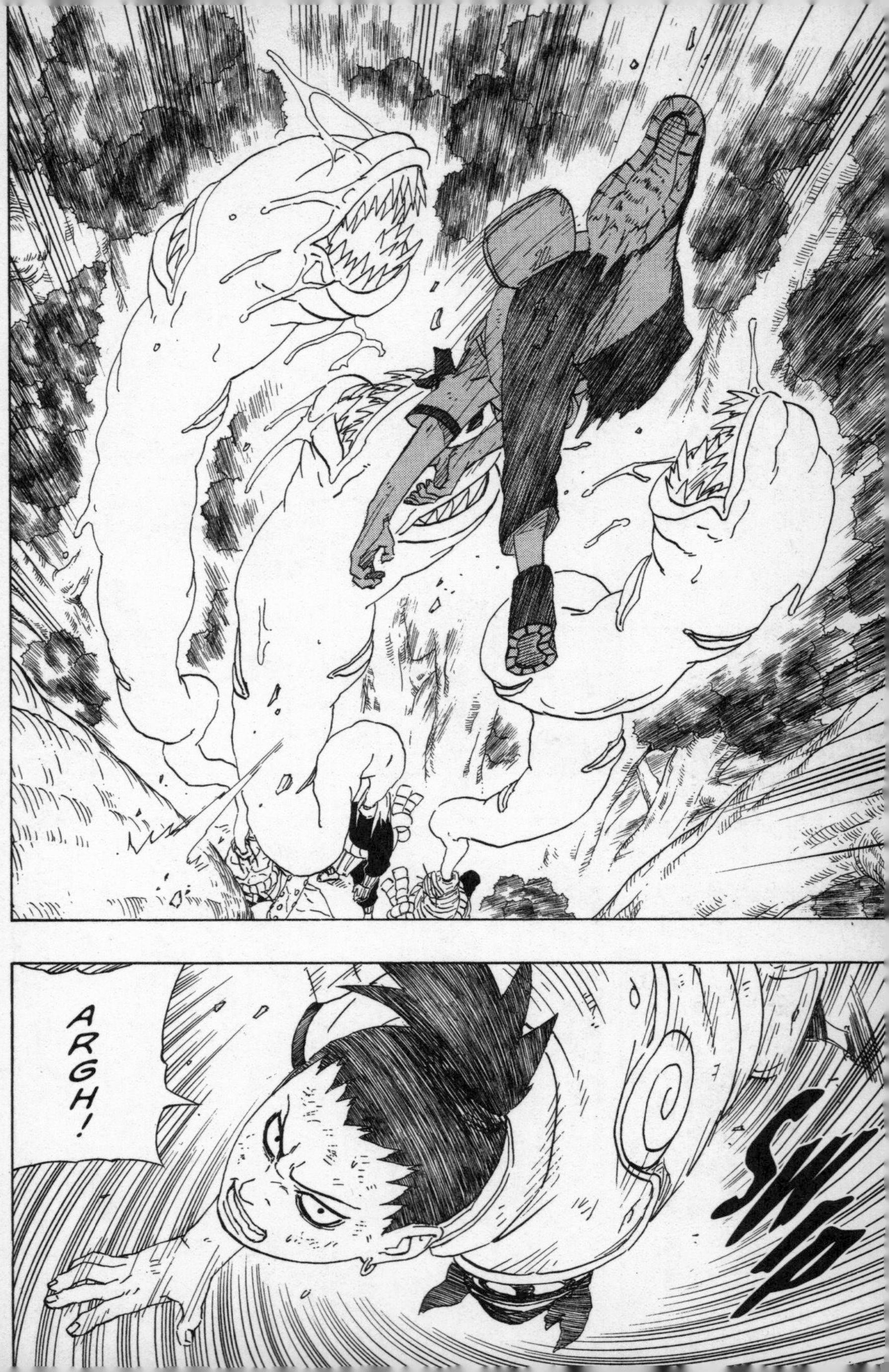
SHP
ARGH!

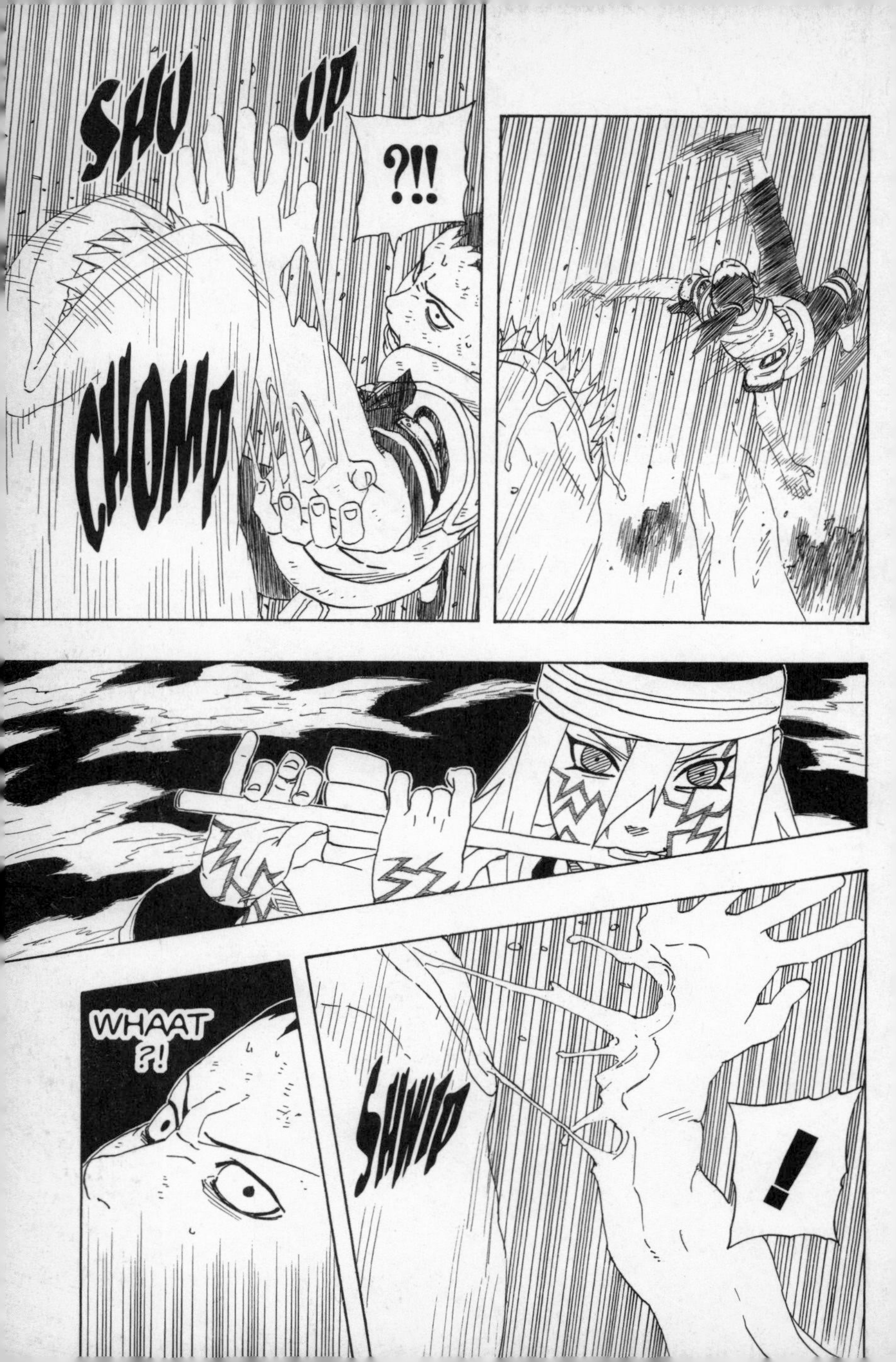
?!!
SHU UP
CHOMP
!
SHWIP
WHAAT ?!

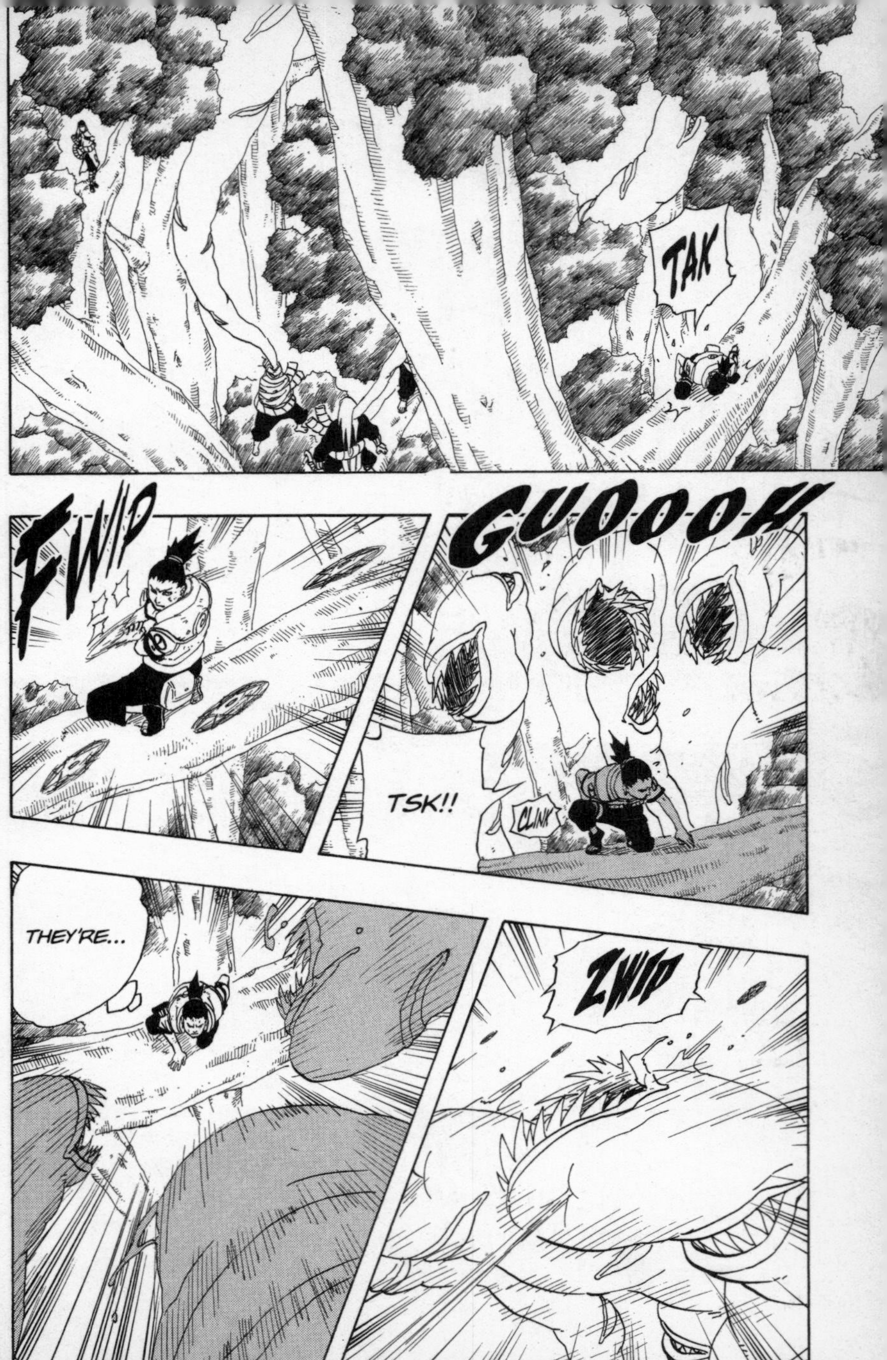
TAK
GUOOOH
TSK!!
CLINK
FWIP
ZWIP
THEY'RE...

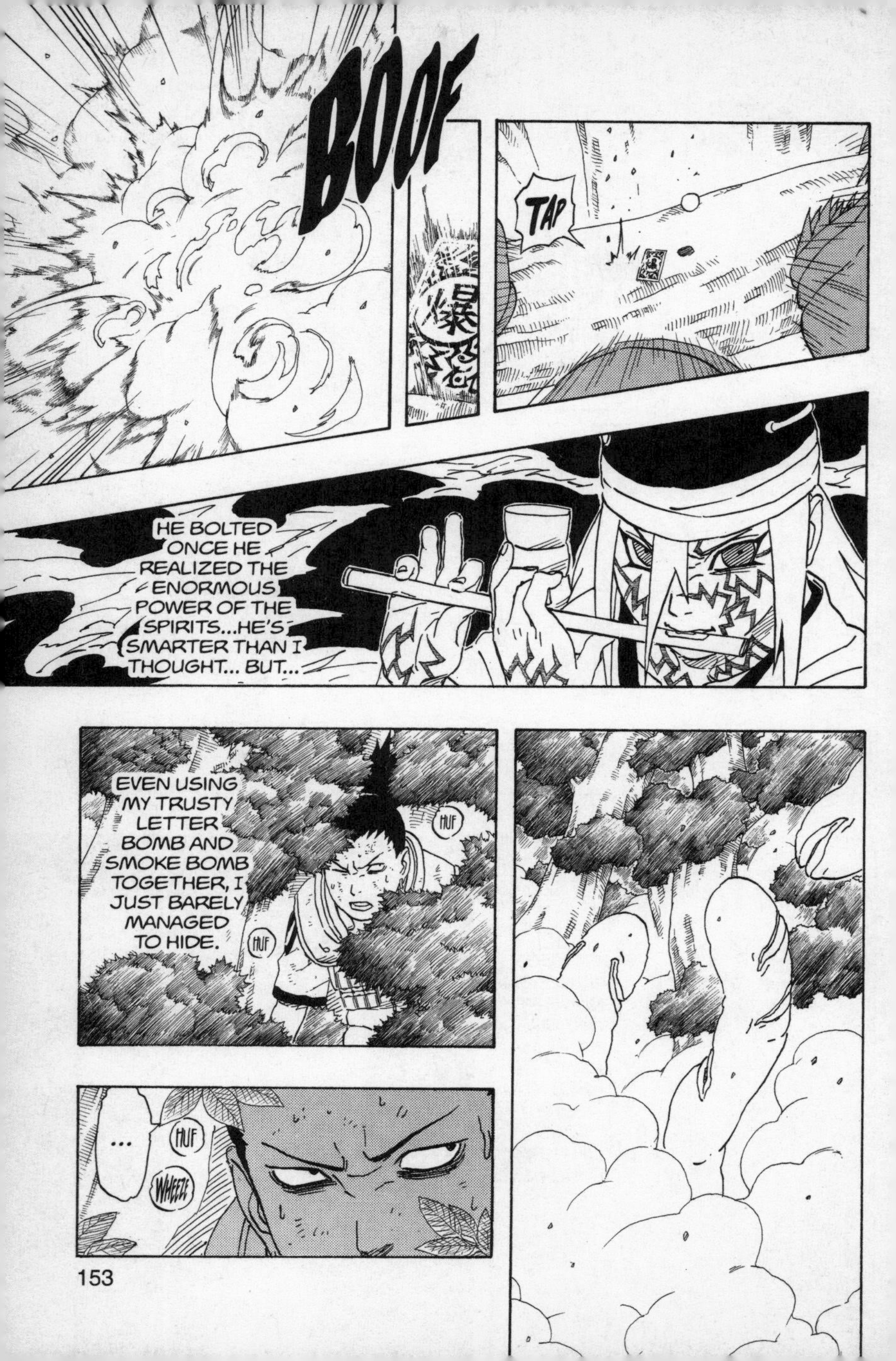
TAP
BOOF
HE BOLTED ONCE HE REALIZED THE ENORMOUS POWER OF THE SPIRITS...HE'S SMARTER THAN I THOUGHT... BUT...
EVEN USING MY TRUSTY LETTER BOMB AND SMOKE BOMB TOGETHER, I JUST BARELY MANAGED TO HIDE.
HUF
HUF
...
HUF
WHEEZE

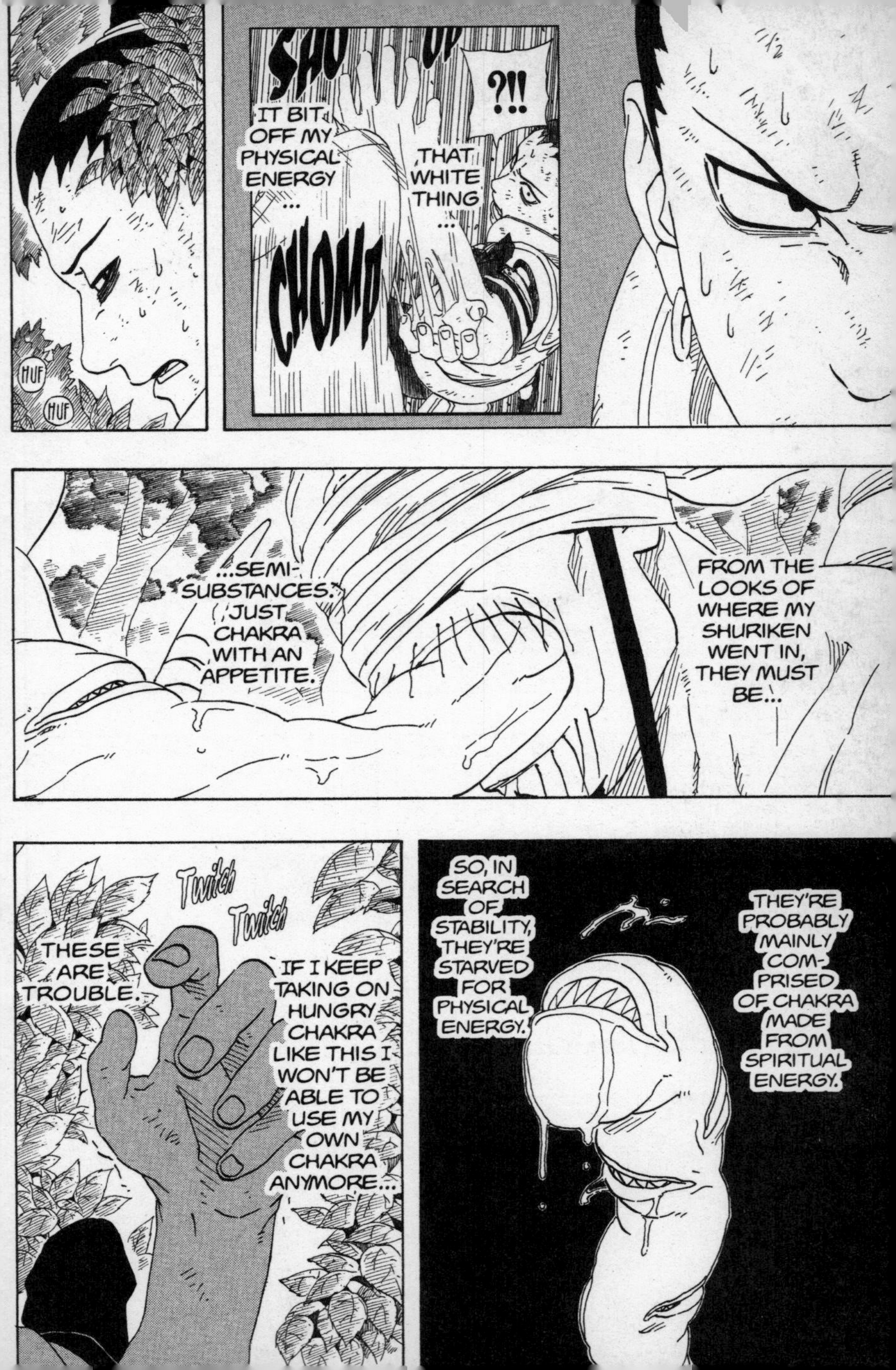
?!!
THAT WHITE THING...
IT BIT OFF MY PHYSICAL ENERGY...
CHOMP
HUF
HUF
FROM THE LOOKS OF WHERE MY SHURIKEN WENT IN, THEY MUST BE...
...SEMI-SUBSTANCES. JUST CHAKRA WITH AN APPETITE.
THEY'RE PROBABLY MAINLY COMPRISED OF CHAKRA MADE FROM SPIRITUAL ENERGY.
SO, IN SEARCH OF STABILITY, THEY'RE STARVED FOR PHYSICAL ENERGY.
Twitch
Twitch
IF I KEEP TAKING ON HUNGRY CHAKRA LIKE THIS I WON'T BE ABLE TO USE MY OWN CHAKRA ANYMORE...
THESE ARE TROUBLE.

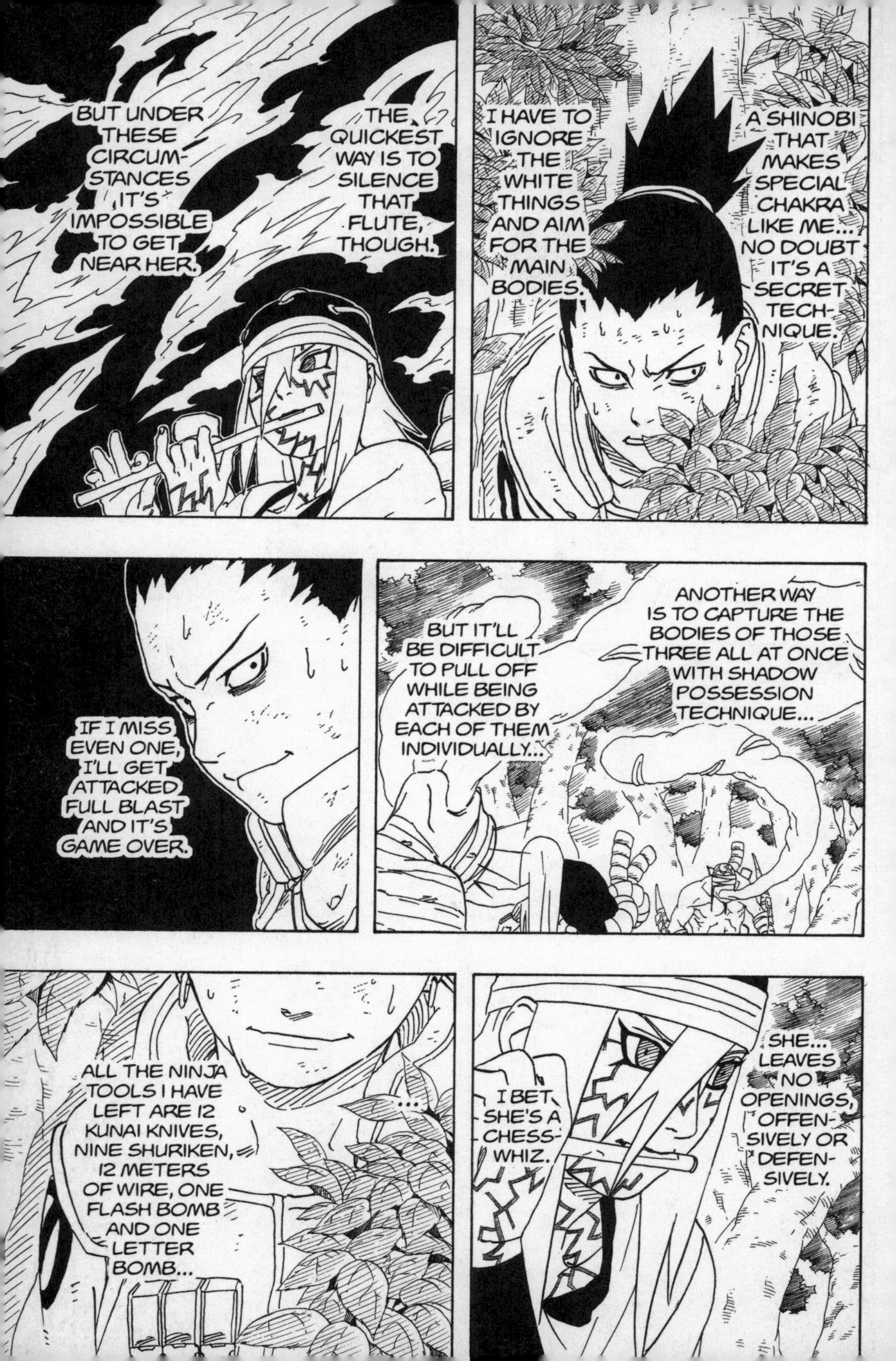
A SHINOBI THAT MAKES SPECIAL CHAKRA LIKE ME... NO DOUBT IT'S A SECRET TECHNIQUE.
I HAVE TO IGNORE THE WHITE THINGS AND AIM FOR THE MAIN BODIES.
THE QUICKEST WAY IS TO SILENCE THAT FLUTE, THOUGH.
BUT UNDER THESE CIRCUMSTANCES IT'S IMPOSSIBLE TO GET NEAR HER.
ANOTHER WAY IS TO CAPTURE THE BODIES OF THOSE THREE ALL AT ONCE WITH SHADOW POSSESSION TECHNIQUE...
BUT IT'LL BE DIFFICULT TO PULL OFF WHILE BEING ATTACKED BY EACH OF THEM INDIVIDUALLY...
IF I MISS EVEN ONE, I'LL GET ATTACKED FULL BLAST AND IT'S GAME OVER.
SHE... LEAVES NO OPENINGS, OFFENSIVELY OR DEFENSIVELY.
I BET SHE'S A CHESS-WHIZ.
...
ALL THE NINJA TOOLS I HAVE LEFT ARE 12 KUNAI KNIVES, NINE SHURIKEN, 12 METERS OF WIRE, ONE FLASH BOMB AND ONE LETTER BOMB...

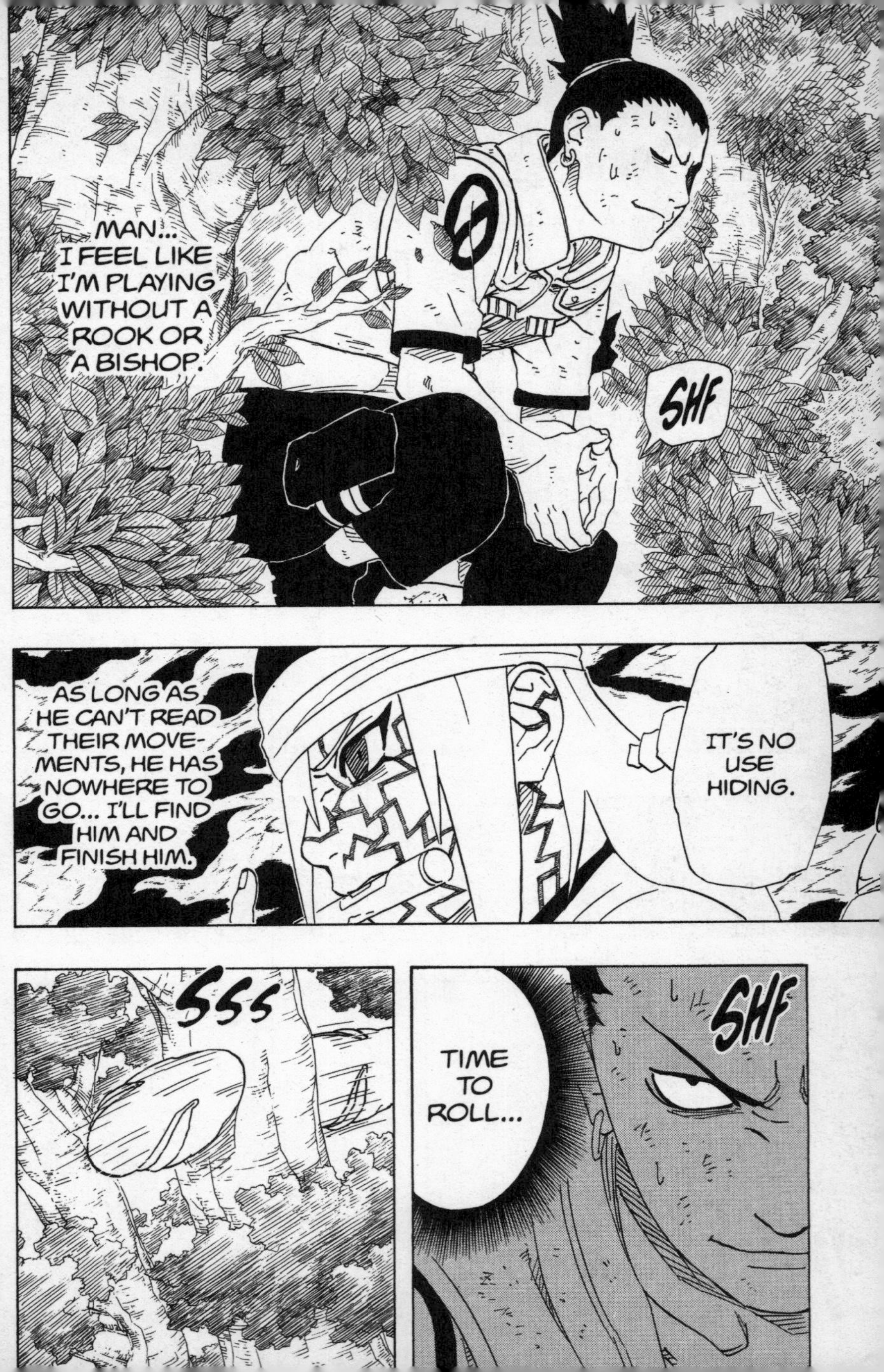
MAN... I FEEL LIKE I'M PLAYING WITHOUT A ROOK OR A BISHOP.
SHF
IT'S NO USE HIDING.
AS LONG AS HE CAN'T READ THEIR MOVEMENTS, HE HAS NOWHERE TO GO... I'LL FIND HIM AND FINISH HIM.
SHF
TIME TO ROLL...
SSS

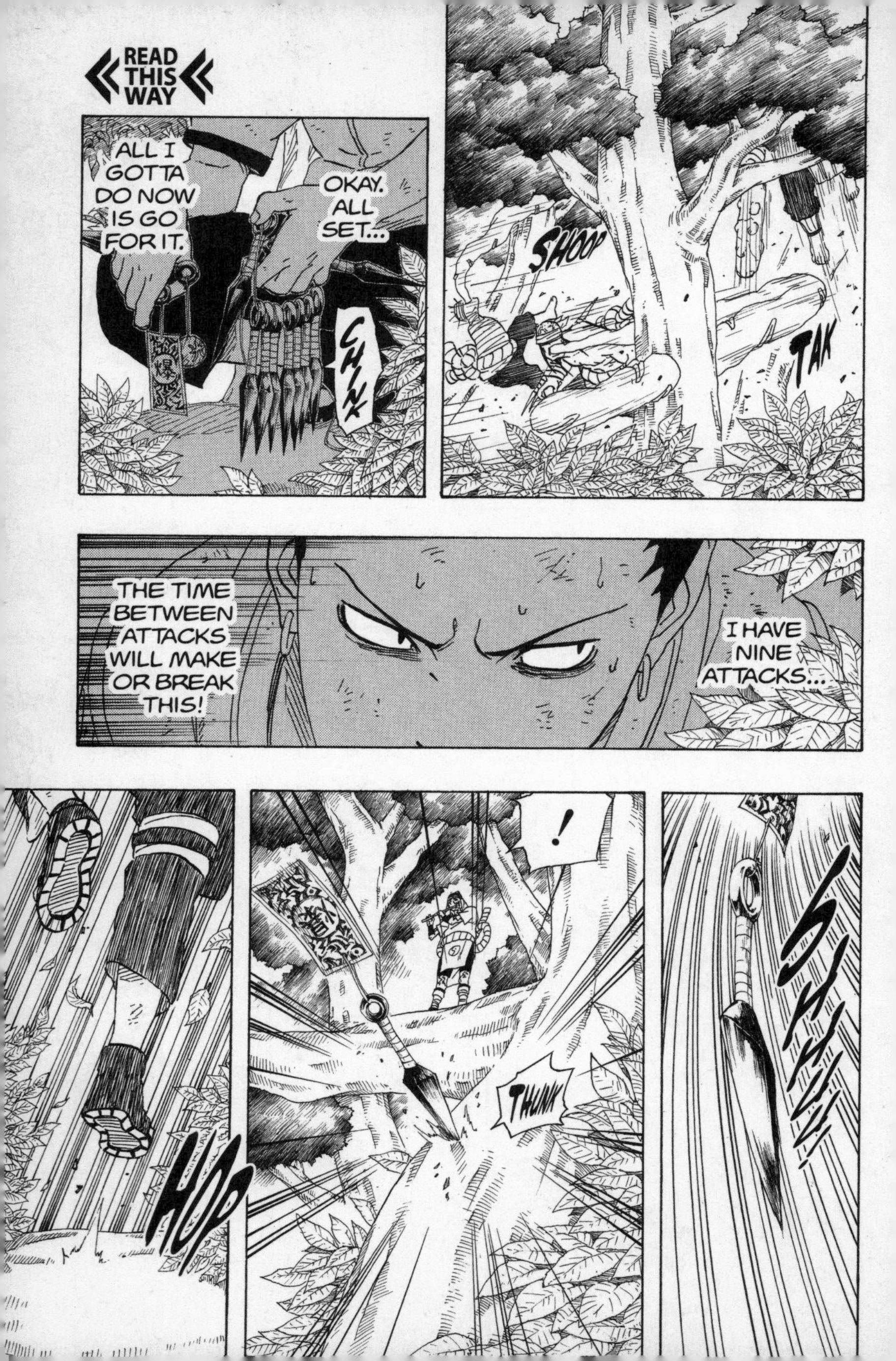
READ THIS WAY
SHOOP
TAK
OKAY. ALL SET...
ALL I GOTTA DO NOW IS GO FOR IT.
CHINK
I HAVE NINE ATTACKS...
THE TIME BETWEEN ATTACKS WILL MAKE OR BREAK THIS!
!
THUNK
HOP

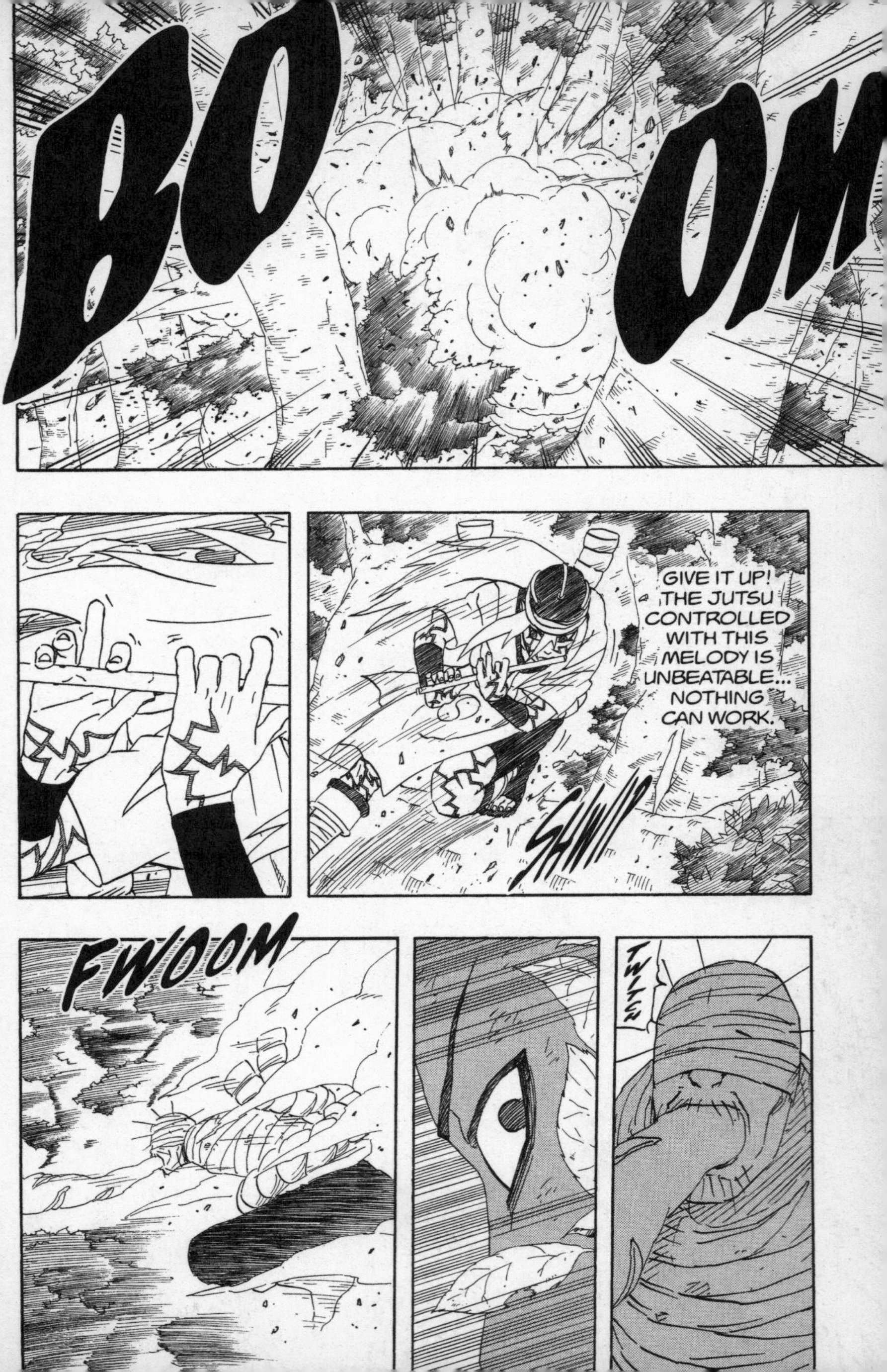
BOOM
GIVE IT UP! THE JUTSU CONTROLLED WITH THIS MELODY IS UNBEATABLE... NOTHING CAN WORK.
SHWIP
TWITCH
FWOOM

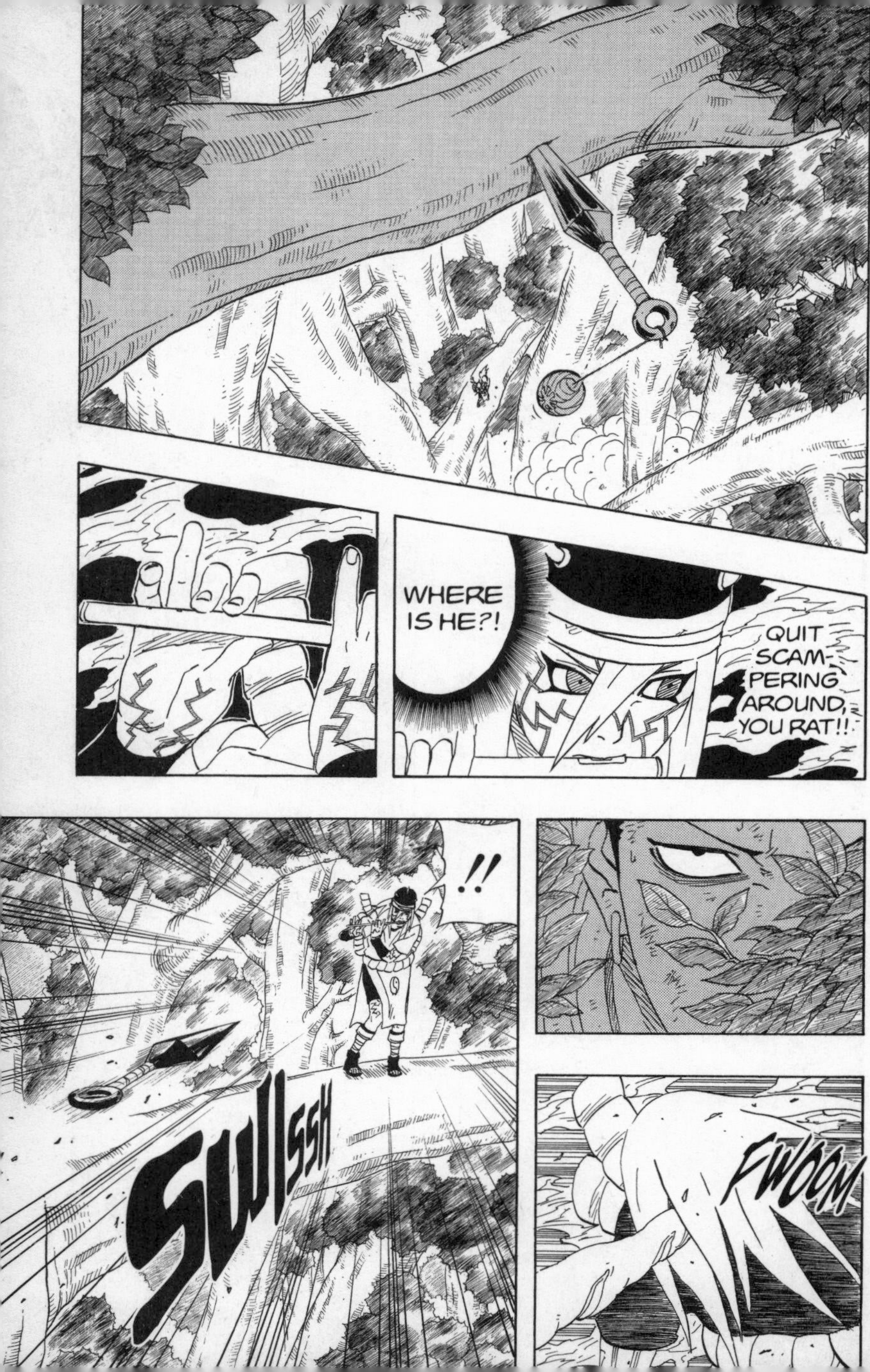
QUIT SCAM-PERING AROUND, YOU RAT!!
WHERE IS HE?!
FWOOM
!!
SWISSH

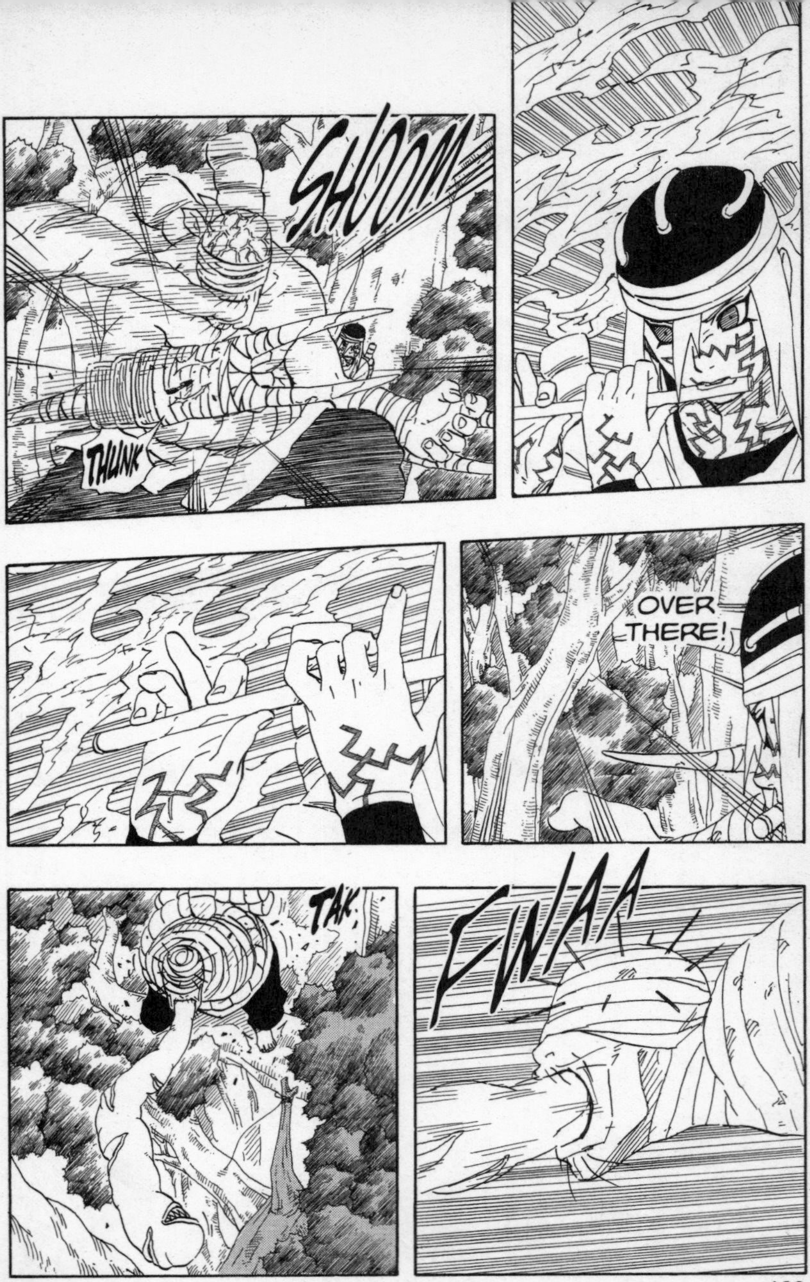
SHOOM
THUNK
OVER THERE!
FWAA
TAK

READ THIS WAY

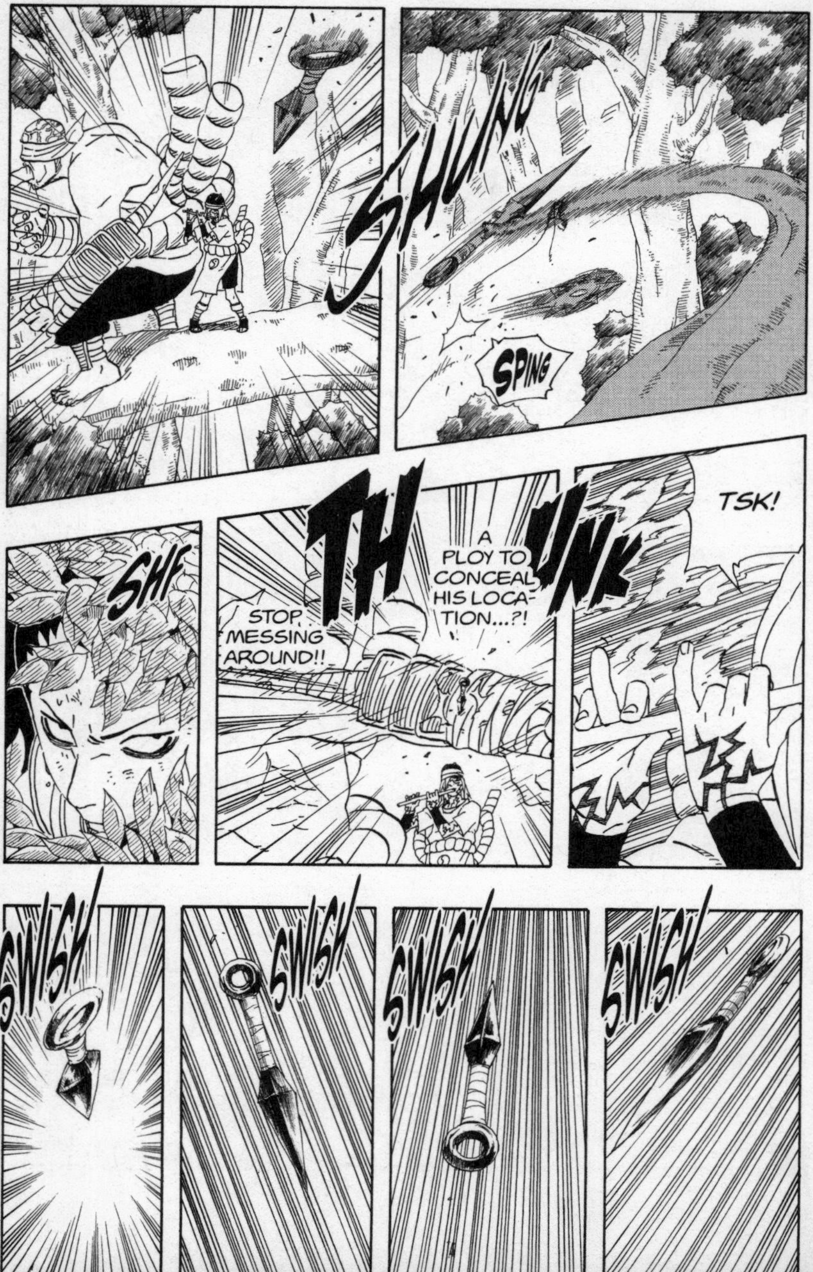
SHUNG
SPING
TSK!
THUNK
A PLOY TO CONCEAL HIS LOCATION...?!
STOP MESSING AROUND!!
SHF
SWISH
SWISH
SWISH
SWISH

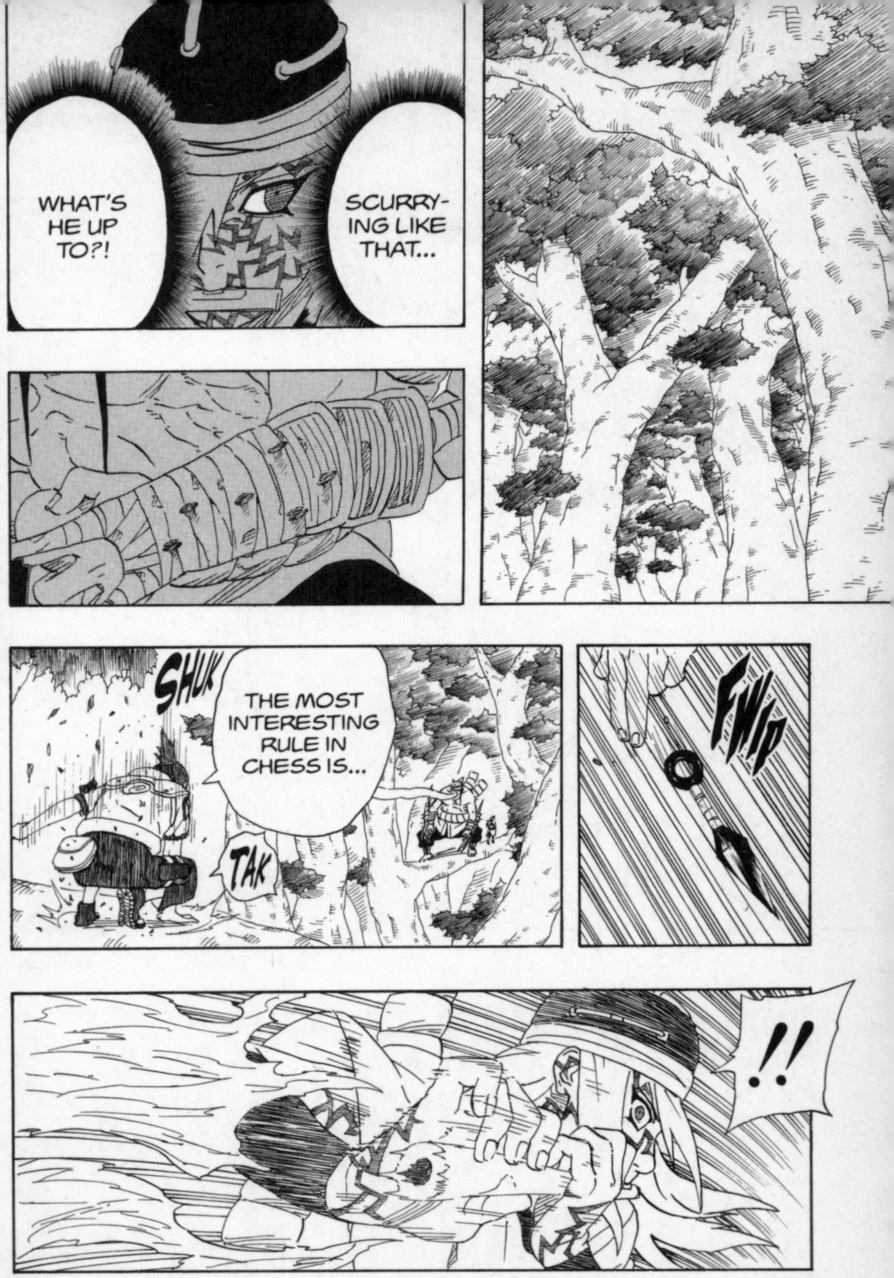
SCURRY-
ING LIKE
THAT...
WHAT'S
HE UP
TO?!
FWIP
THE MOST
INTERESTING
RULE IN
CHESS IS...
SHUK
TAK
!!

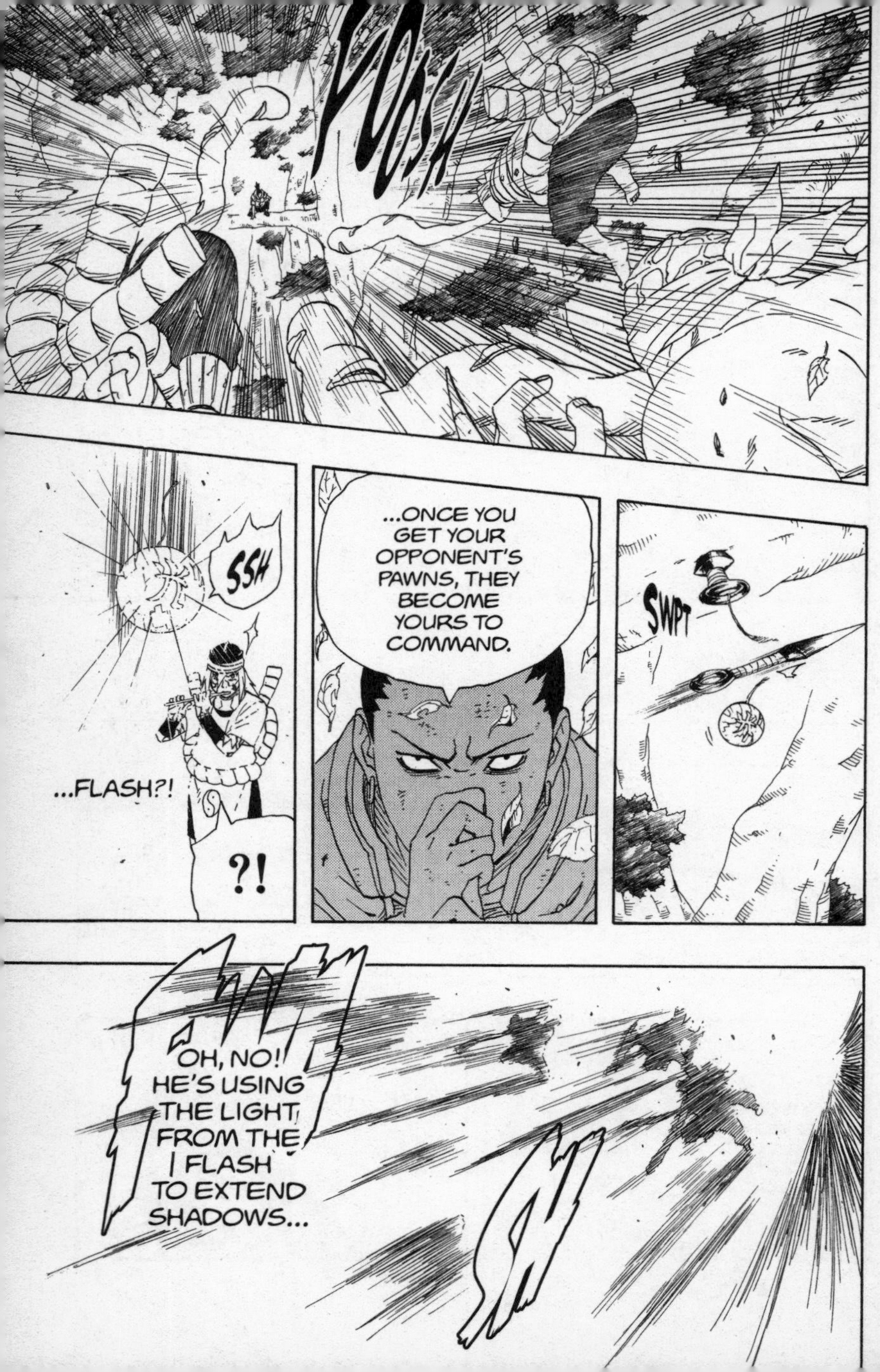
YOSH
SWPT
...ONCE YOU GET YOUR OPPONENT'S PAWNS, THEY BECOME YOURS TO COMMAND.
SSH
...FLASH?!
?!
OH, NO! HE'S USING THE LIGHT FROM THE FLASH TO EXTEND SHADOWS...

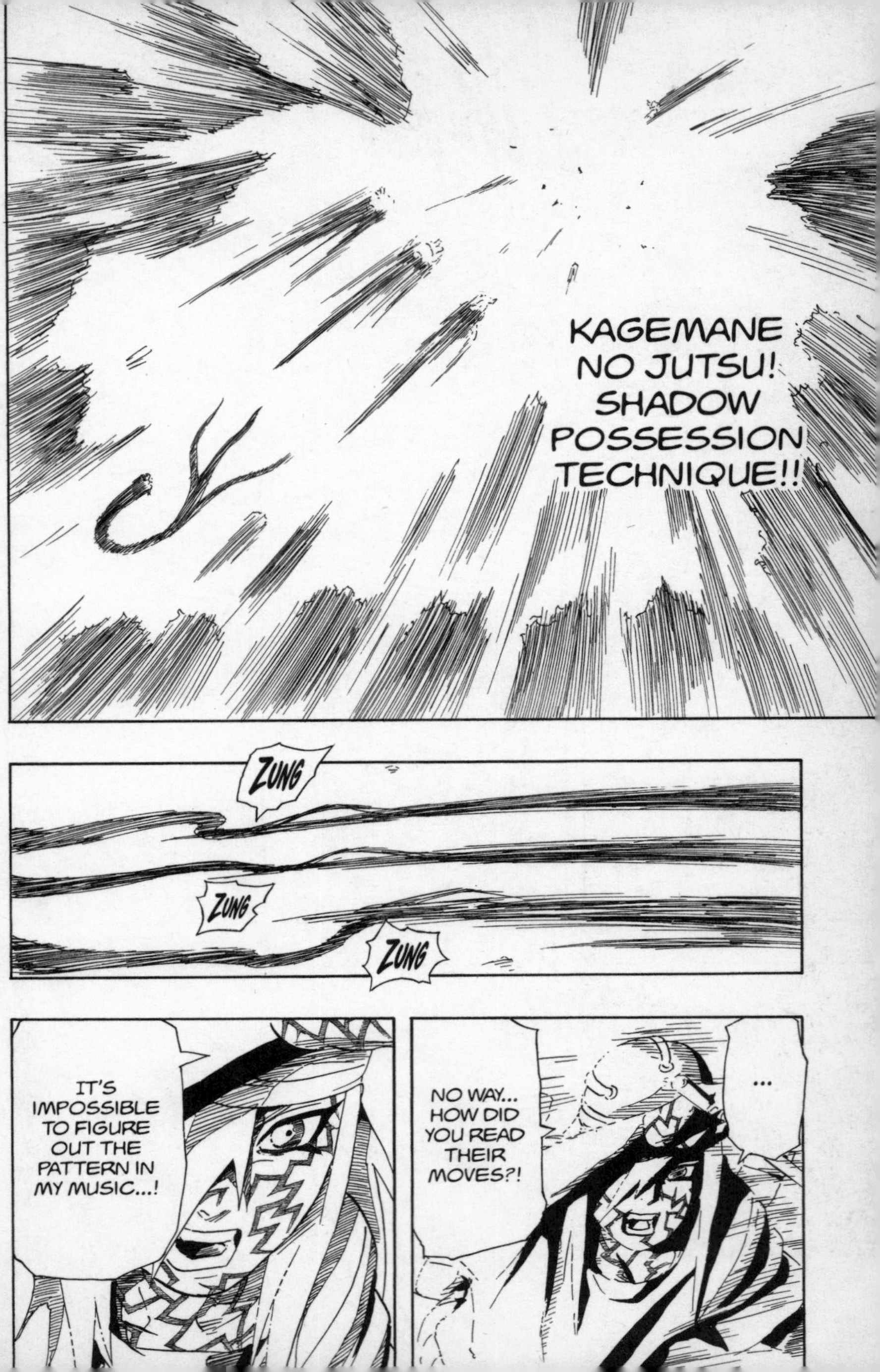

KAGEMANE NO JUTSU! SHADOW POSSESSION TECHNIQUE!!
ZUNG
ZUNG
ZUNG
...
NO WAY... HOW DID YOU READ THEIR MOVES?!
IT'S IMPOSSIBLE TO FIGURE OUT THE PATTERN IN MY MUSIC...!

READ THIS WAY

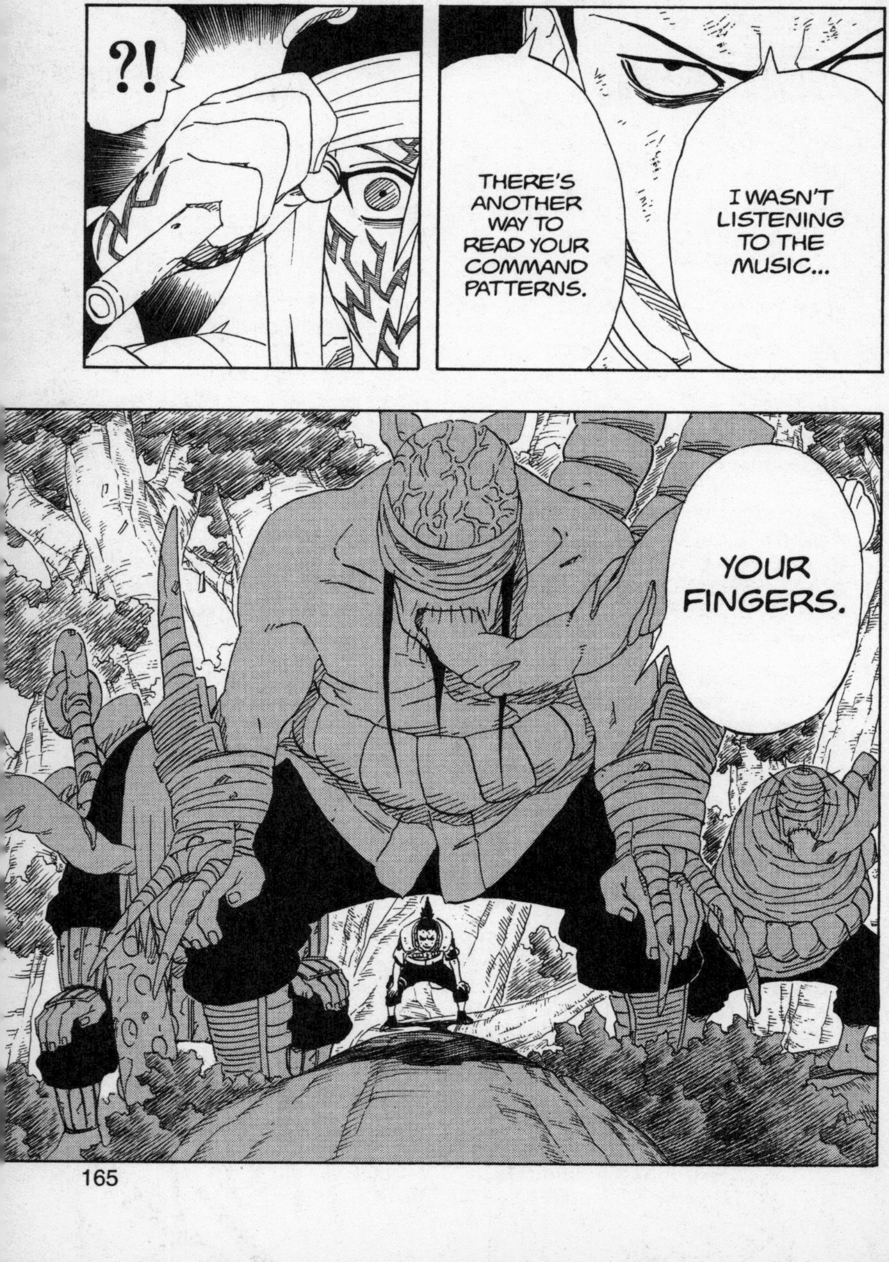
I WASN'T LISTENING TO THE MUSIC...
THERE'S ANOTHER WAY TO READ YOUR COMMAND PATTERNS.
?!
YOUR FINGERS.

THE WORLD OF KISHIMOTO MASASHI
MY PERSONAL HISTORY: A STORY TOO EMBARRASSING
TO WRITE DOWN, PART 2

FOR THE ALMOST ONE YEAR I DECIDED TO IDENTIFY MYSELF
WITH VULPANTHER, I ENCOUNTERED MANY DIFFICULTIES.
VULPANTHER IS YELLOW. BOTTOM LINE, HE'S SYMBOLIZED
BY THE COLOR YELLOW! SO, WHENEVER I HAD TO CHOOSE
A COLOR, I CHOSE YELLOW! ANYTHING AND EVERYTHING
HAD TO BE YELLOW!

VULPANTHER WORE A YELLOW JACKET SO, OF COURSE,
I WORE YELLOW CLOTHES. BUT... THE YELLOW CLOTHES
LOOKED WORSE THAN I THOUGHT.

VULPANTHER IS [SYMBOLIZED BY] CURRY. BOTTOM LINE, HE
LOVES CURRY AND RICE! SO, EVERY TIME SOMEONE ASKED
ME, "WHAT'S YOUR FAVORITE FOOD?" OF COURSE I
ANSWERED "CURRY AND RICE!" ... FOR SOME REASON,
IN THIS KIND OF SENTAI SERIES, MANY CHARACTERS WHOSE
SYMBOLIC COLOR WAS YELLOW LIKED CURRY AND RICE.
THE YELLOW RANGER OF THE GO RANGERS (MIGHTY
MORPHIN POWER RANGERS IN ENGLISH) WAS NO EXCEPTION.

VULPANTHER IS A CHARACTER THAT EATS TONS OF CURRY
AND RICE AND ALWAYS ASKS FOR SECONDS. HE PILES UP
PLATES ONE AFTER ANOTHER, EATING AS FAST AS WANKO
SOBA SPEED-EATERS. AS FAR AS I CAN REMEMBER, HE
WOULD PILE UP ABOUT 20 PLATES. BASICALLY, ONE LOOK AT
HIM REVEALED CLEARLY THAT HE LOVED CURRY AND RICE.

SO YOU CAN IMAGINE HOW EXCITED I GOT ON DAYS WHEN
CURRY AND RICE WAS SERVED FOR DINNER!! A WANNABE
VULPANTHER DEFINITELY HAD TO ASK FOR SECONDS NO
MATTER WHAT, EVEN WHEN HE FELT LIKE THROWING UP OR
THAT HIS STOMACH WAS GOING TO BURST. THEN I WOULD
SAY TO MY MOTHER, "SECONDS, PLEASE! NEXT PLATE!"
MY MOTHER WOULD SAY, "...? WHAT ARE YOU TALKING ABOUT?!
IF YOU WANT SECONDS, PUT IT ON THE SAME PLATE YOU
HAVE NOW!! NO NEED TO DIRTY ANOTHER PLATE!!"
I THOUGHT, "...CAN'T ARGUE WITH THAT..."

VULPANTHER ALSO CLIMBS WALLS. HE HAS SHARP CLAWS
AND CAN CLIMB NO MATTER WHAT, EVEN IF THE WALL IS
PERPENDICULAR TO THE GROUND! OF COURSE, I HAD TO
CLIMB ANY PERPENDICULAR WALL I SAW WHEN PLAYING SUN
VULCAN. ...EVEN I, AS A FIRST GRADER, KNEW THAT NO ONE
COULD CLIMB A PERPENDICULAR WALL. BUT, IN FRONT OF
VULEAGLE AND VULSHARK, I HAD NO CHOICE BUT TO GO FOR
IT. AS I RAN TOWARD THE WALL, I THOUGHT, "...HONESTLY,
PLAYING VULPANTHER IS TOUGH..." JUMP!! AND SPLAT,
I FLATTENED MYSELF AGAINST THAT WALL! SCRATCH!
"OUCH!!" ...MY FINGERNAILS GOT TORN OFF.
...FROM THAT DAY FORWARD, I QUIT PLAYING VULPANTHER.

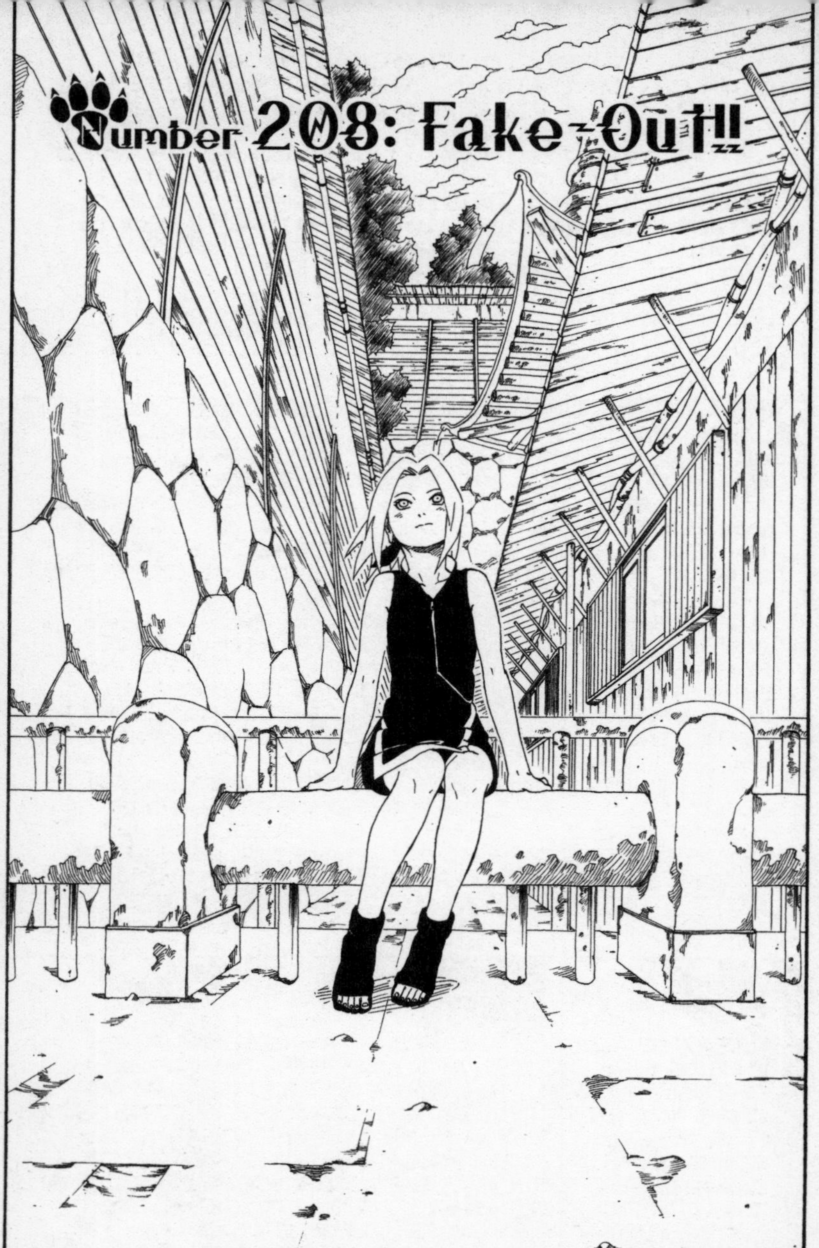
Number 208: Fake-Out!!

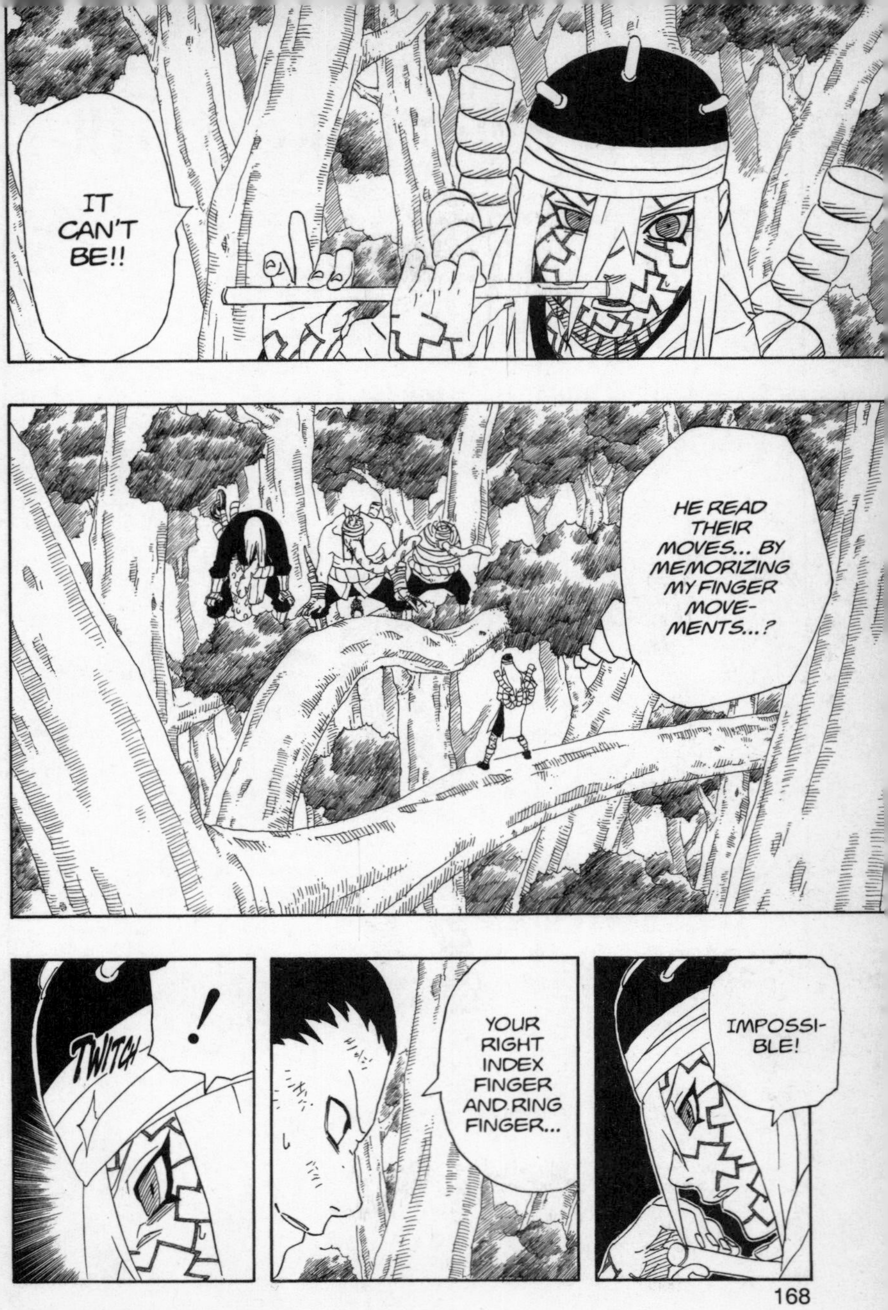
IT CAN'T BE!!
HE READ THEIR MOVES... BY MEMORIZING MY FINGER MOVEMENTS...?
IMPOSSIBLE!
YOUR RIGHT INDEX FINGER AND RING FINGER...
TWITCH
!

READ THIS WAY

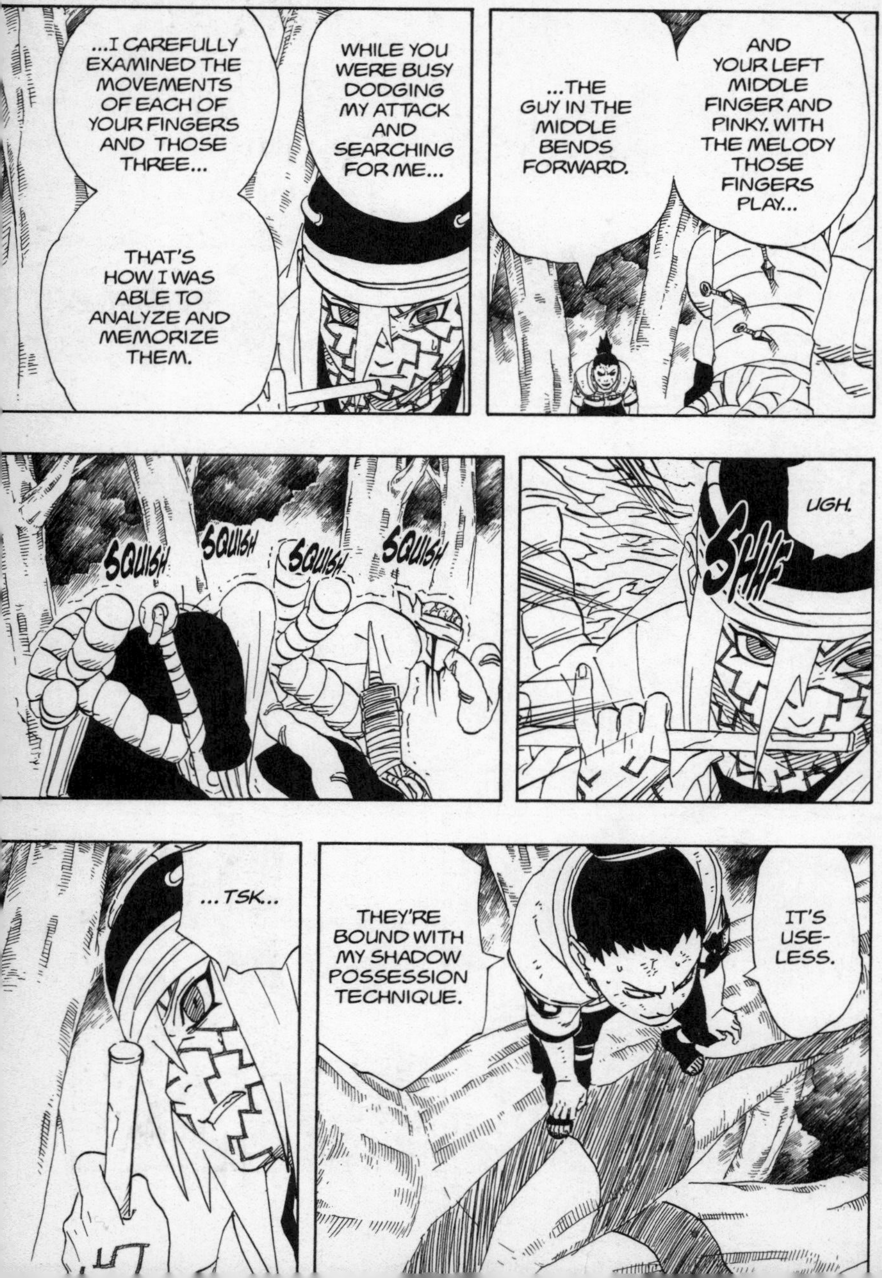
AND YOUR LEFT MIDDLE FINGER AND PINKY. WITH THE MELODY THOSE FINGERS PLAY...
...THE GUY IN THE MIDDLE BENDS FORWARD.
WHILE YOU WERE BUSY DODGING MY ATTACK AND SEARCHING FOR ME...
...I CAREFULLY EXAMINED THE MOVEMENTS OF EACH OF YOUR FINGERS AND THOSE THREE...
THAT'S HOW I WAS ABLE TO ANALYZE AND MEMORIZE THEM.
UGH.
SHHF
SQUISH
SQUISH
SQUISH
SQUISH
IT'S USELESS.
THEY'RE BOUND WITH MY SHADOW POSSESSION TECHNIQUE.
...TSK...

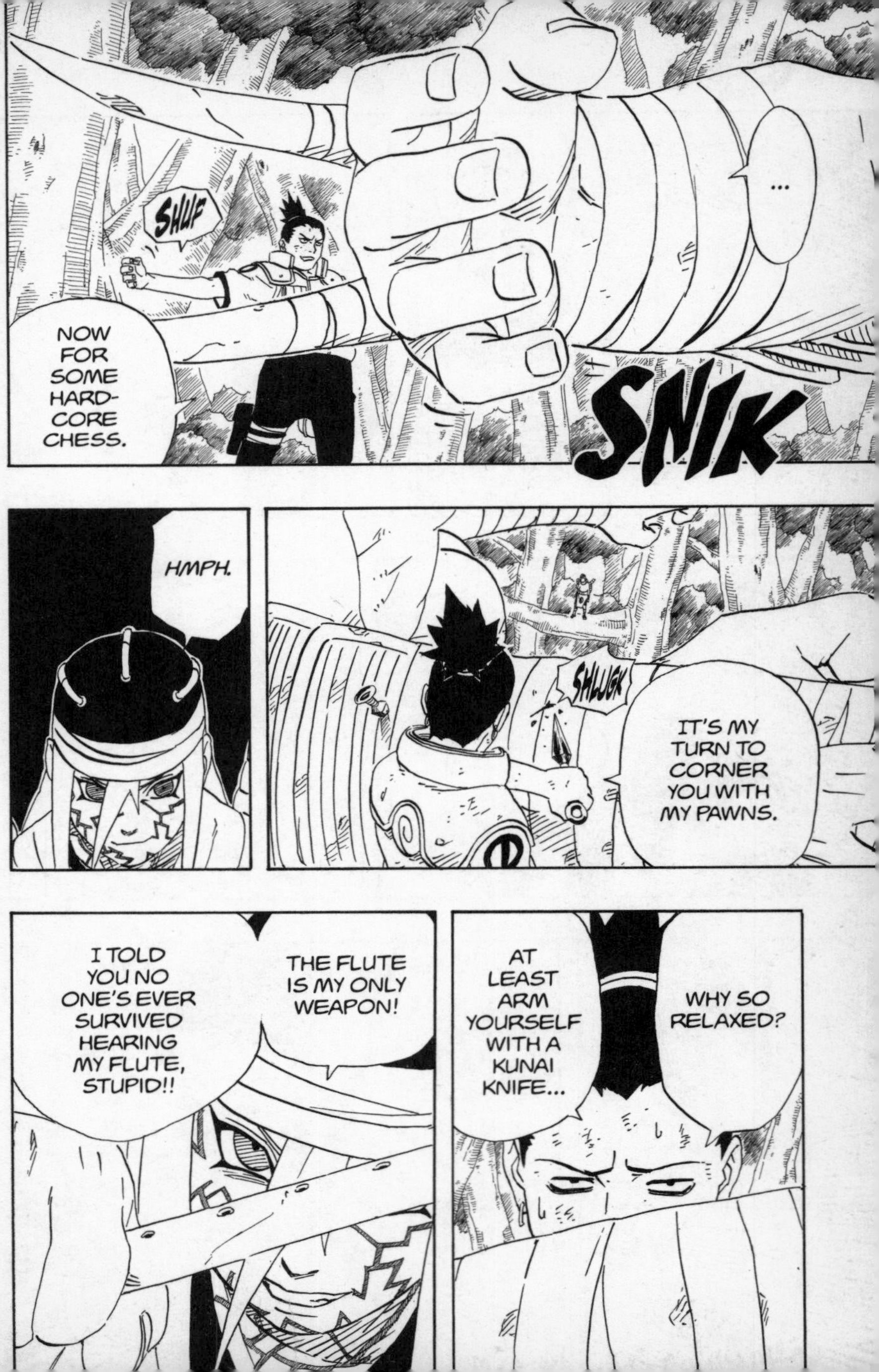
...
SHUF
NOW FOR SOME HARD-CORE CHESS.
SNIK
SHLUGK
IT'S MY TURN TO CORNER YOU WITH MY PAWNS.
HMPH.
WHY SO RELAXED?
AT LEAST ARM YOURSELF WITH A KUNAI KNIFE...
THE FLUTE IS MY ONLY WEAPON!
I TOLD YOU NO ONE'S EVER SURVIVED HEARING MY FLUTE, STUPID!!

READ THIS WAY

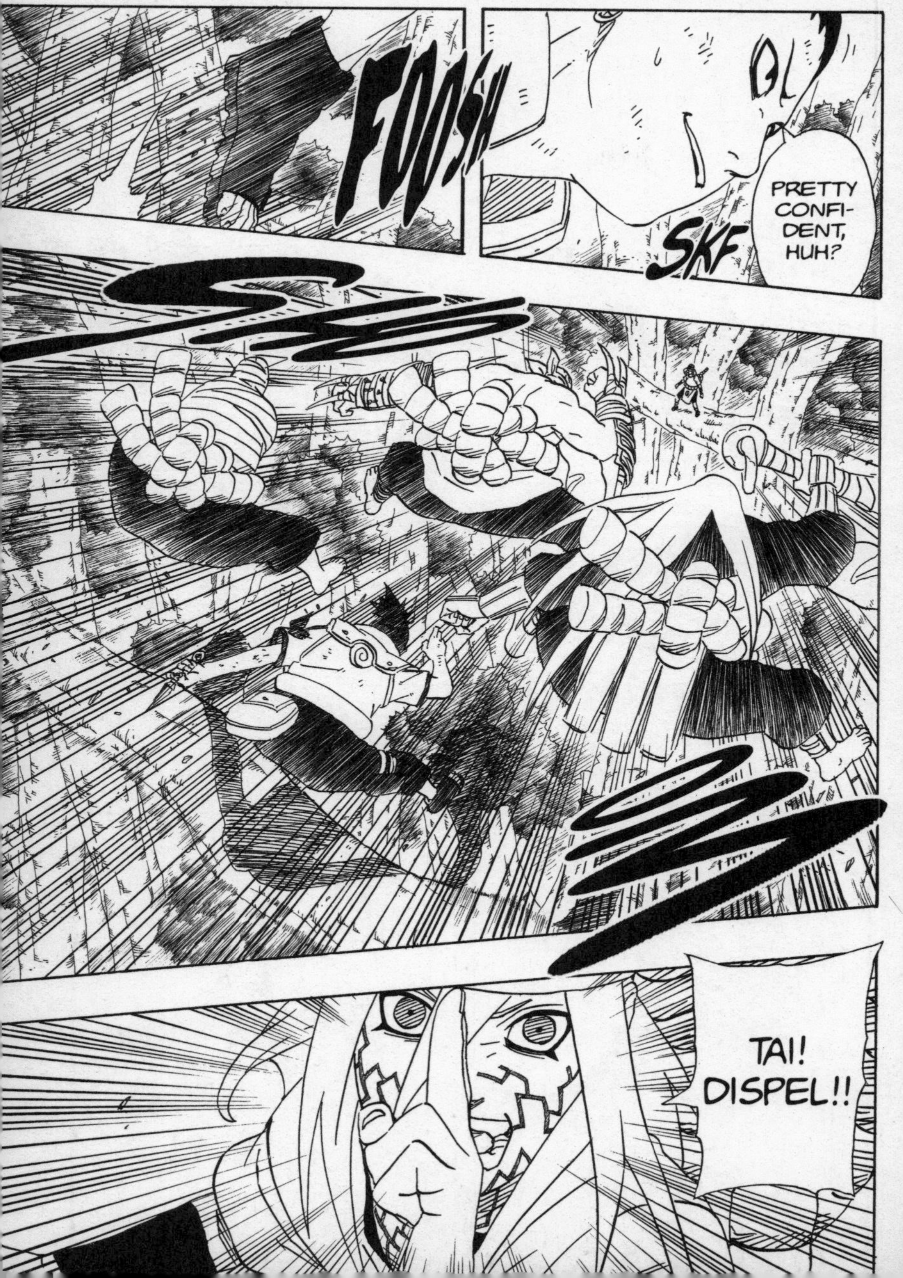
PRETTY CONFI-DENT, HUH?
SKF
FOOSH
TAI! DISPEL!!

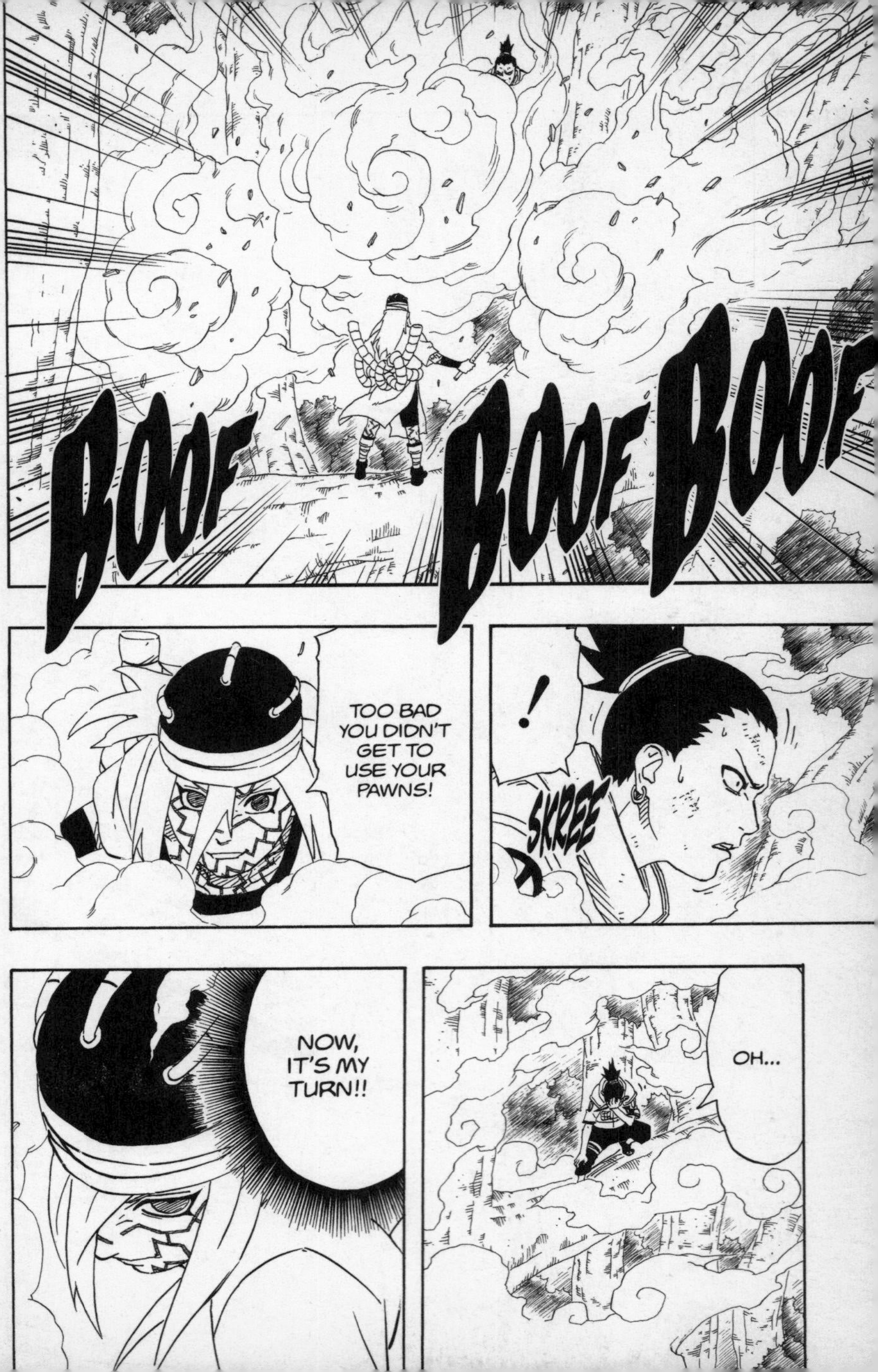
BOOF
BOOF
BOOF
!
SKREE
TOO BAD YOU DIDN'T GET TO USE YOUR PAWNS!
OH...
NOW, IT'S MY TURN!!

READ THIS WAY

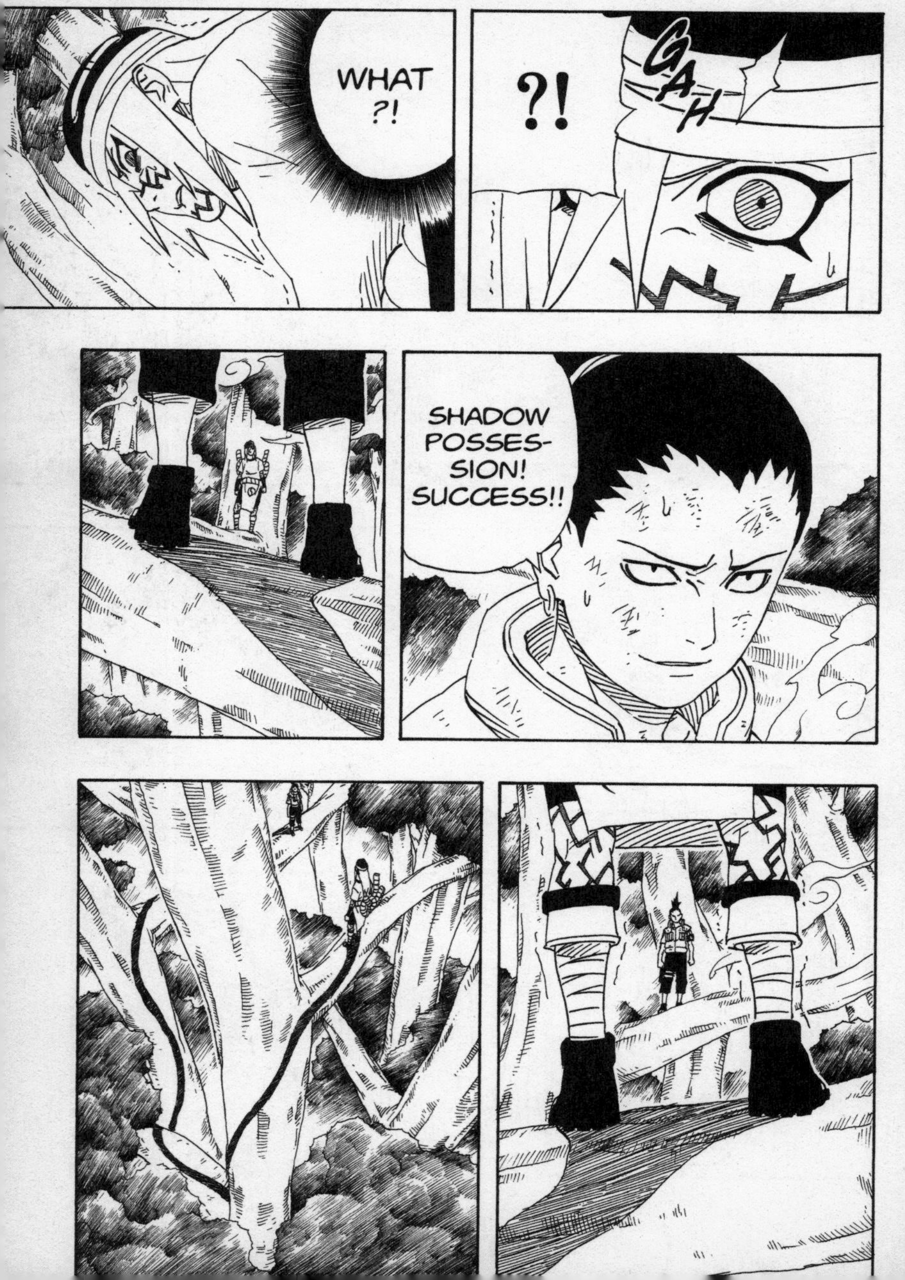
?!
GAH
WHAT ?!
SHADOW POSSESSION! SUCCESS!!

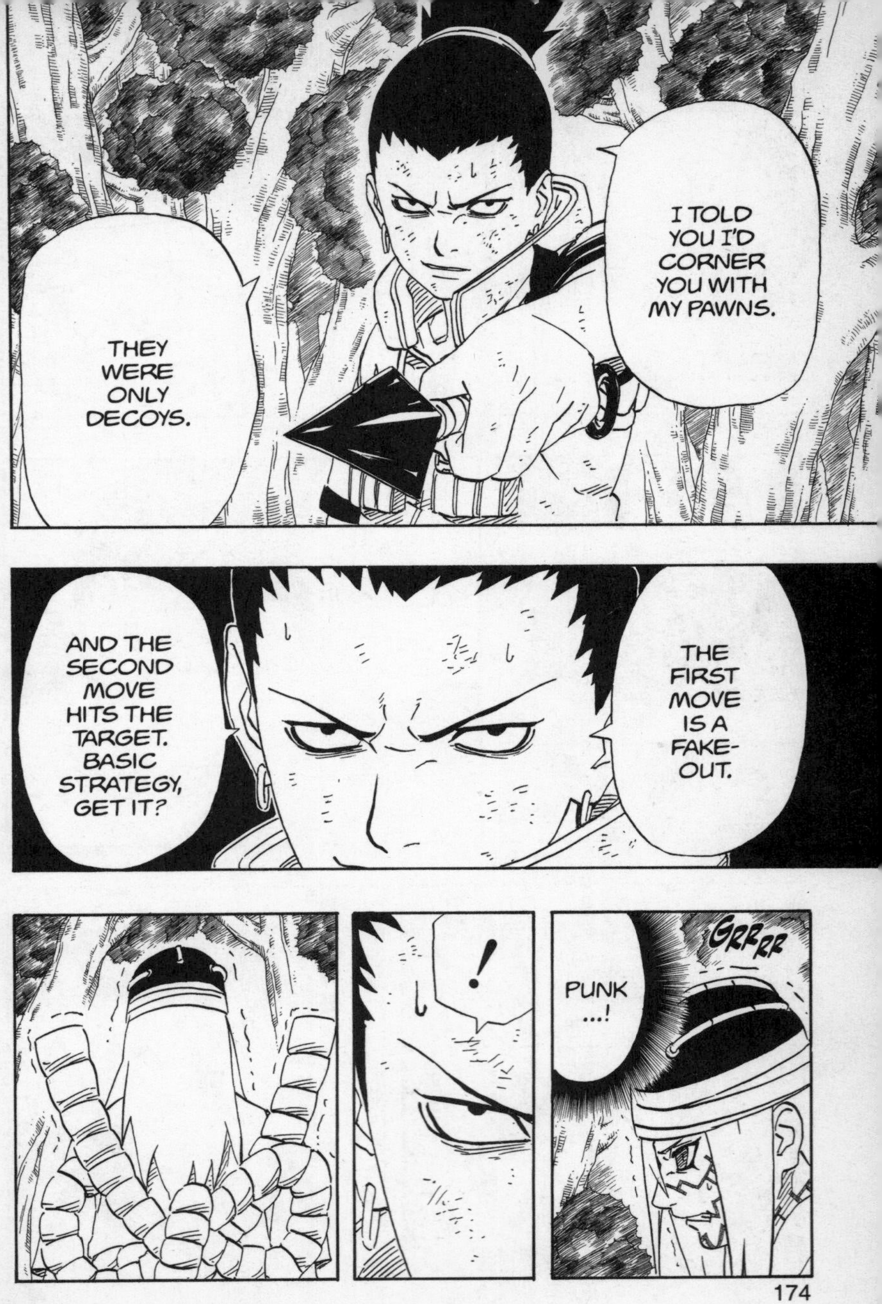

I TOLD YOU I'D CORNER YOU WITH MY PAWNS.
THEY WERE ONLY DECOYS.
THE FIRST MOVE IS A FAKE-OUT.
AND THE SECOND MOVE HITS THE TARGET. BASIC STRATEGY, GET IT?
GRRRR
PUNK ...!
!

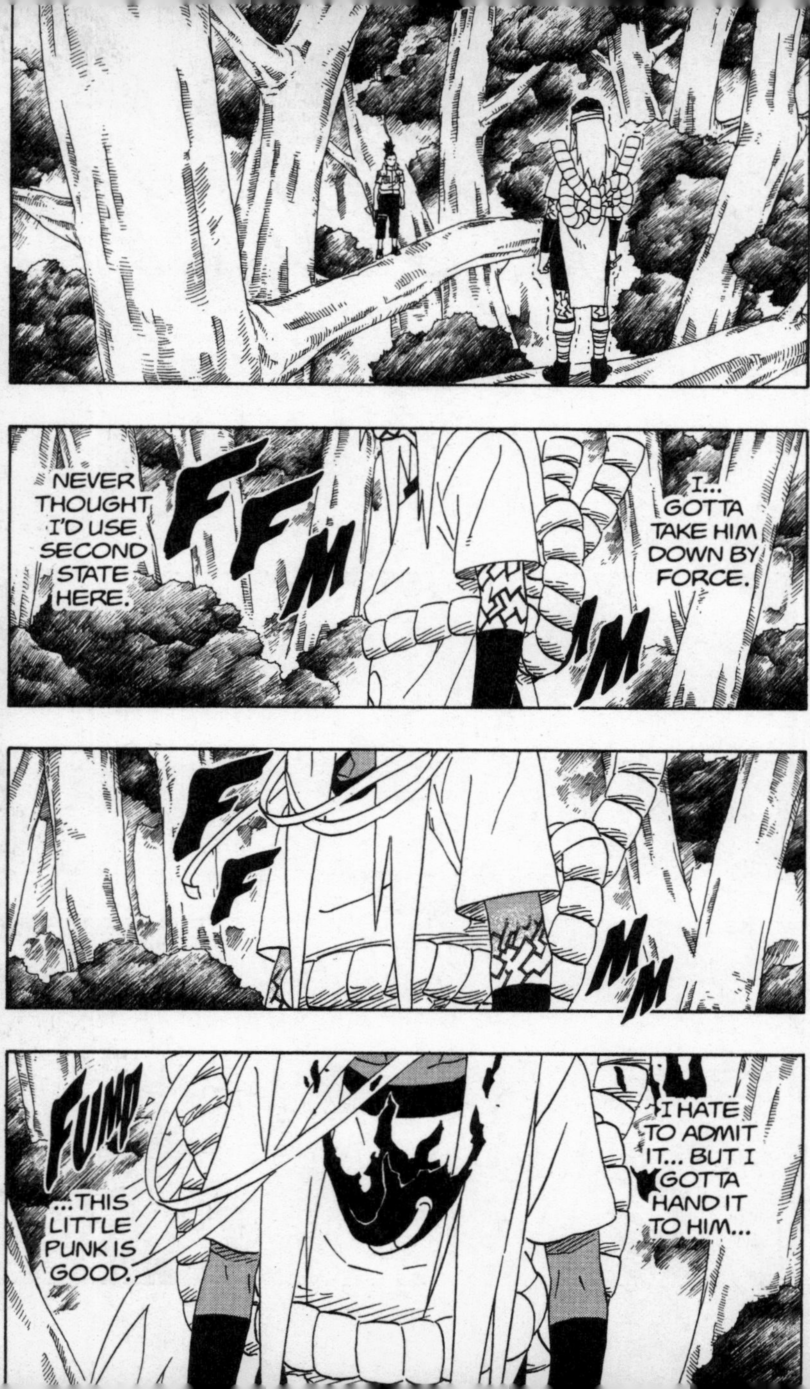
I... GOTTA TAKE HIM DOWN BY FORCE.
NEVER THOUGHT I'D USE SECOND STATE HERE.
FFMMM
FFMM
I HATE TO ADMIT IT... BUT I GOTTA HAND IT TO HIM...
...THIS LITTLE PUNK IS GOOD.
FUMP

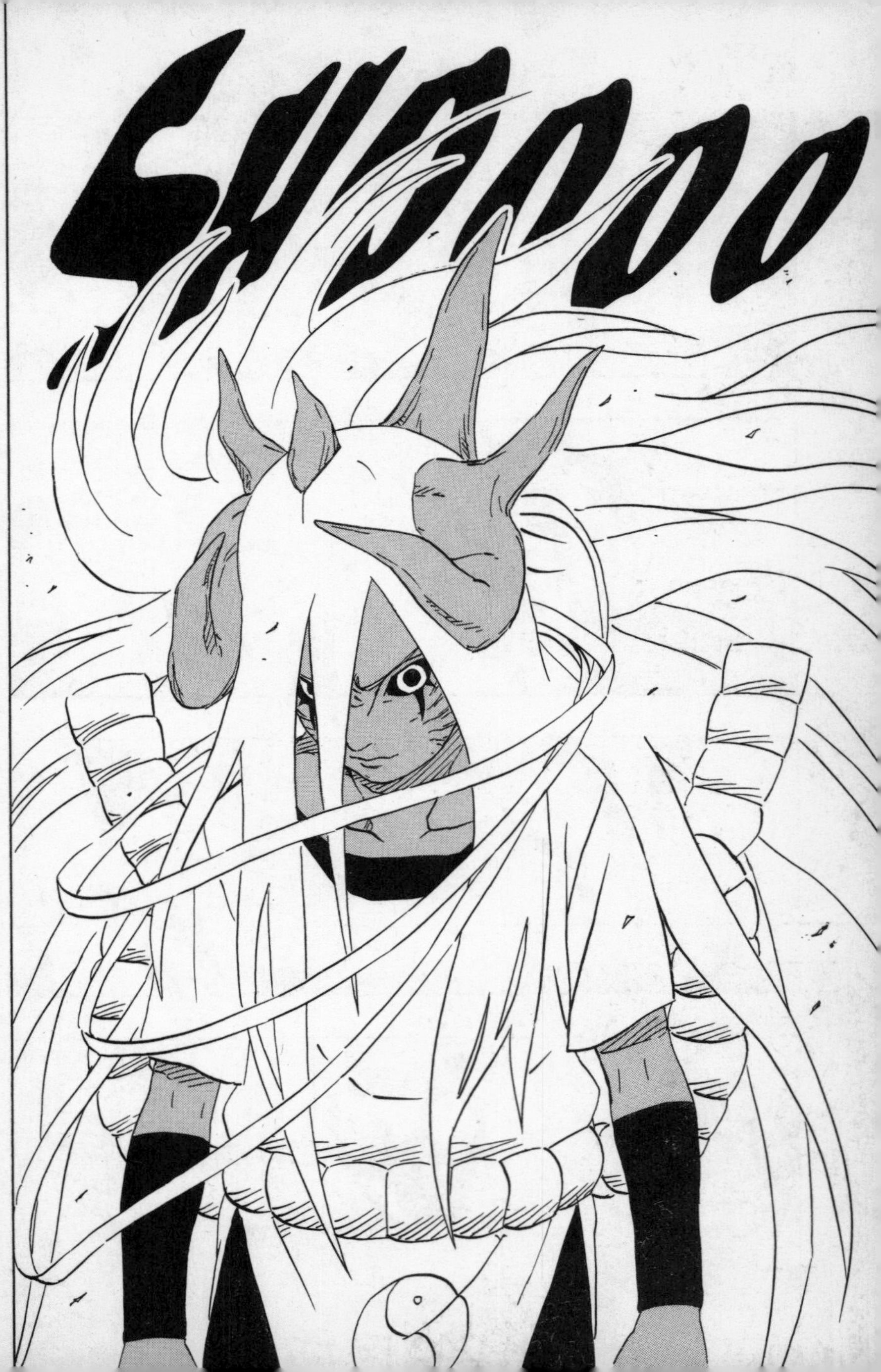
SHOOOO

READ THIS WAY

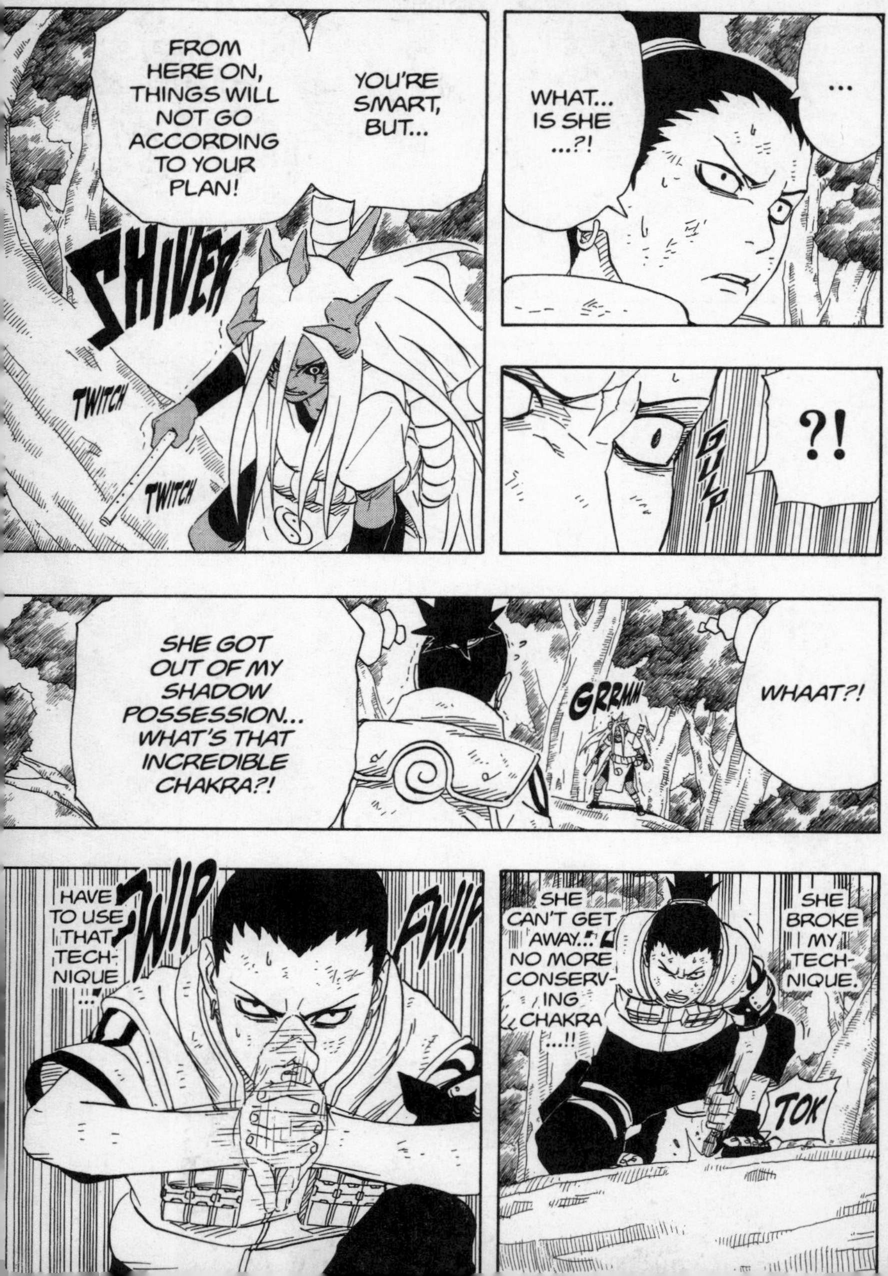
...
WHAT... IS SHE ...?!
?!
GULP
YOU'RE SMART, BUT...
FROM HERE ON, THINGS WILL NOT GO ACCORDING TO YOUR PLAN!
SHIVER
TWITCH
TWITCH
WHAAT?!
GRRMM
SHE GOT OUT OF MY SHADOW POSSESSION... WHAT'S THAT INCREDIBLE CHAKRA?!
SHE BROKE MY TECH-NIQUE.
SHE CAN'T GET AWAY...! NO MORE CONSERV-ING CHAKRA ...!!
TOK
FWIP
SWIP
HAVE TO USE THAT TECH-NIQUE ...!

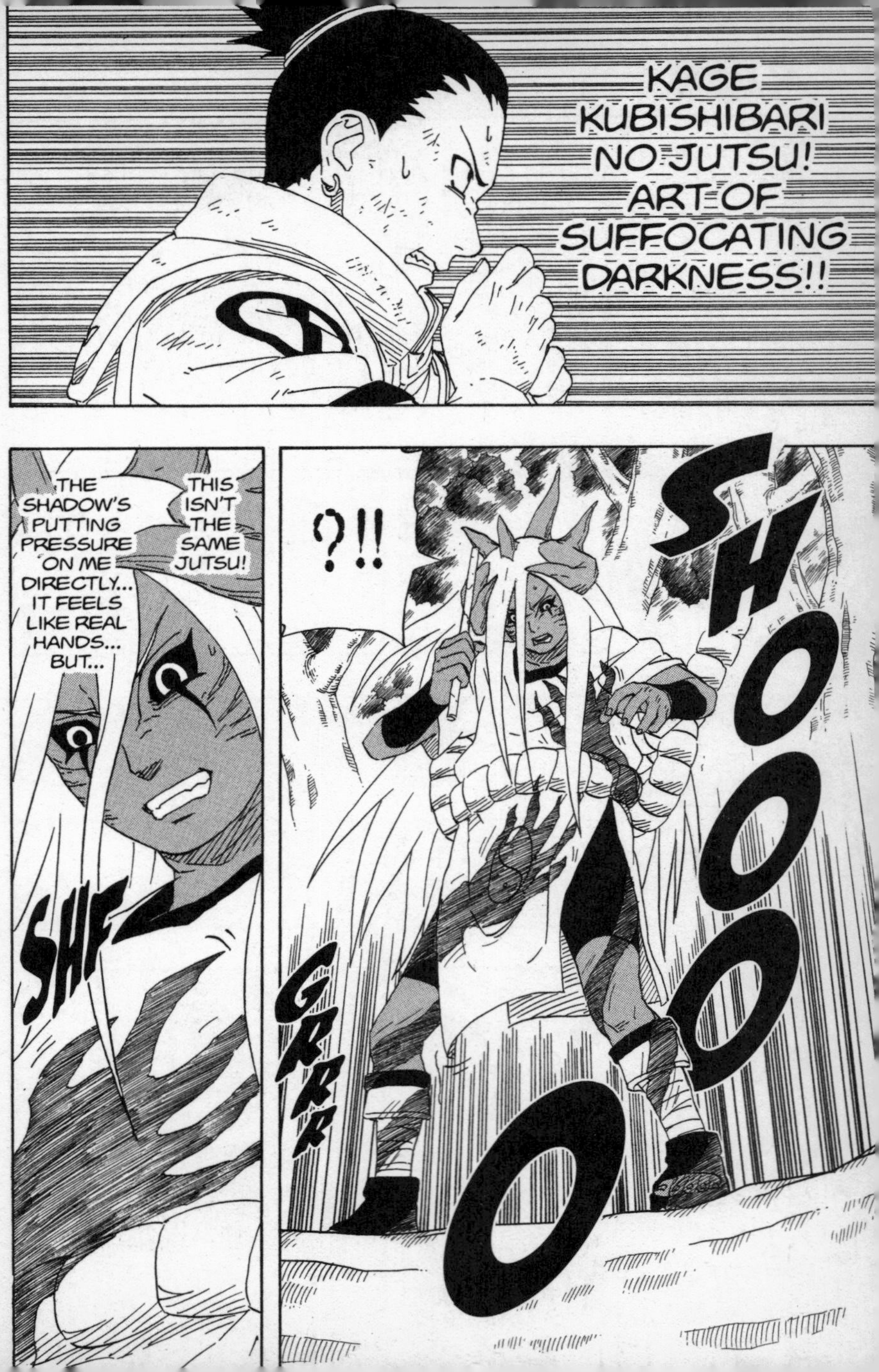
KAGE KUBISHIBARI NO JUTSU! ART OF SUFFOCATING DARKNESS!!
SHOOOOOO
?!!
GRRR
THIS ISN'T THE SAME JUTSU!
THE SHADOW'S PUTTING PRESSURE ON ME DIRECTLY... IT FEELS LIKE REAL HANDS... BUT...
SHF

READ THIS WAY

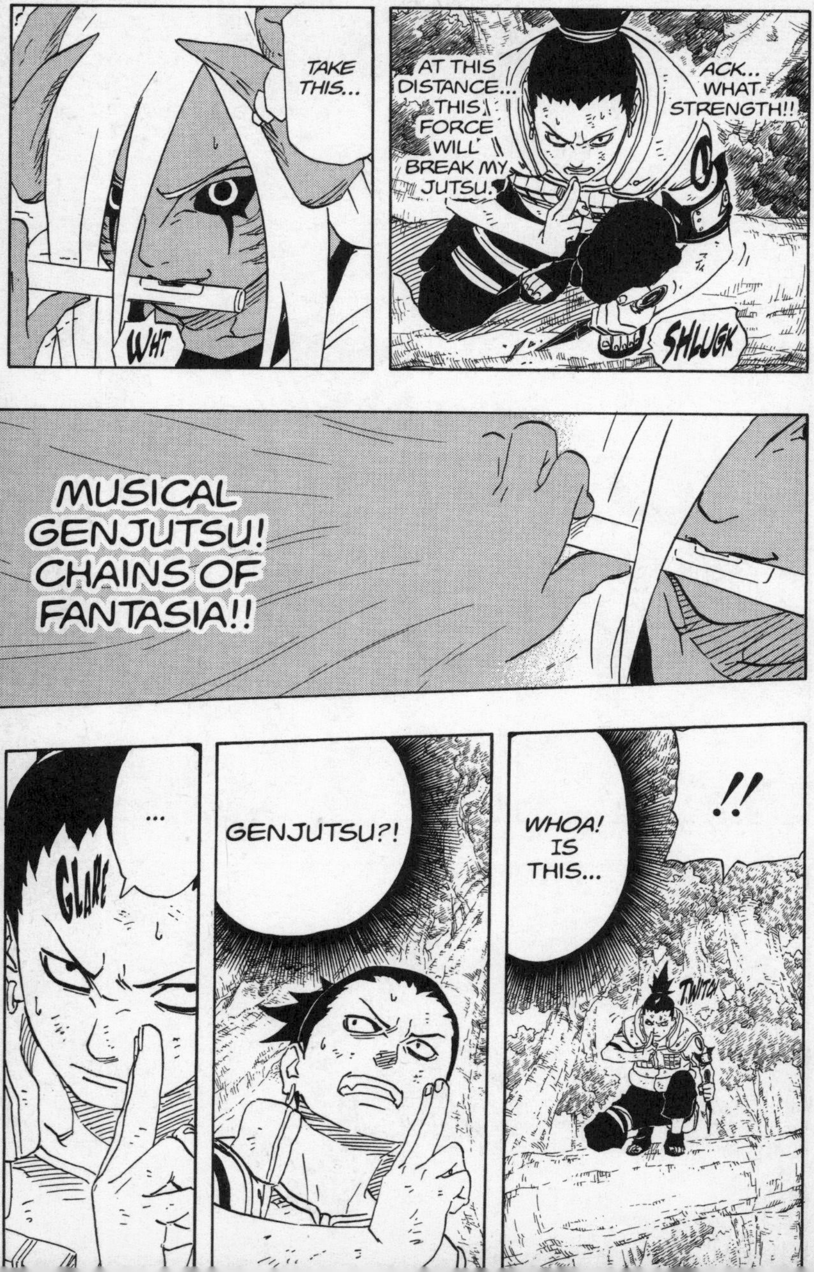
ACK... WHAT STRENGTH!!
AT THIS DISTANCE... THIS FORCE WILL BREAK MY JUTSU.
SHLUGK
TAKE THIS...
WHT
MUSICAL GENJUTSU! CHAINS OF FANTASIA!!
!!
WHOA! IS THIS...
T.WITCH
GENJUTSU?!
...
GLARE

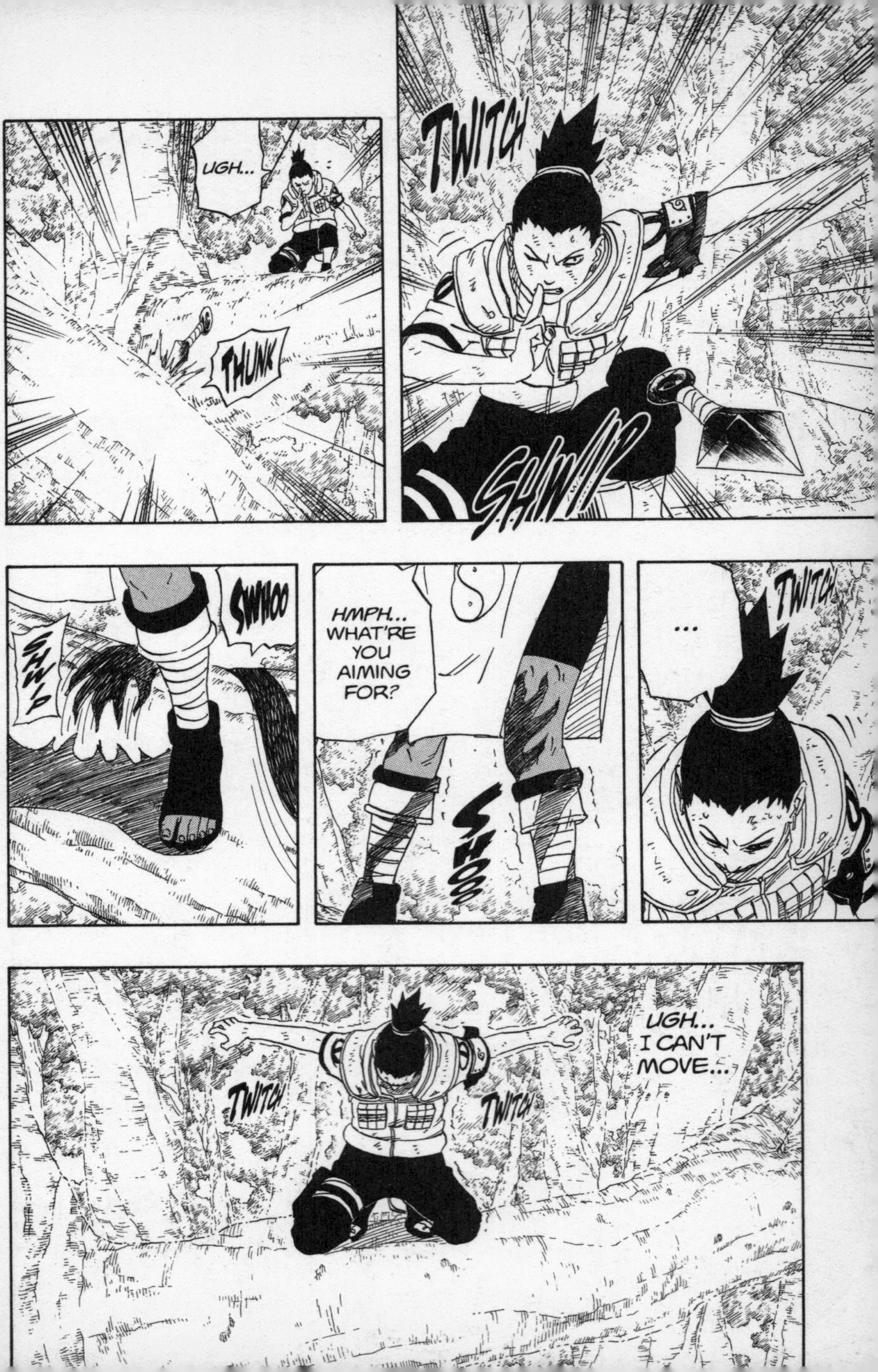
TWITCH
UGH...
THUNK
TWITCH
...
HMPH... WHAT'RE YOU AIMING FOR?
SHWOO
SWHOO
SHWIP
UGH... I CAN'T MOVE...
TWITCH
TWITCH

READ THIS WAY

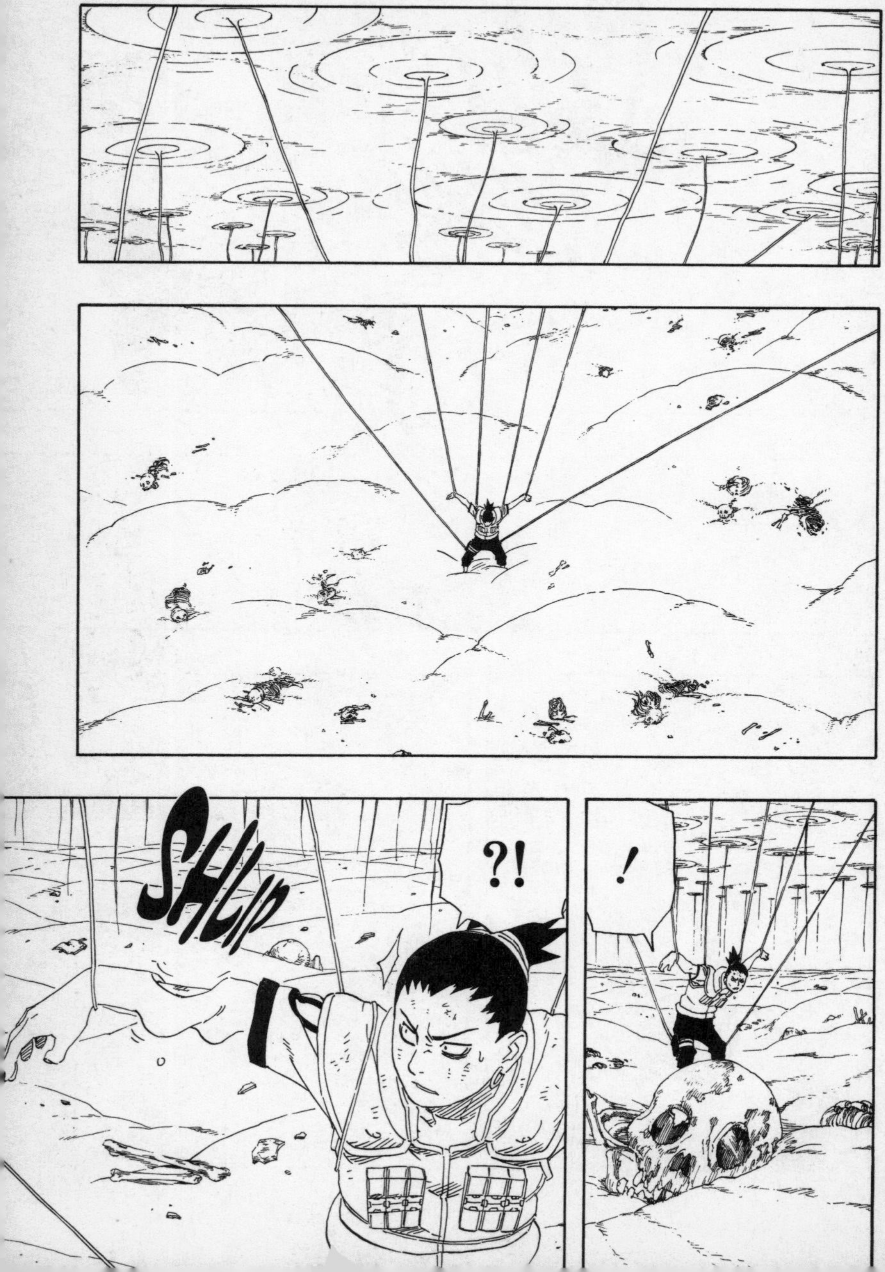
!
?!
SHLIP

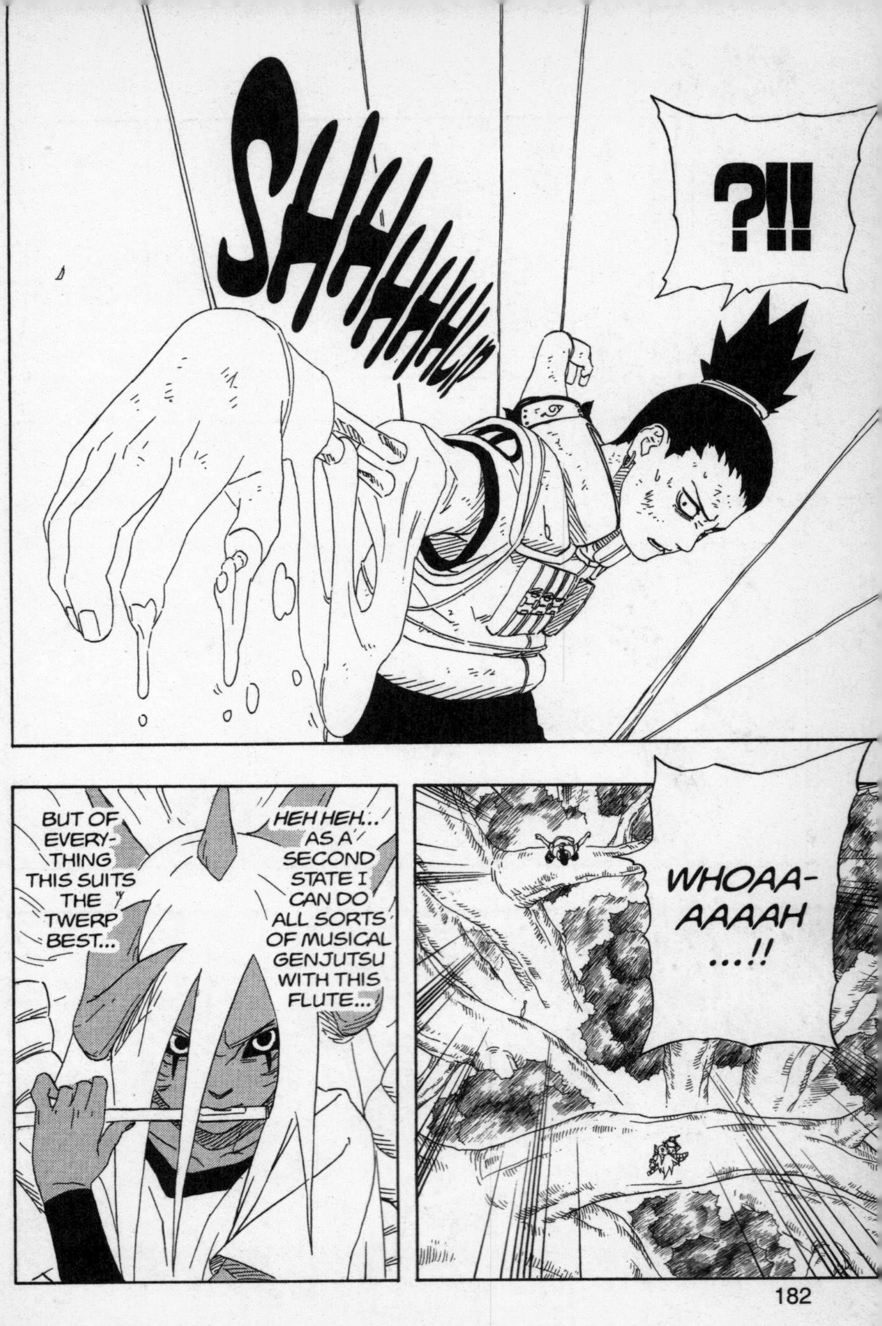
?!!
SHHHHHLP
WHOAA-AAAAH ...!!
HEH HEH... AS A SECOND STATE I CAN DO ALL SORTS OF MUSICAL GENJUTSU WITH THIS FLUTE...
BUT OF EVERY-THING THIS SUITS THE TWERP BEST...

READ THIS WAY

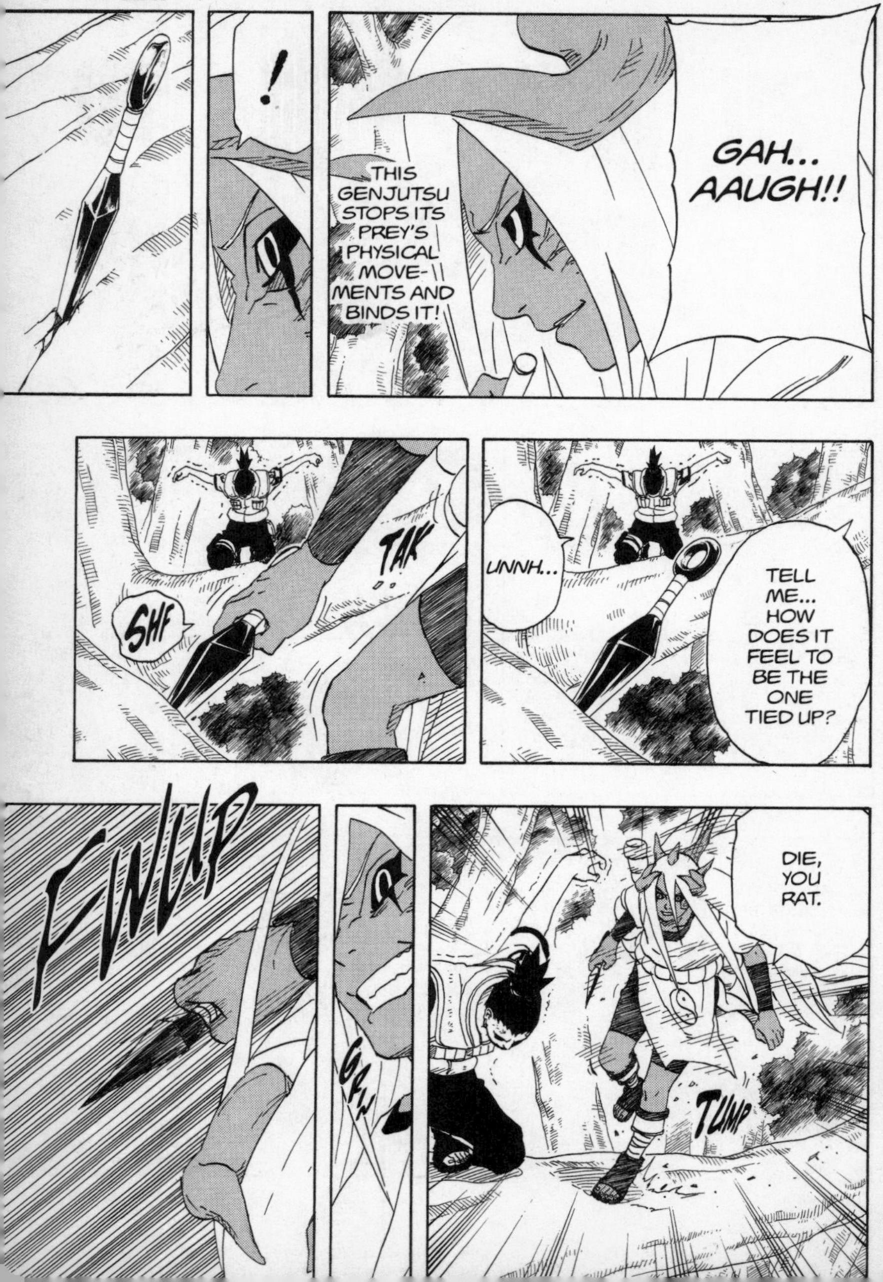

GAH... AAUGH!!
THIS GENJUTSU STOPS ITS PREY'S PHYSICAL MOVE-MENTS AND BINDS IT!
!
UNNH...
TELL ME... HOW DOES IT FEEL TO BE THE ONE TIED UP?
TAK
SHF
DIE, YOU RAT.
TUMP
FWUP

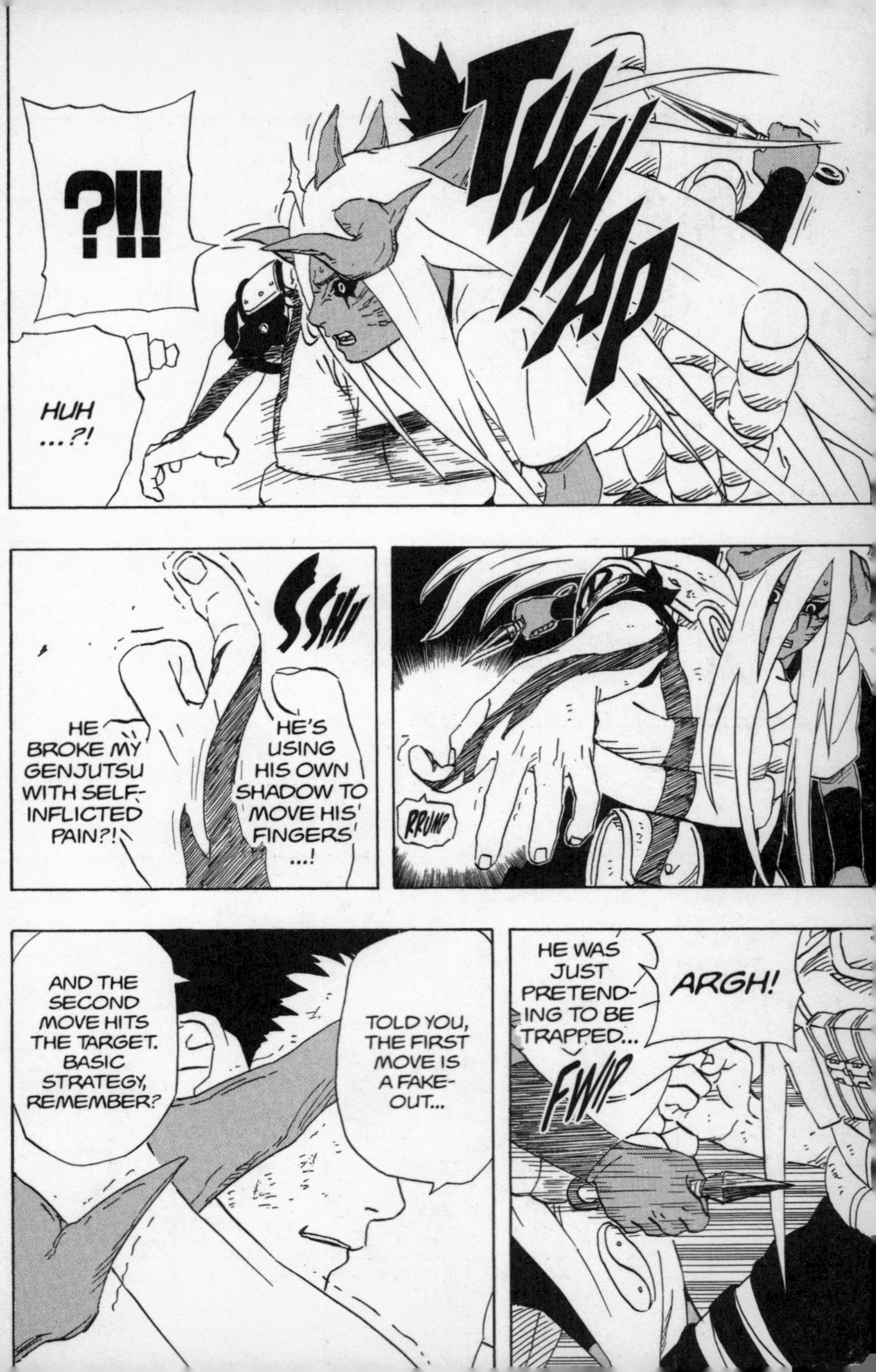
THWAP
?!!
HUH ...?!
RRUMP
SSHH
HE'S USING HIS OWN SHADOW TO MOVE HIS FINGERS ...!
HE BROKE MY GENJUTSU WITH SELF-INFLICTED PAIN?!
ARGH!
HE WAS JUST PRETENDING TO BE TRAPPED...
FWIP
TOLD YOU, THE FIRST MOVE IS A FAKE-OUT...
AND THE SECOND MOVE HITS THE TARGET. BASIC STRATEGY, REMEMBER?

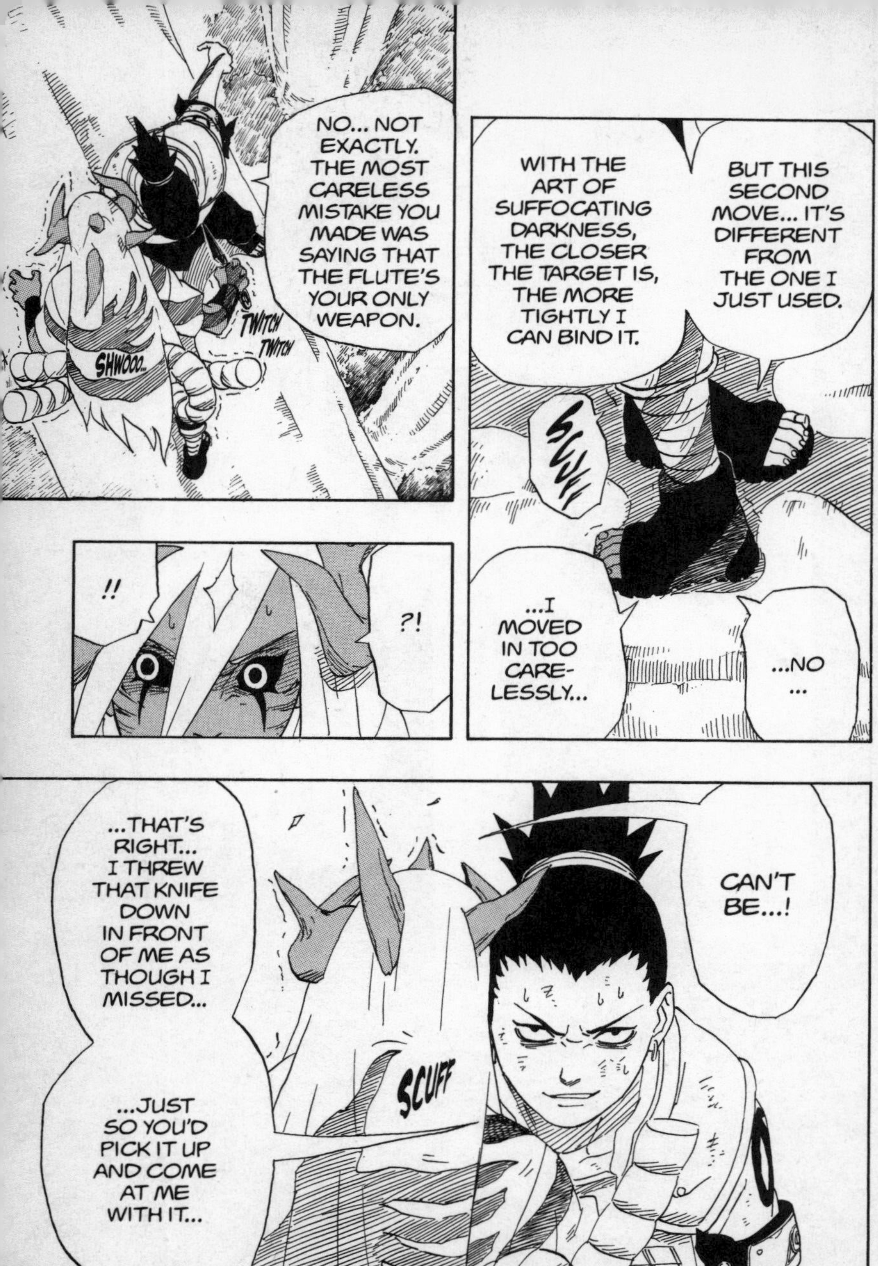
BUT THIS SECOND MOVE... IT'S DIFFERENT FROM THE ONE I JUST USED.
WITH THE ART OF SUFFOCATING DARKNESS, THE CLOSER THE TARGET IS, THE MORE TIGHTLY I CAN BIND IT.
SCUFF
...NO ...
...I MOVED IN TOO CARE-LESSLY...
NO... NOT EXACTLY. THE MOST CARELESS MISTAKE YOU MADE WAS SAYING THAT THE FLUTE'S YOUR ONLY WEAPON.
TWITCH TWITCH
SHWOOO...
?!
!!
CAN'T BE...!
...THAT'S RIGHT... I THREW THAT KNIFE DOWN IN FRONT OF ME AS THOUGH I MISSED...
...JUST SO YOU'D PICK IT UP AND COME AT ME WITH IT...
SCUFF

TO BE CONTINUED IN *NARUTO* VOL. 24!

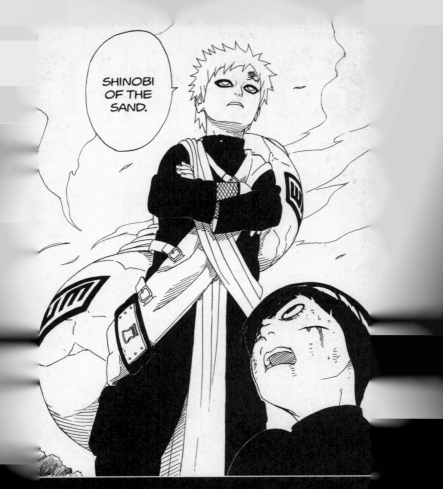

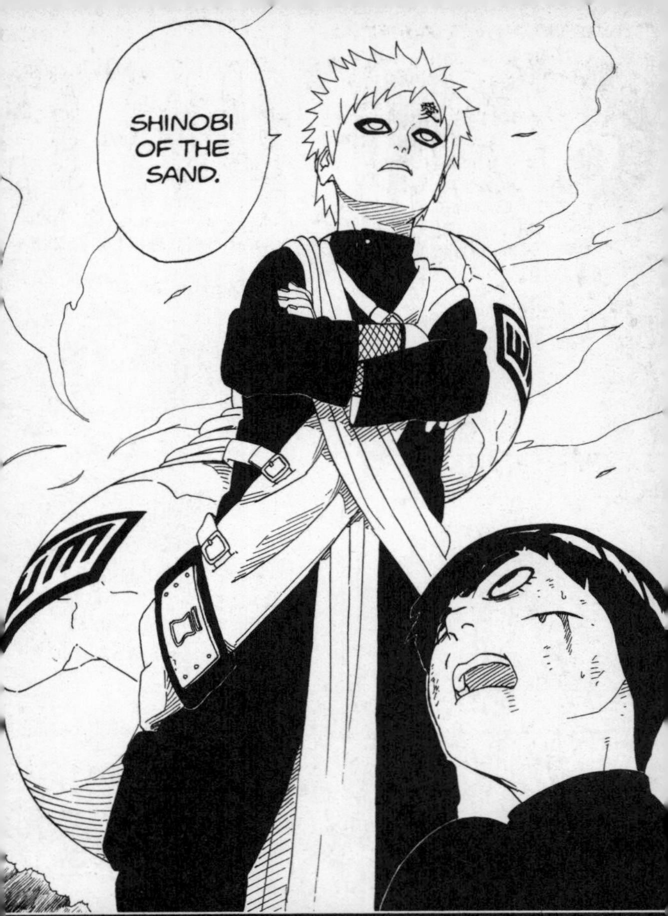
SHINOBI OF THE SAND.

N THE NEXT VOLUME...

JNORTHODOX

Kankuro, Temari and Gaara unexpectedly aid Konohagakure against :he Sound Ninja. Could they have another purpose besides rekindlin :he old alliance between Leaf and Sand?

AVAILABLE NOVEMBER 2007!

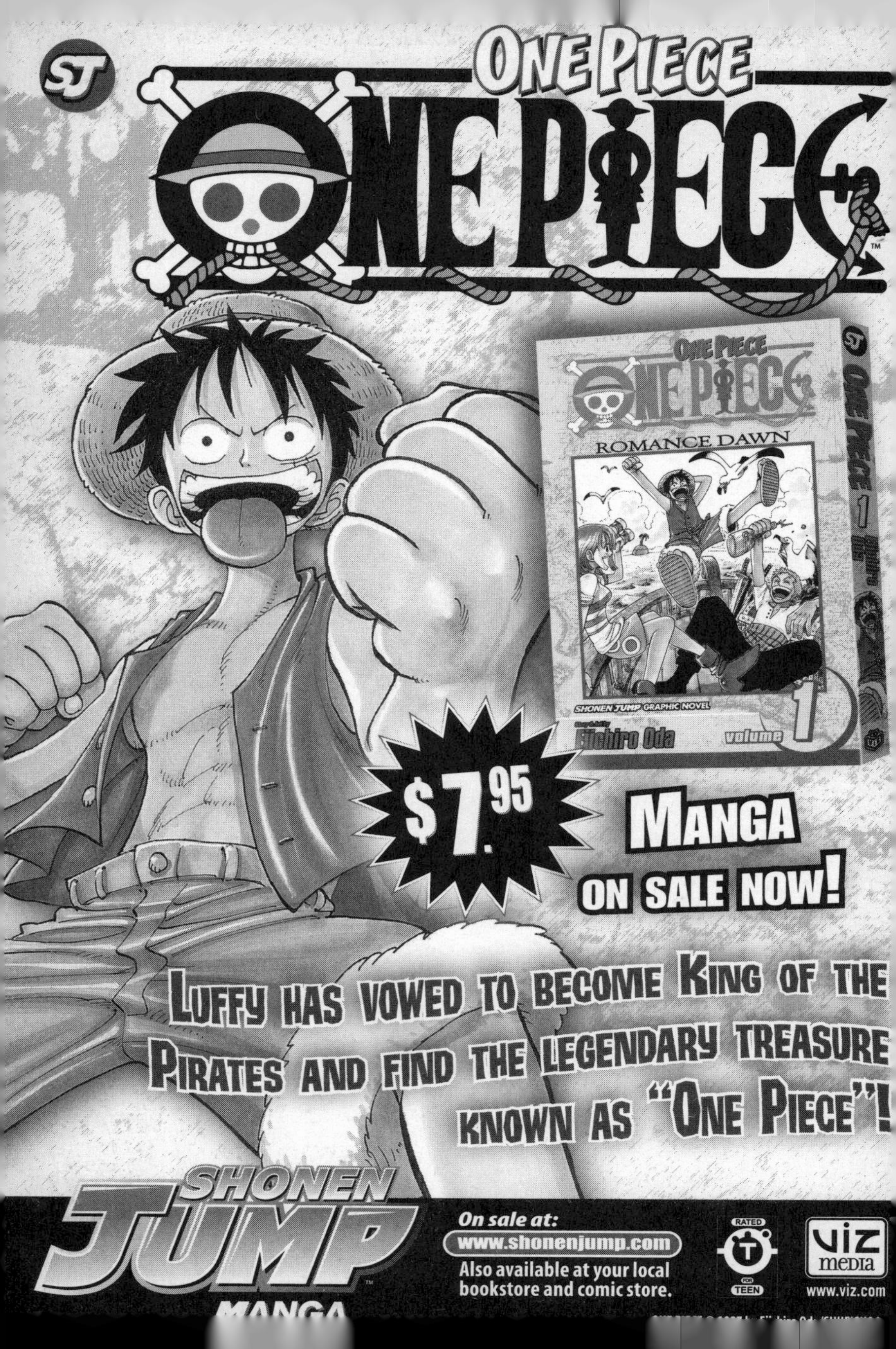

SJ
ONE PIECE
ONE PIECE
ONE PIECE
ONE PIECE
ROMANCE DAWN
SHONEN JUMP GRAPHIC NOVEL
Eiichiro Oda
volume 1
$7.95
MANGA
ON SALE NOW!
LUFFY HAS VOWED TO BECOME KING OF THE PIRATES AND FIND THE LEGENDARY TREASURE KNOWN AS "ONE PIECE"!
SHONEN JUMP
MANGA
On sale at:
www.shonenjump.com
Also available at your local bookstore and comic store.
RATED T FOR TEEN
VIZ media
www.viz.com

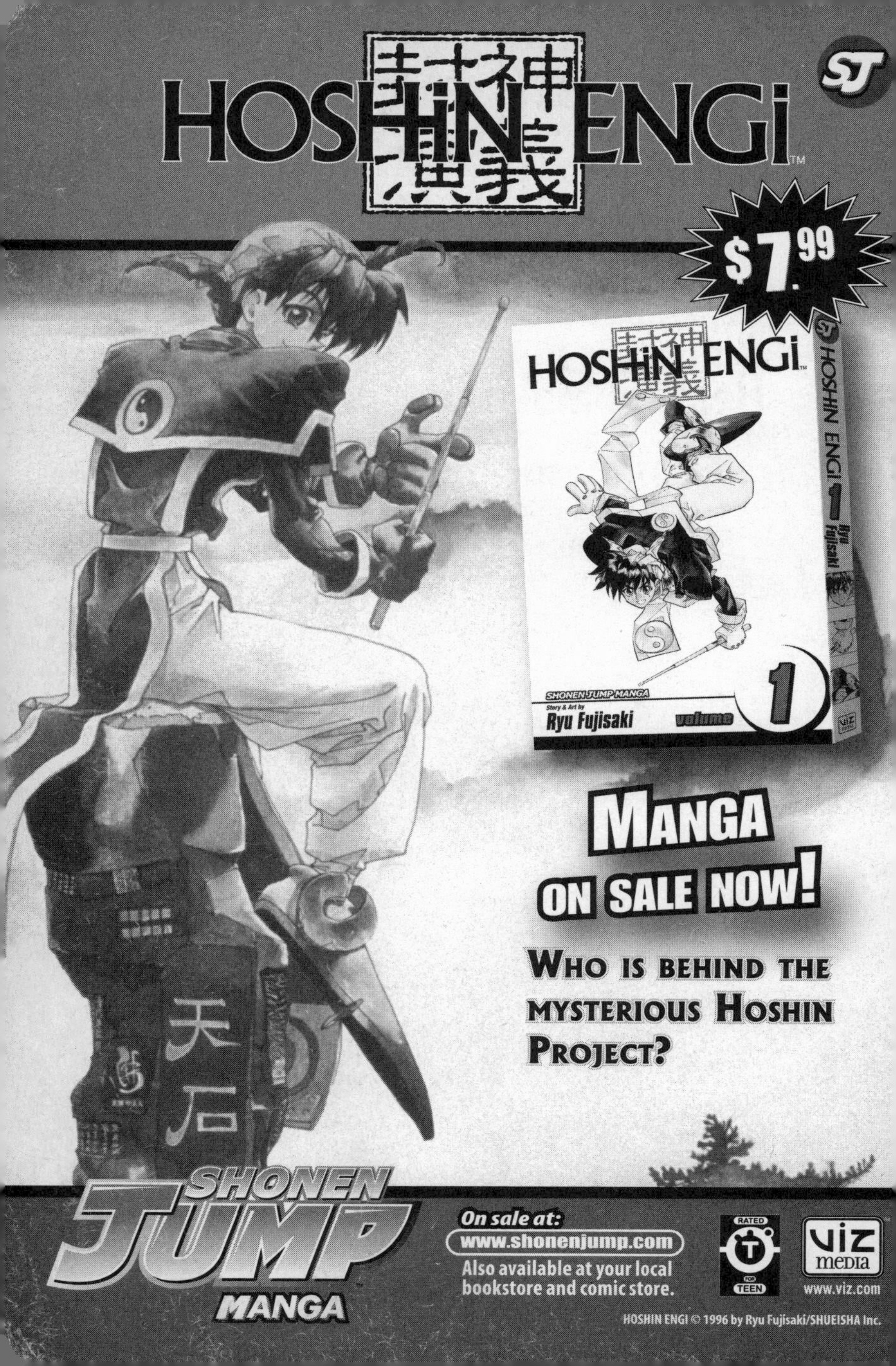
HOSHIN ENGI™
封神演義
SJ
$7.99
HOSHIN ENGI
Shonen Jump Manga
Story & Art by
Ryu Fujisaki
volume 1
MANGA
ON SALE NOW!
WHO IS BEHIND THE MYSTERIOUS HOSHIN PROJECT?
SHONEN JUMP MANGA
On sale at:
www.shonenjump.com
Also available at your local bookstore and comic store.
RATED T FOR TEEN
VIZ media
www.viz.com
HOSHIN ENGI © 1996 by Ryu Fujisaki/SHUEISHA Inc.

Tell us what you think about SHONEN JUMP manga!

Our survey is now available online.
Go to: www.SHONENJUMP.com/mangasurvey

Help us make our product offering better!